LUKE

Brazos Theological Commentary on the Bible

LUKE

DAVID LYLE JEFFREY

BrazosPress
a division of Baker Publishing Group
Grand Rapids, Michigan

© 2012 by David Lyle Jeffrey

Published by Brazos Press
a division of Baker Publishing Group
P.O. Box 6287, Grand Rapids, MI 49516-6287
www.brazospress.com

Printed in the United States of America

Library of Congress Cataloging-in-Publication Data

Jeffrey, David L., 1941–
     Luke / David Lyle Jeffrey.
         p.   cm. — (Brazos theological commentary on the Bible)
     Includes bibliographical references (p.   ) and indexes.
     ISBN 978-1-58743-141-8 (cloth)
     1. Bible. N. T. Luke—Commentaries. I. Title.
     BS2595.53.J44 2012
     226.4′07—dc23   2011033945

12   13   14   15   16   17   18   7   6   5   4   3   2   1

It dates from day
Of his going in Galilee;
Warm-laid grave of a womb-life grey;
Manger, maiden's knee;
The dense and the driven Passion, and frightful sweat:
Thence the discharge of it, there its swelling to be,
Though felt before, though in high flood yet—
What none would have known of it, only the heart, being hard at bay,
Is out with it!

        Gerard Manley Hopkins, "The Wreck of the *Deutschland*"

CONTENTS

Discernment of Spirits

Expectation and Reversal

Passover and Atonement

Resurrection and Recognition

SERIES PREFACE

Near the beginning of his treatise against Gnostic interpretations of the Bible, *Against Heresies*, Irenaeus observes that scripture is like a great mosaic depicting a handsome king. It is as if we were owners of a villa in Gaul who had ordered a mosaic from Rome. It arrives, and the beautifully colored tiles need to be taken out of their packaging and put into proper order according to the plan of the artist. The difficulty, of course, is that scripture provides us with the individual pieces, but the order and sequence of various elements are not obvious. The Bible does not come with instructions that would allow interpreters to simply place verses, episodes, images, and parables in order as a worker might follow a schematic drawing in assembling the pieces to depict the handsome king. The mosaic must be puzzled out. This is precisely the work of scriptural interpretation.

Origen has his own image to express the difficulty of working out the proper approach to reading the Bible. When preparing to offer a commentary on the Psalms he tells of a tradition handed down to him by his Hebrew teacher:

> The Hebrew said that the whole divinely inspired scripture may be likened, because of its obscurity, to many locked rooms in our house. By each room is placed a key, but not the one that corresponds to it, so that the keys are scattered about beside the rooms, none of them matching the room by which it is placed. It is a difficult task to find the keys and match them to the rooms that they can open. We therefore know the scriptures that are obscure only by taking the points of departure for understanding them from another place because they have their interpretive principle scattered among them.[1]

---

1. Fragment from the preface to *Commentary on Psalms 1–25*, preserved in the *Philokalia*, trans. Joseph W. Trigg (London: Routledge, 1998), 70–71.

As is the case for Irenaeus, scriptural interpretation is not purely local. The key in Genesis may best fit the door of Isaiah, which in turn opens up the meaning of Matthew. The mosaic must be put together with an eye toward the overall plan.

Irenaeus, Origen, and the great cloud of premodern biblical interpreters assumed that puzzling out the mosaic of scripture must be a communal project. The Bible is vast, heterogeneous, full of confusing passages and obscure words, and difficult to understand. Only a fool would imagine that he or she could work out solutions alone. The way forward must rely upon a tradition of reading that Irenaeus reports has been passed on as the rule or canon of truth that functions as a confession of faith. "Anyone," he says, "who keeps unchangeable in himself the rule of truth received through baptism will recognize the names and sayings and parables of the scriptures."[2] Modern scholars debate the content of the rule on which Irenaeus relies and commends, not the least because the terms and formulations Irenaeus himself uses shift and slide. Nonetheless, Irenaeus assumes that there is a body of apostolic doctrine sustained by a tradition of teaching in the church. This doctrine provides the clarifying principles that guide exegetical judgment toward a coherent overall reading of scripture as a unified witness. Doctrine, then, is the schematic drawing that will allow the reader to organize the vast heterogeneity of the words, images, and stories of the Bible into a readable, coherent whole. It is the rule that guides us toward the proper matching of keys to doors.

If self-consciousness about the role of history in shaping human consciousness makes modern historical-critical study critical, then what makes modern study of the Bible modern is the consensus that classical Christian doctrine distorts interpretive understanding. Benjamin Jowett, the influential nineteenth-century English classical scholar, is representative. In his programmatic essay "On the Interpretation of Scripture," he exhorts the biblical reader to disengage from doctrine and break its hold over the interpretive imagination. "The simple words of that book," writes Jowett of the modern reader, "he tries to preserve absolutely pure from the refinements or distinctions of later times." The modern interpreter wishes to "clear away the remains of dogmas, systems, controversies, which are encrusted upon" the words of scripture. The disciplines of close philological analysis "would enable us to separate the elements of doctrine and tradition with which the meaning of scripture is encumbered in our own day."[3] The lens of understanding must be wiped clear of the hazy and distorting film of doctrine.

Postmodernity, in turn, has encouraged us to criticize the critics. Jowett imagined that when he wiped away doctrine he would encounter the biblical text in its purity and uncover what he called "the original spirit and intention of the authors."[4] We are not now so sanguine, and the postmodern mind thinks

2. *Against Heresies* 9.4.

3. Benjamin Jowett, "On the Interpretation of Scripture," in *Essays and Reviews* (London: Parker, 1860), 338–39.

4. Ibid., 340.

interpretive frameworks inevitable. Nonetheless, we tend to remain modern in at least one sense. We read Athanasius and think him stage-managing the diversity of scripture to support his positions against the Arians. We read Bernard of Clairvaux and assume that his monastic ideals structure his reading of the Song of Songs. In the wake of the Reformation, we can see how the doctrinal divisions of the time shaped biblical interpretation. Luther famously described the Epistle of James as a "strawy letter," for, as he said, "it has nothing of the nature of the Gospel about it."[5] In these and many other instances, often written in the heat of ecclesiastical controversy or out of the passion of ascetic commitment, we tend to think Jowett correct: doctrine is a distorting film on the lens of understanding.

However, is what we commonly think actually the case? Are readers naturally perceptive? Do we have an unblemished, reliable aptitude for the divine? Have we no need for disciplines of vision? Do our attention and judgment need to be trained, especially as we seek to read scripture as the living word of God? According to Augustine, we all struggle to journey toward God, who is our rest and peace. Yet our vision is darkened and the fetters of worldly habit corrupt our judgment. We need training and instruction in order to cleanse our minds so that we might find our way toward God.[6] To this end, "the whole temporal dispensation was made by divine Providence for our salvation."[7] The covenant with Israel, the coming of Christ, the gathering of the nations into the church—all these things are gathered up into the rule of faith, and they guide the vision and form of the soul toward the end of fellowship with God. In Augustine's view, the reading of scripture both contributes to and benefits from this divine pedagogy. With countless variations in both exegetical conclusions and theological frameworks, the same pedagogy of a doctrinally ruled reading of scripture characterizes the broad sweep of the Christian tradition from Gregory the Great through Bernard and Bonaventure, continuing across Reformation differences in both John Calvin and Cornelius Lapide, Patrick Henry and Bishop Bossuet, and on to more recent figures such as Karl Barth and Hans Urs von Balthasar.

Is doctrine, then, not a moldering scrim of antique prejudice obscuring the Bible, but instead a clarifying agent, an enduring tradition of theological judgments that amplifies the living voice of scripture? And what of the scholarly dispassion advocated by Jowett? Is a noncommitted reading, an interpretation unprejudiced, the way toward objectivity, or does it simply invite the languid intellectual apathy that stands aside to make room for the false truism and easy answers of the age?

This series of biblical commentaries was born out of the conviction that dogma clarifies rather than obscures. The Brazos Theological Commentary on the Bible advances upon the assumption that the Nicene tradition, in all its diversity and controversy, provides the proper basis for the interpretation of the Bible as Christian

---

5. *Luther's Works*, vol. 35, ed. E. Theodore Bachmann (Philadelphia: Fortress, 1959), 362.

6. *On Christian Doctrine* 1.10.

7. *On Christian Doctrine* 1.35.

scripture. God the Father Almighty, who sends his only begotten Son to die for us and for our salvation and who raises the crucified Son in the power of the Holy Spirit so that the baptized may be joined in one body—faith in *this* God with *this* vocation of love for the world is the lens through which to view the heterogeneity and particularity of the biblical texts. Doctrine, then, is not a moldering scrim of antique prejudice obscuring the meaning of the Bible. It is a crucial aspect of the divine pedagogy, a clarifying agent for our minds fogged by self-deceptions, a challenge to our languid intellectual apathy that will too often rest in false truisms and the easy spiritual nostrums of the present age rather than search more deeply and widely for the dispersed keys to the many doors of scripture.

For this reason, the commentators in this series have not been chosen because of their historical or philological expertise. In the main, they are not biblical scholars in the conventional, modern sense of the term. Instead, the commentators were chosen because of their knowledge of and expertise in using the Christian doctrinal tradition. They are qualified by virtue of the doctrinal formation of their mental habits, for it is the conceit of this series of biblical commentaries that theological training in the Nicene tradition prepares one for biblical interpretation, and thus it is to theologians and not biblical scholars that we have turned. "War is too important," it has been said, "to leave to the generals."

We do hope, however, that readers do not draw the wrong impression. The Nicene tradition does not provide a set formula for the solution of exegetical problems. The great tradition of Christian doctrine was not transcribed, bound in folio, and issued in an official, critical edition. We have the Niceno-Constantinopolitan Creed, used for centuries in many traditions of Christian worship. We have ancient baptismal affirmations of faith. The Chalcedonian definition and the creeds and canons of other church councils have their places in official church documents. Yet the rule of faith cannot be limited to a specific set of words, sentences, and creeds. It is instead a pervasive habit of thought, the animating culture of the church in its intellectual aspect. As Augustine observed, commenting on Jer. 31:33, "The creed is learned by listening; it is written, not on stone tablets nor on any material, but on the heart."[8] This is why Irenaeus is able to appeal to the rule of faith more than a century before the first ecumenical council, and this is why we need not itemize the contents of the Nicene tradition in order to appeal to its potency and role in the work of interpretation.

Because doctrine is intrinsically fluid on the margins and most powerful as a habit of mind rather than a list of propositions, this commentary series cannot settle difficult questions of method and content at the outset. The editors of the series impose no particular method of doctrinal interpretation. We cannot say in advance how doctrine helps the Christian reader assemble the mosaic of scripture. We have no clear answer to the question of whether exegesis guided by doctrine is antithetical to or compatible with the now-old modern methods of

8. *Sermon* 212.2.

historical-critical inquiry. Truth—historical, mathematical, or doctrinal—knows no contradiction. But method is a discipline of vision and judgment, and we cannot know in advance what aspects of historical-critical inquiry are functions of modernism that shape the soul to be at odds with Christian discipline. Still further, the editors do not hold the commentators to any particular hermeneutical theory that specifies how to define the plain sense of scripture—or the role this plain sense should play in interpretation. Here the commentary series is tentative and exploratory.

Can we proceed in any other way? European and North American intellectual culture has been de-Christianized. The effect has not been a cessation of Christian activity. Theological work continues. Sermons are preached. Biblical scholars turn out monographs. Church leaders have meetings. But each dimension of a formerly unified Christian practice now tends to function independently. It is as if a weakened army had been fragmented, and various corps had retreated to isolated fortresses in order to survive. Theology has lost its competence in exegesis. Scripture scholars function with minimal theological training. Each decade finds new theories of preaching to cover the nakedness of seminary training that provides theology without exegesis and exegesis without theology.

Not the least of the causes of the fragmentation of Christian intellectual practice has been the divisions of the church. Since the Reformation, the role of the rule of faith in interpretation has been obscured by polemics and counterpolemics about *sola scriptura* and the necessity of a magisterial teaching authority. The Brazos Theological Commentary on the Bible series is deliberately ecumenical in scope, because the editors are convinced that early church fathers were correct: church doctrine does not compete with scripture in a limited economy of epistemic authority. We wish to encourage unashamedly dogmatic interpretation of scripture, confident that the concrete consequences of such a reading will cast far more light on the great divisive questions of the Reformation than either reengaging in old theological polemics or chasing the fantasy of a pure exegesis that will somehow adjudicate between competing theological positions. You shall know the truth of doctrine by its interpretive fruits, and therefore in hopes of contributing to the unity of the church, we have deliberately chosen a wide range of theologians whose commitment to doctrine will allow readers to see real interpretive consequences rather than the shadow boxing of theological concepts.

The Brazos Theological Commentary on the Bible has no dog in the current translation fights, and we endorse a textual ecumenism that parallels our diversity of ecclesial backgrounds. We do not impose the thankfully modest inclusive-language agenda of the New Revised Standard Version, nor do we insist upon the glories of the Authorized Version, nor do we require our commentators to create a new translation. In our communal worship, in our private devotions, in our theological scholarship, we use a range of scriptural translations. Precisely as scripture—a living, functioning text in the present life of faith—the Bible is not semantically fixed. Only a modernist, literalist hermeneutic could imagine that this modest fluidity is a liability. Philological precision and stability is a consequence of, not a basis for, exegesis. Judgments about the meaning of a text fix its literal sense, not the other way around. As a result, readers should expect an eclectic use of biblical translations, both across the different volumes of the series and within individual commentaries.

We cannot speak for contemporary biblical scholars, but as theologians we know that we have long been trained to defend our fortresses of theological concepts and formulations. And we have forgotten the skills of interpretation. Like stroke victims, we must rehabilitate our exegetical imaginations, and there are likely to be different strategies of recovery. Readers should expect this reconstructive—not reactionary—series to provide them with experiments in postcritical doctrinal interpretation, not commentaries written according to the settled principles of a well-functioning tradition. Some commentators will follow classical typological and allegorical readings from the premodern tradition; others will draw on contemporary historical study. Some will comment verse by verse; others will highlight passages, even single words that trigger theological analysis of scripture. No reading strategies are proscribed, no interpretive methods foresworn. The central premise in this commentary series is that doctrine provides structure and cogency to scriptural interpretation. We trust in this premise with the hope that the Nicene tradition can guide us, however imperfectly, diversely, and haltingly, toward a reading of scripture in which the right keys open the right doors.

R. R. Reno

AUTHOR'S PREFACE

This is not a form-critical or closely argued philological commentary for the professional biblical scholar. I seek here to represent Luke's Gospel as, by faithful men and women for more than nineteen centuries, it has been normatively read—namely, as a faithful report of the life, ministry, and person of Jesus the Christ—and to do so with an eye to providing insights from those who would read it in "the company of the saints and faithful of all ages." It will thus be clear that, far from seeking to be original, my effort here has been, in the spirit of our author himself, "to set forth in order a declaration of those things which are most surely believed among us, even as they delivered them unto us" (Luke 1:1–2 KJV). Luke here refers, of course, to the immediate eyewitnesses and "living voices" he consulted, as well as, perhaps, to already transcribed narratives of which he could approve, while I will be drawing on the preachers, teachers, and commentators who, following Luke in apostolic succession and purpose, have been regarded and may still be regarded as one with him in his desire that all Christian readers "may know the certainty of those things in which [we] were instructed" (1:4). The 2003 volume of extracts from earlier commentators compiled by Arthur A. Just has been a welcome index, while the 2009 *Catena Aurea* of Thomas Aquinas, a more extensive anthology, has been indispensable. I have, of course, delved still farther into the riches of past commentary, and I am grateful to be able to share some of this treasury with my readers. I have dared to assume that a love of learning and a desire for God comparable to that of these earlier readers of Luke will have prompted a majority of those who take up this book.

In format, taking advantage of the latitude afforded by our general editors, I have not reprinted the text of Luke in discreet pericopes immediately above the pertinent section of commentary, as is often the practice, nor have I done it verse by verse, as did Jaroslav Pelikan in the Acts volume for this series. Because of the rhetorical power, historical resonance, and continuing presence of the (Authorized) King James Version and the Coverdale Bible in many English liturgical, literary, and musical settings, I have used their nearest modern equivalent, the New King James Version, as my normative English translation, supplementing with Revised Standard Version, King James Version, and (very rarely) my own translation when clarity seemed to require it. In all biblical citations I have modernized capitalization; divine pronouns are thus lowercased. It will thus be desirable for the reader to have a favorite Bible on hand when using this commentary. I recommend reading a chapter in Luke before consulting the relevant chapter in this commentary. Then again, my method of exegesis and exposition are here, in literary fashion, interwoven and varied according to the Lukan material immediately in hand. I quote Luke's text in my own text discursively, which I hope will provide for some approximate sense of the natural intimacy that for centuries has characterized the dialogue between Christian readers as they have corporately pondered the scriptures. This method permits also some notice of the larger narrative structure and argument in Luke.

By profession I am first a literary scholar, having spent much of my life studying the influence upon literature and art of scripture and its historical interpretation. All the more so then, I come to the challenge of direct interpretation with no little caution and much prayerfulness, for the accountability of an expositor of the biblical text far exceeds that of the literary scholar expounding his own more secular texts. What Jesus says in Luke 12 is more than enough to make one's examination of conscience on this point a serious and daily business. Nevertheless, I confess, with the famous teacher of Paul, that it is a wonderful privilege to be able to turn my mind to the place my heart has been so many years; as Gamaliel observed: "How beautiful to study scripture [Torah], and how happy along our earthly journey" (*yafeh talmud torah k'asher imah derech eretz*). My own tent-making, if a loose analogy is permissible, has had the happy benefit of letting me pitch my tent for five decades not far from those for whom Torah (in the sense of all scripture) was their primary lifework; I have watched with keen interest and much affectionate admiration their labors. It is to what has seemed to me the best of their work more than my own insight that I would bear witness. There are, just so, limitations upon my ingathering. An effort even to represent faithful readers down through the ages (one could not hope to be inclusive, needless to say) constitutes a considerable challenge. The constraints of appropriate focus and orderly exposition require many omissions, even of work that remains worthy in whole or in part. For the attenuations and exclusions that have seemed to me necessary I ask in advance the forbearance of my fellow scholars and, when an omission on my part may prove rather than merely seem a *lapsus calumni*, above all the forgiveness of God. But it is my prayer and earnest hope that what follows in these pages will not only make some "rough places plain" for others but also, by attunement to the sheer symphony of the gifted appreciation of great Christian readers of all ages, provide added reason to rejoice in the beauty and truth of the gospel, and so with shared thanksgiving, subtended by the Holy Spirit, to enter into a deeper fullness of the joy of the Lord and the knowledge of his Christ.

I am grateful to several whose comments have been helpful to me at various points in the writing of this commentary. These include Jeff Fish, Mikeal Parsons, David Garland, Daniel H. Williams, Phil Donnelly, Barry Harvey, Julia Dyson Hejduk, Eleonore Stump, Michael O'Brien, Anthony Thistleton, Robert Wilken, and Rusty Reno, the latter two editors for the Brazos Theological Commentary on the Bible. Bill and Mary Jo Robbins, by their remarkable and largely invisible generosity to so many of the poor and underprivileged, have been an encouraging reminder to me whilst I was working on this commentary that taking one of the central messages of Luke's Gospel to heart is now as ever a hallmark of authentic devotion to Jesus Christ. Finally, Katherine Jeffrey has been of unmatched assistance to me by her generosity of critical intelligence, her thoughtfulness as a fellow reader of scripture, and her unswerving love for truth.

ABBREVIATIONS

General

KJV   King James Version
NKJV   New King James Version
RSV   Revised Standard Version
TDNT   *Theological Dictionary of the New Testament*. Edited by G. Kittel and J. Friedrich. Translated by G. W. Bromiley. 10 vols. Grand Rapids: Eerdmans, 1964–76.

Biblical Books

Acts	Acts	Gen.	Genesis
Amos	Amos	Hab.	Habakkuk
1 Chr.	1 Chronicles	Hag.	Haggai
2 Chr.	2 Chronicles	Heb.	Hebrews
Col.	Colossians	Hos.	Hosea
1 Cor.	1 Corinthians	Isa.	Isaiah
2 Cor.	2 Corinthians	Jas.	James
Dan.	Daniel	Jer.	Jeremiah
Deut.	Deuteronomy	Job	Job
Eccl.	Ecclesiastes	Joel	Joel
Eph.	Ephesians	John	John
Esth.	Esther	1 John	1 John
Exod.	Exodus	2 John	2 John
Ezek.	Ezekiel	3 John	3 John
Ezra	Ezra	Jonah	Jonah
Gal.	Galatians	Josh.	Joshua

Jude	Jude		Phil.	Philippians
Judg.	Judges		Phlm.	Philemon
1 Kgs.	1 Kings		Prov.	Proverbs
2 Kgs.	2 Kings		Ps.	Psalms
Lam.	Lamentations		Rev.	Revelation
Lev.	Leviticus		Rom.	Romans
Luke	Luke		Ruth	Ruth
Mal.	Malachi		1 Sam.	1 Samuel
Mark	Mark		2 Sam.	2 Samuel
Matt.	Matthew		Song	Song of Songs
Mic.	Micah		1 Thess.	1 Thessalonians
Nah.	Nahum		2 Thess.	2 Thessalonians
Neh.	Nehemiah		1 Tim.	1 Timothy
Num.	Numbers		2 Tim.	2 Timothy
Obad.	Obadiah		Titus	Titus
1 Pet.	1 Peter		Zech.	Zechariah
2 Pet.	2 Peter		Zeph.	Zephaniah

INTRODUCTION

Luke as Author

Luke does not identify himself as the author either in this Gospel or in the second work attributed to him, the Acts of the Apostles. What he does tell us is that he was not himself an "eyewitness" (*autoptēs*) of Jesus's ministry; these are the people he has consulted (1:2–4). He also tells us, however, that he was a traveling companion of Paul (Acts 16:10–17; 20:5–15). Paul, correspondingly, so identifies Luke (Phlm. 24; Col. 4:14). It is early church writers who name him as author of both Luke and Acts (e.g., Irenaeus, *Against Heresies* 3.13.1; other early attributions come from Origen, Clement of Alexandria, Tertullian, and Eusebius); their verdict is virtually unanimous. Another witness is the Muratorian Fragment, a second-century Christian document written in Latin, which identifies Luke with the "third book of the gospel" and describes him as a "physician" who "wrote down what he had heard" since he "had not known the Lord in the flesh, and having obtained such information as he could he began his account [*narratio*] with the birth of John."[1] The uncontested identification persists, with Jerome in the fourth century adding that Luke's place of origin was Antioch, that Luke was fluent in Greek, and that he wrote his Gospel while in Achaia and died in Boeotia (Patrologia latina 23.650; 26.17).[2] Paul had already confirmed that Luke was a physician and a Gentile (Col. 4:10–14), which would make him the only identified author of a canonical New Testament work who was not Jewish by birth. To this remarkable fact we should add that Luke's is by far the longest of

---

1. Cited in the *Navarre Bible: St. Luke's Gospel* (Dublin: Four Courts, 1988; New York: Scepter, 2005), 11.
2. This was the same region that produced his younger contemporary Plutarch, who died there around AD 120.

the Gospels and that together with his second volume, the Acts of the Apostles, his work comprises about 28 percent of the New Testament canon.[3]

Perhaps Eusebius (late-third-century bishop of Caesarea and father of church history) has done more than any early commentator to suggest that Luke's profession as a physician added a special dimension to his writing. In a nice rhetorical turn, Eusebius offers insight into the particular spiritual character of Luke's writing: "Luke has left us concerning that medicine which he had received from the Apostles . . . two medical books, whereby not our bodies but our souls may be healed" (*Ecclesiastical History* 3.4). The analogy suggested to later commentators, Bonaventure and Thomas Aquinas among them, that Luke's secondary concern was the spiritual health of his readers, as of the church in general, and that his Gospel, when read rightly, is what medieval pastors and humanist scholars would have called a *psychopharmacon* ("therapy for the soul"). Meanwhile, Ambrose, fourth-century bishop of Milan and the teacher of Augustine of Hippo, judged the measured thoughtfulness of Luke's narration to reveal a concern for both historicity and spiritual significance: "Truly, St. Luke kept . . . a certain historical order and revealed to us more miracles of the Lord's deeds," Ambrose writes, "so that the history of his gospel embraced the virtue of all wisdom" (*Exposition of Luke* 12). On this account, Luke was understood to have preserved both the truth of the events themselves and their spiritual meaning. In Luke more than the other Synoptics or John, theology does not so much order narrative as arise from it.

All commentators equipped to read the text in Greek, from Jerome in the fourth century (*Epistle* 20.4) to Thomas Aquinas in the thirteenth (*Catena Aurea* 3.2), attributed to Luke both polish and a tone of secular eloquence. Down to the present, commentators have agreed that if Luke was not quite a Hellenistic *belle-lettrist*, his Greek was at the least formal and precise, exhibiting a "balanced Greek periodic style" (Bock 1994–96: 1.51). It is clear to me that in his vocabulary (at almost every turn in his text there are instances of New Testament *hapax legomena*—words occurring in his texts alone in the biblical canon), Luke reveals a command of Greek literature and vocabulary unmatched by the other Gospel writers, and even Paul. He uses several hundred words found in no other New Testament writer, though most may be found in Hellenic secular texts.[4] This range of classical vocabulary permits him a richness and verbal nuance not so readily available to the other evangelists, for whom Greek is not their first language.

---

3. Charles H. H. Scobie, "A Canonical Approach to Interpreting Luke," in *Reading Luke: Interpretation, Reflection, Formation*, ed. Craig Bartholomew, Joel B. Green, and Anthony Thiselton, Scripture and Hermeneutics 6 (Milton Keynes, UK: Paternoster, 2005), 331.

4. R. Morgenthaler, *Statistik des Neutestamentlichen Wortschatzes* (Zurich: Gotthelf, 1958), notes 266 words peculiar to Luke, 60 found in Luke and Acts only, and 415 found in Acts alone. There remains important work to be done in exploring Luke's use of a richer Hellenistic vocabulary, but it is not appropriate to the present volume. The otherwise excellent guide, *Luke: A Handbook on the Greek Text* by Martin C. Culy, Mikeal C. Parsons, and Joshua J. Stigall (Waco: Baylor University Press, 2010), does not identify or source these distinctive items in Luke's vocabulary.

Luke's textured literary fluency comes through to attuned ears; for contemporary American Catholic novelist Ron Hansen, for example, "Luke is the most writerly of the evangelists."[5] The virtues of this stylistic advantage are perhaps less visible in some English translations (except perhaps KJV and NKJV, which I have used preponderantly in this work), but the characteristic compositional features of educated Hellenistic narrative style, as we shall see, show through well enough in most translations. Yet—and the importance of this point can scarcely be overemphasized—even so carefully historical a Gospel narrative as Luke's has not been received by the church primarily as a resource for historical, philological, or archival purposes. Nor, as with post-Enlightenment academic study of the Bible generally, was the Gospel imagined for nineteen centuries as a text-critical laboratory for posing a set of problems in the verification of historical details.

Luke in Ecclesiastical Tradition

The early church saw the four Gospels, taken together, as enacting a perpetual worship of God in their presentation of Christ. Symbolically, they were identified with the "four living creatures" of Rev. 4:6–8: the first like a lion, the second a calf, the third with a human face, and the fourth "like a flying eagle." Irenaeus, second-century bishop of Lyons (died 200), was among the earliest to suggest Luke's connection with "a calf, signifying the Son of God's sacrificial and sacerdotal office" (*Against Heresies* 14.1–4; 3.11.8), partly on account of his own spiritual reading of the parable of the prodigal son and the feast of restoration in Luke 15. The ox or calf symbol became useful for iconographic purposes in early church liturgy and art, and so stuck. Ambrose repeats it, linking Ezekiel's vision (1:5–12; 10:14) with John's vision of the throne of God, seeing the calf as "the priestly victim" (*Exposition of Luke* prol. 7–8). Aquinas will later summarize these connections typologically, saying that the sacrifice of the calf in Old Testament worship prefigures Christ, "sacrificed for the life of the whole world" (*Catena Aurea* 3.1, following Augustine, *Harmony of the Gospels* 1.2.6). But by then the associations had long been established. Illuminated medieval title pages for manuscripts of the Gospel of Luke, such as in the early eighth-century Lindisfarne Gospels, typically show Luke writing his Gospel in the company of a winged ox bearing a book symbolic of the word, pointing thus to its ultimate revelatory purpose, an adoring, exclusive, worshipful focus on Christ, the Living Word, eternal God incarnate.

Manuscript illustrations from this time through the fifteenth century often place the evangelist anachronistically in a scholar's study, surrounded by books, writing at a desk. This too is consciously symbolic, though it is particularly appropriate in the case of Luke, who is unique in telling his reader that he has, in

5. Ronald Hansen, *A Stay against Confusion: Essays on Faith and Fiction* (New York: HarperCollins, 2001), 19.

the manner of a careful scholar, consulted a variety of sources before setting pen to paper.[6]

Yet another traditional association for Luke should be mentioned, likewise highly symbolic but, as we shall see, richly suggestive for generations of Christian artists. Very early painted representations of Jesus as a child in the arms of the Virgin Mary were alleged to have been done by Luke (Hornik and Parsons 2003–7: 1.17–21, 26nn29–33), and, however implausible this may seem at the literal level, it is certainly understandable that Luke's particular focus on Mary, the annunciation, and the nativity and childhood scenes of the life of Christ, along with his considerable literary skill in depicting the events in Jesus's ministry and teaching throughout, should have together suggested portraiture of a detailed, artistically satisfying character. In one fanciful but genuinely moving private Renaissance devotional painting by Botticelli, Mary holds the child Jesus and simultaneously writes upon the page of Luke's text. The imagined composition is, of course, her beautiful poem, the Magnificat.[7] Such images have served to remind Christian readers of the distinctive inclusions in Luke's Gospel, the great beauty of his depictions, and his distinctive attention to the psalmlike poems of Mary and Zacharias, the beloved Magnificat and Benedictus respectively, of Christian liturgy since the sixth century.[8] In this way we may say that, esthetically, Luke's Gospel not only responds to some of the most beautiful poetry of the Old Testament (particularly from Isaiah and the Psalms), but that in the canon of the New Testament Luke's Gospel corresponds to the stylistic virtues of those Old Testament books particularly in pointing his reader consonantly to the beauty or "glory" (*doxa*) of the Lord.[9] It achieves this particular New Testament register of the theological transcendental in something like the way in which the Epistle to the Hebrews corresponds to Exodus, revealing the beauty of the Lord's holiness foreshadowed there, now in his one-for-all sacrifice.

Prayer and the Holy Spirit

About half the content of Luke is not found in the other Gospels. Some of this matter is new and some elaboration, but other elements are matters of distinctive

---

6. An illustration of this sort is found in Wolfram von den Steinem, *Homo Caelistis: Das Wort der Kunst im Mittelalter*, 2 vols. (Munich: Franke, 1965), 1. pl. 83a. See also Hornik and Parsons 2003–7: 1.1–5.

7. For a discussion of this painting see Ronald Lightbrown, *Sandro Botticelli: Life and Work* (New York: Abbeville, 1989).

8. The Benedictus (Luke 1:68–79) has been sung in the Western church since early times, at lauds. Anglican usage in the Book of Common Prayer preserved it for morning prayer. The Magnificat (1:46–55) is so named, in the manner of the Benedictus, from its opening word in Latin. Since the time of Benedict (early sixth century) it has been the canticle sung at vespers in the Western church (evensong in the Book of Common Prayer).

9. Hans Urs von Balthasar, *The Glory of the Lord: A Theological Aesthetics*, 7 vols., trans. Erasmo Leiva-Merikakis (San Francisco: Ignatius; New York: Crossroad, 1982–90).

detail. For example, few readers will have failed to recognize the greater frequency of situations in which Jesus is shown praying in Luke's account. This not only sets a certain tone but also reveals an important dimension of Jesus's relationship with God the Father and models this means of relationship for his followers. In Luke, prayer precedes decision: while Matthew and Mark also show Jesus withdrawing to pray from time to time during his public ministry (Matt. 14:23; Mark 1:35; cf. Luke 5:16), only Luke tells us that Jesus prays at the time of his baptism and that he "continued all night in prayer to God" (6:12) before choosing the Twelve; likewise, only Luke shows Jesus "alone praying" before the transfiguration (9:18–36). But the emphasis is pervasive: there are also distinctive parables about prayer unique to Luke (11:5–8; 18:1–8; 18:9–14). In Luke, the exemplary prayer given by Jesus to his disciples follows in response to the example of Jesus's own prayer, and only Luke reports the last words of Jesus as prayer (23:34, 46). The theme of prayer and answered prayer is evident from the beginning in the annunciation and nativity narratives peculiar to Luke: Zacharias's prayer is answered (1:13), Simeon's prayer is a prominent prayer of grateful benediction (2:22–28), and the poems of both Mary and Zacharias (her Magnificat and his Benedictus) are highlights of Luke 1.[10] When at his baptism Jesus prays, the heavens open and the dove of the Holy Spirit descends (3:21–22); when Jesus prays from the cross, the temple veil is rent from top to bottom (23:44–46).

The connection of prayer to a powerful presence of the Holy Spirit is thus especially prominent in Luke's writing. We may think, of course, of Acts 2. But the promise of the infilling of the Holy Spirit is already there in the words of the angel Gabriel to Zacharias as he serves at the altar (Luke 1:15), and the Spirit is promised to Mary on her prayerful acquiescence (1:35–38) and then comes to Elizabeth and the babe in her womb simply at Mary's greeting (1:41); Simeon is filled with the Holy Spirit as he prays (2:26–32). These connections are not all unique to Luke (e.g., Matt. 18:20), but they are certainly prominent enough when taken together that we may regard the prayer of the Lord, the prayer of his disciples, and the presence of the Holy Spirit as among the major themes Luke chose to emphasize.

Date and Canonical Placement

A variety of early Christian sources concur that the Gospels of Mark and Matthew were written before Luke began to write, and this accounted for the placement as third Gospel, despite the obvious fact that Luke's is the first of a two-volume work. The second, his Acts of the Apostles, is likewise dedicated to Theophilus,

---

10. A close study of this motif by Craig Bartholomew and Robby Holt is too rich to recount here in further detail; see "Prayer in/and the Drama of Redemption in Luke," in *Reading Luke: Interpretation, Reflection, Formation*, ed. Craig Bartholomew, Joel B. Green, and Anthony Thiselton, Scripture and Hermeneutics 6 (Milton Keynes, UK: Paternoster, 2005), 350–78, esp. 352–58.

and it refers back to this Gospel. We might well have expected the church to have paired them together rather than having John's Gospel intervene, and much speculation about the placement of Luke can be found in the annals of biblical scholarship down through the centuries. It is clear enough, however, that Luke's intention in his first volume was to focus on Christ in an ordered chronological fashion and in his second volume to chronicle the first years of the life of the church. For the first task he had to resort to the reports of eyewitnesses and the written accounts of others; in the second instance he was an intimate participant in much of what he records.

Though a wide range of dates has been proposed at various times by Luke-Acts scholars,[11] the reader can be comfortable with imagining composition taking place somewhere between AD 62–63, just prior to the release of Paul from prison in 63 (Acts 28:16), and, at the latest, about AD 80 (Bauckham 2006: 14). A brief summary of the various arguments made for dates along this spectrum may be found in Bock's detailed study (1994–96: 1.16–18).[12] I have come to think a date in the early to mid-60s is probable, all obvious factors considered (including Luke's omission of any mention of the destruction of Jerusalem in AD 70).

Luke's Gospel links the fourfold Gospel of the evangelists to Acts, and, as noted, Acts in turn introduces the writing of the four main authors of the rest of the New Testament, namely Paul and the apostles Peter, James, and John. This makes his work, as one modern scholar observes, "in effect, the lynchpin of the New Testament canon."[13] It is perhaps noteworthy in this regard that even the heretic Marcion, unwilling either to preserve the Old Testament or to read it figuratively as pointing to Christ, and divorcing thus the two Testaments, kept Luke in his shrunken canon—albeit a bowdlerized version, with what he took to be "judaizing" passages excised.[14] This was a nugatory effort: though he was almost certainly indeed a Gentile, Luke's literary methods reflect the characteristic Jewish mode of exegesis know as "pesher," by which, as Jean Daniélou, A. Laurentin, and others observe, "the events of the life of Jesus . . . are brought into line with the Old Testament prophecies which they fulfill."[15] As we shall see, this is nowhere clearer than in the way Luke highlights the covenantal and sacramental theme of the broken marriage between God and his increasingly adulterous chosen and the restoration of that marriage through God's reestablishment of that divine union through a virgin's consent and the fruitfulness of Christ's sacrifice. In

---

11. For a review of the immense scholarship on this question, see François Bovon, *Luke the Theologian*, trans. K. MacKinney, 2nd ed. (Waco: Baylor University Press, 2006), 631–36.

12. For text-critical analysis Bock is both reliable and extensive, perhaps the best of recent commentaries of this type.

13. Scobie, "Canonical Approach to Interpreting Luke," 331.

14. J. N. D. Kelly, *Early Christian Doctrines* (New York: HarperCollins, 1960; repr., Peabody, MA: Hendrickson, 2004), 57.

15. Jean Daniélou, *Christ and Us*, trans. Walter Roberts (London: Mowbray, 1961), 8; citing R. Laurentin, *Structure et théologie de Luc* (Paris: Lecoffre, 1964), 1.25–51.

this light the divine purpose seems primarily ordered so as to redeem his bride. Here, in a fashion distinctive among the evangelists, Luke shows himself to be an extraordinarily sensitive reader of the Jewish scriptures, keenly attuned to their dominant symbols and metanarrative argument. On any number of counts, and for any number of historical reasons, then, Luke's Gospel has proven to be a text of rich theological synthesis; though written by a Gentile, it is acutely attuned to the full Jewish canon of biblical revelation as preserved in the Septuagint text.

The Historian's Task

This is not at all to say that the writerly talents of Luke are insignificant to the theological value of the text as we have it. Quite the contrary: Luke's evident consciousness of literary form has been a great asset to his readers in every age. He calls the genre of his text *diēgēsis*, a term that the great disciple of Calvin, Theodore Beza, rightly associates with the method also announced in Acts 1:1: "Nothing other is meant except that he intends to write in the manner of a historian" (*nihil aliud declaret quam historiam conscribere*) (1642: 150). This alert to the reader, as I have suggested, shows Luke to be advertising his approach as that of a scholar. But it is additionally clear that he understands himself to be a scholar working in a recognizable Hellenistic form of narrative history or historiography. That is, he employs a literary genre and method highly recognizable to his hellenized contemporaries and widely respected among educated readers in his time. This genre should not be taken to be identical to *historia*, strictly a matter of information or for-the-record overview (Bock 1994–96: 1.52–53). Rather, in the first century it was understood to be a narrative account, a digest, we might say, organized so as to reveal design and ultimate significance in the events recollected. Luke's prologue remarks are thus paralleled in works such as 2 Maccabees 2.19–31, Josephus's *Jewish Antiquities* 1.1–4, and the *Letter of Aristeas* 1–8, as well as perhaps the prologue to the apocryphal wisdom book Sirach. Bauckham shows that similar Hellenistic texts make explicit their reliance on testimony and construe the narrator's task as assembling the witness of firsthand observers, drawing them collectively into a well-ordered account (2006: 5–7). In the case of Luke, there is ample reason to believe, on his declaration of genre alone, that his reportage is much closer to the form in which the eyewitnesses told their stories than would be the case for *historia* normatively.

In the genre *diēgēsis*, or ordered narrative account, an established practice in Hellenistic historical writing of the time was to prefer eyewitness accounts orally delivered over written reports. This conforms to the ancient tendency in general to trust verbal testimony given in a face-to-face encounter. Because the verbal bond was still the practice and preference for formal covenants as late as the medieval era, it may be that this aspect of Luke's intention in announcing his genre was better appreciated by pre-Reformation readers than by our own contemporaries, even in the absence of any full command of early Hellenistic comparative texts that would confirm its normative character. Aquinas, for example, responding to 1:2, says "the term 'handed down' ('they delivered') seems to show that the eyewitnesses regarded themselves as having a commission to transmit the truth" (*Catena Aurea* 3.1.9). Bonaventure reinforces this understanding by citing the Jewish tradition of responsible witnesses, and he quotes John 1:1 and 19:35 to say "because they had seen, therefore they gave witness" (2001–4: 1.26).

In one of the most useful of recent scholarly books on the Gospels, Bauckham draws convincing parallels from the early second-century writer Papias, bishop of Hierapolis, to show precisely how evidentiary and authoritative such a work of *diēgēsis* might be (2006: 12–38). Here, consultation with the "living voices" (*para zōēs phōnēs*), especially of those who were eyewitnesses (*autoptēs*), adds authority no mere third-person overview could hope to obtain.[16] In Luke 6:13–16 and Acts 1:13, the listing of "the Twelve" indicates clearly that these were the most privileged of such "living voices" consulted. They are those who, as Luke indicates, have been with Jesus "from the beginning" (Bauckham 2006: 116). This term in Luke 1:2 (*ap' archēs*), Bauckham convincingly shows (2006: 119), is a necessary qualification for obtaining prime authority in the genre as Luke understands it. Additionally, Luke features in his narrative "a much wider group of itinerant disciples than the Twelve" (2006: 129). In passages such as 6:14–16; 8:1–3; 10:1–20; 19:37; 23:49; 24:9, 33; and Acts 1:23, Luke not only gives us Matthias, Joseph, Barsabbas, and Cleopas but also names three of the women: Mary Magdalene, Joanna, and Susanna (Luke 8:2–3), the latter two of whom, like Cleopas, are named only in his Gospel. It seems likely that the named women were both among Jesus's disciples (24:6–7) and among Luke's eyewitness informants (9:18, 43).[17] As Moessner ventures, all these considerations "indicate Luke's intent to write proper Hellenistic narrative, inclusive of Hellenistic auditors' expectations cultivated in the atmosphere of Graeco-Roman rhetoric."[18] What this means for a modern reader in English translation is that the genre of Luke's Gospel is parallel neither to modern biography (Luke's own authorial insight into the life of Jesus is of comparatively little consequence compared to his ability to compile, collate, and accurately reflect the communal view of the Twelve and other eyewitnesses) nor to the official quasi-omniscient overview of an ancient historian such as Tacitus or Julius Caesar. Luke's account is closer to the literary equivalent of a documentary film, in which the narrative method is to arrange and elucidate with clarity the views of others on a topic or event.

In this context it may be helpful for the reader to reflect on an implication of much importance for one who would compare all four Gospels; they are not of

16. Daniélou, *Christ and Us*, 11.

17. Bauckham 2006: 131–32; Bauckham, *Gospel Women: Studies of the Named Women in the Gospels* (Grand Rapids: Eerdmans, 2002), 186–94.

18. David P. Moessner, "Reading Luke's Gospel as Ancient Hellenistic Narrative," in *Reading Luke: Interpretation, Reflection, Formation*, ed. Craig Bartholomew, Joel B. Green, and Anthony Thiselton, Scripture and Hermeneutics 6 (Milton Keynes, UK: Paternoster, 2005), 133; cf. Bauckham 2006: 310.

identical genre or form, and even the other two Synoptic Gospels thus should not be assumed to represent a type of *diēgēsis*. Mark's brief Gospel is an almost breathless account of the events of the life of Jesus as ordered to indispensable redemptive significance, a kind of bare-bones Gospel. Matthew's account is not like this, nor is it so chronologically ordered as Luke. Instead, Matthew moves in and out of the teaching of Jesus, turning his attention with laser-light intensity upon the character of Jesus's language, revealing his disposition to indirect speech, enigmatic wisdom sayings, and figurative suggestion concerning Jesus's interpretation of Torah and liturgical tradition. We might consider the precise detail with which Matthew recounts the Sermon the Mount, which is only summarized by Luke for his different purposes. We might also reflect on the fascinating seminar Jesus gives to his disciples in Matt. 13 regarding his pedagogical purposes in rejecting declarative, propositional discourse in favor of poetic, indirect language in his teaching—a discourse severely truncated in Luke, perhaps because parables seem to Luke to be so overwhelmingly normative to Jesus's literary teaching method that providing a more extended defense of the method seemed to him unnecessary.

John is different again: his primary focus is the interpenetration of word and flesh, spirit and sign, so that in some ways his is the most overtly sacramental of the four accounts; in his Gospel deliberatively, word and deed are both signs of spiritual reality and participate immediately in that reality. John is likewise attuned to the significance of the ministry of Jesus, but in a distinctive, philosophically imagined way: consider the sacramental incarnationalism of his prologue (John 1:1–14), Jesus's tutorial encounter with Nicodemus (3:1–21), the changing of water into wine at Cana (John 2)—all of which prepare us for the sacramental understanding of love and coinherence emphasized in that part of Jesus's teaching on which John's understanding turns, the unparalleled discourse on love (John 14–17), expressed climactically in Jesus's great high priestly prayer (John 17) before his atoning death on the cross. And when, after his resurrection, Jesus in John's account reveals himself first to Mary Magdalene and she mistakes him for the gardener (*o felix culpa*!), we sense John's enraptured, almost mystical focus on the deep mystery of God's abiding love for the fallen, revealed so transparently, as John is at pains to show us, in Jesus's relationships to the unlikely chosen, including Peter.

Luke's narrative purpose is not quite parallel to any of these others, in that by genre none of the others is *diēgēsis*, an attempt at ordered chronology. Attempts to treat the four Gospels as if they were of the same species—either by believers so as to force a conformity to "save the appearances" or by those who wish to discredit the Gospel accounts because they are inconsistent in their narrative inclusions—are an example of what philosophers call a "category mistake" and literary scholars think of as an insensitivity to genre. Luke's specific genre and purpose, simply put, are the only ones that could begin to oblige a more narrowly historical reflection on the reader's part, and even here we must be cautious, for ancient historical method and our modern sense of the obligations of a chronicler are far apart.

It is doubtless the case that Luke's distinctive task was made more possible than most modern Westerners can easily imagine by the prodigiously more refined practices of memorization that obtained widely until the advent of printing. Teachers like Socrates could depend on pupils such as Plato to preserve an exact verbal memory of his teaching;[19] there is wide attestation to precise verbal recall all through the annals of medieval European literature. The "word hid in the heart" would have been particularly apropos for the sayings of Jesus. Indeed, when Jesus said to his disciples, "Let these words sink down into your ears" (Luke 9:44), he was instructing his disciples to employ a habit widely practiced in both the Jewish and Gentile cultures of his time. Luke could count on a precision of memory no modern Western writer could hope for after the invention of moveable type made memory less essential.

For these reasons, among others, the work of the *Formgeschichte* critics that largely dominated the latter nineteenth and twentieth centuries in academic biblical studies is a historically bounded phenomenon that has become largely now of tertiary importance to a theological and literary commentary such as this. For those seeking further warrant for largely setting most of it aside in a context such as this one, I am happy to recommend Goulder's work as an example from within that field of sensible skepticism about spectral, hypothetical *Urtexts* such as Q (supposedly influential in varying degrees on the Synoptic Gospels).[20] Though there has been a dominating preoccupation with such matters for more than a century, now, in the pursuit of literary and theological engagement of Luke's text, we may here leave it to others to debate the merits of the hypotheses typically offered and to argue with the Jesus Seminar. To some readers, perhaps, an exclusion of so much scholarly endeavor will seem jarring, for even though "nearly all the contentions of the early form critics have been convincingly refuted," the training of most New Testament scholars has to the present still largely depended on their dominant paradigms (Bauckham 2006: 242). Certainly many excellent insights have resulted from the labors of these scholars, and in my own preparation and pursuit of this study I remain gratefully indebted to many whose labors have been primarily in this type of endeavor: Darrell L. Bock, François Bovon, F. W. Danker, Joseph A. Fitzmyer, I. Howard Marshall, David P. Moessner, John Nolland, Mikeal C. Parsons, and Charles H. Talbert among them. Yet in a work such as the present volume, intended rather for the serious layperson and pastoral teacher, I think my readers will be better served by reading the canonical text, first, in the light of Luke's own guidance in his prologue, hence in the light of an understanding of the genre in which he was writing; second, in the light of Old

19. Francis Yates, *The Art of Memory* (Chicago: University of Chicago Press, 1974); and Mary Carruthers, *The Book of Memory: A Study of Memory in Medieval Culture*, 2nd ed. (Cambridge: Cambridge University Press, 2008).

20. Michael D. Goulder, *Luke: A New Paradigm*, 2 vols., Journal for the Study of the New Testament Supplement 20 (Sheffield: JSOT Press, 1989). See the review by John Nolland in *Scottish Journal of Theology* 43 (1990): 269–72.

Testament scriptures and first-century Jewish thought; and, third, in the light of evidently empathetic and, as we might well say, "Spirit-directed" exposition of faithful readers of scripture down through the centuries. Not only will this help us keep our focus just where Luke would have it, namely on the person, sayings, and deeds of Jesus the Christ, but it will have the happy second-order benefit that we will become much more appreciative of the literary craftsmanship and rich detail for which Luke's Gospel has become so beloved among the New Testament writings by the church in all ages.

LUKE'S PROLOGUE
AND TWO NATIVITIES

LUKE 1

Luke's Prologue (1:1–4)

Although we may speak of formal prologues in canonical scripture—Isa. 1:1–20 and John 1:1–14 are examples—these are of a different type from what we have in Luke. Isaiah's prologue essentially outlines the argument and dialogical strategy of that book, and it is wonderfully useful as a guide to the underlying rhetorical unity of an otherwise generically diverse and superficially nonlinear composition.[1] John's prologue is a philosophical recapitulation and, at the same time, a proclamation of the cosmic significance of the incarnation as personal revelation of the divine Logos who originates and imbues creation and all history with significance.[2]

The prologue to Luke is different from either of these—more literary, focusing more narrowly on method in research, establishing order in terms of ultimate significance, and announcing writerly purpose with a specific, named reader in mind. "Most excellent Theophilus" (1:3) recurs, moreover, at the outset of the second volume of Luke's two-volume record, as Luke dedicates his Acts of the Apostles to this same evidently esteemed person (conceivably a patron, perhaps a Greek-speaking Roman official by whom an *apologia* may have been required). Knowing something more about Theophilus would be of great historical interest to us; unfortunately, no positive indicator of his identity has survived (Bock 1994–96: 1.15).[3] For practical purposes, then, we will have to assume that whoever Luke's intended reader may have been, anyone who is a "friend of God" (*theo-*

---

1. David Lyle Jeffrey, *People of the Book: Christian Identity and Literary Culture* (Grand Rapids: Eerdmans, 1996), 29–35.

2. Claude Tresmontant, *The Hebrew Christ: Language in the Age of the Gospels*, trans. K. D. Whitehead (Chicago: Franciscan Herald, 1989); and Craig A. Evans, *Word and Glory: On the Exegetical and Theological Background of John's Prologue*, Journal for the Study of the New Testament Supplement 89 (Sheffield: JSOT Press, 1993), 100–145.

3. In a captivating novel, *Theophilos* (San Francisco: Ignatius, 2010), Michael D. O'Brien speculates that Theophilus was a kind of foster-father to the evangelist and, in a convincing re-creation of the

philos) may be the reader implied by Luke and that we may count ourselves to be thus implicated if we answer to the compliment.

Luke's care to lay out his principles, historical context, genre of discourse (*diēgēsis*, "narrative account"), and authorial purpose to provide a reliable history have, however, survived with clarity, and in such a way as to influence centuries of reflection upon literary aspects of the sacred writer's work. One does not need to be a literary scholar to notice the precise language Luke employs.

First, he acknowledges the existence of previous accounts ("as many have taken in hand") written with the intent to declare fundamental elements of shared belief in the Christian community, "a declaration of those things which are most surely believed among us" (1:1 KJV). Commentators throughout church history have recognized that Luke was clearly aware of the diversity of first-century efforts to narrate the signal events and in some instances to interpret them or construe them erratically as well. Ambrose also was aware of other defective accounts, such as "Gospel of Basilides," "Gospel of Thomas," and another written "according to Matthias" (*Exposition of Luke* 17). These are later texts, but Ambrose, like Eusebius before him (*Ecclesiastical History* 3.4), sees Luke as sorting through such disparate materials, perhaps including noncanonical texts in some stage of their development, and finding some more trustworthy or useful than others.

There are medieval versions of our contemporary "study Bibles with notes," of which one of the most widely used was the *Glossa Ordinaria*; its marginal annotations, written beside the text of medieval manuscript Bibles (during the twelfth century and after), are representative, regarding 1:1–4, in stating a firm consensus that had by then emerged and has since endured. Luke's purpose was to consider everything he could discover of what Jesus did and taught and to weave from these many details a faithful account (*quam historiae texerunt veritatem*) containing not everything that might be unearthed but those things both confirmable and necessary for an understanding of the faith (*Glossa Ordinaria* 243b). Pertinently, the point of the *Glossa Ordinaria* itself was to be, as it was sometimes called, a *glossa communis*, a gathering together of a consensus of understanding in the faithful church, diachronically, in a fashion reflective of Luke's own announced method. Such blended or gathered citations form what was sometimes called a *catena*, of which the *Catena Aurea* ("golden chain") of Thomas Aquinas is perhaps the best known medieval example, while the glossed polyglot Bible (Greek, Old Latin, and Vulgate) of Calvin's scholarly successor Theodore Beza provides a leading Reformation example of the same sort of marginal scholarly commentary. All such editions literally surround the text on each page with an exegetical frame, what the editor considers the best interpretative comments of faithful Christians through the ages. Among Protestants at least as far forward as the work of Matthew Poole (1635), and among Catholics through to the great Jesuit commentator Cornelius

---

Hellenistic culture of that time, gives a good sense of how the events of the gospel might have been received by an educated Gentile.

Lapide (1639), it was nearly impossible to imagine a text of the Gospel author entirely bereft of the long, prayerful, and self-correcting conversation of faithful readers surrounding it in the margins, page after page.[4] Luke's careful, scholarly prologue is a forerunner for this kind of framing commentary, and it is worth noting that the ongoing practice is an important point of reference for us in this series of commentaries as we continue to seek a reading of the text *in communio*.

Among these running commentaries are a number of notable historic discussions of Luke's prologue; in them we may discern various types and degrees of attunement to what Luke himself was attempting to achieve as well as what he was offering by way of assistance to his reader. It is impossible to reflect on them all here, but the approaches of Thomas Aquinas, Bonaventure, and John Calvin are particularly illuminating in our own context.

Aquinas frames his own *Catena Aurea* of noble commentators by numerous contextual remarks and by establishing an overall exegetical framework. He quotes Isa. 50:3–4 as a kind of epigraph to identify what he calls "the object and condition of the writer," and here the key sentences are "I will clothe the heavens with blackness and make sackcloth their covering. The Lord hath given me the tongue of the learned, that I should know how by my word to uphold the weary." We can sense the apropos Aquinas has in mind: the ultimate subject matter of Luke's Gospel is of course the passion of Christ, at which literally there was darkness as a result of which (he cites Ambrose) the faith of the disciples was shaken and clouded. Luke's special gifts, Aquinas suggests, include his learning and his precise distinctions, which "uphold the weary" (*Catena Aurea* 3.1).

Calvin's preface is considerably more compendious and attends in Renaissance humanist fashion to the genre of "gospel" as he understands it to be defined by Paul (Rom. 1:2), and it is superior in technical treatment to Aquinas, though everywhere also more polemical in tone. Distinctively, Calvin entirely excises the early commentators included by Aquinas from his own declaration on the text:

> There were tyrants on all sides, threatening to obstruct the course of the true teaching by terror and oppression. It was a time for Satan and his crew to spread clouds of error all over, to spoil the true light. And as the commonalty had little concern for preserving the purity of the gospel, and few took careful note of what Satan plotted, [or] the danger that lurked in such deceptions, so it was that any man who stood out for his exceptional faith and distinctive gifts of the Spirit had to take the responsibility of greater study and care upon himself, to play a man's part in keeping religious truth free and unspotted from any corrupting influence. Such men were chosen of God, not unlike holy guardians of the law, faithfully to hand down to future generations the heavenly teaching entrusted to them. (Calvin 1972: 1.1)

---

4. Beza 1642; Poole 1685; Lapide 1639; see S. Pagano, "Analysis Notionis Inspirationis S. Scripturae apud Cornelium a Lapide," *Revue de l'Université d'Ottawa* 15 (1945): 65–85. The Ancient Christian Commentary on Scripture (gen. ed. Thomas Oden [Downers Grove, IL: InterVarsity]) is a gesture of return to this early model.

Bonaventure's approach is not less deliberate than that of either Aquinas or Calvin. Like Thomas, he chooses a key biblical text to begin his general preface, in this case a citation by Jesus, in Luke 4:18, of Isa. 61:1. While the Lord's reading of the prophet is his pretext, it is actually the Isaiah text itself rather than Luke 4 that Bonaventure cites: "The Spirit of the LORD is upon me, because the LORD has anointed me." Bonaventure's commentary is not formally a *catena*, but on every page it is imbued with a rich *texera* or weaving of quotations from the full range of scripture and the fathers of the church, a virtual symphony of responses to the gospel as ongoing witness to Christ. His preface is bathed in prayer and invokes the Holy Spirit; he is explicit in his desire that his readers should not regard his commentary as either a complete reflection of faithful commentators or in any sense a last word (2001–4: 1.23–24). But in perhaps the most literarily lucid of premodern expositions, he parses Luke's prologue so as to identify "his [Luke's] intention with regard to four points: that with regard to his motive, what prompted him to write, the direction he took, and his consummate goal" (25).

It is remarkable how Bonaventure is attuned to all the issues discussed thus far: the genre requirements of a "narrative historian" (2001–4: 1.27), the necessity of eschewing unreliable sources (26), his own appreciation of Luke's "orderly, adequate, and diligent process," yet his deep sense, notwithstanding all scholarly diligence, that Luke's Gospel was written "at the prompting of the Holy Spirit" (27–29).

All three approaches—that of Aquinas, Bonaventure, and Calvin—are representative of historic Christian commentary, and each can contribute something to our understanding of the Gospel of Luke. For it is the understanding of the reader, especially any reader who may, like Theophilus, be described fairly as a "lover of God," that Luke was keeping most clearly in mind from the outset, providing accordingly a "declaration of those things which are most surely believed among us" (1:1 KJV). Having acquired a "perfect understanding" of all things from the very first events he records (1:3), Luke sets it as his purpose that his reader should be able to come to know "the certainty of those things" in which he has already been instructed (1:4).

Accordingly, we too, as Ambrose suggests, should remember that "whoso separates the Word from God tears the garment; . . . whoso separates Christ from God tears the garment." The suitably prepared reader today is one in spirit like unto the original intended reader: "So the gospel was written to Theophilus, i.e., to him whom God loves. If you love God, it was written to you; if it was written to you, discharge the duty of an Evangelist. Diligently preserve the pledge of a friend in the secrets of the Spirit. Frequently consider and often discuss the good things committed to your trust by the Holy Spirit who is given to us [2 Tim. 1:14]" (*Exposition of Luke* 23). Such, says Ambrose, is the conversation into which we are invited by Luke, even as by the Lord himself. We will find that this point is echoed by all the lineage of Luke's faithful readers.

Zacharias and Gabriel (1:5–25)

Among Franciscan exegetes of the thirteenth century it was sometimes observed that, in the plan of salvation and the life of the redeemed, "nothing happens for the first time."[5] Strictly speaking, of course, this is hyperbole. Yet it captures a principle in the divine pedagogy that has fascinated readers of scripture down through the centuries. Pairing (or juxtaposition) and intensification in a sequence of parallels are important features of biblical narrative. Even as the events of the New Testament are presaged by events with messianic portent in the Old—typology as we think of it—so also there is imitation or fulfillment of New Testament events in the life of those who subsequently live *imitatio Christi*, in the imitation of Christ. While the stigmata of Francis is a luminous example of strict imitation outwardly symbolized, the patterning of event and foreshadowed event, type and antitype, is actually basic to our understanding of the New Testament from the perspective of a Jewish reader also. One remarkable feature of Luke's Gospel and his history of the early church in Acts is the fine attunement that he, as a Gentile convert, shows to this Jewish principle of reiteration. Nowhere is this understanding more evident than in the opening chapters of his Gospel.

Luke's unique focus on the manner of Jesus's birth and his early infancy, as well as on the parallel events concerning the annunciation and conception of Jesus's cousin and forerunner John, suggests the possibility that among his informants was either Mary herself or someone very close to her. While in Jewish culture the witness of women was normally inadmissible where evidence was required, this was less the case in Hellenic Gentile culture. More to the point of Luke's interest, perhaps, may have been his keen awareness that one distinguishing feature of Jesus's own life and teaching was the countercultural attention he paid throughout his ministry to women, something that Luke, as a Greek living in Palestine, would also have appreciated as an evident departure from Semitic norms.[6] In any case, much of Luke's narrative in 1:5–2:52 is most plausibly imagined as the first-person recollection of a woman singular in importance to the entire biblical narrative, namely that one who had, until her recounting to Luke, "kept all these things in her heart" (2:51). Thus, though Matthew's account is typically Semitic in recounting the circumstances of Jesus's birth from Joseph's perspective, Luke's vantage point is strikingly different. Rather than offering a customary patriarchal genealogy, Luke gives a more intimate family history of Jesus and focuses on the annunciation and birth itself, details missing from the other Gospel accounts.

He does this by "doubling," pairing early events that have interrelated significance, and in a total of six episodes, four of them explicitly paired: two annunciations, two births, two circumcisions, and two temple scenes. Other narratives are

---

5. This reached its most extreme form in Joachism, but the tendency is prominent in all Franciscan exegesis. See David Lyle Jeffrey, *Franciscan Spirituality and the Early English Lyric* (Lincoln: Nebraska University Press, 1975).

6. Jean Daniélou, *Ministry of Women in the Early Church*, 2nd ed. (London: Faith Press, 1974).

of course unique to Jesus in the immediate context: namely, his birth having been revealed to the shepherds, the presentation at the temple, Simeon's and Anna's momentous prophecies, and finally the account of Jesus left behind in the temple at the age of twelve, where he discourses with the elders. Luke keeps close company with the other three canonical Gospels, however, in forbearing comment on the hidden years in Nazareth. (Stories concerning these years are a primary feature of narratives rejected by the church, including those ascribed to Thomas, James—the so-called Protevangelium—and the unascribed "Infancy of Jesus Christ." Luke may have rejected such stories, or he may not have heard of them, since the extant texts of such narratives are all of later composition.)

Luke is scrupulous to locate the events surrounding Jesus's birth precisely in the reign of Herod the Great, the puppet Jewish ruler in Roman-occupied Judea from 37 BC to 4 BC. Herod's commission from Mark Anthony and the Senate was to bring Galilee, Syria, and part of Perea as well as Judea under a more unified Roman provincial authority (Tacitus, *Histories* 5.9). The Venerable Bede, eight centuries later, was historically astute in noting that Herod's rule was a secular displacement of the ruling power of the priesthood, which was now limited to worship functions alone. Thus, in every political sense, to begin with Zacharias is for Luke to begin his narrative in a poignant but terribly pertinent recollection that only a vulnerable remnant of Jewish life in Jerusalem was still focused on temple worship. In terms of the great metaphor for faithfulness and covenant relationship of the Old Testament, in which the prophets and poets of Israel had seen the chosen people as "married" to God, Israel has by now largely forgotten the love of its "betrothals" (Jer. 2:2), has "polluted a land with your harlotry and with your wickedness" (3:2), even "committed adultery with stones and trees" (3:9). In a context in which only a remnant of the faithful can recall Jeremiah's lament that "the virgin of Israel has done a most appalling thing" (18:13), perhaps few now remembered to think of their God as the prophets represent him, a grievously wounded lover who in many places is recorded as saying, as he does in Jeremiah, "for the brokenness of the daughter of my people I am broken; I mourn, dismay has taken hold of me" (8:21), and yet who has also reminded his faithless spouse that despite her countless infidelities his own love is everlastingly faithful (31:3–4).[7] In the prophecy of Hosea he had promised that he will on his own initiative one day renew the broken covenant: "'I will betroth you to me forever . . . in loving-kindness and mercy; I will betroth you to me in faithfulness, and you shall know the LORD. It will come to pass in that day that I will answer,' says the LORD. . . . 'I will say to those who were not my people, "You are my people!"'" (Hos. 2:19–23). Even in the dark days of the Roman occupation there remain a few in Israel who remember, and the worship of this remnant sets the stage for a drama whose full effect is available to us, as to them, precisely to the degree that we understand what the prophets have spoken as crucial prolegomena to what

7. Jeremiah quotations in this paragraph are from the New American Standard Bible.

is recorded here. As Luke turns to the first scene of his *diēgēsis* and the curtain rises, we are introduced to our first sign that the true husband of Israel is about to show his hand.

Zacharias

Zacharias's name probably means something like "Yahweh has remembered again." This tacit connection to the language of the prophets escapes Luke's explicit comment, yet the old priest's faithfulness of lineage does not go without note: Zacharias is of "the division of Abijah," a lineage (established 1 Chr. 24:10) itself historically undistinguished, yet treated here as worthy of note, perhaps not least in that Zacharias has married Elizabeth, "a daughter of Aaron." There were at one time as many as eighteen thousand priests ordained to temple service in rotation; only irregularly and by lot were such priests chosen to offer incense at the morning and evening sacrifice. It would be almost certainly a once-in-a-lifetime experience. Zacharias was not, however, the high priest, as some early fathers (e.g., Ambrose and Chrysostom) thought, unduly influenced as perhaps they were by such noncanonical apocrypha as the Protevangelium of James. Searching for spiritual significance in the detail, Bede, typically more accurate in his historical understanding, is also prepared to think that in "the course of Abijah" being the "eighth lot" we have a symbolic suggestion of the new covenant subtly embedded in the text (*Homilies on the Gospels* 2.19.191). While historical precision and spiritual exegesis are often fruitfully commensurable, in this case the principal point more probably lies right on the surface of Luke's narrative. That is, the key to Luke's careful account of John's parentage is the obedience and faithfulness of Zacharias and Elizabeth themselves: "And they were both righteous before God, walking in all the commandments and ordinances of the Lord blameless" (1:6). Such a commendation from the point of view of halakic (moral, ritual, and domestic) requirements not only sets the old couple apart from the general faithlessness that had become commonplace but also establishes that in his parents John the Baptist, last of the prophets, would have a holy nurturing. It also establishes succinctly and without elaboration that Zacharias's offering on behalf of the people would be by a man disposed to "offer rightly" and thus, as one obedient to the law, to become a fitting witness to God's grace breaking into human history—a pattern to be echoed tacitly in the subsequent narrative of the annunciation to Mary. According to Ambrose (*Exposition of Luke* 1.18), we should not think of Elizabeth and Zacharias as especially prominent in the eyes of their contemporaries but rather as significant simply by virtue of their grateful faithfulness in being chosen. They are representative of a remnant whose righteousness was apparent "before God . . . who cannot be deceived."

And yet we cannot help but observe that even here we have revealed a universally characteristic feature of biblical narrative concerning those whom God chooses: their common humanity, more than their perfection, is typically underscored.

The histories of the patriarchs are pithy with foibles of all kinds; alabaster saints they are not, not even worthies such as Abraham, Jacob, Moses, David, or Elijah. Zacharias is, as far as we know, less to be censured than any of these, perhaps, yet at the very moment when God's miraculous intervention is announced, even as at the height of the evening sacrifice the angel Gabriel appears to him, he of all people flinches with disbelief.

That Elizabeth was barren and that she and Zacharias were both old are other key features of Luke's narrative. There were precedents of which every faithful Jew, and certainly every priest, would be aware: Abraham and Sarah (Gen. 17), Hannah, and even (as John Chrysostom will later note, *Homilies on Genesis* 49) Rebecca and Rachel—all of whose barrenness preceded God's granting of sons and heirs to the covenant (cf. Origin, *Homilies on Genesis* 12.1). In the most notable case of Abraham and Sarah, a doubt similar to that of Zacharias is a prominent feature of the story; here, perhaps, because of his failure to be instructed by such precedents so as to accept the angel's promise at face value, Zacharias is punished. One of the few voices for the remaining faithful is silenced. Thus, we have both a familiar pattern repeated and yet also an intensification concerning the require-ment of faith: such a silencing is without precedent.

That the offering of incense by Zacharias was probably made at the evening sacrifice is suggested by mention of the large crowd waiting in the outer court praying until the officiating priest should emerge. Normally this evening worship would take place within a predictable period of time; on this occasion there is a delay. At first, Zacharias alone understands why. Suddenly, standing at the right side of the altar the angel Gabriel has appeared, as if out of nowhere. The old priest is frightened, and his trepidation occasions the first of several "comforting words" in Luke: "Do not be afraid, Zacharias," says the angel, "for your prayer is heard" (1:13). Then follows the astonishing promise that Elizabeth shall bear a son, whose name is to be John and whose birth is to be a source of joy not only to his parents but to many others (1:14). As the crowd waits outside, the delay is further prolonged, this time in part by Zacharias's incredulity. He hears that the child is to be filled with the Holy Spirit, even from his mother's womb, to live as a Nazirite, and to be a means of restoring many in Israel to faithful obedience, even fulfilling the eschatological promise of a returned Elijah who will reconcile the generations before the Messiah comes (1:15–17; cf. Mal. 4:5–6). Clearly, this is a lot of astonishing information for Zacharias to absorb in a few moments. Yet in terms of the longing of the faithful for their redemption it is overwhelm-ingly good news, and so when Zacharias blurts out his response not as praise or thanksgiving but rather in an importunate demand for some sign or warrant of the truth of what the angel has said, it is almost as though he is unsure that an angel at the altar might not be trying to trick him (Luke 1:18). His reflexive lack of trust, despite what he should remember of the ways of God, brings about a rebuke (1:19–20). He, whose very name means "God has again remembered," has himself forgotten that God—who is "yesterday, today, the same forever"—has done just such shocking, counterintuitive things before in Israel's past. The implicit irony here heightens or intensifies the great biblical parallels invoked, even as his delay in coming out to the people (1:21) and his mute countenance and sign language when he does emerge all suggest to Zacharias's as yet unwitting audience that something mysterious and dramatic has doubtless occurred (1:22).

Gabriel

The angel Gabriel, whose name means "power of God" or "emissary of God," appears four times in the canonical scriptures, each time with a messianic message. For a Jewish audience, it would probably have been of interest that he appears also in intertestamental literature (*2 Enoch* 24.1; *1 Enoch* 40.9) and in the Qumran scrolls (1QM 9.15–16). For talmudic tradition Gabriel is the angel who stands directly before the throne of God, and his special guardianship is over Judah (*Numbers Rabbah* 2.10). Also, he is associated with "the man clothed with linen" in Ezek. 10:2 (*Leviticus Rabbah* 26.8; Babylonian Talmud, tractate *Ta'anit* 3.41, 84) and is credited in Jewish commentary with being the figure who wrestled with Jacob and gave Israel its "new name" (*Genesis Rabbah* 78.3; *Zohar* 2.41b). Perhaps most pertinently, Gabriel's presence was thought by Jewish teachers to indicate proximity of the Shekinah itself, the glory of God's own presence (*Sanhedrin Rabbah* 2.5; 32.9; *Genesis Rabbah* 97.3; also Trypho, in Justin's *Dialogue with Trypho* 20, 28). How much of this Luke knew we can only guess, but the associations are largely consistent with the two canonical Old Testament references that he doubtless did know and that clearly identified Gabriel with God's direct agency in delivering messianic assurance (Dan. 8:15–27). Readers will remember that Gabriel appears a second time in Dan. 9:20–21 to further clarify the eschatological significance of Daniel's vision, precisely when Daniel is praying in repentance for the sins of the people "about the time of the evening offering." In Luke 1:11, Gabriel appears just as Zacharias is offering the evening sacrifice of incense; the reiteration is unmistakable. That the angel is "standing on the right side of the altar of incense" suggests that he stood nearest the entrance to the holy of holies, as if he had come directly from the presence of God.

It is characteristic in all of biblical literature that an encounter with an angel is profoundly unsettling. The doubled verbs used in 1:12 (*etarachthē . . . phobos*, literally "terrified with fear") suggests something even stronger. It is equally characteristic that when bringing a message of consolation or promise the angel will say, "Fear not!" (cf. Dan. 10:12, 19). This echoes the "fear not" assurances of God speaking to Abram and Moses (Gen. 15:1; Num. 21:34), the destitute Hagar (Gen. 21:17), and the insecure Isaac (26:24). "Fear not!" is often on the lips of prophets who announce to a distraught and suffering Israel that their salvation is coming (Isa. 41:10, 13; 43:5; 44:8). All these associations reverberate in Gabriel's assurance to Zacharias, even as later to Mary (Luke 1:30). (When the shepherds on the hills of Judea are frightened by an angel, even before a host of angels appears

in the skies above them singing, the same assurance is given [2:10].) Such fear
at the sight of an angelic being is hardly irrational; deeper than the element of
surprise, being startled or caught off guard is surely for most who experience it
an instantaneous apprehension of being confronted by a presence of the holy and
knowing oneself unprepared for such an encounter. As John Chrysostom notes,
"The most righteous of men cannot see an angel without feeling fear" (*On the
Incomprehensible Nature of God*), and Calvin suggests of Zacharias that "he was
frightened to the point of collapse" (1972: 1.8). The assurance "fear not!" presup-
poses at an intuitive level the recognition that, as at the first Passover, angels can
be emissaries of God's judgment, of death and destruction. Yet fear of an emissary
of God is also, in its way, reflexively consistent with fear of the Lord himself. Assurance that there is no need to fear God's immanent judgment is then already a
sign of grace, coming redemption, and future hope.

Gabriel's assurance continues with a word of comfort, both for the community
and for the priest: the prayer of Zacharias has been heard, and Elizabeth will bear
a son—despite being, like her husband, well past the age for such an event to
occur naturally (1:7). Augustine understands the prayer that has been heard to
relate to the priestly prayer of repentance for the sins of the people and the word
about a son to be an answer to the separate, private prayers of Zacharias and Elizabeth (Sermon 291: "For the Nativity of St. John the Baptist" in Patrologia latina
38.133). This seems to be the appropriate interpretation. Yet the longed-for birth
of a son is not here envisioned just as fulfillment for his parents' sake, since "many
will rejoice at his birth. For he will be great in the sight of the Lord" (1:14–15).
That is, here is a case in which there is to be one answer to two prayers, a fusing
of private desire and representative desire for the common good for Israel—for
which an answer is to be bodied forth in the person of a prophet and a preacher
who will call the people to that very repentance (perhaps we should say "eschatological repentance") for which intercessors have for centuries been praying at
the time of the evening sacrifice.

Gabriel specifies the fashion in which John is to be prepared for that purpose,
notably his Nazirite vows. But he adds something else: John will "be filled with
the Holy Spirit, even from his mother's womb" (1:15). This is an arresting detail. It is possible that Zacharias would have remembered what the Lord said to
Jeremiah at the time of his calling: "Before I formed you in the womb, I knew
you; before you were born I sanctified you; I ordained you a prophet to the
nations" (Jer. 1:5). The Hebrew word translated "sanctified" is there literally
"set apart." Here in Luke the conception of a prenatal consecration is intensified: Zacharias is told that even in Elizabeth's womb the child will already "be
filled with the Holy Spirit" (Luke 1:15). Though the plain sense makes Calvin
uncomfortable, Ambrose more representatively notes (*Exposition of Luke* 1.33)
that later, when John leaps in his mother's womb when Mary comes to visit
Elizabeth (1:44), it is a confirmation of the Spirit's indwelling in John already
while in the womb.

Further, John "will turn many of the children of Israel to the Lord their God" (1:16), the very thing for which, in the evening sacrifice, Zacharias has been praying, namely repentance (cf. Jer. 3:7; Dan. 9:13), and precisely in the fashion called for in the prophecy in Mal. 4:5–6 that before the Messiah will come, God "will . . . send Elijah the prophet . . . [to] turn the hearts of the fathers to the children, and the hearts of the children to their fathers." As Gabriel frames this prophecy concerning John, "he [the messianic forerunner] will also go before him in the spirit and power of Elijah, 'to turn the hearts of the fathers to the children,' and the disobedient to the wisdom of the just, to make ready a people prepared for the Lord" (Luke 1:17; cf. Ps. 24). At this point in Gabriel's proclamation the messianic portent is overwhelming.

Yet it is at just this high point that Zacharias, faithful priest though he has been, stumbles. He is not, of course, the first to doubt such a promise of God, given that it runs against the probabilities of nature. Chrysostom, Bede, and others see Zacharias's demand for a sign as the reflex of an incipiently rebellious spirit (Greek *tolma*, Latin *audacia*), a contrary to faith. While this reading seems entirely plausible, the reader will also immediately think of analogous biblical stories. A difference between this story and the most obvious parallel, the assurance to Abraham of a son and heir by Sarah, is that Abraham's laughter is face down in the dirt and his articulation of fundamental doubt is "in his heart" (Gen. 17:16–17). Zacharias asks aloud, like Gideon (Judg. 6:17), for a sign, and yet, in a way unprecedented in either that or the Abraham story, the angel messenger is in this case offended enough to punish him for his doubt. Gabriel now identifies himself and his purpose as plainly as one might to one with no knowledge of Jewish history at all and tells him that Zacharias himself shall be unable to say another word until the child is born, because, he says, "you did not believe my words which will be fulfilled in their own time" (Luke 1:19–20). Bede sees the irony: Gabriel "gives him the sign he asks for, that he who spoke in unbelief might now by silence learn to believe" (*Homilies on the Gospels* 2.20). The silencing of Zacharias also serves, as Marshall notes (1978: 61), to conceal the revelation from everyone else—perhaps including even the apparently embarrassed Elizabeth—until the event takes place. That this is one of the ironies of providence that everywhere characterize the unfolding master design of biblical grand narrative is suggested by the words *plēroō* ("to fulfill") and *kairos* ("appointed time"). Gabriel's stern judgment, as well as his good news, thus hangs over the whole of the narrative from this point. Zacharias tries in vain to communicate with the waiting worshipers when he comes out from the inner court; shortly afterward, his service completed, he retreats home. The child is conceived. Elizabeth's pregnancy is hidden for more than five months. Suspense gathers concerning the outcome.

But the looked-for birth is not to be before suddenly Gabriel appears again, this time in the most surprising fashion of all—not in the temple, nor even in Jerusalem, but in an undistinguished village, to an apparently unheralded young woman with no evident connection to either the ruling or the religious institutions of Israel.

Mary and Gabriel (1:26–38)

As the curtain rises on this second scene, Mary is described simply as "a virgin
betrothed to a man whose name was Joseph, of the house of David" (1:27). That
is all. There is no description of her domicile; it is simply inferred from the verb
(*eiselthōn*, "entering," typically used with reference to "coming into" a house) that
she is at home privately, precisely as one would expect a young woman of that
time to be, in seclusion from the gaze of men. In such a culture, the virginity of
a young woman was both her own and her family's central concern, a matter of
honor. We, who live in a time of sexual laxity more resembling Roman than a
normatively halakic Jewish culture, may too easily underestimate the degree to
which sexual purity was then integral to both personal and family honor. It is
exceedingly unlikely that a man other than her father or younger siblings would
have access to a young woman in her familial home. Thus, we should not be at all
surprised that Mary was taken aback by the appearance of the angel Gabriel. Here
we need to bear in mind that there is no reason for us to imagine that Mary was
confronted with one of the angels as imagined by the painters, whose wings are
visual attributes designed to distinguish them symbolically from humans: Dan.
9:21, for example, refers to "the man Gabriel." That he was not, however, human
but a divine emissary must have been suggested by his bearing or radiance.

Luke tells us nothing about Mary's parents; her family is indicated only through
Elizabeth, now in her sixth month of pregnancy (that historical detail is of importance to him). There is nothing to indicate a special household or an extraordinary life prior to the annunciation. Indeed, Mary's is a hidden life, even as her
extraordinary choosing is to be itself hidden, by contrast with the annunciation
to Zachariah, which is immediately a subject of public knowledge. As Calvin puts
it, this crucial prophecy was "buried in the heart of one girl only" (1972: 1.21).
Calvin is surely right that this is not the way our own imagination runs; a novelist or propagandist would want to make a narrative case for her special virtue,
her noble family, or some other auspicious foreshadowing. Here, we get a stark
reversal of that expectation; the family of the forerunner or herald is much more
auspicious in its circumstances than is the proleptic family of the Lord.

That Mary is a virgin, moreover, is emphasized by repetition of the term *parthenon*.[8] This firm identification heightens the sense of the extraordinary in the
event of Gabriel's direct address to Mary (Hebrew Miriam), since, as we have seen,
it was so unusual in Jewish culture for any man, let alone a strange man, to salute
a woman, especially an unmarried woman, directly (Lightfoot 1979: 3.25). But
what he says is still more extraordinary: "Rejoice, highly favored one, the Lord is
with you; blessed are you among women!" (Luke 1:28). The term *kecharitōmenē*
("highly favored one") is highly unusual, precedented in the Septuagint only in

---

8. This is a strong term; some Hellenic readers would associate it with the Parthenon, the Athenian
temple to the goddess of wisdom, Athena, and the connection may have been remembered in later references to the Virgin as *sedes sapientiae* ("seat of wisdom").

Dan. 10, where Gabriel is likewise the speaker, and it establishes here a connection between Mary as singular "chosen one" and her most saintly Old Testament predecessor in relationship to the eschatological fulfillment of God's purpose to redeem his people. Mary is perhaps to all outward appearances quite ordinary, but in the divine perspective she is to be revealed as extraordinary on a level yet unimagined in her culture. (Gabriel's form of address to her, his calling her *kecharitōmenē*, suggests in historic Catholic exegesis her having found favor *before* the angel declares it; the parallel with Daniel supports that implication.)

The subversion of normative cultural expectation is heightened in several ways, some highlighted by the pairing of this narrative with that of the announcement to Zacharias of John's birth: special births in scripture had always been announced to the father to be; this time it is the woman who hears first. Gabriel says to Mary, "The Lord is with you," not merely in greeting but in the context a strong affirmation of her chosenness. The following phrase, "blessed are you among women" (Luke 1:28), is missing from some manuscripts but anticipates the response of Elizabeth in 1:42. All of this together makes the angel's greeting a stunning indication of Mary's importance to what follows.

That Mary is "troubled at his saying" should hardly, given this context, be surprising to us. What is more remarkable is that she does not swoon, cry out, or flee from the room. Instead, in Luke's phrase, she "considered what manner of greeting this was" (1:29). In this simple descriptive phrase we are given an important insight into her remarkable composure and alert presence of mind. When the angel then says, "Fear not, Mary, for thou hast found favour with God" (KJV), his calm clarification not only assures her he means no harm but also heightens further the gravity of his address; when he then tells her that she will conceive and bear a son whose name is to be Jesus, one who will not only be called great but will be "the Son of the Highest," that this son will be given the throne of "his father David" and will be the eternal ruler of Israel, she must have been astounded at the eschatological magnitude of what was being said to her. After all, the earthly throne of David had been supplanted by the Herodians, and the Romans now occupied the land.

But when she asks, "How can this be?" it should be apparent to the reader that her mind is far from being directed principally to these political circumstances or probabilities. She may, as Calvin suggests, simply be "struck with a feeling of sudden wonder." Or it may also be that she is simply referring to the obvious personal realities: she is betrothed but not married; a woman espoused but still a virgin, she "know[s] not a man" (KJV). *Ginōskō*, like its Hebrew counterpart, *yāda'*, is the polite but practical euphemism of a modest culture for sexual relations. Perhaps her actual marriage is as yet some time off: how could she be pregnant?

The suggestion of some ancient commentators that she had previously made a vow of perpetual virginity has no support in Luke or any other first-century or canonical scripture. *Ginōskō* is present tense; in Luke's narrative, Mary does not say she is already or will be a dedicated virgin. The suggestion of the apocryphal

Protevangelium of James (ca. AD 140) that Mary was "devoted to the Lord from her infancy" (2.10), lived in the temple (3.3), had daily "conversation of angels" (5.2), and had formally pledged her virginity at the age of fourteen (5.5–6) attempts to lay the groundwork in that text for Gabriel indicating here that Mary has "found favor with the Lord" because she has already made virginity her choice of life (7.9, 16).[9] That is, in the later apocryphal text, a relationship between meritorious and formal religious life and the divine choice is putatively established, and her previously consecrated role is made to be of more public knowledge than anything in Luke; it is worth pondering that all of this retrospective material actually contradicts the central emphasis of Luke's presentation.

There are reasons, of course, for the continuing appeal of the apocryphal text, even after its exclusion under Pope Gelasius (492–96). They are deeply rooted in Hellenistic and Roman (that is, Gentile) anthropology. We should appreciate that to normative Gentile thinking in Mediterranean culture in that period, virginity, in particular female virginity, was not only highly valued in the premarital domestic context (that would be if anything more true in Israel) but also had long been associated with the highest state of Gentile religious life and practice. The apocryphal account seemed more natural to some than any view that might exclude altogether the question of publicly established merit and choice of life in the establishment of Mary's preannunciation "holiness." The Protevangelium of James in its Latin translation was widely copied and circulated, and knowledge of it accounts for statements such as that of Gregory of Nyssa, who, in response to Mary's question to Gabriel, "How can this be, since I do not know a man?" says that she deemed "her inviolability a more precious thing than the Angel's declaration" (quoted in Aquinas, *Catena Aurea* 3.1.155). One may doubt this inference, the preciousness of virginity notwithstanding. In a Jewish context, nothing would be regarded as more precious than to be the addressee of a divine word. Though Luke would have been as aware as any Greek that the priestesses of Artemis Hymnia in Arcadia and those of Heracles at Thespiae in Boeotia[10] were to remain virgins throughout their lives, he makes no suggestion of this possibility in his own narrative concerning Mary. That idea, a recurring motif in medieval art and legendary, comes from the Protevangelium of James distinctively, and we can imagine that it must have seemed to many Mediterranean readers a natural analogy with the Gentile religions they knew. Among those to whom it seemed natural were Jerome (Homily 87) and John Chrysostom (*Homilies on Genesis* 49), but much of the emphasis on Mary's perpetual virginity develops still later (Vatican II, *Gaudium et spes* §46).

Another point worth pondering here is the frank biological realism that undergirds Mary's question in 1:34. The angel Gabriel does not, as in the case of

---

9. Quotations and numbering of the Protevangelium of James follow Frank Crane, *The Lost Books of the Bible* (New York: Alpha House, 1926).

10. It is believed that Luke died there. See Roger Steven Evans, *Sex and Salvation: Virginity as a Soteriological Paradigm in Ancient Christianity* (Lanham, MD: University Press of America, 2004).

Zacharias, regard her question as an expression of doubt in the authority of the divine word to her but rather as a genuine desire for clarification concerning something that she would recognize as without precedent even in biblical history. Yet there is a hint of that history in Gabriel's response: "The Holy Spirit will come upon you, and the power of the Highest will overshadow you" (1:35). The clue is in the verb *episkiasei* ("will overshadow"). In the Septuagint, as Bock notes, this verb "refers either to the Shekinah cloud that rested on the tabernacle (Exod. 40:34–35; Num. 9:18; 10:34) or to God's presence in protecting his people (Ps. 91:4 [LXX 90:4])."[11] Thus, the divine presence in the holy of holies, which Zacharias did not himself encounter, is here made to "overshadow" and inhabit, as tabernacle, the person and womb of the Virgin. Thus, "that Holy One who is to be born will be called the Son of God." There is a doubling or reiteration in these paired events, but also significant intensification.

When Gabriel tells Mary of her aged cousin Elizabeth's pregnancy, it serves to signify that "with God nothing will be impossible" (Luke 1:37); this immediate analogy with another providential event in her family seems intuitively confirming for Mary, just as the typological element in Gabriel's speech provides confirmation for Luke as narrator (Aquinas, *Catena Aurea* 3.35, quotes Chrysostom to this effect). Much in Gabriel's proposal is drawn together in very few words, and the response to it by Mary is now immediate: "*ecce ancilla Domini*" says Mary in the famous Vulgate Latin translation: "Behold the handmaid of the Lord" (KJV). Mary here offers herself as the *doulē*, or "bondservant" of the Lord, in words that recall Hannah (1 Sam. 1:11) as well as anticipate the exuberant citation of Joel's prophecy cited in Acts 2:18. These echoes strengthen our appreciation that Mary's words are a prayer, offered not to Gabriel himself but to the Lord; she adds a distinctive remark that clarifies her understanding that what is said to her, as in all of these other parallels, is a fulfillment of the word of God himself. For two millennia her words have signified for Christians the obedient heart that remains exemplary for all the faithful: "Be it unto me according to thy word" (KJV). Medieval painters, for whom this scene is cherishable, found it appropriate for altarpiece painting precisely because it reveals that through her obedience the Word is made flesh. Accordingly, they developed a visual iconography that is faithful to Luke's narrative in such a way as to make of their work a verbal as well as a visual icon. In the *Ghent Altarpiece* of the Van Eyck brothers, for example, Mary's *ecce ancilla Domini* appears over her head as she looks up, praying, but the words are upside down and reversed, so as to indicate that she speaks neither to us nor to the courtly Gabriel but directly to the Lord. Typically, when Gabriel "appears" in annunciation paintings (especially after Giotto), his courtly body language bespeaks the posture of a royal suitor; also typically he finds Mary reading a psalter or the prophecy of Isa. 7:14; her "be it unto me according to

11. Bock 1994–96: 1.122 also notes a repetition of the verb in Luke 9:34, referring to the cloud of the transfiguration.

thy word" is often signified by her hand held, palm down, over the open page of scripture (e.g., Roger Van de Weyden, *Three Kings Altarpiece*).[12] In this context, we are led both by Luke's narrative and such well-composed painterly commentaries to see Mary as a devout virgin being "courted," and her willing obedience as an exemplar for all faithful persons in whom, in a real and analogous sense, the word of the Lord seeks also a nuptial habitation. Calvin reflects a long tradition of earlier biblical readers: "Now if the holy virgin showed herself the handmaid of the Lord precisely in submitting herself freely to his command, then it is the greatest insult if we deny him, by fleeing from him, such obedience as he deserves and asks" (1972: 1.31).

Medieval and renaissance painters of biblical subjects can often be a useful guide to the way a particular passage has been read by exegetes and theologians. This is particularly the case with Luke, whose close attention to details of the sort we have been considering here led him, as noted earlier, to be thought of as an artist and hence to be a natural patron for Christian artists. With regard to Mary, the painter may treat her as a prefiguration of the church, following Ambrose (*Exposition of Luke*); an example is Petrus Christus's *Annunciation* in which Mary, prayer book in hand, is represented as standing on the porch of a church (the typical medieval place for a wedding ceremony) when Gabriel arrives. Here Mary is the bride of Christ, representatively as well as proleptically the mother of the church. In other contexts, as Bede (*Homilies on the Gospels* 1.3) emphasizes, she is a reversal of Eve; though Eve was seduced by the deceitful archtempter, Mary affirms the divinely appointed courtship of Gabriel, so that primal disobedience may be countered by obedience—a feature often reflected in art by framing the annunciation with scenes from the garden of Eden (as in the *Ghent Altarpiece*). But the wider preeminence of Mary as an exemplar for faithful obedience owes in significant measure to the influence of the commentaries of the Venerable Bede and Bonaventure. Bede strongly emphasizes Mary's faithfulness as a model for all Christians: "Imitating her voice and mind to the best of our abilities, beloved brothers, let us recall that we are Christ's servants in all our actions and intentions. Let us subject all the members of our body in service to him, and let us direct the whole gaze of our mind to the fulfillment of his will" (*Homilies on the Gospels* 1.3).

It may be Bonaventure who most strongly emphasizes the conversation between Mary and Gabriel as reflecting the decorum of gracious medieval courtesy. Giotto picks up this emphasis in his Arena Chapel *Annunciation*, by showing Gabriel kneeling in the fashion of a medieval courtier, white lily in hand (to signify Mary's virginal purity). Bonaventure's primary theological contribution is his emphasis on Mary's free will—her agency. As he summarizes it, Mary's fruitfulness "took place *through God's action*, the *angel's annunciation*, and the *virgin's consent*, so that the restoration might correspond to the fall" (2001–4: 1.1.40). Bonaventure

---

12. See my introductory essay in *The Sacred, Suffering, and the Sublime*, ed. Faith Holly Nelson et al. (Waterloo, ON: Wilfrid Laurier University Press, 2009), 3–21.

---

is not original here—he acknowledges his debt to Bernard of Clairvaux as well as to Bede—but he develops the point more fully. To the many virtues of Mary celebrated by the great Cistercian, Bonaventure adds an emphasis on Mary's active intelligence, so that the reader cannot fail to appreciate that when the Virgin says, "Be it unto me according to thy word," it is as "the perfect consent of love . . . a sign of desire, not an expression of doubt." It is at the precise moment of the Virgin's consent, for Bonaventure, that "the Son of God was conceived" (2001–4: 1.1.70).

For medieval and Renaissance readers, aware as they were of myriad pagan stories of the gods (perhaps especially the numerous stories of rapes of mortal women by a disguised Jupiter or Zeus), this was a distinctive feature of Luke's narrative depiction of the annunciation, and one with large theological implications.[13] Mary's free agency is thus theologically foregrounded in a way that makes her a contrary not only of Eve but also of faithless Israel, the would-be espoused of God who went off into harlotry, disdaining her chosenness with grotesque infidelities. Mary's intelligence and faithful obedience are figured by the painters in so frequently representing her as a reader of scripture, even though they knew as well as we do that historically Mary's having access to a copy of the scriptures, scroll or codex, was more than a little unlikely at the literal level. Yet this imaginative representation beautifully and insightfully reminds the viewer of Mary and Jesus as fulfillments of what the Law and the Prophets have promised. Robert Campin's *Merode Altarpiece* shows a young Mary as if she were a university student (also literally impossible), so absorbed in reading scripture that when the angel arrives, only when the wind from his beating wings has snuffed her candle does she begin to lift her eyes: she is intent upon the law, yet the painter has captured her at the moment she is about to be surprised by grace. Campin here reflects an integral understanding of the relationship of the Old Testament language by which Israel is called as a virgin bride to faithfulness and fruitfulness in conjugal union with God himself: Mary is the perfect foil to Old Testament imagery of the faithless Israel gone a-whoring after alien gods; just so, she is a concrete manifestation of the ideal virgin bride of Israel, the wise virgin, not the foolish woman or the harlot long departed from her fidelity. As in this lovely image the girlish Mary focuses upon the scriptures, her Bible is wrapped in a cloth, anticipating the coming swaddling cloth; in her obedience she who has sought the indwelling word in her heart is now to know the Word made flesh in her womb.[14]

Subtly, but certainly, such elements of emphasis shift our focus from the apocryphal accounts of early vows of temple virginity as a preparation for her response to a more representative desire for spiritual union with the God of Israel and declare

13. Mary's personal agency is often denied her by modern painters, as in Dante Gabriel Rossetti's *Ecce Ancilla*.

14. For Pierre Bersuire, the fourteenth-century Franciscan commentator, writing in his dictionary of Christian symbols, "Christ is a sort of book in the skin of the virgin . . . a book spoken in the disposition of the Father, written in the conception of the mother, expounded in the clarification of the nativity" (*Repertorium morale* [Cologne, 1730]), 1.

that the Word now become reality in her is the ultimate fruitfulness. While such artistic interpretations may depart considerably from Luke's narrative at its literal level, it may be that their way of providing figurative significance, pointing to Mary's free agency, adds a rich reflective dimension for biblical understanding of Mary as the faithful bride, the daughter of Israel to whom the prophets had pointed.

Mary and Elizabeth (1:39–56)

The "visitation" of Mary to Elizabeth, as it has been called for centuries by commentators and painters alike, is a narrative episode of tremendous liturgical importance. Because it yields up both a memorable address from Elizabeth to Mary echoed in the Ave Maria,[15] and because of Mary's Magnificat, her poem of thanksgiving and praise to God that, as Bede notes (*Homilies on the Gospels* 1.4), has been part of the communal prayer at least since the early eighth century, "chanted daily by everyone along with the psalmody of the evening office" (vespers, or evening prayer), this passage was among the most familiar portions of Luke for centuries of Christian worship.[16] Fra Angelico, Giotto, Dietrich Bouts the Elder, Roger Van der Weyden, Rembrandt, and the contemporary French Catholic painter Arcabas are among the dozens of painters who have beautifully rendered the tender scene of their meeting, and there are literally hundreds of illustrations in medieval books of hours as well as etchings in early Protestant devotional books to signify the importance of this moment for Christian history.

A rich human intimacy pervades the whole episode. Mary travels four days into the hill country of Judea to an unidentified village where her old cousin and Zacharias live, doing what women kinfolk in any close family might do, namely helping a mature mother-to-be to negotiate the last trimester of an entirely unanticipated pregnancy. When they meet there is much joy and an instant recognition of realities beyond what the eye can see. At the first sound of Mary's voice, the infant in Elizabeth's womb suddenly leaps; Elizabeth is as suddenly "filled with the Holy Spirit" (1:41), and she exclaims loudly, "Blessed are you among women, and blessed is the fruit of your womb!" (1:42). The strength of the exclamation and the Hebraism "fruit of your womb" indicate a particularity of recall that is noteworthy. In fact, from 1:39 to the end of the passage there are a great many Hebraisms, and a close reader of the Greek text may well imagine that this part of the narrative derives from a different eyewitness reflected in the first half of

---

15. The Ave Maria began to be used liturgically in the eleventh century, but the phrase "pray for us" was added only in the sixteenth century.

16. While in the English Book of Common Prayer (1549; 1662) the Magnificat was part of the service for evening prayer, in the Greek tradition it occurs in the morning office. It has served as the inspiration for some of the finest music in European tradition, including settings by Monteverdi, Schütz, Buxtehuse, Vivaldi, Bach, and Mozart.

the chapter. But we are not told. Here are just the trace elements themselves of a verbally precise recollection. The coda to Elizabeth's brief speech is theologically rich from a Jewish perspective: "Blessed is she who believed, for there will be a fulfillment of those things which were told her from the Lord" (1:45). Echoes of the faithfulness that accords with God's blessing reaching back to Abraham are here present, even as are the promises that in the fullness of time God would bring about all that to which he had committed himself in his word to the prophets. Elizabeth's short speech is a summary, even as her "blessed are you among women" is a more immediate echo of Gabriel's words to Mary (1:28).

Mary's Magnificat is a glorious lyric, a poetic summary from scripture, filled with Old Testament phrases and praises of the God who keeps his own covenanted faithfulness and brings his word to fulfillment (Gen. 17:19; 1 Sam. 2:7–8; Pss. 138:6; 71:19; 126:2–3; 111:9; 103:17; 98:1; 118:15; Isa. 41:8; Hab. 3:18). Echoes of Torah, of the rejoicing of Hannah, but most of all of the psalms of David are woven together into an exuberant poem. And it seems fitting that one who is to bring into the world the "word from the beginning," the long-awaited "David's royal son," should be among women a poet and human author of a seminal scripture herself. As with the song of her namesake predecessor Miriam (Exod. 15) and the psalms of her ancestor David, so Mary's song is poetry attuned for joyous praise; in it God is found to be greater than all our frail imaginings of him. Ambrose remarks that everyone should aspire to "the spirit of Mary, so that he may rejoice in the Lord" (*Exposition of Luke* 2.2c). Botticelli has a painting, *Madonna della Magnificat*, in which (also "poetical") Mary is shown writing her great poem into Luke's book as the evangelist holds her inkwell! Spiritually, this painting echoes the comment of Ambrose. The Hebraic verbal echoes are deep and resonate already in the greeting of Gabriel and Elizabeth: "Blessed is the man . . . [whose] delight is in the law of the LORD" (Ps. 1); blessed is the man, and so also blessed is the woman who is found in the way of complete openness to the word of God. Bonaventure's summary seems most apt: "Her canticle shows that the fulfillment of all promised blessings has come about, and therefore brings about the fulfillment of all praise and canticles and even of the [entire] Scriptures" (2001–4: 1.1.100).

As almost always in scripture, Luke's narrative is spare. We are told that Mary stayed with Elizabeth "about three months" before returning home (Luke 1:56) but not whether she was present to assist at the birth of John; though that seems likely, it is here at most implied.

Elizabeth and Zacharias (1:57–80)

Elizabeth's seclusion was evidently such that when her child was born, neighbors and even relatives were surprised as well as overjoyed (1:58). Here, to a woman already old and childless, a tremendous gift had been given. One imagines also a great party eight days later for the circumcision. As on other occasions in Jewish history (e.g., the birth of Isaac), the naming of the child is rich with theological portent. As in the case of Isaac ("he laughs"), where the name functions as a sign of divine irony, recalling Sarah and Abraham's bemused incredulity, here too the name shows that God, so to speak, always gets the last laugh. The name "Isaac" is a comment on what has happened and is an assurance that God is faithful to fulfill his word. Here, wonder concerning the name on the part of kinfolk must have been intensified by it having been withheld until the circumcision (unusual for Jews) and Zacharias's being mute up till that moment. When Elizabeth tells the crowd that their expectation that he would be named for his father is not to be realized, they are taken aback. "John?" they respond. "There is no one among your relatives who is called by this name" (1:61). That they motion to Zacharias to respond may suggest that he had lost hearing as well as speech; in any event he picks up a writing tablet (a wax-covered board) and writes, "His name is John" (1:63). In the Greek of Luke's narrative, the verb is *estin* ("is"); Zacharias does not say, "His name shall be John," but by the tense indicates that the child's name had been established earlier with the angel's annunciation in the temple (Bock 1994–96: 1.168). John (Aramaic/Hebrew *Jochanan*) means "God is gracious," and so the whole narrative bespeaks God's mercy and kindness in a retrospect here focused on the unchanging character of God despite the changeability of those called to serve him.

"Immediately,"[17] writes Luke, Zacharias's "mouth was opened and his tongue loosed, and he spoke, praising God." Understandably, the crowd of kinfolk was awed, and the news traveled far and wide (1:64–66). But the loosened tongue of Zacharias is now employed in a fashion notably parallel to that of Mary in her Magnificat. He "was filled with the Holy Spirit, and prophesied, saying: 'Blessed is the Lord God of Israel, for he has visited and redeemed his people'" (1:67–68). This hymn, along with the Magnificat, establishes the theological leitmotifs for Luke's entire Gospel, and perhaps for Acts as well. It is, as the *Meditations on the Life of Christ*, a late-thirteenth-century Gospel paraphrase, puts it, worth pondering that in one little house somewhere in the hills of Judea, "two beautiful canticles were created" that remain part of Christian liturgy to this day (Pseudo-Bonaventure 1961: 25). The song of Zacharias, reflecting not so much his personal joy as gratitude for God's graciousness to all Israel in "remember[ing] his holy covenant" (1:72), is a public proclamation of God's faithfulness even as it forms a prophetic charge concerning the preparatory ministry of John "to give knowledge of salvation to his people by the remission of their sins, through the tender mercy of our God" (1:77–78). The recollection here of the Hebrew word for God's "loving-kindness" (*hesed*) is but one of many Hebraisms in the song we now know as the Benedictus. Though the song clearly divides into two units, the

---

17. Luke loves to use this word; it occurs ten times in Luke, frequently in connection with narratives of miracles performed by Jesus. It occurs six times in Acts, but beyond that only once in the other Gospels (Matt. 21:19–20).

first in praise of the God of Israel and the second characterizing John's specific role in repairing the hearts of the people, like a second Elijah, for repentance and forgiveness before the advent of a Messiah, there may be another element drawing both parts together. The name "Zacharias," meaning "God has remembered again," seems to be echoed in "remember his holy covenant" (1:72); "Elizabeth" ("God is my oath") is likewise reflected in the "oath which he swore to our father Abraham" (1:73); and "John" ("God is gracious") is congruent with "the tender mercy of our God" (1:78). Inscribing significance via the meaning of key names is a familiar element in the Jewish scriptures but typically lost in the Greek of the Septuagint. Thus, while the typifying or eponymous character of such names would have been aurally evident to Hebrew speakers like Zacharias, even in colloquial Aramaic, their reflection in Luke's translation into Greek is more muted.

The Benedictus, as this canticle of Zacharias was called by the early church for its first word in Latin, entered the liturgy about the same time as the Magnificat, in the seventh century. In the office of the Western church it is sung at lauds and was taken into the Anglican Book of Common Prayer to be part of the service of morning prayer. (In the Eastern church it is also prescribed for the first office.) The music of these two canticles, along with the psalms of David, have been on the lips and in the hearts of Christian worshipers now for centuries, such that one can say of those Judean hills that for the faithful church they had come alive with the sound of a music that would endure for all time.

John grew, Luke says, and went to live in the desert until his ministry was to begin. Some have thought it possible that he lived with a sect of the Essenes, such as those who formed the community at Qumran (Bock 1994–96: 1.198). It is just possible, for the asceticism and emphasis on repentance and purification is distantly similar. But Luke does not say so; he feels no compunction to record any details of a potentially digressive character. This is one of those cases in which perhaps what we learn in another context qualifies our understanding: John is elsewhere reported early on (John 1:31) as saying he did not know Jesus. Since he was close kin to Jesus, we must infer that he had long been apart; whether or not in a specific desert community, he could not likely have been spending much time near his larger family. And yet, when Jesus came to him to ask to be baptized, there was sudden recognition of an order that deepens the mystery (Matt. 3:14): how did John then recognize the one whose coming he foretold?

LUKE 2

In the bleak mid-winter,
Frosty wind made moan,
Earth stood hard as iron,
Water like a stone.

So wrote the English poet Christina Rossetti (1830–94) in her beautiful and still often sung Christmas carol. Disappointingly, perhaps especially for Christians in the northern hemisphere, we have nothing in Luke to suggest that the birth of the Lord was in winter, and scholars now largely doubt it. The date assigned to the Feast of Christmas, what John Chrysostom was pleased to call "the most holy and awesome of all feasts . . . the mother of all holy days" (*On the Incomprehensible Nature of God* 6.23–24), was fixed late, in AD 354 in the Philocalian Calendar. December 25 seems to have been chosen to counter the midwinter solstice celebrations associated with the Roman Saturnalia, specifically the pagan imperial *Natalis Solis Invicti*; for Christians, the rising of "the Sun of Righteousness" (Mal. 4:2) is part of the poetic language integrated into the liturgy, an ingredient in the rich tapestry of Old Testament metaphors attached by the Gospels and their early commentators to the nativity of the Lord. That is to say, the choice of the date itself, its cold, dark season, is itself a part of the spiritual interpretation of the birth of the Messiah. It has been of the essence of commentary on this event, particularly as narrated in Luke, that some of the most beautiful passages in the prophecy of the Hebrew scriptures and the simple narration of Luke have been interwoven in a masterful symphony or chorus of interpretative praise; accordingly, much of the historic commentary reads like poetry, and the poets in their turn have created poems and carols that are themselves an important part of historic Lukan interpretation.

Almost all of this rich tradition of commentary sees the incarnation as an irreducible mystery. Ordinary words fail to capture such mystery, especially the supercharged entrance of God himself into the world that he made, not as an imperial magnificence beyond imagining but as a helpless peasant child. The paradox has proven dizzying for the most intelligent and probative of exegetes. The library of commentary on this event is massive and ripples down the centuries like a gathering stream; here only a tiny sample must suffice. Ambrose writes, "He was a baby, a child, so that you may become a complete, mature person. He was wrapped in swaddling clothes, so that you might be freed from the bonds of death. He was in a manger, so that you may be on the altar. He came to earth so that you may be in the stars. He had no place in the inn, so that you may have in heaven many mansions. He, being rich, became poor for your sakes, that through his poverty you might become rich." And he adds, touchingly, "You see that he is in swaddling clothes; you do not see that he is in heaven. You hear the cries of an infant, but you do not hear the lowing of an ox recognizing its Master—for the ox knows his owner and the ass his Master's crib [Isa. 1:3]" (*Exposition of Luke* 2.41–42).

From Origen, who may have been among the first to connect Isa. 1:3 to the scene in the Bethlehem stable, through Cyril of Alexandria, Bede, Bonaventure, and others, commentary on such passages is lyrical and poetically textured precisely for the reason that the conceptual magnitude of the incarnation, the mystery of the birth of the Redeemer of the world, far exceeds the capacity of mere literal exposition alone to register it. Medieval painters love to show the manger scene with the ox and ass looking over the manger with the Christ child; their audience remembered, as perhaps we do not, that this was a gesture of visual theology, intended to help us see the nativity as long prepared for and beautifully heralded in many passages in Isaiah. This itself is a mystery. For the *magnum mysterium*, "even the mystery which hath been hid from ages and from generations, but now is made manifest to his saints" (Col. 1:26 KJV), the discursive intellect is, by itself, insufficient. Yet in conversation with the range of scriptures evoked by this narrative, faithful readers have always recognized the principal paradox, namely that in Christ's birth the hiddenness of God and the revelation of his eternal glory are suddenly coextensive. Aspects of illuminating significance now begin to emerge from the phrases and images that attach to God's promises in the poetry of his prophets. What might not be successfully reduced to a strictly analytical argument or literalist account alone becomes vivid in colors drawn in from the weave of the older texts. Analogies help. One image or phrase informs another. This interweaving, for the ancients, became visible through the work of "spiritual interpretation"; in the light of all scripture, the text of a passage such as this reveals not merely more than we knew but more than we thought possible unless we had encountered it in that light.

At the same time, Luke's account makes clear that the mysteries of revelation, like the facts of history, are supported by external evidence. Jesus is born.

Eyewitnesses see, hear, and bear testimony. But then, as the witnesses learn how to see what they are looking at, to listen to what they hear, a symphony starts, and as the music of it swells, we see that the divine mysteries beyond our ken are not simply a matter of disconnected truths lying out beyond the realm of natural things; rather, as German theologian M. Scheeben wrote more than a century ago, all elements are grace notes of "a higher, heavenly world, a mystical cosmos whose parts are united in living harmony."[1] For a full appreciation, we begin with the historical event of Jesus's birth as a Jewish baby in very humble circumstances, but then we look up, cupping our ears for a far-off ethereal music. Maximus the Confessor puts it like this: "So, if the swaddling clothes seem tawdry in your eyes, admire the angels singing praises together. If you are inclined to despise the manger, raise your eyes a little, and behold the new star in the heaven proclaiming to the world the Lord's nativity. If you believe the mundane things, believe also the mighty; if you are tempted to dispute about those matters which signify his lowliness, look with reverence on what is high and heavenly" (*Sermon on the Nativity* 4). Paradox is not obfuscation, not an insoluble puzzle, but a striking breakthrough toward synthesis: at the heart of the mystery of the incarnation we are to see the glorious reconciliation of apparent contraries, even of opposites.

Modern readers of Luke's account of Christ's nativity are likely to be quite familiar with spiritual exegesis without having much thought about it. They know it from old Christmas carols, from juxtaposed readings of the Old Testament in the liturgy, and sometimes from memorable sermons. They also know the prevalence of analogy in common Christian terminology and will hardly be surprised when Bede says, "For in a mystery, those shepherds and their flocks signify all teachers and guides of faithful souls" (*Homilies on the Gospels* 1.6). Or perhaps they will have experienced a version of John Chrysostom's pastoral observation concerning this evidence of God's tendency to choose the simple and undistinguished of this world to show the way to higher wisdom: "There is a certain road," he says, "which leads by innocence to philosophy" (*On the Day of Christ's Nativity*, quoted in Aquinas, *Catena Aurea* 3.1.69). History, allegory, moral insight, and eschatological foreshadowing (anagogy) are richly interwoven in the scriptural commentary of our Christian forebears in a natural way that we could with much profit relearn. The Christmas story is an excellent place to begin, for here if anywhere we read still just a little more like early Christians, and the way of the faithful readers of earlier ages seems less estranged from us or we from it.

But let us begin a little closer to home, with a poem by American poet Richard Wilbur (now also set as a hymn) exemplary of a Christian reading habit of long standing, which may serve as an introduction to the enriched exegesis and

---

1. M. Scheeben, *Die Mysterien des Christenthums* (Frieburg, 1889); cf. J. A. McHugh and Charles J. Callan, eds., *The Catechism of the Council of Trent* (Baltimore: Tan, 1983).

paradoxical wisdom proclaimed in the gospel itself. Wilbur's "A Christmas Hymn" is occasioned by a reference to a much later part of the narrative, Luke 19:39–40, given as an epigraph to the poem. This passage describes the response of Jesus to the insistence of "some of the Pharisees" that he constrain the joyful proclamations of the "good news" by which his disciples have been, in effect, echoing the shepherds and the angels: they have been enthusiastically exclaiming, "Blessed is the King who comes in the name of the Lord!" (a quotation of Ps. 118:26 in Luke 19:38), adding "Peace in heaven and glory in the highest!" (cf. 2:14). Jesus says to these properly religious but unhappy Pharisees, "I tell you that if these should keep silent, the stones would immediately cry out" (a quotation from Hab. 2:11, where the prophetic rejoinder is, in fact, a rebuke to false religious counsel). For Wilbur, thinking quite precisely in the manner of early church Christians, namely that the scriptures are an interwoven tapestry of continuous and cumulative disclosures pointing to the birth of Jesus as the very hinge upon which history turns, such an intertextual connection to Luke's account of the nativity is completely natural. The juxtaposition in Jesus's retort of the prophetic words of Habakkuk with the angels' song at the time of his birth thus invites Wilbur's reverential astonishment at the master paradox itself:

> A stable lamp is lighted
> Whose glow shall wake the sky;
> The stars shall bend their voices,
> And every stone shall cry.
> And every stone shall cry,
> And straw like gold shall shine;
> A barn shall harbor heaven,
> A stall become a shrine.
>
> This child through David's city
> Shall ride in triumph by;
> The palm shall strew its branches,
> And every stone shall cry.
> And every stone shall cry,
> Though heavy, dull, and dumb,
> And lie within the roadway
> To pave his kingdom come.
>
> Yet he shall be forsaken,
> And yielded up to die;
> The sky shall groan and darken,
> And every stone shall cry.
> And every stone shall cry
> For stony hearts of men:
> God's blood upon the spearhead,
> God's love refused again.

> But now, as at the ending,
> The low is lifted high;
> The stars shall bend their voices,
> And every stone shall cry.
> And every stone shall cry
> In praises of the child
> By whose descent among us
> The worlds are reconciled.[2]

In a way actually closely parallel to the method of early readers of the scriptures, Wilbur here connects the dots for us, reminding us that in the literal event of the birth of Jesus in Bethlehem we see the spiritual meaning of many passages of earlier scripture, a clarification of confusing events in earlier history, and above all the spiritual meaning of all history. The interplay of time and eternity of which paradox is a chief expression grants to that history and all of its events also an anagogy, a meaning pointing forward to the culmination of history in eternity. Accordingly, in this recent American poem, as in medieval carols on the same subject or early Christian commentaries on Luke's narrative, we recognize the birth of Jesus as *clavis David*, the key to a spiritual interpretation of all history as, in effect, salvation history. Outside a deeply spiritual understanding of scripture we are likely to think of such paradoxical features as either counterintuitive or flatly contradictory. Inside a deeply spiritual appreciation of scripture as history *sub specie aeternitatis* we see in the Bethlehem manger the ultimate reconciliation of otherwise incommensurable realities and recognize this reconciliation to be both astonishing and yet more real than any other reality we know.

The Birth of Jesus (2:1–20)

It is nonetheless the case, as medieval interpreters like Nicholas of Lyra were constantly reminding readers in their marginal commentaries, that the spiritual sense is contained within the literal or historical plain sense of the text. One striking thing about Luke 2 is another, starker juxtaposition: the holy can appear in the midst of much that is public and profane. Rome's imperial power, proclaimed in the decree of Caesar Augustus "that all the world [hyperbole for Roman Empire] should be registered" (2:1; KJV's "that all the world should be taxed" reflects the reason for the census), is a reminder of the rule over Judea of an alien secular power. Caesar's proclamation itself was hardly good news. There was a species of peace to be sure (*pax Romanum*), the kind of brutally enforced social quietude often found under tyranny. Quirinius, the governor of Syria, decreed the Roman census that, though first enforced in this district, was not the first ordered by Caesar. Nor was the idea that everyone should go to his own city unusual for

2. Richard Wilbur, "A Christmas Hymn." Used by personal permission of the poet.

such a Roman census, though it may indicate an expedient adaptation to Jewish custom by which registration in one's ancestral home would seem a natural way to pay taxes. It is also possible that Joseph had ancestral property in Bethlehem, rented out in his absence, perhaps, to kin.

Although Bethlehem may derive its name from a pre-Jewish settlement, it has the sense in Hebrew of "house of bread"—an etymology of interest to later commentators. The Septuagint does not in fact refer to it as a "city of David"; that appellation is found only in the Masoretic Text, yet another reminder that Luke is indebted to Semitic sources. Yet Luke does not mention the prophecy in Mic. 5:1–2, even though he continues to stress (cf. Luke 1:31–35) the lineage tracing to David. Details concerning the attempt of Joseph and Mary to find a temporary dwelling (usually translated "inn") are sparse, and it can be helpful to a modern reader to know some of the pertinent cultural context. The Greek term *katalyma* signifies a building that is probably not in our sense an "inn" but rather a public shelter. The former would be designated a *pandocheion*, a commercial inn such as is designated in Jesus's parable about the good Samaritan. A *katalyma* is not like this; it is rather a sort of guestroom in a private dwelling, and to stay there one would presumably have to know the owner. If Joseph had been renting out his own ancestral property, he might well have expected to be able to stay in its *katalyma* while in town for the census. Moreover, the laying of Jesus in a "manger" or feed trough may not indicate, as typically imagined, a barn or "stable" in our Western conception of those terms, as the repeated term might seem to warrant. Bailey shows that for Joseph and Mary to have been turned away from an already occupied *katalyma* ("guestroom") almost certainly indicates that their intended hospice was in a simple family dwelling. A typical Palestinian family home would have a larger family room adjacent to a "stable" or animal shelter, it being at a lower level, with an opening, at head height for the animals, into the general family room. Hollowed out of the tufa rock along the ledge separating the stable from living quarters were the feed troughs. The animals would actually have their heads in the family room as they ate. There is a mundane sense in which an ox could hardly avoid knowing his owner, or an ass his master's crib (Isa. 1:3); this adds to the bite in the taunt of the Lord as recorded by Isaiah, a recollection of which carries a homely poignancy in this manger scene. The slope of the overall Palestinian dwelling was a practical requirement since animals were kept at the lowest level; typically the guestroom would be at the highest level, literally "an upper room."[3] To the early Christian mind, especially for Palestinian followers of Jesus, the connection of this hospice to the "upper room" of the Last Supper in which Jesus himself would eventually play the part of host, and thus of Bethlehem, the "house of bread" to the "bread of life" of the Thursday supper and Eucharist, would have come more naturally from the literal sense than it does for most of us.

3. Kenneth E. Bailey, *Jesus through Middle Eastern Eyes: Cultural Studies in the Gospels* (Downers Grove, IL: InterVarsity, 2008), 30–33.

Luke implies that Joseph had come to his hometown with his "betrothed" or "espoused" wife. This suggests that the *ketubah* or marriage contract had been signed and that her ensuing legal responsibility dictated this difficult journey at an unpropitious time. Luke's specification that Mary was *emnēsteumenē* has occasioned debate among modern as well as earlier commentators. Some (e.g., Cyril of Alexandria) take the term at face value as meaning "betrothed" but not married and referring to the vows she had made to Joseph before her conception through the Holy Spirit. Many early and medieval commentators pass over it altogether, as does Calvin. Some modern commentators are troubled that Mary should have taken so long a trip from home in an as yet unmarried state and are inclined to think that Luke's use of the term refers to marriage rather than betrothal, but "that the marriage is not yet consummated and thus implies a virgin birth" (e.g., Bock 1994–96: 1.205–6). This uncertainty underlies a Christian doctrine concerning Mary that Luke himself does not clarify but that tradition has incorporated into belief that Mary is "ever virgin" (*aeiparthenon*). The doctrine of Mary's perpetual virginity is attested in extracanonical writings of the second and third centuries and is later affirmed by Gregory of Nyssa, Didymus of Alexandria, Epiphanius, Athanasius (*aeiparthenon* is a term in the Athanasian Creed), Ambrose (*Exhortation to Virginity*), and Jerome (in his defense of this doctrine against Helvidius in *On the Perpetual Virginity of Mary*). By the fourth century it had been firmly established, and it entered formally into the articles of faith of both Eastern and Western churches by the sixth century (Fifth Ecumenical Council of Constantinople in AD 653). Calvin and Luther continue in acceptance of this tradition; after the fourth century, speculation concerning the "brothers" of Jesus appears much later, primarily in Protestant writers after the eighteenth century.[4] Luke's own interest, it must be said, falls elsewhere. (When he describes the child as *prōtotokos* ["firstborn"] in 2:7 we should bear in mind that this term was commonly used of only children as well.)[5] Bede gives the enduring interpretation:

> [He] calls the Lord "firstborn," not because we should believe that Mary gave birth to other sons after him, since it is true that she was memorable for her unique perpetual chastity with Joseph her husband. But he properly names him "firstborn" because, as John says, "But to as many as received him he gave them power to become sons of God" [John 1:12]. Among these sons he rightfully holds the primacy who, before he was born in the flesh, was Son of God, born without beginning . . . that "he should be firstborn of many brothers" [Rom. 8:29]. (*Homilies on the Gospels* 1.6)

Mary wraps the infant firstborn of the universe in swaddling clothes and lays him in a manger in Bethlehem; this child, as Cyril says, was to become the bread of

---

4. John McHugh, *The Mother of Jesus in the New Testament* (New York: Doubleday, 1975); and Hugo Rahner, *Our Lady and the Church*, trans. Sebastian Bullogh (New York: Pantheon, 1961).

5. Raymond Brown, *The Birth of the Messiah: A Commentary on the Infancy Narratives in Matthew and Luke* (New York: Doubleday, 1977), 398; and Fitzmyer 1981–85: 1.407.

life for all who would come, like simple creatures, to recognize their master's crib (*Commentary on Luke* 1).

Meanwhile, a mile or so away by scholarly reckoning, shepherds out in the fields, "keeping watch over their flock by night" (Luke 2:8), see something completely extraordinary: "And behold, an angel of the Lord stood before them, and the glory of the Lord shone around them, and they were greatly afraid" (2:9). Small wonder—these were not patriarchs or prophets or high priests, but simple men. That the *doxa* ("glory, beauty") of the Lord should shine around humble shepherds on a Judean hillside is an event of enormous portent and hugely counterintuitive to normative religious thinking. The shepherds are understandably unprepared, as would anyone be in their place, for they can only relate what they see to the bright Shekinah glory of God's holy presence in the tabernacle (Exod. 16:10; Ps. 63:2; Isa. 40:5; Ezek. 1). How should such a presence be borne by unhallowed men? This is not the painters' image of angels hovering in the sky (cf. Heb. 2:7–9) but a picture of one, perhaps like Gabriel, standing on the earth, as in Daniel or in the visitations to Zacharias and Mary. As in those instances the angel says, "Fear not!" Then he adds, "For behold, I bring you good tidings of great joy, which shall be to all people" (Luke 2:10 KJV)—"shall be," because what comes first to the chosen people (the "all" refers to them in this instance) is then, of course, to come to all peoples who will receive him as Christ. "For there is born to you this day in the city of David a Savior, who is Christ the Lord" (2:11); "this day," or "today," emphasizes present fulfillment of that which had long been promised, a "savior" (*sōtēr*) who is the *christos* and *kyrios*; these three messianic terms are brought together for the first time in reference to Jesus in the form of a divine title. Strictly speaking, a *sōtēr* is one who delivers people from their enemies; Calvin notes pertinently that the translation in some Latin texts, *servator*, is insufficient to carry the weight of the meaning here and prefers *salvator* (1972: 1.76). The term "savior" is not in the Old Testament applied to the Messiah (Hebrew *māšîaḥ*, Greek *christos*); the Anointed One is the clarification that the historic role of God as the ultimate deliverer of his people is here conjoined to his "Sent One," his Christ, who is now to be understood as "God with us," "Emmanuel," and hence also Lord (Hebrew *ădonay*, Greek *kyrios*). There can be no mistaking the comprehensive character of the divine name here, even perhaps for humble shepherds; in definitive language it draws all of salvation history and the holiness of God to a very specific place and time as "fulfillment." Bock notes (1994–96: 1.218n12) that *kyrios* is used more than 9,000 times in the Septuagint, of which 6,150 translate the untranslatable *yhwh*. *Sōtēr/sōtēria/sōtērion* is Luke's indicative christological title for Jesus (Luke 1:47, 69, 71, 77; 2:11, 30).

But, accommodating human frailty, there is for the shepherds not only a manifestation and an announcement but also a "sign": they will find the infant wrapped in "swaddling cloths, lying in a manger" (Luke 2:12). What a strikingly appropriate sign for shepherds! And yet not only to those shepherds (Latin *pastores*); as Bede reflects, "in a mystery, those shepherds and their flocks signify all teachers and guides to faithful souls" (*Homilies on the Gospels* 1.6). His allegory continues by describing Jesus as the Bread of Life, and the shepherds' discovery of "the virgin beauty of the church, that is, Mary; the manly company of the spiritual doctors, that is, Joseph; and the lowly coming of Christ contained in the pages of holy scripture, that is the infant Child Christ, laid in the manger." This is characteristic homiletical application, the bare letter of Luke's text employed as a guide to those whose work it is, like all faithful "shepherds," to proclaim the good news (2:17–18) and to encourage its embodiment in the living church.

Meanwhile, back on that Judean hillside, there is suddenly a whole "multitude of the heavenly host," choirs of angels praising God: "Glory to God in the highest, and on earth peace, good will towards men" (KJV). The "glory" (*doxa*) the angels proclaim (Luke does not say "sing," though that sense is possible) clearly proffers here an invitation, much as in the Psalms, to join in the praise, to "glorify" God by reflecting his glory. "In the highest" (*hypsistois*) can mean either "in the highest, most noble way" or "in the highest place." I think we can take it here to mean both; Bonaventure, thinking in this way, changes the Vulgate's *altissimus* to *in excelsis* (2001–4: 1.161), better to reflect in this way the Greek as he understands it, and it is this term that survives in the liturgical Gloria and in hymns of the church. The shepherds are invited to join in a cosmic chorus of men and angels glorifying God for what he has done. Von Balthasar says memorably that the angels here at once "reflect the heavenly glory of the Son of Man . . . and make visible the social character of the Kingdom of Heaven, into which the cosmos is to be transformed."[6] The angels' salutation is of "peace" (*eirēnē*), an echo of the *šālôm* promised by the prophets (Isa. 26:3; Jer. 16:5; Ezek. 34:25–31); evidently, as Jerome says, it is a peace most likely to be understood among men of goodwill, "that is, among those who acknowledge the birth of Christ" (*On the Nativity of Our Lord*). Calvin picks up on this understanding: "Certainly [the angels] are not speaking of outward peace, as men keep it with themselves, but they mean that the earth has been pacified when men are reconciled to God inwardly, and are quiet in their own minds" (1972: 1.77). To those who understand only the *pax Romanum*, this will surely be a peace that passes *political* understanding. But it is also, contrastively, a promise that one day the true Prince of Peace will come again in glory, over all to reign, bringing a peace in which the will of the Father will at last be done on earth as it is in heaven. That anagogical sense is of the essence of the good news too, in any Jewish or Christian understanding.

The shepherds come "with haste" and find, just as the angels said, "Mary and Joseph, and the Babe lying in a manger" (Luke 2:16). In Luke there are no angels hovering over the crib, as in so many beautiful paintings that compress these narratives together with their pastoral applications (e.g., Giotto, Piero della Francesca)—just a quiet tableau, the holy family and an undisclosed number of

---

6. Hans Urs von Balthasar, *The Glory of the Lord: A Theological Aesthetics*, trans. Erasmo Leiva-Merikakis (San Francisco: Ignatius; New York: Crossroad, 1982–90), 1.675.

doubtless motley shepherds. Luke records no conversation between them. What he does record is that they are transformed by what has been made known to them into active evangelists, making "widely known the saying which was told them concerning this child" (2:17). Moreover, "all those who heard it marveled at those things which were told them by the shepherds" (2:18); we may reasonably surmise that some of those who heard were among the eyewitnesses to whom Luke spoke (Bonaventure 2001–4: 1.169 connects this passage to Isa. 9:6). If Luke were a modern historian, he would footnote his sources. But his focus is clearly on the events themselves as, in effect, transformative of history as to meaning and thus irreducible to any naturalistic understanding of the historical event dependent on outward appearance alone.

As still water runs deep, so Mary: she "kept all these things and pondered them in her heart" (Luke 2:19). Bede takes this sentence to imply her inward reflection on scripture, on the way in which God's promises to his people were being fulfilled, "comparing those things which she had read were to occur with those which she recognized as already having occurred" (*Homilies on the Gospels* 1.7). This has seemed plausible enough that no better thought has been offered; for a woman in the line of David to meditate upon the word of the Lord, "day and night" in this way, seems entirely suited to her blessedness, her status as *kecharitōmenē* ("highly favored") in a way far transcending any Rachel or Rebecca, howsoever beautifully "well favored" we may imagine them to have been.

The Circumcision of Jesus and Temple Presentation (2:21–40)

Early in Christian culture physical circumcision was discontinued as a practice of covenant obedience, faithfulness under the old law since the time of Abraham. Paul, in his rejection of the persistence of the practice among some of the Galatians (Gal. 5:1–12; cf. Rom. 3:1), is particularly scathing. Baptism had become the new "sign" (*sēmeion*) of the new covenant.[7] That was not yet the situation, of course, at the time of the birth of Jesus.

The Jews were by this time not singular in the practice of circumcision; almost every people of the western Semitic areas except the Philistines practiced it, as did Egypt, and in all cases it had both a cultic and a hygienic origin. While many of these cultures practiced circumcision as a rite of puberty, in preparation for marriage, in Jewish life since the time of Moses it was practiced as an infant initiation, typically on the eighth day according to the law (Lev. 12:3). It is clear that the adherence of Mary and Joseph to the law was scrupulous. Retrospectively, bearing in mind that Christians generally had discontinued the practice after Paul,

---

7. Cyril of Alexandria gives a representative explanation: "[Now] circumcision is the symbol of the faithful when they are established in grace, as they cut away and mortify the tumescent arousal of carnal pleasures and passions by the sharp surgery of faith and by ascetic labors. They do this not by cutting of the body but by purifying of the heart" (1983: Homily 3).

most commentators take the view of Bede, namely that Jesus did not disdain the provisions of the law; rather, he submitted to it "not because of necessity but for the sake of example," even as he submitted in an analogous way to the waters of baptism (*Homilies on the Gospels* 1.11). Cyril of Alexandria draws out the theological application by way of picking up the Torah theme of ransom in what will become New Testament terms:

> "God sent forth his Son, born of a woman, born under the law, to redeem them that were under the law" [Gal. 4:4–5]. Christ therefore ransomed from the curse of the law those who being subject to it, had been unable to keep its enactments. And in what way did he ransom them? By fulfilling the law. To put it in another way: in order that he might expiate the guilt of Adam's transgression, he showed himself obedient and submissive to God the Father in our stead. For it is written, "that as through the disobedience of the one man, many were made sinners, so also through the obedience of the one, many shall be made just" [Rom. 5:19]. (Homily 3)

The "presentation at the temple," as it becomes known in traditional Christian nomenclature, is similarly occasioned by conformity to the law: Mary waits for the full forty days of postpartum purification (Lev. 12:2–8), then the family travels to Jerusalem to offer a sacrifice. Since "every male who opens the womb shall be called holy to the Lord" (Luke 2:23; cf. Deut. 18:4; Exod. 13:2, 12, 15), a substitutionary sacrifice is required—a lamb, for those who can afford it, or "a pair of turtledoves or two young pigeons" (Luke 2:24; cf. Lev. 12:2, 8). It seems probable that Joseph and Mary could not have afforded the provision of a five-shekel ransom for the firstborn presented to the Lord (Num. 18:15–16). The citations of the law do not follow the Greek (Septuagint) text, and we may reasonably assume that Luke's language here reflects the report of his informants, possibly in a condensed form. But it is clear that in addition to the purification of Mary and the presentation of their firstborn, there is a formal dedication of Jesus to the service of the Lord (cf. 1 Sam. 1–2). Since the offering for the firstborn did not require the presence of the child (though the distance from home may have), but dedication would certainly require it, it may be that Luke means to say that the offering of the poor for Mary's purification (the two doves) was paid, but that Jesus was in fact dedicated thus, like the child Samuel, to the service of the Lord (Marshall 1978: 117). This possibility certainly makes sense of the conflation. That the Greek text of Luke 2:22 uses the plural *autōn* ("*their* purification") rather than *autēs* ("*her* purification") suggests that Joseph may have assisted at the birth of Jesus, rather than a midwife, in which case mishnaic law would require also his participation in the purification rite.

All of this takes place seventy weeks after the announcement of John's birth to Zacharias by Gabriel, forty days after the birth of Jesus. Now there is an unexpected element. An unanticipated figure arrives, designated unusually as both "just" (*dikaios*) and "devout" (*eulabēs*), but not described by Luke as a priest (as in the apocryphal Matthew and Protevangelium of James). Calvin identifies Simeon with "that remnant which God tells us has been preserved according to God's free election," adding that his song shows plainly that Simeon "beheld the Son of God with eyes other than the flesh" (1972: 1.91). His name (Hebrew "God has heard") fits beautifully with what follows (it is also assonant with Greek *sēmeion*, "sign"), though Luke draws no special attention to that. He does say that Simeon was, perhaps with an unusual intensity, "waiting for the Consolation of Israel" (2:25). Some commentators note that a Rabbi Simeon, the son of Hillel, was alive in Jerusalem at the time, but not much more about him (Lightfoot 1979: 3.40; cf. Calvin 1972: 1.91).[8] What Luke says next, however, is of indisputably greater significance: "And the Holy Spirit was upon him." Further, he tells us that the Holy Spirit has separately revealed to Simeon that he would not die "before he had seen the Lord's Christ." The verb here (*kechrēmatismenon*, "had been revealed") intriguingly also contains a near homonym with the mysterious Simeon's name, which to a Greek ear, as noted, also resembles "sign" (*sēmeion*). The words that Simeon uses (2:34) in describing Jesus himself are *sēmeion antilegomenon*, for which the best translation might be "a sign of contradiction" rather than, as more prosaically, NKJV's "a sign which will be spoken against" (cf. K. H. Rengstorf in *TDNT* 7.238); this too is aurally harmonious, even as it points to the disharmony the Messiah will occasion, since Jesus is "destined for the fall and rising of many in Israel" (2:34). Cyril of Alexandria, a Greek speaker commenting on this passage in Greek, refers to Septuagint Zech. 10:8, adducing the words "I will make signs unto them, and receive them, because I will ransom them" (1983: 60). Whatever the phonological play in this passage, it is evident that the unexpected appearance of Simeon is, in his role and recorded words, very much a "sign" for Luke himself. Congruently, Basil will understand Simeon's words as anticipating the ultimate "sign of contradiction," the cross (*Homily* on Ps. 61:2).

Strikingly, even before the offering for the firstborn can be accomplished by his parents, Simeon takes Jesus up in his arms, blessing God and saying, "Lord, now lettest thou thy servant depart in peace, according to thy word. For my eyes have seen thy salvation, which thou hast prepared before the face of all people; a light to lighten the Gentiles, and the glory of thy people Israel" (Luke 2:29–32 KJV). I cite the KJV here because of its proximity to the language of the liturgy in the Book of Common Prayer (1662) and thus primarily to draw attention among English speakers to this passage being the fourth poetic or hymnic passage encountered thus far in Luke to have entered into Christian liturgy. It has been part of daily prayers since the fourth century; in the Eastern church it is said at vespers, in Western use generally at compline, from which it enters the Book of

8. A late-third- or early-fourth-century inscription on a large, ancient burial monument in Jerusalem is inscribed with Luke 2:25; it says that the tomb is of "Simeon, who was a very just man and very devoted, who was waiting for the consolation of the people." This phrasing corresponds to the version found in the Codex Sinaiticus, the fourth-century biblical text. Historically the tomb has been thought to contain his body, that of Zacharias, and that of the Apostle James.

Common Prayer. Simeon's benedictional praise poem has thus also itself become a "sign to many" for two millennia.

The wonder that Joseph and Mary feel in these words must have been tempered somewhat by Simeon's "blessing" on them (2:34–35), which includes his words about division in Israel and an enigmatic prophecy to Mary that "a sword will pierce through your own soul also, that the thoughts of many hearts may be revealed." The word for "sword" here is *rhomphaia*, a particularly lethal two-edged broadsword—not the word used in Heb. 4:12 (though that passage's *makaran distomon*, "two-edged," may mean the same thing essentially)—but some early and Reformation interpreters (e.g., Ambrose, *Exposition of Luke* 2.61; Calvin 1972: 1.97) made the connection (cf. Ambrose on Heb. 4:12), whereas others, such as Bede, see Mary in this prophecy as already figurative for the church: "Now, even down to the close of the present time, the sword of severest tribulation ceases not to go through the soul of the church, when with bitter sorrow she experiences evil speaking directed against the sign of faith" (*Homilies on the Gospels* 1.18).

Now suddenly appears yet another surprising figure, namely Anna (Hebrew Hannah, meaning "grace"). Luke tells us that she is a prophetess and, more remarkably, that she has spent most of her long life in the temple precincts, "serv[ing] God with fastings and prayers night and day" (Luke 2:37). She is a widow, her husband having died seven years after her marriage. She is of the tribe of Asher and a daughter of Phanuel (whose name is a variant of "Peniel," recalling Gen. 32:30: "face to face [*pānîm el-pānîm*] with God"), and it appears that, most unusually for any woman, she has effectively been an intercessor at the temple for more than sixty years. She is eighty-four at least (the syntax here is ambiguous); for Luke it is evidently a fact of interest that she is so advanced in age. Later commentators, possessed of the conviction that no apparently incidental number would have been included in the narrative by the biblical writers unless there was a spiritual reason for it, sometimes treat the number as symbolic or figural and see Anna's responsive thanksgiving as constituting her as a mystical sign of the church (e.g., Bede, *Homilies on the Gospels* 2.38: seven [a number for the "fullness of time"] multiplied by twelve [a biblical number for revelation of God's purposes]). Be that as it may, all commentators see her appearance as highly significant to Luke. In some deep sense, Jesus is an answer to the prayers of Anna, even as to those of Simeon. Arriving on the scene precisely at the moment of Simeon's prayer she acts as what dramaturgists call "fifth business"; in her words she not only gives thanks to God but, Luke adds, like the shepherds, also immediately begins to spread the good word "to all those who looked for redemption in Jerusalem" (2:38). Calvin sees the examples of Simeon and Anna also as prefiguring the evangelical joy of the church, "that the faithful may encourage each other to sing God's praises with one voice, and mutually to take up the strain" (1972: 1.98). About Anna's personally spreading the good news Calvin is more somber, seeing in Luke's phrasing a suggestion that the remnant of those who still looked to God to deliver Israel must now have been very small.

Jesus's Childhood (2:41–52)

Luke, like all the canonical Gospel writers, has nothing to say about the early child-hood of Jesus. (The apocryphal accounts, by contrast, feature spurious miracles and lack Luke's emphasis on Jesus's maturation, especially his being "filled with wisdom.") Luke does record in close detail one event that particularly anticipates the adult ministry of Jesus and that contains his first recorded words in the New Testament accounts. Chrysostom observes, counter to the claims of the apocryphal accounts, "The Lord truly did no miracle in his childhood, yet this one fact Luke mentions, which made men look with wonder upon him" (*Homilies on John* 20). The fathers see this episode as evidence not only of the passage of time and of Jesus's physical growth but also as a manifestation of a gradual revelation of the significance of the wisdom of the eternal Logos becoming more apparent. Cyril of Alexandria puts it thus: "He is said to increase because the human nature of the word increased in him" (*On Thessalonians* 1.10.c7). Though the twelfth year is sometimes seen as a spiritual number because of its recurrence in the twelve tribes and twelve disciples, or because in the twelve gates of Jerusalem the number takes on the property of revelation, becoming a number for patterns of divine disclosure, or because it conforms to the pattern of the later bar mitzvah, the focus of these commentators closely follows the most literal purport of Luke's text. Calvin likewise follows closely, observing that there is no warrant in Luke's text for jejune speculation about "latent intelligence" in the young Savior or to suspect his gradual maturation as evidence of some early taint of original sin. Rather, as Calvin puts it, "Growing up gradually is part of what the Lord took on himself in condescending to our human condition: He freely took what cannot be separated from human nature" (1972: 1.107). But Calvin speaks for the whole of Christian tradition in what he says out of his knowledge of the extraordinary character of Jesus's conversation with the "teachers" (*didaskalōn*) of Israel: "There must have been beams of divine radiance openly shining on the boy for him to have been allowed to sit by these proud men. Though it is likely he sat on a bench, and not on the doctors' level, these haughty men would never have granted him an audience in public assembly if some divine force had not driven them to it" (1972: 1.108). It is almost as though Calvin had been thinking of Giotto's fresco painting, *The Finding at the Temple*, a depiction that he doubtless had never seen.

Jesus is more precisely a listener in Luke's account. He enters into the conver-sation, however, that led the ancients to parallel this scene with Socratic teach-ing, hence the later visual analogies to Socrates and his disciples in some early representations. Whatever their motive, as the conversation went on, says Luke, the teaching elders "were astonished at his understanding and answers" (2:47).

But Luke's attention falls almost equally on the natural tension between the anxiety of his parents, imagining him with other families in the returning party and discovering only at nightfall after a day's journey that he was missing, and Jesus's calm absorption in his conversations in the temple. It would be a poor parent who would not feel the gravest concern in such a situation, and after a full day's journey back they look for him everywhere for another day before finding him in the temple, calmly discoursing on scripture. Mary, speaking for both parents, exclaims, "Son, why have you done this to us? Look, your father and I have sought you anxiously" (2:48) (*odynōmenoi* carries the sense of pain and distress, just as it does in the Classical Greek of Homer). His reply is as astonishing as it must have been to them bewildering: "Why did you seek me? Did you not know that I must be about my Father's business?" (2:49). Many a parent, understanding or not (2:50), might in such a circumstance have been moved to anger. Not so Mary, as far as Luke tells us. Moreover, he leaves the phrase "about my Father's business"—so freighted with tension vis-à-vis the silent but nurturing Joseph and with mystery concerning all that Jesus may mean by it—without further comment. It is as though, for the discerning reader, further comment is unnecessary. As with Mary, so with Luke's sensitive reader: "these things" are to be kept inwardly and pondered in the heart. This phrase seems to suggest Mary herself as a possible source for Luke for this episode or, if not, at least a member of her family. Like the sentence that follows, it also serves to heighten the reader's expectation: "And Jesus increased in wisdom and stature, and in favor with God and men" (2:52).

For many a devout Christian reader, however, this verse has raised another question that Luke does not directly answer, and in this case it can occasion a serious theological conundrum. If the incarnate Lord "increased in wisdom," does that mean that he was not, as a child, aware of his status as second person of the Trinity? Or, did he only gradually *become* who he was as God made man? For if he was not aware, or not yet fully God at the time of his birth, surely this would create serious christological problems.

This verse was, in fact, one of those used by Arius and his followers against those who ultimately prevailed at the Council of Nicaea (AD 325). How could Jesus be the Logos (John 1:1–14), they asked, the eternal wisdom of God (Prov. 8:22–31 as per the commentaries), and at the same time so evidently human as to require to learn things, to be said to "increase in wisdom"? The apparent contradiction and division of opinion among Christians posed a nontrivial challenge, not least for the politics of the Roman Empire under Constantine, who had made Christianity "official" in AD 313. Arius attracted numerous followers, especially in intellectual centers such as Antioch and Syria, where the influence of Platonic thought and perhaps especially Aristotelian rationalism made this humanistic view of Jesus seem more natural, and, it must be said, less radical a departure from pagan notions of emperors (such as Caesar Augustus) who had themselves sought to be seen and worshiped as divine. But surely this kind of humanistic analogy would undercut the claim of Jesus, as recorded in the Gospels, of his oneness with God: "I and my Father are one" (John 10:30), not to mention the doctrine of Paul and later writers that Christ was "truly God" as well as "truly man."

The Council of Nicaea was called largely to address this and related problems. A champion for the orthodox position was Athanasius, who takes up the controversy at length in his *Orations against the Arians* and makes an especially masterful use of a wide range of scriptures to show that Christ's identification with the common lot required of him a *kenōsis*, a self-emptying assent to quite radical constraints upon his deity, without which the incarnation could not have occurred. The humanity of Christ for Athanasius, his willingness to identify with our mortal lot, is as necessary for our salvation as his divine nature, and the two cannot be separated. He became an infant, frail and weak; he grew to manhood and acquired wisdom in such ways as are consistent with human learning. If he displayed an extraordinary command of the scripture in his session with the elders in the temple, this may owe in part to his special attunement to divine purpose in the texts, but it certainly does not indicate that his maturation was *merely* human or that it contradicted his unity with the Father. Nor did his being "of one substance with the Father," as the Nicene Creed would phrase it, cancel out the ordinary humanity that he submitted to in his experience. That has been the abiding understanding of the church ever since concerning the incarnation of the Word.

OLD AND NEW ADAM

LUKE 3

Luke's precision in establishing a historical context for the beginning of John the Baptist's ministry is entirely congruent with his method and genre (*diēgēsis*). It is more than the context in imperial history as he knows it, but the context of Jewish history and especially the Old Testament promise of a messianic disclosure of God's purpose in salvation history that prompts the way in which he has organized this episode in his Gospel. Luke clearly understands the time of John's ministry to be propitious in this larger sense of being the "fullness of time" long promised, a time charged with the guiding hand of providence at work, as yet unrecognized, in the lives of Gentiles and Jews alike.

John the Baptist (3:1–2)

Among the evangelists, Luke is unique in his detail and precision in these matters; we are given the names of seven historical rulers at the time John begins his ministry. This is something that has parallels among Greek historians, however (e.g., Polybius 1.3; Thucydides 2.2). It is precisely "the fifteenth year of the reign of Tiberius Caesar," which, when correlated with Roman histories and that of Josephus, suggests that John enters upon the public stage in AD 29. This date was known among early Christian commentators; Bede notes further that Pontius Pilate had begun his ten-year stint as procurator of Judea in the twelfth year of Tiberius and that Herod, Philip, and Lysanius, all sons of Herod the Great, king at the time of Jesus's birth, did not take power at their father's death but only after a ten-year interval of Archelaus (*Homilies on the Gospels* 2.23). But as Josephus notes, Archelaus had been charged with having imperious designs of his own, before Augustus was exiled to Gaul. Thus, the chronological point not to miss in Luke's account is his designation of each of the three younger sons of Herod as *tetrarch* (*tetra* + *archos*), indicating the division of the Jewish province now into four provinces subordinate to the Roman authority, indubitably reflecting the Roman instinct to divide as a means of control. Bonaventure understands this divided condition as a form of political punishment (2001–4: 1.3.3). Any visible political unity in the Jewish nation is gone, even geographically; Pilate has direct control over the most important district, namely Judea, and is a Roman; Herod the Younger is tetrarch of Galilee, the scene of much of Jesus's ministry and the home of several disciples; Philip is tetrarch of Iturea and Trachonitus; and Lysanius is tetrarch of Abilene. Josephus provides our medieval commentators with a confirming account (*Jewish Antiquities* 14.330–36; 15.88–95). Luke's own political map shows us two things: the Jewish nation has been broken up; and, to add insult to injury, a Gentile, Pilate, clearly has the supremacy. Over the entirety of the events Luke will narrate then hangs the shadow of Roman imperial power; as a careful historian, Luke makes it abundantly clear that he is keenly aware of the phenomenon that Rémi Brague, among others, calls *romanitas*, here the Romanization of occupied Palestine.[1] Though there are two high priests (Annas, an *éminence grise* and not officially in office after the ascension of Caiaphas, is probably still honored by that title), the dissipation of Jewish religious as well as political identity is a harsh reality. Luke's picture also suggests an ethos of sordid compromise. While Bede's suggestion that Annas and Caiaphas had each purchased their positions from the Romans is far from provable, it is not improbable. That the Romans may have wanted to keep Annas around for their own purposes would be consistent with the character of the times.

Repentance and Baptism (3:3–14)

To anyone familiar with the Jewish scriptures there was something about John the Baptist that ineluctably echoed the prophets of old. For one thing, the "word" (*rhēma*) or revelation came to John in the desert. This already has a prophetic connotation (cf. Jer. 1:1–14). For another, it wasn't just that John preached the need to repent. It was, at least in part, that he preached it out in the desert, "in the wilderness" (Luke 3:2). Luke makes explicit the connection of John to Isaiah, citing an evidently messianic passage (Isa. 40:3–5). Here Luke puts together the judgment voice of Isaiah's condemnation of Israel and calling it to repentance (cf. Isa. 11) with the consolatory mood of Isa. 40 ("comfort ye my people") in a striking juxtaposition. John is here not only acting, as Malachi had predicted, as an agent to turn "the hearts of the fathers to the children, and the hearts of the children to their fathers" (Mal. 4:6; Luke 7:27), but in a more radically transgenerational way calling the dispirited and scattered Israel of his time to repent. Then he invites the penitents to be baptized as a sign of cleansing from their sins so that these individuals may become the faithful Israel long ago covenanted in a spiritual marriage to Israel's most holy God.

1. Rémi Brague, *Eccentric Culture: A Theory of Western Civilization* (South Bend, IN: St. Augustine, 2009).

This message could hardly have come at a time when the Jewish political fortunes were at a lower ebb—at least since the Babylonian captivity and perhaps the "abomination of desolation," the setting up by Antiochus IV Epiphanes of a statue of Zeus Olympus on the altar of burnt offerings. As Gregory the Great and Bonaventure have it, it was clear to all that "Judea had come to an end, for it was subjected and divided into so many kingdoms" (Bonaventure 2001–4: 1.5.228). Jerusalem was now again possessed by an alien power; all manner of vile judgment had fallen on it, and when the authentic voice of a prophet as of old was heard to cry out in the desert, many who were despondent but yet yearned in their hearts for the peace of Jerusalem went out to hear this prophet for themselves.

They cannot have gone out to be flattered, or even entertained. John the Baptist would not have done well in a culture-affirming, therapeutic religious environment. He not only calls those who come to hear him a "brood of vipers," warning them "to flee from the wrath to come" (3:7), but also makes it clear that a verbal repentance will not do; there must be concrete actions consistent with it to be authentic. Nor will typically Jewish protestations of a covenant lineage be of any use (3:8). In a passage that presages what Jesus will say to some Pharisees (19:39–40), John tells them that God is able to raise up authentic sons of Abraham from the very stones on the ground; the pun in Aramaic and Hebrew (John would not here be addressing his hearers in Greek) adds ironic pith to his declamation: *benayya'* ("children") and *'abnayya'* ("stones") (as well as, allusively, *bānâ*, "to build up and to discern") play off each other in the words Luke understands John to have spoken. (These puns will return in later chapters, with Jesus as the speaker.) The Baptist's declaration that already "the ax is laid to the root of the trees" and that "every tree which does not bear good fruit is cut down and thrown into the fire" (3:9) also anticipates Jesus's own words (e.g., Matt. 7:19).

The Greek word for repentance is *metanoia*; it relates to Hebrew *šûb* ("to turn"), as found in passages such as Isa. 6:10 and Amos 4:6–8. Augustine, in *Confessions* 8, makes use of the Latin equivalents: *vertere* ("to turn"), *revertere* ("to turn again"), and *convertere* ("to convert"). But repentance here is coupled with the explicit sign of purification: "Wash yourselves, make yourselves clean" (Isa. 1:16; cf. 2 Kgs. 5:10; Ps. 51:7; Acts 22:16). Thus John's distinctive hallmark, and the name by which we know him. But unlike Jewish purification rituals of the *mikvah* ("bath"), which cleansed the worshiper in preparation for sacrifice, John's baptism seems to have been a one-time event, signifying in effect a "new life," but with eschatological overtones (Bock 1994–96: 1.289). Christians through the centuries have not always seen John's baptism as an act that in itself conveyed forgiveness of sins (Gregory the Great, *Homily* 20.2 in *Patrologia latina* 76.1160–61; also Bonaventure 2001–4: 1.3.9.231): that has usually been reserved for the baptism of Christ. Nevertheless, in Luke's text we plainly have "for the remission of sins." How are we to understand this? The answer requires a context, and it may be helpful to have it before we take up Luke's account of the baptism of the Lord (3:21–22).

The word "baptism" is derived from the Greek word *baptizō* ("to immerse, dip"). This is the aspect of John's baptism captured in 3:16—distinguishing water baptism from the baptism of Christ to come "with the Holy Spirit and with fire"—that provides the key, as will the baptism of Jesus by John that follows (3:21–22), in which the Holy Spirit "descended in bodily form like a dove upon him, and a voice came from heaven which said, 'You are my beloved son; in you I am well pleased'" (3:22). In Matt. 3:12–17, we are told that John, recognizing who Jesus is, questions how it is that he should baptize Jesus and not the reverse. Jesus makes it clear that he identifies, as God's only begotten Son, with the unfaithful sons of Israel who are newly repentant and thus seek "to fulfill all righteousness" (Matt. 3:15). The baptism that Jesus later commanded his disciples to perform after teaching in "all nations" is, by contrast, distinctively apostolic and is to be in the name of the Trinity—Father, Son, and Holy Spirit (Luke 24:47; cf. John 20:22–23; Matt. 28:19; Acts 2:38–41). There is no record of Jesus performing such a baptism himself; this is a charge to the apostles to baptize converts, but following their own baptism by the Holy Spirit and with fire. By comparison, John's baptism was still, though striking, a baptism of the old dispensation; Ambrose reflects a widespread view among early commentators that John is here "a type of the law, because the law could denounce sin, but not pardon it" (*Exposition of Luke* 2.68; cf. Calvin 1972: 1.11).[2] Later he adds, "there is therefore one baptism of repentance and another of grace" (*Exposition of Luke* 2.79). Here the baptism is a sign of true and most practical repentance and John's prophetic office: to the penitents' Ezekiel-like question, "What shall we do then?" (Luke 3:10), John's answer to those who have possessions is that they share them (3:11), to the tax collectors for the Roman government that they take no more than is appropriate (3:12–13), and to the soldiers that they should "not intimidate anyone or accuse falsely, and be content with [their] wages" (3:14). Both early and medieval commentators (Origen may have been the first) noted how these three groups of penitents reflected the three basic estates as they understood them: commoners, clerks, and knights (soldiers); these who come to John are thus a representative remnant of Jewish society. This aspect of John's message, namely that a scrupulous ethical life is both necessary for a true repentance and certainly consequent upon it, is recorded uniquely in Luke's Gospel: "fruits worthy of repentance" (3:8) establish that reformed action, not mere membership, is the criterion, and it connects this passage, as Bonaventure notes, to the prospect of God's judgment (2001–4: 1.20.240; cf. Matt. 21:19; Luke 13:7; Dan. 4:11). Here, as earlier in Old Testament contexts, almsgiving is related to the idea that sin incurs indebtedness to both God and neighbor, and gifts to the house of the Lord and to the needy are ways provided by which our indebtedness may be satisfied (Augustine, Sermon 389). This concept will carry over into the teaching of Jesus, as the prayer he taught the

---

2. Cf. Talbert 2002: 27–30, who sees John the Baptist as a prototype of the Christian evangelist.

disciples (Luke 11:2–4) and the repentance of Zacchaeus (19:8–10) make clear.[3] Calvin says that "*good works* are called the fruits of repentance, for repentance is an inward thing . . . but results in the production of fruit by a change of life" (1972: 1.122). In the light of 3:10–14, as read by the church down through the centuries, we cannot doubt that 3:8–9 links the general absence of "works worthy of repentance" in the larger population to Israel's disfavor and God's judgment, and so prompts John the Baptist's prophetic image of "the ax . . . laid to the root of the trees" (3:9). He is here, as we are later told explicitly, the last of the Old Testament prophets (16:16).

The Fullness of Time; Remarriage (3:15–20)

We can hardly overstress the sense in this chapter of an impending great moment; from the eschatological words from Isaiah forward, our sense of the mission of John the Baptist as the one who, like Elijah, would "make ready a people prepared for the Lord" (1:17) has been building suspense in Luke's narrative. Clearly John's ministry and reputation are already seen in that light, for "the people were in expectation, and all reasoned in their hearts about John, whether he was the Christ [Anointed One] or not" (3:15). Since the time of the prophets faithful Jews had been in such expectation, right down to Zacharias, Simeon, and Anna; in the fullness of time "it shall come to pass" (Isa. 2:2–4). Specifically, it had been expected that the Anointed of the Lord would come to deliver his people, and this language is echoed in the New Testament with reference to the redemptive work of the Messiah (Eph. 1:10; Gal. 4:4). The preaching of John and his manner of life appeared as a throwback in such evident ways to the long-deceased prophets that the people most naturally ask if he is the promised Christ (Luke 3:15).

The Baptist's answer is straightforward and yet charged with the deepest possible level of spiritual significance. What does he mean by referring to the sandal strap of the Coming One, saying that he is not worthy to loosen it? Some take it to be a reference to the third-century mishnaic protocol in which it is said that "a disciple will do every service of a slave for his master in regard to his teacher except loosening his shoe" (*Mekilta de Rabbi Ishmael*, tractate *Neziqin* 1 on Exod. 21:2; cf. Bock 1994–96: 1.321), suggesting that John is here saying that he is unworthy to perform even the service of a slave for his master. But for Jews with a knowledge of halakah, religious law, something much higher and of more powerful moment as a *sign* was possibly involved. "To loosen the sandal strap" is, in Old Testament marriage custom, associated with levirate marriage. Although there are only two Old Testament narratives in which this custom is referenced, namely the account of Judah and Tamar (Gen. 38) and the story of the kinsman redeemer (*gōʾēl*) in the book of Ruth, there seems to be warrant for thinking that

---

3. Gary A. Anderson, *Sin: A History* (New Haven: Yale University Press, 2009), 8–9, 15–17, 27–33.

the practice of levirate law (from Hebrew *yābām*, "brother-in-law," translated into Latin as *levir*) laid down in Deut. 25:5–10 may be alluded to here. By loosening the strap of one shoe (cf. Ruth 4:7–8), a man who was closest kin to a widow or "desolate" woman could without blame give up his legal obligation (and right) to marry her;[4] because that does not happen in the case of the sons of Judah, but in fact gross deception occurs, the obligation for redemption reverts to the father-in-law; when Judah also seeks to evade his responsibility, Tamar tricks him into intercourse (Gen. 38:15–19). In Ruth's case the proper procedure is followed, and Boaz becomes the "kinsman redeemer" for Ruth and Naomi. There is a great deal of commentary on these two stories by both Jewish and Christian exegetes (little of which can be represented here), but the attentive reader of scripture will already have noted that John and Jesus are cousins ("brothers" in Semitic parlance) and that the offspring of both Old Testament unions (Perez son of Judah and Tamar, and Obed son of Boaz and Ruth) are mentioned in Luke's genealogy of Jesus, which follows almost immediately in the text (3:32–33). Gregory the Great says (*Forty Gospel Homilies* 6), following Ambrose, that we should understand here a great mystery of which the Old Testament stories are merely a foreshadowing. John the Baptist, last of the prophets, represents fidelity under the law and the covenant. But even as the questions of the people concerning his identity suggest, he is naturally to be associated with Israel's longing for redemption "in the fullness of time"; they seek thus to discover if he is to be their *gō'ēl* ("redeemer"). John's answer that he is not that person is given by reference to the levirate sign, according to Gregory the Great: "John denounces himself as unworthy to loose the latchet of Christ's shoes; as if he openly said, 'I am not able to disclose the footsteps of the Redeemer, and do not presume to take unto myself unworthily the name of bridegroom,' for it was an ancient custom that when a man refused to take to wife her to whom he was obligated, whoever should come to her betrothed by right of kin was to loose his shoe" (*Forty Gospel Homilies* 6). This association is also found in Augustine (Homily 4: "On the Birth of John the Baptist"), Cyprian (*Against the Jews* 2.19), and, as we have seen, Ambrose. Reinforcing this nuptial analogy, John the Baptist is recorded as saying at this precise juncture, "He who has the bride is the bridegroom; but the friend of the bridegroom, who stands and hears him, rejoices greatly because of the bridegroom's voice. Therefore this joy of mine is fulfilled. He must increase, but I must decrease" (John 3:29–30).

But who then is the bride who has been bequeathed by John, last of the prophets, to this one who is "mightier" than himself (Luke 3:16)? Clearly, it seems, the chosen bride is Israel itself, at least that faithful remnant of Israel who has been waiting expectantly, like the five wise virgins, for the bridegroom to appear and the nuptial sacrament to begin (Matt. 25:1). That this image of Israel as a virgin bride covenanted to the Lord is everywhere in the prophets hardly needed to be

4. Roland de Vaux, *Ancient Israel: Its Life and Institutions*, trans. John McHugh (New York: McGraw-Hill, 1961), 22, 37–38.

explained (2 Kgs. 19:21; Isa. 37:22; Jer. 14:17) and that the "virgin of Israel" had notoriously fallen from fidelity is a stock theme of prophetic condemnation (Jer. 2:32; 18:13; Ezek. 16:15; Amos 5:2). The cries of Jeremiah have until now gone largely without response: "Turn back, O virgin of Israel, turn back. . . . How long will you gad about, O you backsliding daughter?" (Jer. 31:21–22). The Hebrew here is much stronger than the translation suggests. But this passage likewise contains the promise of a "new covenant" (31:31), not like the first that Israel has broken, defiling Yahweh's holy right as "husband to them" (31:32). "After those days, says the LORD: I will put my law in their minds, and write it on their hearts; and I will be their God, and they shall be my people" (31:33).

For Luke, evidently so well versed in the scriptures, who begins his narrative (Luke 1–2) with representatives of faithful Israel, culminating in the supreme biblical example of the faithful virgin in Israel, this saying of John's is charged with powerful significance: unmistakably the bridegroom himself is about to return to claim his bride. Old things have passed away, and all will become new. The "fullness of time" is at hand, a time of redemption (Gal. 4:4–7) and marriage. Of this John the Baptist seems indeed to have been a harbinger, a forerunner, a witness as a "friend of the bridegroom"—in contemporary parlance, the "best man." "He was not that Light, but was sent to bear witness of that Light" (John 1:8).

There is much preparation for this imagery in scripture, more than can be commented on here. But it may help us to remember that in the light of the contrast between the pagan cults of fertility and sacred marriage (cf. Prov. 7–9) against which Israel's religion saw corporate Israel as the chaste bride of Yahweh, Ps. 45, a royal epithalamion, was interpreted by the rabbis as an allegory of Israel's betrothal to God, in a similar fashion to their interpretation of the Song of Songs. This interpretation, clearly reinforced by the Revelation to John that concludes the New Testament, was followed by Christian exegetes from Origen and Augustine down through Luther and the New England Puritans, such as Edward Taylor in his "Preparatory Meditations." It is still reflected in the well-known Protestant hymn "The Church's One Foundation," by Samuel J. Stone, in which are the lines:

> She is his new Creation, by water and the Word,
> From heaven he came and sought her,
> To be his holy bride;
> With his own blood he bought her,
> And for her life he died.

This hymn is often sung in a eucharistic setting by Protestants, reflecting a tradition of eucharistic association of the nuptial imagery of scripture going back to the early church and memorably expressed by Augustine in his homily on John 8 (Patrologia latina 35.1452).

Luke's companion Paul will also employ the metaphor of the *paranymphos* ("friend of the bridegroom") to explain his own role in relationship to the mystery of the sacred, sacramental marriage, in which the marriage analogy is to the church as chaste bride of Christ (1 Cor. 11:3; 2 Cor. 11:2–3; Eph. 5:25–32). In Romans, Paul will refer to the condition of grace as distinct from the law by the analogy of a woman, whose former husband was the law, who has "died," freeing her now to be married to another: "Him who was raised from the dead, that we should bear fruit to God" (Rom. 7:1–4). (Here too the levirate analogy is suggested.) Finally, the image of the *parousia* in the teaching of Jesus as a wedding banquet (Matt. 22:1–14), Jesus's own reference to himself as bridegroom (Luke 5:33–35; cf. Matt. 9:14–15; Mark 2:19–20), the description of the heavenly Jerusalem as the bride of Christ (Rev. 21:2, 9), and in the concluding words of the New Testament the invocation: "The Spirit and the bride say, 'Come!'" (22:17)—all help us to appreciate that in a canonical reading of scripture the divine marriage imagery of Luke's Gospel constitutes one of scripture's central themes.

The eschatological theme of judgment is also associated with nuptial imagery in the Old Testament prophets, Matthew's eschatological discourse (Matt. 22–25), and Revelation: John foretells in classically Old Testament metaphors that the coming Redeemer will separate the faithful and unfaithful in a definitive, ultimate fashion (Luke 3:17). Moreover, John's criticism of one representative corruption of faithful marriage, that of Herod with his brother Philip's former wife Herodias, while the legitimate spouses of each were still living, highlights with a dark contrast the persistent theme (3:19). This was no honorable levirate marriage but a public dishonoring of the institution: Eusebius notes (*Ecclesiastical History* 3.23–24) that Herodias had children already by Philip (Salome is the notable example), so that no legitimate remarriage was possible ("for those only were allowed to do this whose brothers had died without offspring"). And there were in Herod's case other contraventions of the law (Lev. 18:16; 20:21). As when Elijah condemned Ahab for a similar corruption of faithful marriage (1 Kgs. 21:17–26), unsurprisingly, John's condemnation did not win him royal approval. Although it is unclear how much later it happened, John was clapped into prison (Luke 3:20).

The Baptism of Jesus (3:21–22)

The baptism of Jesus figures in all four Gospels (Matt. 3:13–17; Mark 1:9–11; Luke 3:21–22; John 1:32–34), and it appears early on as a major motif in Christian art: among the finest examples are the mosaics of the cathedral of Santo Spirito in Ravenna and the octagonal baptistery of Sant' Apollinaire in nearby Classe, in both of which a pagan river god recognizes Christ as the herald of a new order, even as the dove descends. The baptism is more realistically portrayed in Giotto's beautiful fresco in the Scrovegni Chapel in Padua, but the artists in all cases capture the baptism of Jesus in the Jordan River by John as in some sense comparable with other baptisms, yet incomparable with any because it is accompanied by the voice of God out of heaven and the visible descent of the dove, understood to be a manifestation of the Holy Spirit, upon the head of Jesus. Matthew and Mark have it that these "signs" occur *after* Jesus has gone up out of the water (Matt. 3:16). In John and Luke this is not as clear; their compression of the account may contribute to their greater importance to Christian artists of late antiquity through the Counter-Reformation.[5]

The reader of Luke is likely to wonder with John the Baptist himself why it should be that Jesus would want to be baptized in a baptism of repentance, since he "knew no sin." Cyprian comments here: "Although he was himself not a sinner, he did not disdain to bear the sins of others" (*Good of Patience* 6); and Chrysostom adds that the baptism of Jesus "savored partly of antiquity, partly of novelty, for that he should receive baptism from a prophet showed antiquity, but the Spirit's descent denoted something new" (quoted in Aquinas, *Catena Aurea* 3.128). There is a profound sense among the exegetes that in the baptism of Jesus we are at the symbolic hinge point between the Old and the New in biblical theology (e.g., Augustine, *Trinity* 6; Martin Luther, "On the Fourth Sunday in Advent," 39). As John the Baptist says, "He must increase, but I must decrease" (John 3:29–30). The order of the prophets has here given way, in the fullness of time, to that one whose coming they foretold.

Luke's account, like that of the other evangelists, makes it clear that there are distinctive features setting the baptism of Jesus apart; both the voice and the dove are clearly unique, and John's Gospel records John the Baptist as saying that he had been prepared for this remarkable event: "He who sent me to baptize with water said to me, 'Upon whom you see the Spirit descending, and remaining on him, this is he who baptizes with the Holy Spirit.'" John then adds, "And I have seen and testified that this is the Son of God" (John 1:32–34). The divine signature, by voice and by the Holy Spirit descending "in a bodily shape like a dove upon him" (Luke 3:22), indicates beyond doubt for all of the evangelists that, however Jesus may have identified with sinful Israel in its need for cleansing and redemption, the meaning of his own baptism has more to do with bearing witness to divine presence and approval at the beginning of his ministry. Luke emphasizes that "the heaven was opened" when Jesus was praying (3:21). Though bird omens are a well-recognized topos of Hellenic literature,[6] this dove, accompanied by the divine voice out of heaven, seems to have a distinctively Semitic character (Bock 1994–96: 1.338–39). But it is hardly possible to think, as Bock seems to, that the dove is "a simple metaphor without theological significance" (339). Given the memory of the dove in the Noah story, associated there with redemption after the waters of the flood, it seems at the least to be a concrete sign of God's assurance of his presence and imminent deliverance of his people (Ambrose,

5. On this and related art-historical representations of Luke, see Hornik and Parsons 2003–7.

6. James McConnell, "The Rhetorical Use of Oracles in Plutarch's *Lives* and Old Testament Scripture in Luke-Acts" (PhD diss., Baylor University, 2009).

Exposition of Luke 2.92). It is no accident that the dove becomes a symbol for the presence of the Holy Spirit in Christian art; this would seem to be the first New Testament passage in which the Trinity is explicitly present in all three persons. As Bonaventure (2001–4: 1.3.52–56) and other commentators suggest, it is the natural precursor to the Trinitarian formula for baptism commanded by Jesus (Matt. 28:19). Gregory Nazianzus is among many orthodox commentators who point out that the descent of the dove does not indicate that Jesus received the presence of the Holy Spirit only at this point; rather, the baptism of Jesus occurs to give a new significance to baptism altogether. He adds: "Christ comes also to baptism perhaps to sanctify baptism, but doubtless to bury the old Adam in water" (*On Preaching* 39). This shows, as we shall see, that Gregory Nazianzus has been attentive to the distinctive character of Luke's genealogy of the Christ that immediately follows in the text.

The Genealogy of Jesus (3:23–38)

Genealogies such as those in Matthew and Luke can seem largely uninteresting to contemporary readers and, indeed, to even so scrupulous a commentator as Calvin, who passes over it. We might pay it slight attention as well, except for Luke's genealogy having several distinctive features. While Matthew goes back only as far as Abraham (Matt. 1:1–17), emphasizing the covenant, and has the more typical order of descent to the present from an *Ur*-ancestor, Luke reverses this order, going from the present all the way back through Abraham to "Adam, the son of God" (3:38). This has the effect of identifying Jesus not merely with the covenant people but with the whole human race. It also provides, by its ending with such a firm reference to the first Adam, a perfect setting for the temptation of Jesus that immediately follows. One has to wonder if Paul's emphasis on Jesus as Second Adam (Rom. 5:12–21; 1 Cor. 15:20–28, 45–49) is not influenced in some way by discussion with his friend Luke. Of course, conceivably it might just as well have been the other way round.

That Jesus was thirty years old at the time of his baptism is not without a natural significance since it is the normative Mediterranean age of majority. But there are other numbers to reckon with here as well; whereas Matthew's genealogy stresses the Davidic line and groups the names of the ancestors in three groups of fourteen, totaling forty-two, Luke has, beyond Joseph, eleven groups of seven names, for a total of seventy-seven. Biblical scholars tend to see, following rabbinic tradition, the arrangement in Matthew as an example of Jewish *gematria*, by which symbolic significance is found in numbers: the numeric values in the name "David" add up to fourteen. It may well be that Luke, a Gentile raised rather with Pythagorean number symbolism, has something comparable in mind: seven signifies in that context a number of plenitude or temporal fullness, much as in the Bible, while eleven is—as it remained for the Christian Middle Ages—a number of imperfection, even of sinful imperfection suggesting the need for repentance and completion.[7]

Be that as it may, there is a further divergence: whereas Matthew's lineage is to Mary and matriarchal, Luke's is patriarchal and focused on Joseph. It may be that, as Julianus Africanus long ago suggested, Luke is pointing to a *legal* line as distinct from a *genetic* line (cf. Bock 1994–96: 1.352). But there are further curiosities here: many of the names in Luke's genealogy either have marginal significance in Old Testament history or they don't exist in the record at all (cf. Bock 1994–96: 1.353–59). The technical term for such occurrences with regard to unprecedented names is "onomastic *hapax legomenon*"; there are seven of these in the list Luke gives. Perhaps a key to their inclusion is to be found in the idea of levirate marriage mentioned earlier in this chapter. (Bock 1994–96: 1.354–55 thinks this may be a factor in the case of Zerubbabel son of Pedaiah [1 Chr. 3:19], a brother to Shealtiel, being called later "the son of Shealtiel" [Ezra 3:2].) Levirate marriage would account for this element, as well it may for the seven unrecorded names. It also would make sense of Luke's having described Joseph, the legal father of Jesus, as the "supposed" (*enomizeto*) father of Jesus (Luke 2:23). Joseph, legally married to Mary, is quite precisely a levirate father, a kinsman redeemer, and has raised Jesus legally, as his own child. To the degree that this reading seems to be accounted for in the text, it certainly makes a splendid introduction for the great New Testament theme of adoption. This view is anticipated in the fathers, as when Augustine connects levirate marriage to Luke's genealogy to explain the discrepancies and hitherto unknown names (*Questions on the Gospels* 2.5). Augustine also notices the possibility of significance in the numerology: "But most fitly with regard to our baptized Lord does Luke reckon the generations through seventy-seven persons." Eleven is, for him, a sign of the sin of pride and covetousness; and seven he finds to signify the temporal evolution of the human condition (2.6). On this sort of reading, ending the genealogy of Jesus with Adam, temporally the first but disobedient "son of God," makes perfect sense. Jesus is here the younger, appointed to obedience; from Cain and Abel through Ishmael and Isaac, Saul and David, this is an established biblical pattern.

7. The literature on biblical numerology and its medieval commentary is extensive; for an introduction see J. J. Davis, *Biblical Numerology* (Grand Rapids: Baker, 1968); L. E. Dickson, *History of the Theory of Numbers*, 3 vols. (Chicago: University of Chicago Press, 1919–23); and Christopher Butler, *Number Symbolism* (New York: Barnes & Noble, 1970).

LUKE 4

The Temptation of Christ (4:1–13)

Scriptural narrative presents three direct temptations by Satan; these, in canonical order, are the temptation of Adam and Eve, the temptation of Job, and the temptation of Jesus here in Luke's Gospel. Unsurprisingly, these three episodes have been connected by Christian exegetes down through the centuries in various ways, but especially by seeing the resistance of temptation by Jesus as a paradigmatic reversal of the yielding of Eve and Adam in the garden of Eden. That this connection is invited by Luke, arranging and concluding his genealogy of Jesus as he does with Jesus as "the son of Adam, the son of God" (3:38), has seemed to much of Christian tradition an obvious element of his narrative design. Thus, Ambrose speaks for many: "There is here an Adam typology and a Genesis background to this story: as Adam is cast out of paradise into the wilderness, so Christ, the new Adam, goes into the wilderness on our behalf, then to come forth from that temptation to lead us back to paradise" (*Exposition of Luke* 4.7). Parallels with Job are a frequent theme in Protestant theologians and poets such as Henry Oxenden's *Jobus Triumphans* (1656) and especially John Milton's *Paradise Regained* (1671), where the "two Adams" theme nonetheless still predominates: Milton bases his companion to *Paradise Lost* on Luke's rather than Matthew's account with its different order of temptations (Matt. 4:1–11) because it suited what he called his own "grand design" to place the temptation of the tower last. Milton, though influenced by Calvin, is in this preference for Luke's account certainly following the more dominant typology (*Paradise Regained* 2.129–39).

What seems to emerge in these Lukan passages is a strong reminder that in biblical narrative in general there is a cosmic *agōn* or struggle taking place for the human soul (Calvin 1972: 1.135). In the temptation of Jesus, most fully recounted by Matthew and Luke (Mark mentions it only briefly and John not at all), it is as though the fundamental antagonist to God and his creation has been exposed in a face-to-face encounter with the now revealed protagonist of salvation history, the Redeemer, toward whom all the other narratives and prophecies of scripture had long been pointing. This too is a part of the reader's growing sense of the "fullness of time" now appearing. That this confrontation was not an accidental encounter but rather a deliberate showdown willed by the divine author of salvation history is indicated by Luke's beginning his narrative of this event by specifying that Jesus, newly signified from heaven as God's anointed, was "filled with the Holy Spirit" and that it was the Spirit who "led [him] . . . into the wilderness" (4:1).

But there are other threads woven into the episode, and Luke has certainly indicated them. First-century Jews, whether readers of the Septuagint text or simply hearers of the Old Testament scriptures in the synagogue, could not have avoided in the forty days of Jesus's desert fast (4:2) recalling several biblical precedents. Not only does this number recall the forty years of Israel's desert wanderings (Num. 14:33; Deut. 8:2), the forty days of rain in Noah's flood (Gen. 7:4, 12), Ezekiel's forty-day burden of the sin of Judah (Ezek. 4:6), and the forty-day ritual period of purification for a woman postpartum (Lev. 12:1–4), all of which suggest typological connections, but this was precisely the duration of Moses's fast (Exod. 34:28; Deut. 9:9) as well as that of Elijah (1 Kgs. 19:8), each of which held a special prominence in Jewish consciousness (Bock 1994–96: 1.370). Forty is thus a number that in the Jewish imagination was already charged with a sense of trial and testing in preparation for something new. Commentators from Cyril of Alexandria (1983: Homily 12) through Augustine (*Harmony of the Gospels* 4.9) to Matthew Henry (1728: 31) have seen the parallel with the fasts of Moses and Elijah as highly significant, and this is the typological parallel preferred by Calvin (1972: 1.34).

That there are three temptations nevertheless has itself evoked another sense of primal pattern in biblical readers who are used to seeing all of scripture as "one word of God." Bede, as often he does, sees here an archetype of the disposition to sin that is inherently human and that Jesus uniquely overcomes: following the lead of Augustine (*On Psalms* 9.13) and Ambrose (*Exposition of Luke* 4.17–34), who call the temptations "appetite," "boasting," and "ambition," Bede notes further parallels in the three excuses later given by the recalcitrant guests in the parable of the wedding feast (Luke 14:16–24) and in the paradigm given by John the evangelist in 1 John 2:16 as "the lust of the flesh, the lust of the eyes, and the pride of life" (*Homilies on the Gospels* 1.119; cf. Augustine, *Tractate* on 1 John 2:16). All of these are a kind of tropological or moral application in which the summary failures of humankind without Christ are seen as victories achieved *by* Christ, a sense certainly warranted by Luke's account and placement of Christ's temptation in his narrative. Peter Lombard, whose twelfth-century *Sentences on the Gospels* served as a standard for scholars of scripture until the seventeenth century, summarizes the Adamic reversal in this way:

> But in the same way that he [Satan] overcame the first man, he was now subdued by the Second. He tempted him also with gluttony when he said: "Command

that these stones be made bread." He tempted him with vainglory when he said, "If thou be the Son of God, cast thyself down." And with avarice for prominence and power, he tempted him when he showed him all the world, saying, "All these things will I give thee if you fall down and adore me." (*Sentences on the Gospels* 2.21)

Calvin rejects this established emphasis on paradigmatic vices (1972: 1.136–37) but stresses, as does John Milton in *Paradise Regained*, the way in which Christ defeats the perversity of Satan by his more just citation of the words of holy scripture. This aspect has in fact been noticed by a majority of Christian interpreters down through the centuries as they consider the dramatic debate between Christ and Satan in Luke 4:3–13. Though, as Ambrose says in a seminal warning to all Christians, "the devil makes use of the Scriptures not to teach but to deceive," it is crucially instructive that "he who had alleged the testimony of Scripture should by Scripture himself be overthrown" (*Exposition of Luke* 4.24–33). Ambrose concludes by drawing the moral lesson for those who would follow Christ: "Therefore, the Lord first remitted the debt of the ancient wrong, in order that, having shaken off the yoke of captivity, we may learn to overcome our faults with the help of the Scriptures." This application Calvin is happy to echo: "Christ uses the Scripture as a shield against him, and this is the true way of fighting if we wish to win a sure victory" (1972: 1.137). But Ambrose, in a sentence regarding the end of this episode (*Exposition of Luke* 4.13), shows that he understands a profound connection on this point between Luke and Genesis, as well as between Luke and the Pauline epistles (Col. 3:9–10; Eph. 4:22–24) and Heb. 4:1–15, and in so doing underscores Luke's choice of language for the Christology his narrative has been developing: "He [Luke] would not have said that all the temptation was ended, had there not been in the three temptations which have been described the materials for every human transgression ... for the courses of our own [illicit] desires are the delight of the flesh, the pomp of vainglory, and the greed for power" (*Exposition of Luke* 4.35). New Testament scholar David Garland remarked in a May 2010 graduation address at Baylor on the uncanny coalescence of these satanic temptations with the normative seductions of our general culture. The temptations of Jesus are, of course, diabolical drama at the highest level, but in its basic dark stratagems the satanic appeal is representative for any age and culture, and a warning for those who would be faithful disciples of the Lord. Jesus was, in this high desert drama, "in all points tempted as we are, yet without sin" (Heb. 4:15). With however great difficulty, as Luke's narrative goes on to show, every true disciple must seek to imitate Christ if there is to be success in refusing such temptations.

I have emphasized the moral application of traditional Christian readings of this episode because for the church historically spiritual conflict with the adversary has made Jesus's example of defense by a deep sense of scripture an important principle. For Luke himself, it is the distinctive question of Jesus's identity that takes precedence, however. Luke wants us to see that the baptized Christ, divinely ordained to his ministry of preaching the salvation of God, is uniquely, unequivocally God's Anointed One. Jesus, though echoing the prophets, is not their equivalent. He is rather the Son of God who alone overcame by the word of his power. When the archtempter offered just such temptations as those to which we ourselves fall heir, Jesus answered Satan in each case with a definitive word of God, citing, as in the third instance (which is a summary of Deut. 6:16), just the pertinent divine word to answer a distorted citation of that word.

Early artistic representations as often present Satan as an attractive man as by the carnivalesque horned monstrosities of some later medieval manuscript illustrations; later still, painters will represent Satan as an apparently pure and beautiful youth (Titian, *Temptation*, 1545) or as Lucifer, a beautiful fallen angel (Tintoretto, *Temptation of Christ*, Scuola di San Rocco, 1588). But we should not forget that in the text itself it is the all-too-seductive appeal of normative human temptation, couched in apparently biblical language, that Luke has recorded. One can only imagine that he, like Matthew, acquired these diabolically twisted citations and their unarguable divine answers from someone close to the Lord, a disciple to whom Jesus had revealed the substance of his dramatic desert contestation.

The Word Fulfilled (4:14–30)

We know from John's Gospel that Jesus had been ministering for about a year largely in Judea before the event Luke next narrates (cf. Bock 1994–96: 1.386). Jesus had evidently been more recently preaching in the synagogues in Galilee (Luke 4:14–15) and had now returned to his hometown, with his *phēmē* ("fame") having preceded him. It is probable that the synagogue in Nazareth would have been filled with expectant listeners.

The familiar iconic image of Christ as *pantokratōr*, the earliest now extant of which is the encaustic painting found at St. Catherine's monastery in Sinai, Egypt, has myriad versions across the Greek Christian world. A particular feature of these representations is to show Jesus holding a codex of holy scripture. The depiction is not literal, of course, but iconic, and it articulates a visual theology concerning Jesus as the Christ. The image represents him as Lord of the cosmos who creates by the power of his *logos*; at the same time, it calls to mind the precise historical moment when Jesus is called upon by the leader of the congregation to stand up and read the text of Isaiah. In the first century, of course, and for Jewish tradition continuously, the text of scripture was in a scroll (4:17); hence it had to be unrolled until the reader found the place he sought.

Several elements of this scene are best contextualized in historic Jewish worship practice. As one who grew up in Nazareth, Jesus would have been a member of this congregation (*synagōgē*, "gathering together as one," similar to Greek *ekklēsia* and Latin *congregatio*). The order of service following recitation of the Shema (Deut.

6:4–9) included liturgical prayers, followed by a reading from the Torah, followed by another reading, with commentary, by a member of the congregation; this reading was typically from the prophets. Then there would be a benediction. The second reading is called the *haftarah* and the reader, selected for the Sabbath by the ruler of the local synagogue, is known as a *maphtir* (Lightfoot 1979: 3.66–72 provides a summary). In synagogue custom, the Torah reading was probably prescribed; we are uncertain about a specific schedule for the *haftarah* from the prophets. It would be of much interest to know what the Torah reading was, but we do not. (It would make much sense if it had been from Exodus.) What Luke does make clear is that Jesus had a pertinent passage from the prophets clearly in his own mind, for he rolled out the scroll (a time-consuming task, perhaps adding suspense) until "he found the place" for which he was looking (Luke 4:17). Then he began to read from Isaiah. As Luke has recorded it, the main passage read was apparently Isa. 61:1–2, but there are also phrases from 48:8–9 and possibly an allusion to 58:6 (Luke 4:18). It was possible, under synagogue practice, for Jesus to have skipped from place to place so as to bring a larger portion of the prophetic text to mind (Lightfoot 1979: 3.72). The reference of Jesus to "the acceptable year of the Lord" (4:19, citing Isa. 61:2) may have been understood as just one more reminder of the ancient and little-heeded law of the year of Jubilee and the redemption it was to herald for captives and the indebted poor (Lev. 25:1–42). Yet for most this commandment and observance had come to be thought of as an archaic practice, and its mention, sadly, was by now for many in Israel little more than an invocation of religious buzzwords. (Lev. 25:9–10 would also have been an appropriate Torah selection, given the choice Jesus makes for his reading from the prophets.) Provocatively, Cyril of Alexandria suggests that by "the acceptable year of the Lord" Jesus may have been consciously referring to the "joyful tidings of his own advent" (1983: Homily 12). He also connects Jesus's reference to the "poor" to the spiritually poor (cf. Matt. 5:1), especially the Gentiles, but a reader of Luke's Gospel should also connect this opening proclamation of the Lord to the Magnificat of Mary, which surely it echoes (Luke 1:46–55). The crowd, though this is Nazareth, does not likely know Mary's song. Jesus, on the other hand, having spent his childhood years in her company, may know it very well indeed.

While Jesus is reading, all eyes are fixed upon him and all ears attend; here was a passage of enormous portent for Israel, still in captivity, yearning to be set free. When he closed up the scroll, gave it to the attendant, and, as was customary, sat down to comment upon what was written, it is clear from Luke's language that the atmosphere was charged with expectation (4:20). As he begins to speak— "this day is this scripture fulfilled in your ears" (4:21 KJV)—it seems that two responses swept over the crowd in rapid succession; in the first there was a buzz of excitement and appreciation, but almost immediately it seems to have been fol-lowed by second-guessing: is this not just our neighbor, the son of Joseph? (4:22).

Jesus responds to the skepticism he knows is rising in their hearts with a "proverb" (Greek *parabolē*; the Hebrew equivalent, *māšāl*, can mean any figurative saying as well as "parable"). Jesus knows what they really want is for him to do in their own midst some of the miracles he has done up north in Capernaum (4:23). They want to see signs and wonders here and now, in their own village; they have little interest in the larger context. His response immediately points up two things that his audience in Nazareth, as elsewhere, does not like to hear: first, that Israel more often than not has rejected the prophets (4:24) and, second, that, as a result, wonders of the Lord were sometimes then performed by the prophets among the Gentiles instead, as witnessed by Elijah's blessing of the widow of Zarephath (4:25; cf. 1 Kgs. 17:9–24). Jesus is here reminding his hearers pointedly of the same thing John did in the previous chapter (Luke 3:8–9): if Israel thinks its special covenant relationship with God is all that matters, their disobedience notwithstanding, they have not been paying sufficient attention to either the Law *or* the Prophets. Cyril of Alexandria grasps the point firmly: by these two stories of Elijah and Elisha, he says, Jesus is referring to the "heathen who were about to accept him and be healed of their leprosy, by reason of Israel's remaining impenitent" (1983: Homily 12). It seems more than probable that Luke, a Gentile himself, must have noticed these long-standing biblical patterns and pondered over their recurrent frequency in the teaching of Jesus and the ministry of the apostles.

We have to conclude from the suddenly impassioned and violent response of the crowd in the synagogue that, here as elsewhere, any suggestion that God would bypass the Jews and confer his blessing on the hated Gentiles has produced a hair-trigger animosity; Lightfoot's general observations about this reflex suggest that the pattern of response to this message everywhere in the New Testament was well grounded in long-standing Jewish prejudice (1979: 3.59). The enraged crowd drags Jesus out and tries to shove him off a cliff, presumably so as then to stone him. But somehow, mysteriously, he escapes (4:29–30), for, as Bede says, reflecting Luke's words, "the hour of his passion had not yet come" (quoted in Aquinas, *Catena Aurea* 3.1.163).

The Word with Power (4:31–44)

The road from the rocky outcrops of Nazareth down to the Sea of Galilee is indeed a descent, for Capernaum and the neighboring village of Bethsaida were on the shore, more than six hundred feet below sea level (of the nearby Mediterranean). Galilee was home to a rural and practical people, and also a refuge for Zealots and revolutionaries; it was home notably to Simon Peter, born at Bethsaida, a fisherman like many in that place. Capernaum was the larger market town, surrounded by farms and vineyards. People ate well there. Their synagogues were comfortable, if not affluent, and the congregations were themselves an expression of the suspicious independence that Galilee strove to maintain under increasingly difficult conditions imposed by the Romans.

Jesus had been teaching in the synagogue on Sabbath days, and we are told that his hearers "were astonished at his teaching, for his word was with authority [*exousia*]" (4:32). We should not in the least imagine that Luke here is referring to some sort of histrionic or, as we should likely say, "charismatic" pulpit-pounding oratory (which is often a sign that the kind of authority found in Jesus's preaching is conspicuously wanting). The presence of the Holy Spirit in Jesus's teaching was evident rather in the authority of "his word" (*logos autou*). These terms carry us back to Nazareth and, further still, to the response of the temple elders to Jesus speaking of the scriptures with them when he was still a boy. When Jesus spoke, howsoever quietly, there seems to have been a sense of potent immediacy to which the synagogue worshipers were not accustomed, an authorial command and presence that let those hearing know instantly that Jesus was like no teacher they had known. The contrast—here tacit, elsewhere explicit—would have been with such scribes who normally teach the tradition more than the text ("Rabbi Solomon says," "Rabbi Eleazar says," etc.). Jesus, intimate to the word in the words, addressed the text directly. But we should not imagine their "astonishment" (*exeplēssonto*) as occasioned simply by some novel method; it is clear that the *exousia* of God's word was being revealed to them in a new register, qualitatively unprecedented.

If Luke finds Jesus's teaching in the synagogues significant, it is clear also that he regards Jesus's healing people—in the synagogue and on the Sabbath—as a correlative sign of a qualitative difference in the authority of his word. Luke knew, of course, that many of the Jews (especially the Pharisees) regarded healing as a form of work, hence to be excluded from both Sabbath and synagogue. But the healings on this particular Sabbath are only the first of many in Luke (cf. 6:6–11; 13:10–17; 14:1–6). Moreover, by following the Nazareth proclamation of the Jubilee "Sabbath of Sabbaths," with these events Jesus is drawing attention to a signal theme of the good news he has come to proclaim. Ambrose notes that in Luke's Gospel the work of the new creation begins on the Sabbath, just where the old creation had ceased (*Exposition of Luke* 4.58). The point is Pauline, but its applicability to the narrative itself is clear. In part at least, we may take these gestures of apparent contradiction to custom on the part of Jesus as a reversion to the spiritual intent of the law, a course correction that will emerge over a wide range of halakic practices addressed in his teaching. Here, in the most radical sort of demonstration, Jesus is restoring content to the term "holy" ("remember the Sabbath day to keep it holy") by striking right to the core of unholiness to which the congregation had long accustomed itself.

One man possessed by radical unholiness, "a spirit of an unclean devil," was right there in the synagogue. We know nothing about this fellow before the dramatic event of this one Sabbath; we do know that he was admitted to the congregation without a fuss, so that we should perhaps assume that he was a regular, sufficiently qualified to be part of a *minyan* (the number—ten—of Jewish males in good standing required for prayer). But however quiet and compliant he has been with the proceedings on previous occasions, on this day, in his own terrible way, he recognizes that he is in the presence of someone entirely alien to him. What he cried out was perhaps almost involuntary, and certainly fearful: "Let us alone! What have we to do with you, Jesus of Nazareth? Did you come to destroy us? I know who you are—the Holy One of God!" (4:34). Commentators typically observe that the demons know well enough who Jesus is and tremble in fear at his presence. But here there is also an explicit differentiation between whatever the synagogue in Capernaum then represented ("what have we to do with you?") and what Jesus represents. This difference has everything to do with the holiness of God, the very reason for Sabbath observance in the first place, which nonetheless has been forgotten rather than remembered, in contravention of the fourth commandment. The tacit condemnation of religious misunderstanding in this episode could hardly be stronger. For anyone who knew the word of God, moreover, the messianic title should have been enough to set their own knees to trembling: this is that one who the psalmist foretold when he expressed his understanding that God would not permit his Holy One to see corruption; he is that Holy One foretold by the prophets (Isa. 40:25; 43:15; Hab. 1:12; 3:3; Ps. 16:10); the connection will later be made explicit by Peter in his Pentecost sermon (Acts 2:27) and by Paul at Antioch (13:35–37), both of which Luke records.

Jesus rebukes the demon and silences him. It may be, as some earlier commentators thought, that Jesus was refusing testimony from "the father of lies" (John 8:44). But it is also apparent from Luke's overall narrative that Jesus himself is pacing the plot, not wishing to accelerate events toward their climax before he has accomplished by his word of teaching what he has come to proclaim. That we have here a direct confrontation with demonic forces, in the context of Jesus just having been tempted by Satan in the desert, is evidence that Luke understands how profoundly cosmic is the battle between the holiness of God and the utterly profane antiholiness of the adversary. At the risk of pedantry, it should be observed that the term *daimonion* ("demon") occurs twenty-three times in Luke's Gospel. This is not a trivial statistic. Luke will not allow us to read his account of the life of Jesus as other than an eschatological return to his creation by the Lord of creation, who is intent upon throwing out the usurper. For this the synagogue is here both a literal venue and a symbolic microcosm, as also in his own way is the unnamed man possessed by the usurper.

The demons obey Jesus (Luke 4:36); the unnamed man is thrown down, fittingly in the midst of the congregation, as the devil leaves his body. The destruction apparently feared by the demon/man (4:34)—a recurrent theme in biblical demonology—does not occur. The evil spirit is ejected from the man's body, and his body is unharmed. Suddenly, he is whole. No rituals are involved. Jesus does this simply by his word. Small wonder the congregation is amazed. Whether they had known the man to be possessed is unclear; what they do know is that they have never seen "unclean spirits" obey anyone before (4:36). The fame of Jesus, unsurprisingly, travels far and quickly (4:37).

Almost innocuously, it appears that Jesus leaves the synagogue to go to the home of Simon (Peter), there presumably to share in a Sabbath lunch prepared the previous day. But when they arrive, they are met with bad news; Simon Peter's mother-in-law is sick with a high fever (4:38). When the family asks for Jesus's help, he stands over her, rebukes the fever just as he had the unclean spirit, and it leaves her. "Immediately," as Luke likes to say, she gets up and begins to attend to the group. The experience of healing prompts grateful service to others: this too is a paradigm. The homely intimacy of this family event, following as it does upon the highly dramatic public event in the synagogue, serves to make personal the healing power of the Lord in such a way that the reader can begin to identify with it. After all, the cosmic battle touches all of us in one way or another.

It seems more than likely that Simon Peter, who Luke knew well, was his source for these events in Capernaum. What Luke has learned from the household of Simon and here narrates is that Jesus had a very busy Sabbath evening (when the Sabbath is officially ending), at sundown healing all sorts of people afflicted with illness (4:40). The "demons came out of many" (4:41), underscoring the new creation theme; they too recognize that Jesus is the Redeemer, "Christ the Son of God," the messianic "Anointed One," bringing to fullness the metonymic quality of this "day of the Lord" on which, as in Mary's Magnificat, "the arm of the Lord" is being revealed.

At daybreak Jesus goes out into a solitary place, doubtless to pray. The people follow him, however, and clamor for him to stay with them in Capernaum. Their parochialism is just the opposite to that of Nazareth: the people of Nazareth had wanted to kill Jesus; these want to keep him to themselves (4:42). But Jesus resists, indicating that his ministry is to be wider (4:43), and Luke's narrative at this point concludes simply by recording that Jesus went on to preach in other synagogues in Galilee (4:44). We wish we knew what Jesus said and what happened in those congregations, but Luke does not tell us. He does tell us, next, of another event that displays the authoritative word spoken by the Lord, directly this time to creation itself.

DISCIPLINE
AND DISCIPLESHIP

LUKE 5

Fishers of Men (5:1–11)

In Mark's attenuated account (1:16–20), the story of the calling of the fishermen to be disciples of Jesus comes immediately following his temptation and is the first recorded episode in Galilee. Much of great interest would be lost to us without Luke's much more complete account of this event.[1]

Luke's language makes it clear that the intensely positive popular response to Jesus by the Galileans was, however mixed of curiosity and awe, clearly indicative that Jesus was no ordinary religious teacher. They were pressing in close to hear *ton logon tou theou* ("the word of God"). Evidently Jesus was right by the edge of the water with almost no place to stand on account of the press of the crowd. The place itself is rich with historical memory. Lake Genessaret, as it was called by the locals, was known also as Galilee, for the fertile region it drained (Matt. 4:18; Mark 1:16; Josephus, *Jewish Antiquities* 18.27). Currently called el-Ghuweir by Arabic speakers, its Old Testament name had been Chinnereth (Num. 34:11; Josh. 11:2; Calvin 1972: 3.156), and this is the name by which Israelis refer to the lake to this day. (Genessaret seems to be an Aramaic form.) Originally part of the land allotted to the tribe of Naphtali (Josh. 19:35), it was famous for its rich commercial fishery. The lake was fished mostly from boats, mostly at night, and with the aid of cast-nets; the boats, to judge both from historical accounts and one preserved find (Yigdal Allon Museum), were close to thirty feet in length, relatively broad in the beam and flat-bottomed, for stability and draft when fishing near the shore. Two such boats were nearby at the water's edge, but their crew was up on shore, washing the nets (Luke 5:2). To get a bit of distance from the

---

1. Most scholars agree that this event is to be distinguished from the postresurrection draught of fishes given in John 21:1–13. It may even be, as Fitzmyer suggests (1981–85: 1.560), that Mark and Luke are recording distinct events, though that seems to me less likely.

crowd Jesus stepped into the one owned by Simon, and when the boat was moved out a few feet, Jesus sat down and began again to address the crowd. Centuries later, teachers of scripture in monasteries and the early universities would cite this observation of Luke's as having spiritual significance: even when not in a place of worship, the disciple of Christ who teaches should avoid the commanding stance of a public orator and sit, indicating authority rather than a display of power (e.g., Bonaventure 2001–4: 1.4.6–7). Maximus of Turin will say that Jesus's choice of Peter's boat presages his choice for the church (Sermon 49.1–3). There is much medieval wordplay on the Latin term for "boat" (*navis*), for the "nave" of the churches often had ribbed vaults, evocative of a ship upside down. "The ship of Simon," says Bede, "is the primitive church" (*Homilies on the Gospels*). We may find such spiritual exegesis today to be a bit fanciful, but much of it has entered into our hymnody and preacherly illustration quite naturally. There are good reasons for this habit of mind when reading scripture, as the magisterial work of Henri de Lubac, Jean Daniélou, and others shows.[2]

Once Jesus has finished speaking to the people he asks Simon to launch out into deeper water and let down his nets—certainly not a request that would conform to regular fishing practice on this lake. Simon's response is polite, but clearly he is weary after the fruitless night of fishing. Yet his obedience to the counterintuitive command of Jesus is striking: "Nevertheless at your word I will let down the net" (5:4–6). The result of his obedience is startling—even with the aid of the partners in the other boat they can scarcely get the two boats to shore before they sink. As Bede says, "The filling of these ships [the churches] thus goes on until the end of the world" (quoted in Aquinas, *Catena Aurea* 3.1.177). Here more immediately we see that creation, too, obeys the Lord of creation. The huge catch doubtless netted the fishermen a tidy sum—in timely fashion, since they were about to leave their boats and families to follow Jesus—but we do not know whether, as in John Newton's hymn "Casting the Gospel Net" (*Olney Hymns*, no. 10; Newton 1995: 3.473), or among the commentaries of early exegetes, the miracle is regarded as having also a spiritual significance. Thus Gregory the Great: "We must understand the miracles of our Lord and Savior, dearly beloved, so as to believe that they have truly been done, but also that their meaning signifies still something more to us" (Patrologia latina 76.1082b). For Gregory the Great, Bede (*Homilies on the Gospels* 4.76–78), and Bonaventure (2001–4: 1.5.12–19), as with John Newton and many a children's hymn, there is a plain sense in which the apostolic mission of the church to evangelize is figured forth in the miracle of the great draught of fishes. In Luke's narrative itself this connection is unarguably warranted, given what follows.

Peter is immediately aware of the Lord as the Holy One and of himself as unholy, "a sinful man," unworthy to give hospitality to Jesus. It is clear also that his

2. Particularly for readings from the Old Testament in the light of the New, see Henri de Lubac, *Medieval Exegesis*, 3 vols. to date, trans. Mark Sebanc and E. M. Macierowski (Grand Rapids: Eerdmans, 1998–2009); and Jean Daniélou, *From Shadow to Reality: Studies in the Biblical Typology of the Fathers* (London: Burns & Oates, 1960).

partners, James and John, were quite literally frightened by what they had seen. Jesus's calming words pick up a theme from early on in the Gospel: "Do not be afraid," says Jesus; "from now on you will catch men" (5:8–10). The conclusion of this episode could hardly be more emphatic: at the absolute peak of their success as literal Genessaret fishermen, "they forsook all and followed him" (5:11). Luke has established in a variety of ways in this episode that, as Gregory of Nyssa will later say, "the voice of the word is the voice of power, at whose bidding at the beginning of the world light and other creatures came forth" (quoted in Aquinas, *Catena Aurea* 3.1.177–78).

Healer of Humankind (5:12–26)

Luke's ambiguous location ("in a certain city") for the healing of the man "full of leprosy" may or may not be, as Henry suggests, owing to Luke's sense that "it was a reflection upon the government of the city that a leper was suffered to be in it" (1728: 633a). What is beyond doubt is that Luke's phrase, "full of leprosy" (*plērēs lepras*), indicates a severe and advanced case of a disease not merely associated by the law with ritual uncleanness, but that in its final stages was a kind of living death (cf. Bock 1994–96: 1.473). It was, for many, difficult to imagine a condition more antithetical to good health. Bede is surely well within an understanding of this event that, though perhaps not more than subconscious for the crowd, was more apparent to Luke in retrospect: "How typically the leprous man represents the whole human race, languishing with sins (full of leprosy), 'for all have sinned and fallen short of the glory of God' [citing Rom. 3:23]" (*Homilies on the Gospels*). The leprous man in his evident disfigurement was both a present reality and a troubling reminder; his approach to Jesus would have been seen as a public impropriety by anyone present. Jesus, however, sees his approach as an act of great faith, and when the man falls on his face before Jesus, addressing him as *Kyrie* ("Lord"), imploring his aid, we have a supercharged moment in Luke's narrative: the man's faith in Jesus, however legally transgressive or theologically uninformed it may have been, was without reservation or ambivalence: "Lord, if you are willing, you can make me clean" (Luke 5:12).

When Jesus reaches out to touch the man (5:13), making himself thus ritually unclean by the law (Lev. 13–14), many in the crowd must have gasped on that account alone. Though they could not have formulated this with the hindsight of later commentators (e.g., Ambrose, *Exposition of Luke* 5.6: "The law forbids to touch the leprous man, but he who is Lord of the law submits not to the law, but makes the law"), the crowd seems well enough to have understood that something far greater than the law was present. Jesus simply says, "I am willing; be cleansed," and "immediately" the leprosy vanishes. The effect of this transformation on all present would have been stunning. Then Jesus does something that must have jolted them again; having apparently ignored the law by touching the leper, he now invokes it and sends him, healed, according to the requirements of the law (Lev. 13:1–3; 14:2–32), to show himself to the priests. As Augustine says, Jesus would not have been so scrupulous about the law if he hadn't wanted also to approve it (*Harmony of the Gospels* 1.2.3). This event, and perhaps its combination of respect for the law and going beyond it, seems to have set the country ablaze with report and rumor; "great multitudes," says Luke, "came together to hear, and to be healed by him of their infirmities" (Luke 5:15).

But Jesus "withdrew into the wilderness and prayed" (5:16). As we have seen, prayer is a major theme in Luke's Gospel, and the habit of Jesus to retreat from the crowds for personal prayer has become a pertinent insight for Christian discipleship down through the centuries. Spurgeon's pithy comment is consistent with the convictions of many an early father or medieval spiritual writer upon the point, though stated in the negative: "Neglect of private prayer is the locust which devours the strength of the church."[3]

The case of the paralytic man brought by his four friends, which may have occurred sometime later, seems to have been placed here by Luke as a kind of intensifier for the healing of the leper that precedes it. Spurgeon captured in his Baptistic spiritual exegesis a better sense than some twenty-first-century readers that the man's paralysis was at once a physical disease and a symbol of spiritual disease: "We may safely gather from the narrative," he says, "that the root of spiritual paralysis generally lies in unpardoned sin," and he adds that "the bottom of this paralysis is sin upon the conscience, working death . . . paralyzing with despair."[4] Cyril of Alexandria, writing fifteen hundred years earlier, is typical of the earliest commentators in reflexively connecting the disease of the body to disease of the soul, so that most naturally "the man, who since medical art had seemed a failure, was carried by his kinfolk to a higher and heavenly Physician." Likewise Bede, who in the eighth century matter-of-factly observes that "the Lord, about to cure the man of his palsy, first loosens the chains of his sins, that he may show him that it is on account of the bonds of his sins that he has become afflicted with the loosening of his joints, and that unless the former are set free, he cannot be healed with respect to recovery in his limbs" (quoted in Aquinas, *Catena Aurea* 3.1.186). Today in the West we tend to find such views troubling, even to the point of being an insult to those who are physically afflicted. (The thoughts and experiences of our African and Asian fellow Christians on such matters are typically much closer to those of earlier Christians.) Perhaps we should pause over our reflexive modernist aversion to connecting physical and spiritual disease, not because the relation is an invariable axiom (as other New Testament passages seem to indicate; e.g., Jairus's daughter, the raising of Lazarus) but because an aversion to the very possibility of such a connection can make a mockery of prayer for the sick

3. C. H. Spurgeon, *Spurgeon's Sermons* (New York: Carter, 1883; repr., Grand Rapids: Baker, n.d.), 9.26.457.
4. Ibid., 467–68.

even as it ossifies our reading of the Gospel, wherein these connections are both frequent and fundamental to Jesus's ministry in all its aspects as Luke records it.

The crowd who had gathered to hear Jesus teach that day included, however, skeptics of a sort who might well seem more like our modern selves than Luke's narrative will permit us to be happy with: various of the educated religious Jews have become curious. Specifically, these were Pharisees—a kind of superobservant lay fraternity who strove to keep other people attendant to the law—and "teachers of the law" (*nomodidaskaloi*), elsewhere called "scribes" (*grammateus*), who served both the Pharisees and the priests as scholarly, academic interpreters of the law. When Matthew says that Jesus "taught them as one having authority, and not as the scribes" (7:29), he is in part distinguishing between the pedantic literalism of the scribes and the words with power by which Jesus both taught and performed his miracles. Generally speaking, academics do not like miracles and are inclined to suspect deception. When Luke says "the power of the Lord was present to heal them" (5:17), there is tacit irony: such as the Pharisees and scribes are unlikely to be among those looking for healing in any species.

Much has been written on the faith and ingenuity of the palsied man's friends; it is sufficient for our purposes simply to note that their own faith as well as their fidelity to their friend are well attested in their perseverance. When they lower the man in his pallet to the floor of the house before Jesus, *their* faith is what captures the attention of the Lord: "When he saw their faith, he said to him, 'Man, your sins are forgiven you'" (5:20)—giving an unmistakable indication that it has been the intercessory action of the four that prompts the action of Jesus, even before the man can speak (this is the case also in the accounts of Mark 2:3–12 and Matt. 9:2–8). In this, the first use of the word "faith" (*pistis*) in Luke, we have introduced another critical Lukan theme (7:9, 50; 8:48–50; 17:19; 18:42). At the same time, the narrative makes clear overall that faith was not lacking in the paralytic himself, prompting Bonaventure to add to a thought of Bede's concerning the exemplary character of the faith of both parties for the church: "Now, this forgiveness of sins had begun through someone else's faith, but is consummated through one's own" (2001–4: 1.5.47). Luke and Mark record the words of Jesus in closely similar language; Matthew alone has Jesus saying first, "Be of good cheer"—perhaps an indication that depression was a factor in the man's illness. But only Luke has Jesus saying, "Man, your sins are forgiven you" (5:20). This is one of those occasions in which, if we are to take Luke at his word and suppose an *autoptēs* ("eyewitness") account as his source, Jesus's addressing of the man in Hebrew (if not Aramaic)—and the probability of a Hebrew speaker reporting it to Luke—becomes a factor in our understanding, especially given the themes that Luke has already established in his earlier narrative. In Hebrew (paralleled in Aramaic), Jesus would have said to the paralytic, "*'ādām* [man], your sins are forgiven you." Given the old Adam theme established by Luke's version of Jesus's genealogy (3:38) and the tacit suggestion that Jesus is the New Adam, Son of God, a typological connection soon apparent to centuries of Christian readers in the baptism of Jesus and the temptation in the wilderness, it is easy to understand how Luke himself might have seen the healing of the paralytic in symbolic, cosmic, proleptic terms.[5] It is certain that *anthrōpē*, the Greek form for *'ādām* ("man"), is here vocative and suggests affinity rather than any sort of distancing.

The scribes and Pharisees "began to reason" (*dialogizesthai*); we might also construe this as "rationalize," and it would make sense of their discourse as to purpose. They see the evidence that, for Jesus, forgiveness is somehow integral to the man's healing and see the healing itself therefore as blasphemy, since they believe that none but God can forgive sins (5:21). As a species of legal reasoning, given the eyewitness evidence they have chosen to exclude (a miracle has taken place and must owe to some power greater than human reason), their logic is, ironically, "reasonable." This is one of those instances of which one may, however, say with Lord Peter Wimsey (in Dorothy Sayers's novel *Whose Body?*), "There is nothing you can't prove, if only your outlook is sufficiently limited." Jesus knows their mind and motive and reveals them to themselves with one devastating question, "Why are you reasoning in your hearts?" (5:22)—a phrase indicating that he knows well enough that their motive has malice—followed by another: "Which is easier, to say, 'Your sins are forgiven you' or to say, 'Rise up and walk'?" (5:23). Bock is surely right that the logic of Jesus's question is "easy to follow: it is easier to say [or get away with saying] something that cannot be visually verified than to say something that can be visually substantiated" (1994–96: 1.485). The question of Jesus is about the nature of verification and evidence. He then turns to the invalid and says something that puts the skeptical unbelief of the scribes and Pharisees into the starkest of contrasts with the willingness of the sick man to believe: "But that you may know that the Son of Man [Hebrew *ben-'ādām*] has power on earth to forgive sins . . . I say to you, arise, take up your bed, and go to your house" (5:24). And that is just what happens; the man goes off whole to his house, "glorifying God" (5:25). It cannot be an accident that Luke here for the first time in his Gospel uses the divine title "Son of Man" (*ho huios tou anthrōpou*). (The first instance in Mark is in his parallel account in 2:10, whereas the parallel in Matt. 9:6 is the second instance in his case.) But Luke will go on to use this messianic title twenty-five times (Bock 1994–96: 1.485–86). Whether the crowd fully comprehended what they saw and heard we do not know, but Luke tells us that they mirrored the healed man's praise of God and said, "We have seen strange [or wonderful] things today!" (5:26); the word "wonderful" here is the unique appearance in the New Testament of *paradoxa*, from which we get one of our most useful theological concepts for all manner of situations in which reason falls short as a guide to understanding something we nevertheless can see is true.

5. One wonders if Jesus was making use here of local geography, for the nearby Genessaret (granted to Naphtali; Josh. 19:36) was also called Adamah ("earth"). Was this the place Jesus was teaching, and the man thus an exemplar of all that "Adam" might mean—of the earth, earthy, human as from *humus*? We may speculate, but Luke does not tell us.

The Calling of Sinners (5:27–39)

To many a religious expectation—and certainly by the general opinion of Jewish taxpayers—the calling of Levi the tax collector (KJV "publican") to follow Jesus, who after all was thought by most people to be at the least a teacher of righteousness, must have seemed more than paradoxical, even scandalously self-contradictory. Not least problematic for the prejudices of the Palestinian Jewish community was Levi's being a toady of the Roman oppressors, effectively a traitor to his own people. Yet called by Jesus he most certainly was, and from the very customs house where he plied his trade and in which Jesus had been "observing" him (*etheasato*) for some time. It must have rankled the Pharisees that the calling of Jesus seemed so utterly to disregard merit. As with many other things in the culture of that time, their distaste is not without parallels in our own culture. In the fourth play of Dorothy Sayers's radio play-cycle *The Man Born to Be King*, the author captures in her dramatis personae an overtone of the resentment that may have been present at first even in some of the other disciples:

> He has oily black hair and rapacious little hands ... [yet] he has been swept off his feet by a heavenly kindness and beauty of mind which had never dawned, even as a possibility, on his sordid experience. ... He thinks the parable of the Unjust Steward is a frightfully funny story. He gives the account of his own conversion with the utmost sincerity and without any sort of self-consciousness. He is having a wonderful time, and Jesus is wonderful, and he wants everybody to know it. Jesus likes Matthew very much.[6]

Artistic license aside, Sayers here captures something that most modern commentators, anxious for social propriety or else insufficiently attuned to the culture of Palestine in the time of Jesus, just miss. Many earlier commentators, particularly the artists, do better. In one justly famous artistic depiction of the scene, that of the Italian Renaissance painter commonly known as Caravaggio (ca. 1600), all the persons at the counting table seem astonished, but none more so that Matthew himself (*The Calling of Matthew*).

The Gospel of Matthew alone calls Levi Matthew, which Bede thought might have indicated circumspection on the part of Mark and Luke (*Homilies on the Gospels* 1.21). Whether Matthew the evangelist and Matthew Levi are the same person is not absolutely certain, but it seems probable. That Matthew should leave an ugly, disreputable, yet lucrative vocation for the most estimable apostolic calling is in itself dramatic because counterintuitive. All Synoptic accounts show his obedience to Jesus's call to be as spontaneous as complete. Almost immediately he holds a banquet in Jesus's honor and invites his natural circle of equally disreputable friends and business associates. This has seemed delightful to commentators

6. Dorothy Sayers, *The Man Born to Be King: A Play-Cycle on the Life of Our Lord and Saviour Jesus Christ* (London, 1943; repr., Grand Rapids: Eerdmans, 1976), 100.

of all eras, a delight in no way diminished by the irritation of the Pharisees, who complained (indirectly) that the disciples of Jesus ate and drank with "publicans and sinners" (5:30 KJV). That Jesus and the disciples should enjoy themselves in the company of such people was a powerful affront to the Pharisees' sense of "apartness" or purity. Chrysostom grasps the scope of this paradox that the Lord "refutes these charges, showing that so far from it being a fault to mix with sinners, it is actually part of his merciful design" (*Homilies on Matthew* 30). This design, namely to bring healing to the sick and sinful, and not the righteous to repentance (5:31–32), is to the Pharisees more than mere incongruity; it is a direct affront to their own sense of accrued religious merit. Even the disciples of John are like the Pharisees in frequent fasting and prayer: why do those who follow Jesus party it up, and in such unseemly company?

The reply of Jesus to this accusation must have been a further shock and affront, for here Jesus introduces an analogy between the feast provided by Matthew Levi for his motley guests and a wedding feast, even a wedding banquet with eschatological foreshadowing. "Can you make the friends of the bridegroom fast while the bridegroom is with them? But the days will come when the bridegroom will be taken away from them; then they will fast in those days" (5:34–35). Here is one of the contextually enigmatic sayings of Jesus, almost certainly opaque to his immediate hearers. But did Luke, who so clearly built a nuptial analogy into his account of the annunciation, birth, and baptism of Jesus, perhaps have a register of deeper, pervasive meaning, a sense here too of the Lord's design? It seems so, for he will return to it later in his capturing of the sayings of Jesus.

One wishes that it were as easy to understand the reach and connectedness of the parable and proverbial sayings that follow. The first is perspicuous enough, namely the saying (analogy or *māšāl*) about trying to patch an old garment with a piece from a new one: Jesus is suggesting, as Bonaventure puts it representatively, that "new observances, commensurate with a new way of life, are not to be imposed until a person has put off his previous way of life"—a connection Bonaventure readily makes with Paul's language in Eph. 4:22–24 (2001–4: 1.5.83). Trying to patch up a decadent Jewish practice and meritocracy with a few insights from the teaching of Jesus, or trying to synthesize them with the status quo, will not do. But the remaining sayings are more challenging, not just because the futility of putting new wine into old bottles is not analogous with the previous metaphor of the patched garment, but rather because, just where one expects Jesus to say that the new wine is to be preferred, he doesn't. Instead, most memorably for a feast where much wine is being drunk, he says instead what is unarguably true but apparently a contradiction to the whole series of sayings: "No one, having drunk old wine, immediately desires new; for he says, 'The old is better'" (5:39). Does Jesus mean that a palate accustomed to older wine (what in Hebrew parlance of the time would be called "a wine of three leaves" [years] or more; Lightfoot 1979: 3.78) will take slowly to the new, and thus intend his saying as a gesture of accommodation to his bewildered critics? The commentators are far from unanimous, perhaps not least because in both Mediterranean and European vernacular there was a clear preference for wine that had time to mellow with age. A question thus remains about how to understand Jesus's saying at this point. Perhaps he is just saying that he understands their resistance to change.

LUKE 6

There is a focus in Luke's narrative on teaching and events that take place on the Sabbath. We may imagine this as not only reflecting the natural congregation of large audiences that would have been able to hear Jesus teach in the synagogue on those days but also highlighting tensions between Jesus's teaching and the established religious culture of the synagogue. For Jews of this period the synagogue was both a visible sign and the natural locus of instruction in the law and Jewish identity; men came to hear the scriptures read and to hear commentary on it. The Sabbath controversies between Jesus and the Pharisees suggest that their resistance to him stems in part from a certain propriety, a commitment to synagogue culture preeminently as a sign of devotion to the law rather more than as a locus for celebration of the covenant, that is to say, as a place for experiencing relationship to God. Or at least, so it seems in the dialogues Luke records. What the Sabbath teaching and miracles of Jesus do in Luke's narrative is to expose the Pharisees' characteristic preoccupation with the law and, in the interpretations of Jesus, to redirect attention to the purpose such preoccupation with the ordinances themselves tends to obscure, namely that the law was intended to serve rather than to encumber the children of the covenant.

The Sabbath Snack (6:1–5)

Luke seems to have placed the controversy over the plucking of ears of grain by the disciples in a topical rather than necessarily chronological relation to the immediately preceding events (Bock 1994–96: 1.504). Matthew 12:1–8 places it after the gathering of the Twelve, whereas Mark and Luke have it before. The prompting issue for Luke seems to be that the Sabbath controversies, as a group, offer insight into a central point of conflict between Jesus's sense of the law and the legalism scrupulously enforced by the religious leaders of his day. Thus Luke typically begins by designating the Sabbath events as such, so that the extraordinary nature of these events can be all the more readily understood as a flash point for controversy (Luke 6:1).

There is more than a little reason to sense a measure of prejudice in the Pharisees, who have already had Jesus under surveillance for some time. Cyril of Alexandria draws our attention to textual evidence that envy seems, in these exchanges, to be a primary animus in the Pharisees' interventions; memorably, he observes that often in such situations "the nature of an envious person is such that he makes praises of others food for his own disease, and is wickedly maddened by their reputation" (1983: Homily 23). Entrapment is accordingly the Pharisees' wish, and when the hungry disciples decide to snack on a few ears of barley or wheat as they pass by some fields, "rubbing them in their hands" to separate out the husks, they are promptly accused by some of the Pharisees of violating the Sabbath law (6:2). In eating the grain itself (though it is grown in someone else's fields) they haven't broken the law; Deut. 23:25 says: "When you come into your neighbor's standing grain, you may pluck the heads with your hand, but you shall not use a sickle." In doing this on the Sabbath, however, they have transgressed (Exod. 20:8–11), at least according to a strict interpretation that, interestingly, later Judaism will abrogate; the Babylonian Talmud, tractate *Shabbat* 128a–b, permits such activity on the Sabbath as long as no sickle is used. Then as now, observant Jews prepared their Sabbath meals the day before to avoid the problem. Jesus's disciples, however, are in this case not at home but on the road.

Jesus evidently surprised everyone with his rejoinder to the Pharisees, pointing to the occasion on which David and his men asked for the consecrated bread of the tabernacle because they were famished (1 Sam. 21:1–7; 22:9–10). This event, too, is represented in Jewish tradition as occurring on the Sabbath, for the showbread loaves had just been changed (E. Lohse in *TDNT* 7.21; cf. Lev. 24:5–9; Exod. 25:30; 40:22–23; 1 Sam. 21:6). The analogies are clear, but the implication that these events are parallel would have been unsettling to the Pharisees. The disciples, as Bede reasonably observes, "did not have the chance to eat on account of the press of the crowds" (*Homilies on the Gospels* 2.6.1); Bonaventure, likewise, notes that they were compelled by human necessity (2001–4: 1.6.4). This would make their situation similar to that of David and his men, and Luke's narrative implies by their silence that the Pharisees were stumped: if David did this and was excused by Abimelech, how can it be said to be forbidden?

Their troubled silence is broken then by a summary from Jesus: "The Son of Man is also Lord of the Sabbath" (Luke 6:5). In Mark 2:27, we have the additional turn of phrase, "The Sabbath was made for man, and not man for the Sabbath," itself a statement entirely congruent with the rabbinic saying that "the Sabbath is given over to you and not you to the Sabbath" (*Mekilta de Rabbi Ishmael*, Shabbat 1 on Exod. 31:13). While the rabbinic statement comes later, it seems to reflect an established tradition. Thus, on their own rules the Pharisees are for the time being checked and forced to withdraw—though not, of course, for long.

The Withered Hand (6:6–11)

"On another [*heterō*] Sabbath," Luke tells us, Jesus is teaching in a synagogue, and among those gathered is "a man . . . whose right hand was withered" (6:6). Again the Pharisees are watching to see if Jesus will heal someone, because in their way of understanding, for him to perform a healing could be construed as work and thus a breach of the Sabbath. Bock draws attention to the apocryphal "Gospel to the Nazarenes," which suggests that the man was a stonemason whose hand had been injured, thus depriving him of his livelihood (1994–96: 1.528). For Bede, many centuries later, the man is a figure more generally of the basic condition of all fallen people, deprived of their full creational faculties, "withered by the unfruitfulness of good works because the hand of our first parents stretched forth to take the apple" (quoted in Aquinas, *Catena Aurea* 3.1.202), while Ambrose sees in the man a similar moral lesson and suggests that, just as Jesus asks the man to stretch forth his hand (6:10), so too, if we in our diseased state wish to be healed, we will stretch forth our hand often, "to help our neighbor, to protect the widow, to save from injury him who you see the victim of an unjust attack." As the hand is stretched forth to heal others, Ambrose says, it will itself be healed (*Exposition of Luke* 5.40). This moral exegesis has seemed natural to subsequent exegetical tradition. But Ambrose offers another possible clue to our understanding of this episode in its more immediate Jewish context: "Thus Jeroboam's hand withered when he sacrificed to idols; thus it stretched when he entreated God." Here the great bishop of Milan seems to be taking a clue from what Jesus did in the previous episode, so drawing an Old Testament analogy. The story of Jeroboam (1 Kgs. 13:4–6) is perhaps pertinent, given the probable motives in the hearts of the scribes and Pharisees, for Jeroboam's hand had withered when he tried to "lay hold on" a prophet ("a man of God out of Judah by the word of the LORD"; 13:1 KJV); the sudden injury prevented him from doing harm. When he then pleaded with this unnamed "man of God" to restore his hand, the prophet prayed to the Lord, and "the king's hand was restored to him, and became as before" (13:6). That the withering clearly occurred because of malice intended by the king against the "man of God" would, on such a view as Ambrose takes, make the healing of not only typological and moral significance to Luke's readers but also, in the immediate context of the Pharisees' similar disingenuous intent, ironic. This interesting connection is not, however, the primary source of irony in the event as Luke narrates it.

The question Jesus puts to the Pharisees before he heals the man is designed to reveal that they are not themselves entirely faithful to the precepts they claim to invoke, nor even, perhaps, do they fully understand the tradition: "Is it lawful on the Sabbath to do good or to do evil, to save life or to destroy?" (Luke 6:9). This very sort of "good" redemptive action (*sōzō*) to preserve life was not forbidden either by the book of *Jubilees* 11.16–17 (ca. 150 BC) or, it seems, by the Pharisees themselves (Mishnah, tractate *Eruvin*): Sabbath regulations could be abrogated if a life was in danger, and Hos. 6:6 is alluded to in Matthew's version of this story (Matt. 12:7) to suggest that mercy shown on the Sabbath outweighs even sacrifice. In Matthew, Jesus thus calls on the Pharisees' knowledge of their own tradition to say that if it is permissible to rescue a sheep from a pit on the Sabbath then so much more to heal or do good to humans (Matt. 12:11–13). Jesus is here demonstrating that, so far from transgressing the law, he is actually fulfilling its Sabbath purpose even on the Pharisees' own reckoning.

In one of the narrative elements distinctive to Luke, with his fine ear and eye for detail in the reports he has heard, he notes that after this question by which he thwarts the Pharisees, Jesus gazes upon the crowd, "look[ing] around at them all," and *then* says to the man, "Stretch out your hand" (6:10). No one present could have missed either the healing or the contrast between God's redemptive purposes as Jesus sees them and the narrower vision of the Pharisees.

Foiled once again, the Pharisees, Luke notes, are "filled with madness" (KJV), presumably enraged at being outwitted in their attempt to show Jesus to be an unfaithful Jew. They then set themselves ominously to darker strategies and "communed one with another what they might do to Jesus" (KJV). As they had been proven in regard to the synagogue to be prone to "idolatry of the sign," so here also with regard to the Sabbath itself. That which had been given, according to the law of Moses (Exod. 31:17), as an instrumental sign of the relationship between God and his people and his provision for their *šālôm*, or flourishing, has been unconsciously reduced in the imagination of the Pharisees to the status of a legalism; the causal primacy of the relationship having been lost, Sabbath observance for them has become the intrinsic good in itself, rather than the instrumental good it was intended to be. The healing of the man with the withered hand and evidence of Jesus's superior knowledge of the law have shattered their confidence and confounded their strategy. The Pharisees are now, as we say, "out of their minds" with anger, for they have much invested in their point of view, not to mention their institutional control over how such matters are to be understood by the people. From their perspective, one can see how Jesus's challenges put their authority at risk.

Luke's attention to detail we may, I think, imagine to be consistent with his having listened closely for small but significant elements in the accounts of the eyewitnesses on whom he relied. That these *autoptēs* included at this point the disciples themselves seems more probable than any alternative; in any case, Luke's finely detailed account of the healing of the man with the withered hand reveals something of the character that made him seem to the early church the appropriate patron saint of painters, for the additional elements all build up together toward a thematic unity and form the basis for seeing this event just as Luke presents it, not only as a literal but also as a symbolic or iconic healing. Though the event is recorded in Mark and Matthew, in Luke alone do we learn that the event takes place on "another Sabbath," that it occurred while Jesus was teaching in the synagogue, that it was the *right* hand of the man, that the Pharisees and scribes were present, that Jesus "knew their thoughts," and that the man both stood up and stepped out of the crowd in response to Jesus's command to him (6:6–8). We might think that in the careful way he relates such significant detail Luke could readily be an exemplar for historians, dramatists, and novelists as well.

Calling of the Twelve (6:12–19)

Luke adds distinctive elements also to the calling of the disciples. First, as is thematic with him, he records that Jesus went off into the mountain to pray by himself and stayed there all night in prayer (6:12–13). Bock notes (1994–96: 1.540) that the term here in Luke's Greek, *dianyktereuōn*, found only here in the New Testament, is a technical term for an all-night prayer vigil occurring in the Septuagint (Job 2:9c), Josephus (*Jewish Antiquities* 6.311), and elsewhere. The additional phrase *proseuchē tou theou* ("prayer to God") marks Jesus's role as Son of the Father and intercessor; for Luke it is of the essence of our understanding of what follows that we perceive that Jesus has sought the will of the Father specifically before acting. As prolegomena, it is here especially striking: in the words of
· Pope Benedict XVI, "the calling of the disciples is a prayer event; it is as if they were begotten in prayer, in intimacy with the Father."[1]

When we consider the list of those chosen the next morning, and that Judas Iscariot is among those named (though last), we have already sufficient reason to reflect on the wider mystery of the calling of the disciples. Luke will later tell us that they were chosen from a larger group of seventy-two disciples (10:1–12). The participle *eklexamenos* ("chose") functions here to emphasize that the choice of each disciple is deliberate; Judas was therefore no accident. But the factor of divine foreknowledge and the reader's knowledge of the sordid role Judas was to play naturally raise the question: why Judas? Many a commentator has asked the question only to grasp the answer in a fashion similar to Augustine: "Judas the traitor is chosen, not unwittingly, but knowingly, for Christ has indeed taken to himself the weakness of man, and therefore refused not even this share of human infirmity. He was willing to be betrayed by his own apostle, that you, when betrayed by your friend, may more calmly bear your mistaken judgment, your kindness thrown away" (*Harmony of the Gospels* 2.30).

A small anonymous tract of the fourteenth century, incorporated by the Augustinian canon Walter Hilton into his *Ladder of Perfection*, derives another but related insight, suggesting that the choice of Judas offers us an unparalleled opportunity to reflect on what it means when Jesus says later, "Love your enemies" (6:27). Recounting the completely equitable way in which Jesus treated Judas through many stages of his ministry, the text says, "All this charitable love Christ showed to Judas, whom he knew to be damnable—not in any kind of feigning

---

1. Pope Benedict XVI, *Jesus of Nazareth*, trans. Adrian J. Walker (New York: Doubleday, 2007), 170.

or flattering but in truthfulness of good love and pure charity."[2] That the sermon of Jesus with the injunctions to love one's enemies follows immediately on the selection of the Twelve, including Judas, strengthens the force of Jesus's teaching for the Christian reader. The standard for love set by Jesus is very high.

The order of the disciples in all accounts (Luke 6:12–16; Matt. 10:2–4; Mark 3:16–19; Acts 1:13) places Peter first and Judas last. The first four are invariably Peter, Andrew, James, and John (although not always in this order). James and John, sons of Zebedee (Luke 5:10) and perhaps for their personalities called "Sons of Thunder" (Mark 3:17), are cousins to Jesus; their mother is Salome, sister to Mary. All are Galileans except Judas, whose surname "Iscariot" may mean that he comes from a region in Judah called Kerioth (Josh. 15:25; Jer. 48:24), though it is possible that in Aramaic one would hear in his name overtones of the word "false one," or perhaps in Latin translation *sicarius* ("dagger man, assassin"), for the Sicarians, a radical wing of the Zealots (Bock 1994–96: 1.546). Whether those philological overtones were picked up by Luke himself, it is on all counts clear that Judas the Zealot was an outsider from the beginning. Yet even the Eleven, the Galileans, might not seem to any human political wisdom to be ideal candidates for such a crucial mission. Ambrose speaks for many later commentators, nevertheless, when he sees a hidden wisdom in the choices Jesus makes from among his disciples (Luke 6:13): "He chose not wise men, nor rich, nor nobles, but fishermen and tax collectors . . . lest he seem to have seduced some by wisdom, or bought them with riches, or attracted them by the graces of authority, [political] power, and nobility. He did this," Ambrose concludes, "so that the reasoning of truth, not the gift of disputation, should prevail" (*Exposition of Luke* 5.44).

Luke is unique among the Gospel writers at this point in the narrative in calling the Twelve "apostles" (6:13) to distinguish them from the other disciples. The term is found elsewhere only twice in the Gospels (Mark 6:30; Matt. 10:2; cf. variant reading in Mark 3:13), but six times altogether in Luke. Calvin, excellent in his discussion of the calling of the Twelve, is troubled with the tendency of earlier commentators to confuse this passage with Matt. 10 and, depending on Mark 3:13, suggests that Jesus "does not ordain them as Apostles . . . but takes disciples into his company in the hope of Apostleship to come" (1972: 1.165). This view is, however, at odds with Luke's specific use of the term "apostle," and one may reasonably agree with Bock (1994–96: 1.541–42) that Luke, who is after all highly conscious of the history of the early church in Acts, should have quite naturally used this term: Luke sees the event retrospectively and, knowing that these twelve were distinctively "apostles," Judas later to be replaced, uses the term in a historian's sense to refer to those particular disciples to whom Eusebius will also later refer by this term (almost certainly echoing Luke), as those "who from the beginning were eyewitnesses and ministers of the word" (*Proof of the Gospel*

2. David Lyle Jeffrey, ed., *The Law of Love: English Spirituality in the Age of Wyclif* (Grand Rapids: Eerdmans, 1988; repr., Vancouver: Regent, 2006), 291–92.

3.5.120). In effect, for Luke the calling of the Twelve indicates the intention of Jesus to form a community; with the exception of the betrayer, these chosen ones will become the foundation for the church after Jesus has risen from the tomb.

It would seem to be the case that the calling of the disciples recorded here occurred somewhere up the slope, near where Jesus has prayed (6:12), for now Luke describes him as "coming down" with the Twelve and standing in "the plain" (6:17), perhaps better understood as a plateau or level place not far from the bottom where "a great multitude of people" from as far away as Jerusalem and the coast of Tyre and Sidon had come to "hear him and be healed of their diseases" (6:17). That there were twelve who appeared at his side before the crowd must have struck some present as symbolic, for this was "the number of Israel." "In this sense," writes Pope Benedict XVI, "the number twelve is a return to the origins of Israel, and yet at the same time is a symbol of hope."[3] The people who had gathered included many who were "vexed with unclean spirits" (KJV), echoing a persistent theme in Luke's Gospel that the presence of demonic forces has been exposed by Jesus's presence and that his healings include exorcism and a great confrontation of the powers of darkness. It must have been a noisy crowd, with some of those with unclean spirits perhaps having been dragged there against their will, kicking and screaming, while others were doubtless jostling for a better vantage point. "The whole multitude," Luke says, "sought to touch him: for there went virtue out of him, and healed them all" (6:19 KJV). The presence of the living Christ is, now as then, an uncanny but palpable phenomenon: men and women who know yet nothing of what he will say already feel the transforming power of his person and, howsoever darkened in spirit, confused, and sin-sick, sense themselves on the cusp of being forever changed. All this before "he lifted up his eyes toward his disciples," as the Hebraism of Luke has it, and began his discourse in a way clearly directed most of all to the disciples themselves.

Central Teaching of Jesus (6:20–26)

In the audience were at least seventy-two disciples, twelve of whom had just been named apostles, a crowd of other Jews from both Judea and Jerusalem who had traveled to hear him, and a third group, some Gentiles from Tyre and Sidon. But it is to the disciples primarily that he speaks; the *laos*, the other "people," were overhearing a sermon directed primarily at those who were already committed both to follow their master in his life and, by word and example, to become teachers of his teaching. The lifting up of his eyes on them in particular is a powerful way of saying, "Pay attention: I am about to tell you something of critical importance for your mission."

This sermon is omitted in Mark, while the version in Matthew is ampler and, as will be apparent, is there structured differently. If they are the same sermon,

3. Benedict, *Jesus of Nazareth*, 171.

Luke's is a terse summary. For example, he has four beatitudes by contrast with Matthew's eight, and the order differs. And Luke alone adds four "woes," imprecations against those who, for reasons of wealth, creature comforts, and love of amusements and worldly flattery, resist the calling of Jesus.

A huge amount of printer's ink has gone into comparative analysis of Matthew's and Luke's versions. This debate began in the early church, and by the time of Augustine the general tendency had become to assume two separate occasions of teaching, one on a "plain" or "plateau" and the other on a mountain, in which "Christ repeated some words he had already spoken elsewhere," as Augustine puts it (*Harmony of the Gospels* 19.45–46). Bonaventure later offered his opinion that Christ had already given the fuller version of his sermon as recorded in Matthew at the top of the mountain to the Twelve and that, on descending to the others and the crowd at large, he gave an abbreviated version, coupled with warning to those in the crowd, such as the Pharisees and scribes, who were least like the Twelve who had left everything to follow him (2001–4: 1.6.41). Bonaventure argued that Luke's inclusion of warnings and promises suggests a different audience and location from those in Matthew's account (2001–4: 1.6.62). This is a view that some may still find plausible; we may imagine that when Jesus and the Twelve came down from the higher place where they had fuller instruction, some of them might have said in Aramaic to their friends among the larger body of disciples, "We have just heard the most amazing things from Jesus." In such a case, Jesus might well have turned to the larger group, Gentiles among them, and given a truncated version aimed at the different, much more variegated audience. Supporting this Bonaventuran scenario is, among many other considerable discrepancies, Matthew's version (whatever occasion is represented in his text, he was one of the select Twelve on the mountain) having more references to Jewish law overall and also including disparaging references to Gentiles (*ethnikoi*) that are missing in Luke (Matt. 5:47; 6:7). Further, the content of Matt. 6 is not found in Luke's version of the teaching, though several elements from it occur later in his account of the teaching of Jesus (Luke 11:1–4; 12:22–36).

There is no way, I think, to establish definitively whether there was but one sermon, very divergently reported, or whether there were two events. Augustine's "two-occasion" theory remained the consensus until well after the Reformation, with Calvin still holding more or less to Augustine's view of the matter: "Both evangelists had the intention of gathering into one single passage the chief headings of Christ's teaching that had regard to the rule of godly and holy living" (1972: 1.168). But Augustine had also left the door open to the possibility that these were two distinct accounts of the same sermon and that by *topou pedinou* (6:17) the evangelist may simply have indicated, as the Greek literally says, "a level place," a kind of foothold area on the mountain slope big enough to act as a kind of natural amphitheater (*Harmony of the Gospels* 19.47). The point about a "level place" would have pertinence on either understanding. Form-critical scholarship of the last two hundred years on the question is so voluminous that it cannot be reflected here; an admirable summary has been achieved by Bock, and I am content to recommend his digest to the interested reader (1994–96: 1.548–628). For our purposes, an accountable reading of Luke's version is possible on either of Augustine's two views. Bock is inclined (1994–96: 1.556) to Augustine's second, and that position has much to commend it. What is indisputable, it seems to me, is (a) that the sermon as we find it in Luke has as its historic occasion the time immediately following upon the calling of the apostles, an event that is more ambiguously placed in Matt. 10; and (b) that, as all commentators from Augustine forward seem to recognize, the Luke sermon contains a condensed version or core of the teaching of Jesus that commends itself to our understanding. In Luke's version, the force of Jesus's teaching concerns how we are to respond to bad treatment by other people and how we are to regard certain types of deprivation in relation to happiness or human flourishing, which in Hebrew is typically called *šālôm*.

The Beatitudes

"Blessed are you poor, for yours is the kingdom of God" (Luke 6:20): Matthew, famously, has "poor in spirit." Cyril of Alexandria was one of the earliest commentators to suggest that Matthew's phrase seems to suggest people of modest demeanor and perhaps even a depressed mind, whereas Luke's phrase seems to broaden the blessing to those who have been denied worldly wealth or perhaps have forsaken riches for the sake of righteousness (1983: Sermon 27). If he is right, then the phrase in Luke would attach to all those who have left their livelihood behind to follow Jesus and also perhaps to the indigent poor who might be in the crowd (e.g., Ambrose, *Exposition of Luke* 5.53–54). These are, however, the faithful poor, persons like the widow giving her two mites (Mark 12:42; Luke 21:2), who are even in their poverty marked by gratefulness to God. Basil observes that many among the ordinary poor are actually quite "covetous in their disposition," and hence not in fact blessed (*Commentary* on Ps. 33). In his view the "poor" are here properly to be understood as faithful disciples of Christ; this was a view of the desert fathers and early monastics, and later on poverty would be regarded as sine qua non the proper condition of a serious following of Christ by Francis of Assisi and his followers. To borrow a contemporary phrase, a preponderance of the commentary of the early and medieval church understands this first blessing in Luke's version as a promise to the "purpose-driven" poor, those who have deliberately renounced the world to follow in the way of the cross. This view seems to be warranted by the words that follow, since "for yours is the kingdom of God" is strongly contrastive in a fashion that puts the common term (*ptōchos/ptōchoi*) in a substantively eschatological context. Those who for Christ's sake became poor will by his graciousness enter into a spiritual richness that has no equal.

Consistently then, "Blessed are you who hunger now, for you shall be filled" (Luke 6:21). As Ambrose says, Jesus is not here by implication condemning those who are rich in a sweeping way, but, as elsewhere, he is indicating that those who are not encumbered by riches have incentives to fix their aspiration on higher things that the rich person often lacks. The problem with the rich person is not the riches per se—wealth is strictly, in spiritual terms, as neutral as poverty—the difficulty in practice is that many of those who have riches "do not know how to use them" (*Exposition of Luke* 5.69). The principle that Jesus enunciates here as a promise to those who are now genuinely deprived can be much more generally extrapolated, as in Jesus saying, "Lay not up for yourselves treasures upon earth, where moth and rust doth corrupt, and where thieves break through and steal. But lay up for yourselves treasures in heaven, where neither moth nor rust doth corrupt, and where thieves do not break through nor steal. For where your treasure is, there will your heart be also" (Matt. 6:19–21 KJV). This is one of several places in which we can see clearly how Luke's text seems to be a précis, a concise summary of what is given more expansively in Matthew; many of the sayings of Matt. 6 are really a form of midrash by Jesus on the principles given in Matt. 5 as "beatitudes." But we also get a stronger sense of the way in which, for Luke, so many of the major themes in the teachings of Jesus are found earlier in Isaiah; he has already shown these themes to be focused beautifully by the prayers of Zacharias, Simeon, Elizabeth, and above all Mary in her Magnificat. Calvin's comment captures this part of the weaving of Luke's text succinctly: "At the end God will hear their sighs, will satisfy their just desires, as it is his work to fill the hungry with good things, as we see in the canticle of the Virgin" (1972: 1.171).

"Blessed are you who weep now, for you shall laugh" (Luke 6:21): this promise of Jesus is, of course, contrastive, like the others, but laughter is a term that many have puzzled over. I think it is safe to observe, again with the majority of the tradition, that Augustine sets us on the right track that "crying is a requirement, laughter the reward, of wisdom. He [Luke] wrote laughter to mean joy" (Sermon 175.2). Others take it to refer to the joy of the blessed in eternity. Some, like John Chrysostom, associate the weeping with contrition and "repentance to salvation" (Homily 18: "To the People of Antioch"), but a majority of subsequent commentators have seen it as referring to the inevitable adversities that, by the very nature of human sin and its consequences, afflict even those who seek faithfulness to Christ. Following Ambrose closely, for Bede (quoted in Aquinas, *Catena Aurea* 3.1.210–11), this transitions perfectly to the next (and, in Luke, last) beatitude: he sees it as commending those whose faithfulness moves them to maintain Christian virtues even in the face of great adversity.

But what now follows is a harder saying. "Blessed are you when men hate you, and when they exclude you, and revile you, and cast out your name as evil, for the Son of Man's sake. Rejoice in that day and leap for joy! For indeed your reward is great in heaven. For in like manner their fathers did to the prophets" (6:22–23). Now it is clear that this fourth beatitude is not only a promise but also itself a dire prophecy; Eusebius, that always interesting if problematic early historian of the church, had the benefit of hindsight on the intervening three centuries of massive martyrdoms, both in Judea and all around the Mediterranean, when he wrote that in these words Jesus is "fortifying his disciples against the attacks of their adversaries, which they were about to suffer as they preached through the whole world" (*Proof of the Gospel* 3.5.122). The reference to the prophets would certainly have evoked for all of the Jews in Jesus's immediate audience a painful but unarguably well-established history of the rejection of those God sent to call them to repentance. It also keeps the issues of truth and spiritual realism right in the foreground for these hearers, for they knew well enough themselves that, as Bede was to put it, "they who seek the truth commonly suffer persecution" (quoted in Aquinas, *Catena Aurea* 3.1.211).

Here then we have the four blessings in Luke's précis of Jesus's teaching. Regarding the eight beatitudes in Matthew, Ambrose may be correct in suggesting that, as to principle, the eight are contained in Luke's four. He sees the four, moreover, as corresponding formally to the four cardinal virtues—temperance, justice, prudence, and fortitude—suggesting in effect that they are a Gospel counter to these Stoic virtues (*Exposition of Luke* 5.62–63, 68). On this point Calvin, himself a humanist scholar who began his scholarly career with commentary on Seneca's *De clementia* (1532), knew Stoic philosophy well enough to draw the comparison more contrastively between the Christian definition of "blessedness" (*makarios/makarioi*, similar in meaning to Hebrew *bārûk*)—certainly a word that may be understood in a general sense as "happiness"—and the Classical Greek philosophical notion of *eudaimonia* (an achievement of "happiness" or "serenity"). But these, of course, are very different notions, though each reflect a vision of the "good life."[4] Calvin's suggestion provides a point of interest for Christian scholars generally: for the Genevan doctor the distinction between Jesus's notion of the blessed life and that of the Athenian philosophers (one supposes him to be thinking, perhaps, of Aristotle in *Nicomachean Ethics*) shows the spiritual insufficiency of the Greeks. Their conception of happiness (*eudaimonia*), says Calvin, is erroneous to the degree that their definition of happiness is no higher than that of the "common crowd"; they think "the happy man is he who, relieved from all his troubles, in possession of all he asks, leads a happy and a quiet life" (1972: 1.169). While this seems a little unfair to Aristotle (*Nicomachean Ethics* 1175a25), who also was thinking of the optimal conditions for human flourishing as a process, a way of living, it remains the case that Jesus's teaching is certainly in sharp contrast to the general application of Aristotle's principle among the later Stoics as a kind of happiness *in the world*. On Jesus's account, Calvin correctly observes: "It should be the philosophy of Christ's disciples that they may set their happiness beyond this world, and above

---

4. For the Greeks, *eudaimonia* was, in effect, the achievement of godlike serenity (*eudia*), usually through personal discipline, rendering oneself immune to the slings and arrows of fortune. Christian blessedness clearly requires identification in the sorrows of others. Some early Greek fathers took a different view; see Robert Wilken, "Gregory of Nyss, De Beatitudinibus. Oratio VIII: 'Blessed are those who are persecuted for Righteousness Sake, for theirs is the Kingdom of Heaven,'" in *Gregory of Nyss: Homilies on the Beatitudes*, ed. Hubertus Drobner and Albert Viciano (Leiden: Brill, 2000), 243–57.

the desire of the flesh" (1972: 1.169).[5] Calvin sees the two notions of happiness (Classical and Christian) as thus inherently incompatible, yet he insists of Jesus's notion of blessedness that "it is no pipe-dream that he is propounding, like the paradoxical game which the Stoics used to play, but a real-life demonstration of why those who are the truly happy are those whose state is rated most unhappy." In this remarkable excursus Calvin goes on to say of Jesus's teaching, over against Stoic notions of virtue and hence, implicitly, of happiness: "Christ is not stuffing his people's minds with some windy argument, or hardening them with iron-shod determination, like the Stoics, but [he] encourages them to patience by recalling them to the hope of eternal life" (1972: 1.170; cf. 171–73). I think we may recognize in this passage of Calvin's commentary an insight of great pertinence for our appreciation of the way Jesus's teaching might fall upon hellenized ears, such as those in the crowd who, we are told, had come from Tyre and Sidon, and certainly later on the ears of Luke himself.

It is a matter of related interest to those who trace the influence of the Sermon on the Mount generally and the beatitudes in particular through Christian commentary, art, and literature that there is a distinct tradition of homiletical influence arising from each. Broadly speaking, we may say that Matthew's version produces the most extensive commentary and tends to prompt calls to repentance and reformation of the merely nominal Christian life: powerful examples of this tradition are found for example in the 1747 sermon cycle on the Matthew text by John Wesley and the two-volume cycle of sermons by Martyn Lloyd-Jones.[6] The Luke version tends in commentary to be represented in a focus on *askēsis* or disciplined self-denial and struggle in the life of the dedicated disciple. This is the way Dante employs the Lukan beatitudes in his *Purgatorio*, with each beatitude marking out the relationship between personal reformation through penance and the ascent to ultimate blessedness. (Chaucer, by contrast, makes more extensive use of the Matthean version to structure his *Canterbury Tales* as a prospectus for health in the Christian community as it journeys through our present, fallen world.)[7] Dante may well have been following Ambrose, who describes Luke's four beatitudes as "steps of virtues whereby we may ascend from the lowest to the highest" (*Exposition of Luke* 5.60).

The Four Woes

This very Greek way of understanding the shorter list of beatitudes in Luke's account is not without an aspect that nicely corresponds to a Jewish philosophical

5. N. T. Wright, though he does not adduce Calvin, makes essentially the same distinction in *After You Believe: Why Christian Character Matters* (New York: HarperOne, 2010), 103–4.

6. Wesley 1895; D. Martyn Lloyd-Jones, *Studies in the Sermon on the Mount*, 2 vols. (Grand Rapids: Eerdmans, 1960); also Carl G. Vaught, *The Sermon on the Mount: A Theological Investigation* (Waco: Baylor University Press, 2001).

7. David Lyle Jeffrey, "The Beatitudes in Dante and Chaucer," in *The Sermon on the Mount through the Centuries*, ed. Jeffrey P. Greenman, Timothy Larsen, and Stephen Spenser (Grand Rapids: Brazos, 2007), 81–107.

paradigm as well, and it must have occurred to some among Jesus's listeners. The binary structure of Ps. 1, in which the characteristics of the "blessed" man are set off against those of the man who is not ("the ungodly are not so"), declares that the good life, optimal for human flourishing, involves a similar *askēsis*. The blessed man does not go along to get along; he marches to the beat of a different drummer, eschewing the counsel of the ungodly, the gathering places of sinners, and the judgment of mockers and cynics. Rather, he delights in the Torah, the instruction of God, and is completely given over, night and day, to ruminating on its wisdom. His flourishing accordingly is like that of "a tree planted by the rivers of water," fruitful and verdant: "Whatsoever he doeth shall prosper" (Ps. 1:1–3). But the poet David does not stop there; he teaches the virtues of the good or blessed life also by their opposite, namely the "ungodly" life. So here too four calamities are predicted for those who "have already their reward." Once again we can see how consistent is the teaching of Jesus in these matters. Too bad for the rich, for they "have received [their] consolation" already (Luke 6:24)—not, as Ambrose suggests, because they happen to have money but because "the heart of the possessive person is at fault [i.e., wrongly directed]" (*Exposition of Luke* 5.69). Similarly with those who are sated now; they have an experience of hunger awaiting them (6:25). Likewise with those who are able to laugh off the adverse circumstances of others in the world; theirs is an evil laughter, to judge from some uses of this word in the Septuagint (Marshall 1978: 256). The antithesis is intensified when Jesus says that they shall "mourn" (the word suggests for loss of loved ones) *and* "weep" (perhaps for their own dire calamities). Such people may be popular or have a good public reputation, but it is probable that they invite the cajoling of flatterers whose shallow self-interest it is to butter up the rich and influential, and for that species of condoned untruth also there is a judgment coming.

There is nothing equivalent to the four woes in Matthew, and, at the very least, it changes the tone of the sermon to have them here. As Ambrose puts it, Matthew's version, by its emphasis on rewards, calls the people to virtue and faith, whereas Luke also "frightened them from their sins and iniquities by denunciation [of sin and threatening] future punishment" (*Exposition of Luke* 5.72). The four woes not only balance the four occasions of blessedness in Luke in the Jewish fashion of Ps. 1 but also set up the extraordinarily counterintuitive teaching of Jesus that follows. These are in the form of commands, imperatives in the second person plural, which can leave no doubt in anyone's mind that Jesus, so far from being like the vengeful Zealots, has set a standard for faithfulness and righteousness far more challenging than any of his hearers has ever contemplated. It is interesting in this regard that the binary opposition of four beatitudes to four woes reflects a familiar, even dominant rhetorical and structure pattern from the Old Testament, one with which his Jewish hearers should have been intimately acquainted. But thinking of others, the Gentiles, Luke may also have had in mind Greek parallels. In Herodotus 1.87, one of the most famous passages in Greek literature, King Croesus of Lydia learns from Solon that the vices of pride, greed, and complacency, despite the wealth and prosperity (*eudaimonia*, "good fortune") he enjoyed, could lead him to wretchedness (*kakodaimonia*) and a fiery judgment. For the great orator Demosthenes it may be that a man's prosperity "covers a multitude of faults" (2.20), yet the will of heaven will expose his actual *kakodaimonia*. In Aristotle (*Eudemian Ethics* 1.5; *Nicomachean Ethics* 6.13), the material conditions of *eudaimonia* are said to be of no avail in the absence of virtue, effectively becoming *kakodaimonia* despite the appearances. The opposition is at least as old as Hesiod, the bard of Mount Helicon, who in his eclectic wisdom poem *Works and Days* opposes his own proffered conditions of philosophical *eudaimonia*, behavior that conduces to a good reputation, to contrary conditions that rob one of such happiness (*Works and Days* 293–341; cf. 170–201)—idleness, deceit of the neighbor, ill-gotten gains, miscreance with another's wife, and all such things as lead to shame (317–20). The four woes, as Luke presents them, certainly accord with this sort of Hellenistic binary structure in general terms, and their inclusion in Luke's account may suggest that, as an educated Greek, he knew authors such as Herodotus, Hesiod, and Aristotle and perhaps accordingly perceived Jesus's sermon as an astutely multicultural discourse on *eudaimonia*, on pursuit of the good life.

The Commandments of the Lord

"The commandment of the LORD is pure," says the psalmist, "enlightening the eyes" (Ps. 19:8). Perhaps this is why the church has tended to receive the teaching of Jesus in this section as a counsel of perfection, so purely divine in its injunction as to cause us to establish our obligations to righteousness in what for most people will seem an idealistic, unrealizable way. But if we take these commandments of Jesus seriously, we shall surely be challenged to a higher standard than the Greek notion of *eudaimonia*. As Bonaventure puts it: "With regard to the promulgation of these teachings it is to be noted that for a person to be perfect it is necessary for that individual to be perfectly *benevolent*, perfectly *pacific*, and perfectly *beneficent*" (2001–4: 1.6.64).

Perfection in *love* is clearly the key to Jesus's teaching, and it is at the heart of his commandments. As we have seen already, the sort of love of which Jesus speaks is not natural to us: "Love your enemies, do good to those who hate you, bless those who curse you, and pray for those who despitefully use you" (Luke 6:27–28). As Ephraem the Syrian says, "An eye for an eye" is a normative Old Testament notion of "perfection in justice" (*Commentary on Tatian's Diatessaron* 6.11b–12). This teaching of Jesus concerning "righteousness" (*dikaiosynē*), however, seems to turn the received standard of "justice" (*dikē*) completely inside out. Hesiod, for example, gives the normative Greek standard: "Love those who love you, and help those who help you. / Give to those who give to you, never to those who do not" (*Works and Days* 353–54). In some groups of Jews, such as those at Qumran, the right to hate one's enemy was spelled out (Bock 1994–96:

1.588). In the context of Roman occupation, in which every Jew yearned for restitution and the Zealots for retribution and revenge, the injunctions that follow must have seemed especially radical, even opprobrious: we must imagine that for such as Simon the Zealot and Judas Iscariot, not to mention those in the crowd less well attuned to Jesus, there would have been palpable irritation at such sayings as, "To him who strikes you on the one cheek, offer the other also. And from him who takes away your cloak, do not withhold your tunic either" (Luke 6:29). Our familiar proverb about being willing to give the shirt off one's back to another in need has here its source—though for us it is typically spoken in hyperbole. "Almost all of us," as Basil says, "offend against this command" (*Commentary on Isaiah* 1.23).

What follows is sometimes called the Golden Rule. At one level this commandment can be seen as a principle universally understood. John Chrysostom acknowledges this: "Now we have a natural law implanted in us by which we can distinguish between what is virtue and what is vice" (Homily 13: "To the People of Antioch," quoted in Aquinas, *Catena Aurea* 3.1.28). In Judaism, one's "neighbor" was a member of one's own religious community (Lev. 19:18), but clearly it is not so limited a term here. Alert to the distinction, Calvin points out (1972: 1.198) that Jesus does not intend by his commandment in Luke 6:31 to indicate a rule of enlightened self-interest, such as we find recommended by Plato. Here, in its context, there is no suggestion of reciprocal good, but more probably the opposite. Thus 6:32 makes it clear that the worldly model for social virtue, evident to a natural-law understanding, does not come up to the standard of Jesus, for "if you love those who love you, what credit is that to you? For even sinners love those who love them." So also with doing good to others (6:33). Thus, the versions of this principle found in Philo (*Hypothetica* 7.6), Seneca (*On Benefits* 2.1.1), and as far afield as Confucius (*Analects* 15.23) and as near as Rabbi Hillel (Babylonian Talmud, tractate *Shabbat* 31a) are in the teaching of Jesus much more strictly altruistic. The application to lending money or goods is similarly astringent: one is not to lend to another in the hope of a someday quid pro quo (Luke 6:34), but, as Bonaventure suggests (2001–4: 1.79–84), in loving one's enemies and doing good, we are to lend without any hope of reward (6:35). Here too we have a higher standard than the law of Moses, for Deut. 23:19–20 permits lending at interest to the "stranger," though not to the "brother." Jesus asks us to treat the stranger, even the enemy, in the same way as we treat those to whom we are bound as kin or in friendship.[8] That alone is the behavior that permits us to be regarded as "children of the highest" by a God who, after all, is evidently "kind to the unthankful and evil [person]" (Luke 6:35).

---

8. This principle accounts for a general aversion to moneylending as an occupation among some early Christians. Gregory of Nyssa calls borrowing at interest a "destructive monster" and says to those who make their living by it that they should give it up, that they should get their living by work, service, even begging if necessary: "Anything is more tolerable than borrowing upon interest" (quoted in Aquinas, *Catena Aurea* 3.1.220).

The basis for all of this is now made clear; it is not merely another order of social reciprocity, not merely interpersonal, but self-transcending gratitude for the mercy of God. So: "Therefore be merciful, just as your Father also is merciful" (6:36). In Luke, the famous injunction "judge not, and you shall not be judged" (cf. Matt. 7:1) is strengthened by an emphasis on God's mercy and then underscored through the Hebrew parallelisms that follow: "Condemn not, and you shall not be condemned. Forgive, and you will be forgiven" (Luke 6:37). These expansions serve to assure us that, as in so many places in his Gospel, Luke the Gentile is attending closely to the verbal reports of Hebrew-speaking (or Aramaic-speaking) interlocutors. We overhear with a similar precision a Hebraic accent in the illustration that follows: "Give, and it will be given to you: good measure, pressed down, shaken together, and running over will be put into your bosom" (6:38); the echoes of God's goodness to David in Ps. 23, as his "cup runs over," underscore another Jesus principle, a corollary, namely that unstinting generosity toward others will be rewarded by God's favor (*charis*) toward us: "For with the same measure that you use, it will be measured back to you" (Luke 6:38). This precept, which underlies Shakespeare's play *Measure for Measure*, both in its title and its eschatological plot, has become one of the best-known passages of the sermon.

Wisdom for (Future) Teachers (6:39–49)

The rest of the chapter resembles the wisdom literature of the Hebrew scriptures in its use of *māšāl* (Greek *parabolē*), parable or figurative analogies, pointing to the character of wisdom upon which the faithful disciple should seek to build. As Cyril of Alexandria notes, "His disciples were the future teachers of the world, and it therefore became them to know the way of a virtuous life, having their minds illuminated, as it were, by a divine brightness, that they should not be blind leaders of the blind" (1983: Homily 33). Some readers will remember Peter Brueghel's painting illustrating this saying: leadership requires better vision and substantively better sense of the path than does following. Leadership is not easy. A teacher should not be presumptuous. By the same token, students should not quickly imagine themselves to be wiser than their teachers: "A disciple is not above his teacher, but everyone who is perfectly trained will be *like* his teacher" (6:40). *Imitatio Christi* is the essence of the disciples' vocation. But now the caution about judging comes back in a specific warning to those who would presume to offer moral instruction: as in Matthew, the saying about the "mote" (dust speck) and "beam" (*dokon* might be translated "log") is an example of Hebrew hyperbole, indicating, as Cyril says, that the one who teaches others must first show himself to be cleansed of great sins and only then presume to give counsel to others whose sins, after all, may be comparatively much less serious (1983: Sermon 35). Basil summarizes this, in an echo of Socratic wisdom: "In truth, self-knowledge seems the most important of all [requirements]" (*Hexameron*,

Homily 9). To come to the task of teaching without it is inevitably to be (or become) a hypocrite (6:41–42).

The image of the good tree or bush (here again the Jewish hearers may well have thought about the well-nourished tree as an image for the faithful student of the word in Ps. 1; cf. Matt. 3:10; Luke 3:9) is likewise about the conditions of fruitfulness in a disciple who would become a worthy teacher, and the image of the "inner treasure" of the teacher is shown to be like it; habits of mind produce both words and deeds, and all must be consonant in the faithful disciples of Jesus (6:43–45). Bede's thought on this principle is representative and points to a demand for consistency of word and deed that is central to all of Jesus's teaching: "The treasure in one's heart," he says, "is the intention of the thought, from which the Searcher of hearts judges the outcome. . . . Christ subsequently adds force to his pronouncement by clearly showing that good speech without the additional attestation of deeds is of no advantage at all" (*Homilies on the Gospels* 2.25).[9] Therefore, Jesus says, "Why do you call me 'Lord, Lord,' and not do the things which I say?" (6:46). To whom is he speaking here? Not to his chosen Twelve alone, it would seem, though certainly to them and the other disciples primarily. It may be that Bonaventure has indeed given us a plausible way to think about the relationship between Matthew's Sermon on the Mount and the account given by Luke a little lower down. Bonaventure, a Franciscan, would have well understood that a *magister* in his Sorbonne classroom would expound a passage from the Gospel in a formal exposition very differently than he would—if he wished to be followed—in a homily to the laity on Sunday. There would, of course, be overlap and consistency as to substance, but audience would dictate both brevity and restructuring. Thinking of it in this way, it is perhaps not too difficult to imagine Jesus drawing to himself the Twelve, all of whom were Jews living, like Zacharias, in expectation of the kingdom, and then, as Matthew has it, "when he was seated" (5:1) in the usual magisterial posture, teaching his chosen ones in a characteristically rabbinical way. Matthew 10:5–6 tells us later that he sent the Twelve specifically to a Jewish audience: "Do not go into the way of the Gentiles, and do not enter into a city of the Samaritans. But go rather to the sheep of the house of Israel." But when he has come down from the mountain to meet the jostling, noisy mixed crowd of the *hoi polloi*, including the second tier of his own students and some Gentiles from the coastal cities, then we can certainly imagine him delivering his message in terms all could understand plainly enough. Whatever the case, the central teaching of Jesus as we find it in Luke's account, while not contradicting Matthew's, is in important ways rhetorically and even theologically different in emphasis. In Luke, the sermon offers a magnificent example of the way in which Jesus reaches out to Gentiles

9. For a good contemporary discussion of *kardia* ("heart") as both the source of inclination and desire and the wellspring of intellection, see John Topel, *Children of a Compassionate God: A Theological Exegesis of Luke 6:20–49* (Collegeville, MN: Liturgical Press, 2001), 205–8.

and disparate levels of his Jewish audience simultaneously and in terms that put them, so to speak, on a level playing field.

Who is the good student who may, in due course of learned obedience to Christ, become a worthy teacher? Jesus's final parable is again in the form of a binary contrast. The one who both hears Jesus's words and puts them into practice is wise in the fashion of one who builds his house on a foundation dug down to the solid rock (Luke 6:48). For Augustine, the proper place of building is the whole field of holy scripture itself; in that field, he says, "let us dig more deeply until we come to the rock: 'Now the Rock was Christ,'" he adds, quoting 1 Cor. 10:4 (*Tractates on the Gospel of John* 23.1). The foolish man, as the children's hymn remembers it, builds his house upon the sand because it is easier. But then, when the "flashflood" (*plēmmyrēs*) hits, the water tears away the soil at the base of the walls and down it comes in rubble. Bede draws the point: "As far as men trust in their own strength, they fall away, but as long as they cling to the immovable rock they cannot be shaken" (*Homilies on the Gospels* 1.20). This parable, we should notice, is the apt conclusion to what Jesus has to say in Matthew's version as well. It is an epitome of the wisdom one who follows Christ will seek, the only reliable foundation for an authentic Christian philosophy.

LUKE 7

By the end of Luke 6, as the opening of Luke 7 rhetorically marks it, we have come to a point in Luke's narrative at which our own questions about who Jesus is and what the central tenets of his teaching are have been, in principle, answered. A new phase lies before us as readers of Luke's Gospel; there is a certain suspense as to whether and how people will respond to Jesus as, indeed, the very "sent one," the "Anointed" (*christos*) of God. Indeed, the tempo of Luke's narrative begins to quicken as the spectrum of those "on the ground" who will recognize Jesus as the Christ begins quickly to widen, here to include a prominent Gentile; retrospectively, Jesus's identity is also about to be confirmed for John the Baptist and his own disciples. The air seems charged with a kind of electricity; as Jesus ends his discourse and turns toward the city of Capernaum, Luke gives us three events that capture the speed and spell of his spreading word.

The Centurion (7:1–10)

What could be more unexpected for the restive Galileans than that Jesus should next respond not only to a Gentile but to a centurion, a commander in the hated Roman army of occupation? But that is precisely what happens: an action of Jesus that not only illustrates his principle of loving one's enemies and doing good (6:35) but also shows the official "enemy" in a most favorable light. In Luke's account, the centurion (Latin *centurio*, the term used in Mark 15:39, is here *hekatontarchos*) hears about Jesus and sends to him "elders of the Jews" (*presbyteroi*) to ask him to heal his esteemed servant; he does not come himself (cf. Matt. 8:5–13). This is not a matter of pride, as Luke's text makes clear, but scruple: he shows his respect for a Jewish rabbi by not approaching him directly. The Jewish emissaries may be civic leaders, even elders in the synagogue, for these men make the case to Jesus that, though a centurion and a Gentile (cf. Luke 7:9), the petitioner is "worthy" (*axios*) on account of his unusual love for the Jewish people, even to the degree that out of his personal funds he has built a local synagogue (7:4–5).[1] We do not know the name of the centurion's servant, and Luke does not give his nationality; any of several districts from the empire might be possible. He is clearly not a Jew and not (since the events are taking place prior to AD 44) a Roman either.[2] What we are given to know is that Jesus readily agrees to go with the emissaries back to the centurion's house, but that before he can get there, the centurion sends friends to him, with words now known around the world from their paraphrase in the eucharistic liturgy: "Lord,... I am not worthy that you should enter under my roof.... But say the word, and my servant will be healed" (7:6–7). The sense this Gentile has of Jewish law concerning the conversation of rabbis especially with Gentiles, and the risk of breach of the purity law for Jesus to enter a Gentile domicile, is evidence of knowledgeable respect for Jewish religious culture (cf. Acts 10:28; 11:12). His extraordinary confidence in the power of Jesus's word is an indication of remarkable faith.

Above all, the centurion recognizes Jesus's superior authority as one who is clearly sent from God. By his analogy he exhibits his understanding of the nature of true authority and of Jesus's possession of it: he likewise is a man "under authority" and has been given authority over others as a consequence (Luke 7:8). The analogy, even if it is limited, captures something important. A Roman centurion had, more or less, one hundred men at his charge, as the term suggests. He in turn is one of sixty centurions in a legion; he is responsible to train and provision his men and to command them both in their post and in battle. His sense thus that Jesus is "a man ... under authority" like himself shows that while he has not yet a full appreciation of who Jesus is, he grasps a critical principle, and Jesus realizes this. But the trust he expresses in Jesus is regarded as truly exemplary. Luke says that on hearing what the centurion has said, Jesus "marveled" and "turned about" (*strapheis*), a dramatic gesture that marks, as did his fixing the whole crowd with his gaze before healing the man with the withered hand, that this is a teaching moment. He says to the disciples, "I have not found so great faith, no, not in Israel" (7:9 KJV). The point here, then, is not only a healing but a lesson: even a Gentile who, presumably, has not seen Jesus can exemplify a completeness of faith greater than those who have been specifically called from among the Jews. It is a lesson that will be repeated in Acts and elsewhere, and it is a moment that, for the fathers of the church, is charged with significance for those of the adoption everywhere. This lesson also connects faith with an appreciation of authority and the dignity of office, a concept that many in our own culture do not grasp (or wish to grasp). Bede has an application that extends the connection between faith and authority to the historic life of the church: "But we of the Gentles who

---

1. A Roman centurion might earn as much as one hundred times the salary of a common soldier; often they were wealthy men.

2. A. N. Sherwin-White, *Roman Society and Roman Law in the New Testament*, Sarum Lectures 1960–61 (Oxford: Clarendon, 1963), 123–24.

believe cannot ourselves come to the Lord, whom we are unable to see in the flesh, but ought to approach by faith; we must send the elders of the Jews, that is, we must by our suppliant entreaties gain as patrons the greatest men of the church [apostles, early martyrs] who have gone before us to the Lord, who bearing witness that we have a care to build up the church, may intercede for our sins" (quoted in Aquinas, *Catena Aurea* 3.1.236). Bede's application goes beyond Luke's account, perhaps, but not by much. He sees, as do all who read this remarkable passage, a great exemplification of faith with its requisite appreciation of the nature of Jesus's authority. A lesson for the Jews especially is that an exemplary faith can come from among those who have not with their own eyes seen or with their own ears heard, yet who have believed the report of faithful witnesses.

The Widow Bereft (7:11–17)

One senses not only that the tempo is picking up in Luke's narrative but also that "the joining of miracle to miracle," as Cyril of Alexandria puts it, involves an intensification (1983: Sermon 36). The very next day, Jesus, accompanied by his followers, is approaching the small village ("city" seems a compliment to a place that has only about two hundred inhabitants today) of Nain (present-day Nein). There has been a death of a young man whose widowed mother is now left bereft of protection and sustenance (7:12). As Gregory of Nyssa puts it, Luke has here given us "the sum of misery in few words" (quoted in Aquinas, *Catena Aurea* 3.1.238). The crowd of mourners coming out the city gate is large, and they meet there the crowd of those who followed Jesus. Luke does not say this, but it is likely that the time is late afternoon, since burial often occurred at this time on the day of death. The corpse is being carried on a bier (*soros*), really just a plank upon which the shrouded body was removed as promptly as possible for burial. Jesus—this is the first time Luke describes him narratively as "the Lord" (*ho kyrios*)—sees the widow mourning and approaches her directly; Luke notes that "he had compassion on her" and said, "Do not weep" (7:13 KJV). In almost any context but that which follows, this remark would seem inappropriate. Coming closer, Jesus "touched the bier" (7:14), a striking act that everyone present realized would bring on him ritual defilement according to the law (Num. 19:11, 16). Arrested by this action in midstride, it seems, the pallbearers come to a halt. Jesus then says, "Young man, I say to you, arise," at which point "he who was dead sat up" (*anekathisen*, a term of recovery found in medical literature to describe recovery from incapacitating illness and that, as such, would be familiar to Luke). He then "began to speak" (Luke 7:15). One wonders if the pallbearers dropped the plank and ran. Luke simply records, calmly, that Jesus "delivered him to his mother" (KJV), the natural completion of his gesture of compassion.

For the crowd, however, there is more to notice. Whether or not some ran, Luke's informants have told him that they were overcome with "fear," yet also glorified God.

The terms for "delivered him to his mother" are a verbatim equivalent of the Greek used in 1 Kgs. 17:23, when Elijah healed the son of the widow of Zarephath. It is clear that the connection between the ancient and present event occurs to some in the crowd; they say, "A great prophet has risen up among us" and "God has visited his people" (Luke 7:16). The report of this miracle spreads like wildfire, reaching even into the desert places, where it comes to that "second Elijah," John the Baptist, imprisoned at Macherus, Josephus tells us, east of the Dead Sea (*Jewish Antiquities* 18.116–19).[3] Now it is John's turn to wonder, and he sends two emissaries of his own to Jesus, to ask what all of this means. Again, the pace quickens, but now by way of bringing the earliest part of Luke's narrative back to bear on the question: Who, really, is Jesus? A great prophet? Or someone much greater?

John the Baptist and His Disciples (7:18–35)

It is not hard to imagine why John, imprisoned and most probably, given his denunciations of Herod's scandalous marriage, sensing time's immanent foreclosure for himself, should now wonder about the character and outworking of the messianic ministry to which he has been the herald. John's own situation hardly accorded with the promised "liberty to the captives" (4:18–19); his own disciples, moreover, must have been demoralized when Herod arrested their leader, and they would have questions, doubtless, of their own. John, in an earlier assurance to his disciples, had described himself as the rejoicing "friend of the bridegroom" and had said, "He must increase, but I must decrease" (John 3:29–30), but now it looked surely as though "decrease" might mean disappear altogether. Where was the promised kingdom?

From the point of view of a narrative whose purpose it is to present Jesus as the *christos*, the doubts of John's disciples and perhaps of John himself are a potentially embarrassing inclusion; Luke's detailed report of it suggests that he was not, however, in any way trying to minimize the questions raised by John's disciples about the true identity of Jesus. We may regard this fairly, I think, as principled on Luke's part; his narrative will not exclude challenges to the truth he is proclaiming. Luke's readers should grasp in this narrative an important distinction: a pursuit of righteousness with faith in God's unfolding plan for redemption is good, but superior to it is a recognition that Jesus is the singular standard for righteousness and the only focus for saving faith. In John 1:35–40,

---

3. John's arrest, imprisonment, and beheading by Herod Antipas are given in Mark 6:17–29 (cf. Matt. 14:3–12). In Western art, the account of Herodias's daughter dancing before Herod, gaining as boon the head of John the Baptist on a platter, has provided subject matter for countless gory paintings from the Middle Ages to the decadent period, with Gustave Moreau and Aubrey Beardsley. The name given to the dancing girl is, in tradition (it is not biblical), Salome, and the play *Salome*, written in French by Oscar Wilde, brings out the lurid possibilities of this account as vividly as the paintings of Titian, Andrea del Sarto, and Moreau.

we learn that many of John the Baptist's disciples transferred their allegiance to Jesus, perhaps some even earlier than the event recorded here in Luke, yet there is further evidence in Acts 19:1–7 that this was not universally the case; some persisted as John's disciples well after Jesus's resurrection and ascension and the events of Pentecost. Here in Luke it is clear that both possibilities of response to the divine plan were available to virtuous men and yet that only one of these possible responses fully approaches the truth.

The question John the Baptist's disciples ask is straightforward: "Are you the Coming One, or do we look for another?" (Luke 7:20). Jesus might well have answered with an apodeictic claim to his divine office, but rather than that, he asks them simply to be observers of what he is doing at the very moment and thus come to a conclusion for themselves. (As Jesus says elsewhere, the verbal "witness" one bears to oneself is not of much authority; John 5:31–32.) Cyril of Alexandria sees in Jesus's answer an example of divine pedagogy, what he calls "the beautiful art of the Savior's management. He does not simply say, 'I am.' If he had spoken this, it would have been true. He leads them to the proof given by the works themselves" (1983: Homily 37). Here we may see an instance in which Luke's authorial principles, namely to order his account of Jesus truthfully and thus not to pass over questions about Jesus's authenticity from within the community of faith as well as without, are modeled on the teaching of the Lord himself about appropriate verification. There are thus three levels of purpose regarding truth in this passage: that of the disciples of John, complex or straightforward as they may have been in their questioning; that of Luke, in his scruple to relate their challenge fairly; and that of Jesus himself in "the beautiful art of his management," as Cyril describes it, asking to be judged on the works that he does. The church continues to be instructed in all of these to the degree to which it does not privilege any of them exclusively but sees "all things working together" under God's providence to give us a more textured, more complete sense of how theological truth may be grasped.

"In that same hour" (KJV), Luke attests, Jesus performed many miracles of healing, cast out demons, and restored sight to the blind (7:21). Then he commanded John's disciples to return to him with a report of what they had seen. But the words Jesus uses echo the messianic predictions of Isa. 33:5–6 and 61:1–3 in such a way that the truth of Isaiah's prophecy is confirmed irrefragably (Luke 7:22). Then he adds, "Blessed is he who is not offended [*skandalizō*, literally "tripped up"] because of me" (7:23).

When the messengers have turned and headed back to John the Baptist, Jesus speaks to the crowd to ensure that they do not, as a result of the engagement to which they have been witness, undervalue the legitimate prophetic ministry John has had. John himself obviously more than justified the crowds going out into the desert to see him; he is neither a mere reed in the wind (King Herod's insignia on coins of his minting was a reed) nor some sort of sumptuously attired royal messenger (7:24–25). He is a true prophet, says Jesus, and much more, the very forerunner whose ministry caps and brings to its highest achievement the work of all the prophets (7:26–27). Jesus quotes Mal. 3:1 (cf. Isa. 40:3) to make the point clear, then explicitly declares of John—in a classic Hebraism—that "among those born of women there is not a greater prophet." And yet, "he who is least in the kingdom of God is greater than he" (Luke 7:28). The sense of culmination for "all that the law and the prophets have spoken" could hardly be more clearly stated, yet the declaration that now there was a new order of God's providence is equally sharply set forth. This distinction has led Ambrose to see John the Baptist, in effect, as a summary type of the law (*Exposition of Luke* 5.94). But what then must we make of Jesus, in view of this passage and its chief distinction? Here I think Benedict XVI's recent summary comments are most helpful: "Jesus' claim entails that the community of his disciples is the New Israel. How can this not unsettle someone who has the 'eternal Israel' at heart? The issue of Jesus' claim to be Temple and Torah in person also has implications for the question of Israel—the issue of the living community of the people in whom God's word is actualized."[4]

Pope Benedict is here in sympathetic dialogue with a deeply serious son of Israel, Jacob Neusner.[5] Neusner's position (especially his objections to the claims of Jesus) bears a close affinity with the sense of opprobrium felt by the Pharisees, but it is not far removed from the uneasiness reflected also in the crowds and prompted by the questions of the disciples of John the Baptist. Jesus does not do away with the Torah; he fulfills it as to divine intention from the beginning. And yet, as Benedict says, "There is a fundamental difference. . . . It is not the universally binding adherence to the Torah that forms the new family. Rather, it is adherence to Jesus himself, to his Torah."[6] He is, in this sense too, the Word made flesh, and, as Neusner recognizes, "only God can demand of me what Jesus is asking."[7] Blessed indeed, who does not find in this Jesus a *skandalizō*, an occasion of offense. Jesus is here unmistakably, even to the perplexed, claiming to be God. To those who understand "the baptism of John" (7:29) in this way, the implications of Jesus's "signs" and his comments on John's role and place in the divine plan are going to lead them ineluctably to recognition of Jesus as their Messiah long promised. For the scribes and the Pharisees, who at least as clearly as Rabbi Neusner know where all of this is leading, "reject[ion of] the counsel of God against themselves" (KJV) creates an impasse. Accordingly, they have not been baptized by John, which is to say, they have not felt the need for repentance (7:30).

The analogy Jesus gives for "this generation" (7:31) is, at one level, to compare them to children who will not join in a game they have not themselves initiated; since the game is not of their choosing, they will, as we say, take their marbles and go home. At another level, the reference to pipes and dancing, evocative of a marriage feast, alludes to the bridegroom, bride, and friend of the bridegroom—imagery to which, as we have seen, Luke has been attentive all along (7:31–32). And yet Jesus

---

4. Pope Benedict XVI, *Jesus of Nazareth*, trans. Adrian J. Walker (New York: Doubleday, 2007), 111.

5. Jacob Neusner, *A Rabbi Talks with Jesus* (Montreal: McGill-Queens University Press, 2000).

6. Benedict, *Jesus of Nazareth*, 115.

7. Neusner, *Rabbi Talks with Jesus*, 68.

says also, "We mourned to you, and you did not weep." Some, he suggests, have not lamented the state of Israel for the pertinent reasons or responded to their predicament in the right way—by contrition and repentance. The contrast the Pharisees make between John and Jesus seems mostly a matter of style to them, and yet they appear to be pointing out a more problematic discrepancy when they observe that John's disciples live a penitential lifestyle, fasting and abstaining, whereas the disciples of Jesus are celebratory, "eating and drinking" (to excess, they imply). Jesus gently mocks their scorn when he says that they are, in effect, aloof to either option. Rather, they hold back from both ways, skeptical, critical, and disdainful (7:33–34).

Jesus's concluding remark might seem opaque, an obscure saying. It is not. When Jesus says to them that "wisdom is justified by all her children" (7:35), he is saying that there is no wisdom in the Pharisees' own standoffishness but much wisdom in the character of both John the Baptist's and Jesus's disciples and their respective means of declaring what God requires. The "lawyers/scribes" (*hoi nomikoi*) know the law; that was the key to their authority. But they have not internalized it. When Jesus refers to himself as "the Son of Man" (*ho huios tou anthrōpou*), he is suggesting quite another order of authority—and thus of wisdom. Augustine gets us much closer: "If you ask who those children are, read what is written: 'the sons of wisdom are the church of the just'" (Letter 36); he elaborates this to observe "that the children of wisdom understand that righteousness consists neither in abstaining from, nor eating food." Bonaventure, having observed that Augustine is here quoting an intertestamental book, completes the quotation instructively: "The children of Wisdom are the congregation of the just, and their nation [is characterized by] obedience and love" (2001–4: 1.7.61, quoting Sirach 3.1). Following Paul, who says that Christ has been made for us "wisdom, and righteousness, and sanctification, and redemption" (1 Cor. 1:30 KJV), Bonaventure adds that in context the "children of this Wisdom are the Apostles, begotten by the word of this Wisdom and vivified by the Holy Spirit." Ambrose suggests further that the Son of God is personified wisdom available to us "when it is not rejected through obstinacy, but through righteousness is acknowledged as the gift of God" (*Exposition of Luke* 6.1). Putting these comments together we begin to get a sense of how it is that the early church will come to regard Jesus as the very wisdom of God. This wisdom, taught by faithful Jews for centuries as beginning in "the fear of the LORD" (Prov. 1:7; Ps. 111:10), is now made manifest in Jesus. As he is the Torah of God fulfilled by God, so also he is the wisdom of God revealed from the beginning in creation (Prov. 8:22–36). There is such a wealth of coalescence of the Law, Prophets, and Wisdom of God in this discourse that his hearers must be forgiven—even his disciples—for being slow to take it all in. But we cannot say of Luke that he has himself failed to understand: his ordered narrative makes this coalescence in Jesus especially clear to readers already attuned to the scriptures. Wisdom of God that begins in fear of the Lord and grows to maturity in obedience to him becomes utterly compelling, however, when its ultimate manifestation is love. And this is precisely the point of Luke's next episode.

The Fallen Woman Much Forgiven (7:36–50)

When a Pharisee invites Jesus to dinner, it is hard to be sure what motives other than pure hospitality may have been in his mind. It is clear enough in Luke's narrative, however, that his house is not a place we might have expected, given the accusations leveled against Jesus, to encounter what follows. Or is it? We know that by the time of Jesus both Hellenic and Roman culture had significantly affected Jewish culture in Palestine and that especially among the more affluent, mosaic tiles, hellenized furnishings, and even social customs were all incorporated. This may help us understand better the dinner Simon the Pharisee had invited Jesus to attend, and it may go some way toward explaining certain features of the conversation that ensues. It seems that the kind of special meal to which Jesus has been invited is not a family meal, at which people would have sat (Jeremias 1963: 126), perhaps around a cloth on the floor. Rather, since the woman who enters is able to stand behind Jesus and wash his feet, the guests are reclining (*kateklinē*), the normal position for a special meal (cf. 9:14–15). Jeremias suggests that this may well be a Sabbath meal in honor of Jesus, as a teacher. But several elements raise questions about the strictness of Simon's Judaism, or, to put it in another way, they help explain that his motive may have been to some degree shaped by his domestic familiarity with the Hellenic custom of the *symposium*, a formal banquet whose conversational intention was philosophical, even as there was food, wine, and other entertainments. (In Greek culture this included music, and the so-called flute-girls who served wine typically were hired to provide sexual entertainment.) Guests reclined to eat. In the Roman version of this custom, the *comissatio*, little had changed; the food and wine, the cup rituals and libations, were all similar; guests sat around a horseshoe-shaped low table, reclining on couches, with their feet away from the table, and the flute-girls were now called *haetera*, a higher class of courtesan. That Jews in Palestine at this period would have been familiar with these Gentile customs is obvious; that Luke, a Gentile, would have been familiar with such a setting for serious conversation and high feasting in a pagan context is inevitable. But in the house of a Pharisee on the Sabbath? The reader can be forgiven for finding the connection dishonorable.

Yet it is there in our text. Not only the Sabbath meal, but even the Passover *seder* of this period had incorporated many elements from the contemporary form of Greco-Roman symposium. In the Babylonian Talmud, the Jewish version is called *afikomen*, a transliteration of the Greek *epikōmos/epikōmion* ("upon the revelry"), indicating at that time a "ritualized upper class banquet and intellectual dialogue, including reclining on couches ... ritual hand-washing ... a series of ritual wine libations, a sumptuous meal, and a series of questions as a starting point for an intellectual discussion of a designated topic." Because the *afikomen* concluded frequently in the Gentile fashion, "the Sages, not wanting the aftermath of the Seder to degenerate into the bawdy and lascivious behavior of the komos, realized that it was necessary to avoid the excesses of the symposium"; hence the Mishnah forbade the additional revelries at the Passover Seder.[8] All of this points to the distinct possibility that the Pharisee, though a Pharisee, had absorbed some distinctly Greco-Roman cultural practices and had invited Jesus to a banquet whose ostensible purpose was philosophical discussion of a sort to tease out the character of his teaching or even of the nature of his evident claims concerning his identity. It is almost as if Simon the Pharisee were to say, "All right now, miracles of healing and such aside, come to my house and let us have a serious, rational conversation about your philosophical position." That the syncretistic nature of the symposium or *afikomen* to which he had invited Jesus might prove to be a prime example of Jesus eating and drinking with sinners (cf. 7:34) is perhaps an irony that had not crossed his mind. It has, however, crossed the mind of the Lord, and Luke draws our attention to it.

When Luke next says that "a woman in the city who was a sinner [*hamartōlos*]" came to the house to see Jesus, he is telling us what Simon the Pharisee clearly has known for some time: she is a "public woman" or prostitute. That she possesses "an alabaster box of ointment" (KJV) is indicative not only of her trade but also probably of her success in it. In the similar story in Matt. 26 and Mark 14, where the host happens also to be named Simon (an extremely common first name) but is a leper (and therefore ineligible to be a Pharisee), a woman pours a box of ointment on Jesus's head, and the disciples see it as a ridiculous extravagance, for the money it would bring was sufficient (Mark 14 says "three hundred denarii") to alleviate the want of "the poor." The manner in which the woman in Luke accomplishes her gesture, however, is in some ways still more powerful, though the presenting issue is not a concern about money for the poor.

Because typically at a banquet of the sort we surmise was here taking place the guests recline at table, their bared feet behind them and away from the table, the woman is able to approach Jesus from behind without him noticing her (there would have been servers, presumably, attending to the guests). But the question of how a woman of her known reputation gained such ready access to the house of a Pharisee raises other questions, questions most reasonably answered in the light of Greek (*symposium*) and Roman (*comissatio*) analogues to the *afikomen* as it had developed in hellenized Jewish culture. But it is equally clear that, so far from appearing in the context of plying her trade, she is behind Jesus weeping (*brechō* suggests sobbing, almost uncontrollably). But she goes much further. Clearly having loosed her hair, an action charged with an aura of intimacy and regarded as an act of immodesty in public (Lightfoot 1979: 3.376), she now washes his feet with her tears and wipes them with her hair, an act that defies social custom, Jewish or Gentile. Then she anoints his feet with her precious ointment (7:38). All of this action together expresses extravagantly a profound gratitude and affection,

8. Gil Marks, "All about Afikomen," in "Emunah of America," online at emunah.org/magazine_detail .php?id=64. Today, the word *afikomen* is employed only as a reference to the final matzah of the *seder* meal, and no longer as something forbidden; this modern usage first occurs in Rashi in the twelfth century (*Responses*) and, eliding the original Palestinian custom, was formalized by the *Shulkan Arukh*, the normative code for halakic observance, in 1555.

perhaps for forgiveness in one who has long seen herself as trapped in her opprobrious social role, but now has repented (both Nolland 1989–93: 1.354 and Bock 1994–96: 1.697 see a subconscious sense of ritual here). Gregory the Great sees beauty as well as irony in the account, for though "she had once used ointment for the perfume of her body; what she unworthily applied to herself she now laudably offered to the Lord" (Homily 33). The whole of her gesture would have taken some time to unfold; the guests must have noticed, perhaps with varying degrees of curiosity and discomfort. Meanwhile, as perhaps they might expect of such a woman at such an event, she says not a word. She just weeps, washes, and anoints the feet of Jesus—however long that takes.

After some time the host cannot forebear voicing a hitherto unspoken reflection that may hint at his having sensed yet another way to entrap Jesus: "This man, if he were a prophet, would know who and what manner of woman this is who is touching him, for she is a sinner" (7:39). But Jesus has read his mind and accordingly opens the dialogue on an unexpected tack, in which it is Jesus, not Simon the Pharisee, who sets the agenda. Perhaps in an extension of the intimacy of the moment, Jesus addresses his host by his first name: "Simon, I have somewhat to say to you." And the host replies respectfully: "*Didaskale* [teacher], say it" (7:40). Jesus's parable that then follows is a dialogical excursus of the sort that, in Luke's Gospel particularly, characterizes his teaching, the particular wisdom or philosophy that he declares unfolding here in a fashion not entirely dissimilar to that of Socrates in *The Symposium*. In the discussion moderated by Socrates the topic had been love (*eros*), and the parable retold by the "servant-girl" Diotima a means of theorizing such love; here too the topic is love, but not the eros Simon or perhaps the reader imagines. The word employed by Jesus in the parable and in reference to weeping woman is *agapa* (7:42, 47). There are two debtors, Jesus says, one who owes five hundred denarii, the other fifty, but both are effectively bankrupt and cannot repay. The creditor utterly uncharacteristically (we should not try this on our bankers) forgives (*charizomai*) both their debts. So Jesus concludes with his Socratic question: "Tell me, therefore, which of them will love him [the lender] more?" (7:41–42). The answer is obvious; Simon gives it, and Jesus commends him for the rectitude of his judgment (7:43). But we can be pretty sure that Simon either had not seen what is coming next, not least from the caution in his voice, or fears that he will be trapped by his own right answer: "I suppose [*hypolambanō*]," he says carefully, "the one whom he forgave more."

The irony in this passage carries its deep meaning. "Simon," Jesus now says, "have a look at this woman." Simon, of course, has been doing nothing else. Then Jesus points out that what is clearly a breach of hospitality in Jewish culture (though not so clearly in Greek or Roman culture), the failure of his host to provide for a ritual washing of feet before the dinner, has been remarkably made up for by the extravagant action of a "sinner." Simon, perhaps out of the cautious suspicion he has of his guest, has not given the usual polite kiss as an expression of friendship (cf. Gen. 33:4; Exod. 18:7), something now also more extravagantly supplied by the woman kissing

Jesus's feet (Luke 7:44–45). Finally, though such polite and formal gestures would have been an unmistakable sign of honor at a banquet in the Jewish context (cf. Ps. 23:5), here "you did not anoint my head with oil, but this woman has anointed my feet with fragrant oil" (Luke 7:46). All this to say: Simon, you have actually fallen short of the normative generosities of hospitality in our Jewish tradition, but this woman, evidently of a dishonorable profession, has more than made up for it.

The conclusion that follows opens to the reader's understanding a very Jewish notion of the relationship of sin and indebtedness as suggested by Jesus's parable, a dialogical example to set beside the actual occasion of the Pharisee's critical view of Jesus in relation to the woman's extravagant actions: "She is obviously *that* kind of sinner, and he does not know it." But Jesus does know it, and while in one respect her sin is clearly more flagrant than that of many, perhaps in particular the sin of Simon, "her sins . . . are forgiven, for she loved much." But the corollary holds also as instruction to the point, namely that "to whom little is forgiven, the same loves little" (7:47). Anderson shows how extensively in Second Temple Judaism the biblical metaphors for sin shift from it being a "burden" to a "debt" (Hebrew ḥôb); the Aramaic word for sin (ḥôba) is the term used also for indicating the debt one owes a lender and is clearly a cognate.[9] The prevalence of this fiscal metaphor, familiar thus to the Pharisee, helps us to understand the force of what Jesus is saying here. As Anderson goes on to point out, Simon, as host, was "obligated or indebted [hayyab] to provide for the washing of his guests' feet"; this particular hospitality was a gesture toward the poverty of Christ that might have done him credit, so to speak. Jesus's story of canceled debt is already a story about forgiveness; the idea of canceled debt (charizomai) will recur forcefully in Paul's letter to the Colossians, when he speaks of Christ's forgiveness of our sins as "the erasure of the bond of indebtedness" (Col. 2:14, author's translation). When Jesus says to the woman, "Your sins are forgiven [apheōntai]" (Luke 7:48), the verb is perfect tense; she is already forgiven. This may mean either that before the occasion of the meal Jesus had forgiven her or that the transaction has just occurred. But when the other guests react with, "Who is this who even forgives sins?" (7:49), the verb is present tense, aphiēsin ("is forgiving"), which probably means that they think the forgiveness has just occurred. But the question they ask is for them unanswered: only God can forgive sins, they believe, and they cannot accept that Jesus would be such a one as could claim to forgive without the claim being blasphemy. But the woman herself is given assurance in words that echo both the history of Jewish righteousness and the present tense of Jesus's teaching as Luke records it: "Your faith has saved you. Go in peace" (7:50). We may nowadays resist somewhat the typological interpretation of Gregory the Great, namely that the Pharisee, "presuming upon his pretense of righteousness, is the Jewish people," while the sinful woman "represents the conversion of the Gentiles" (Homily 33). But we who know ourselves to be included among the "all" who "have sinned and fall short of the glory of God" (Rom. 3:23)

9. Gary A. Anderson, *Sin: A History* (New Haven: Yale University Press, 2009), 27.

must acknowledge that she is a dramatic representative of the grief for sin and the enraptured sense of forgiveness we too experience in Christ. It is she, the courtesan, who is the "everyman" figure in this narrative, not Simon the Pharisee.

Who was this woman? Because Mary Magdalene appears immediately following in Luke's text, many interpreters suggest this identity. Others identify both with Mary of Bethany.[10] Partly this is philological: *m'gadd'la* ("hairdresser") was as common a euphemism for prostitute, as was "flute-girl." The connection to Mary of Bethany, sister of Martha, is suggested notably by Gregory the Great, but since Origen (*Commentary on Matthew* 27:55–56) it has also been resisted; both Bernard of Clairvaux and Calvin follow Origen in this regard. Lightfoot was content with the Magdalene association (1979: 3.85) and cites various rabbinic writings in identifying "Magdalene" with Magdala Zebaim, a place said to have been "destroyed because of its adulteries" and "whoredoms" (3.375). Lightfoot also locates a woman of the time so named by talmudic sources as the adulterous wife of one Papas Ben Judah, a contemporary of Gamaliel (1979: 3.86). While none of this is definitive, Luke's narrative order at least opens up the possibility that the weeping woman and Mary Magdalene are one and the same. Commenting in his poem "Marie Magdalene" on the scene just considered, the seventeenth-century poet-pastor George Herbert finds the value of the connection rooted in the combined action of repentance, forgiveness, and love:

> When blessed Marie wip'd her Saviours feet,
> (Whose precepts she had trampled on before)
> And wore them for a jewell on her head,
>   Shewing his steps should be the street
>   Wherein she thenceforth evermore
> With pensive humblenesse would live and tread:
>
> She being stain'd her self, why did she strive
> To make him clean, who could not be defil'd?
> Why kept she not her tears for her own faults,
>   And not his feet? Though we could dive
>   In tears like seas, our sinnes are pil'd
> Deeper than they, in words, and works, and thoughts.
>
> Deare soul, she knew who did vouchsafe and deigne
> To bear her filth; and that her sinnes did dash
> Ev'n God himself: wherefore she was not loth,
>   As she had brought wherewith to stain,
>   So to bring in wherewith to wash:
> And yet in washing one, she washed both.

10. An intriguing linkage between this passage, the account of Jesus at Mary and Martha's house in Bethany, and the resurrection of Lazarus is elaborated by Eleonore Stump as a final chapter in her *Wandering in Darkness: Narrative and the Problem of Suffering* (New York: Oxford University Press, 2010).

EVANGELISM
AND ITS ENEMIES

LUKE 8

Certain Women (8:1–3)

An unspecified time has intervened, but presumably not long after the meal at Simon's house Jesus sets out once again throughout the Galilee region "preaching and bringing the glad tidings of the kingdom of God" (8:1). Evidently his retinue of followers is increasing. Luke specifies "the twelve" but now adds that there are "certain women who had been healed of evil spirits and infirmities" with him (8:2), among whom Luke names three of the more prominent figures. The first of these is Mary Magdalene, "out of whom went seven devils" (KJV). Bede and Gregory the Great, among others who identify Magdalene with the weeping penitent of Luke 7, suggest that the "seven devils" may be understood as a reference to seven vices (Bede, *Homilies on the Gospels* 2.4) or to a universal proclivity to a life of vice (Gregory the Great, *Homily on the Gospels* 33). Luke's text itself, however, suggests in the episode of the Gadarene swine that ensues that something more dramatic, however unspecified in his narrative, may have been involved. In any case, Luke is here naming a woman whose repentance and spiritual transformation were especially noteworthy and whose utter faithfulness to Jesus would see her both among the few remaining at the cross itself and, after Jesus's resurrection, as the one to whom first he would appear, in an episode recorded only in John's Gospel. Magdalene clearly occupies a place of respect among the disciples. About Chuza, the steward of Herod, we know little; that his wife, Joanna, should have left the court precincts to follow Jesus indicates that she also may have had "substance" at her disposal with which to provision the Twelve and Jesus. She seems to have become a friend of Mary Magdalene, and she is later named with Mary Magdalene and the other women who returned from the open tomb to inform the disciples (Luke 24:10). Susanna appears by name only here. All of these women "ministered" (*diakoneō*) to Jesus "from their substance" (KJV). The phrase here can mean simply "to wait on tables," but clearly this is insufficient to explain the role of these women. Though they may have provisioned the group with food, the itinerary does not well support the imagination of cooking and serving at tables; "from their substance" sounds much more like their having had sufficient money to buy food and periodically, perhaps, to rent lodgings. This is one of several moments in Luke's narrative in which he reminds us of the mendicant poverty of Christ and the Twelve; Henry comments aptly when he remembers in this context another text: "'Though he was rich, yet for our sakes he became poor,' and lived on alms" (1728: 657).

To see women in such a group of disciples may perhaps have aroused curiosity in itself; Jewish culture normatively restricted women's privileges even to speak in public social gatherings, and a woman could not so much as enter a synagogue or pray the Shema (Fitzmyer 1981–85: 1.696). Jesus is different. Accordingly, women play an important part in Luke's narratives. Here is a visible sign that Jesus is creating a holistic representation of membership in the kingdom, showing it to be a real *koinōnia*. All of these people, men and women together, were being trained by example to become productive members of the body of Christ, even as they, though in a material sense poor, were being exposed to the riches of Jesus's pedagogy. It is clear that here, as in Luke 6 at the choosing of the disciples, Luke shows us that Jesus has been consciously building up a community of complementarity in roles and gifts, endowing them with instruction and good purpose so that they could become the church. What they were learning together was not just *what* he taught but *how* he taught. Not all of this, of course, would be easy for them.

Parables (8:4)

Teaching by parable was not unprecedented in Jewish culture; far from it. Although there are many Old Testament examples of this genre, most readers of scripture will find Nathan's parable to David among the most powerful and memorable. Regarding the rich man with many sheep who steals from a poor man his only ewe, which he has cherished almost as a child, the murderous and adulterous King David makes an enraged judgment. Yet as Nathan then shows, he has but judged himself (2 Sam. 12:1–15). Herbert's superb insight, namely that the Old Testament *māšāl* ("figurative teaching") "had a clearly recognizable purpose: that of quickening an apprehension of the real as distinct from the wished for," applies very well to the parable teaching of Jesus.[1] Rabbinic teachers whose works have survived in Mishnah and Talmud clearly continued to use *māšālîm*—a form of indirect discourse that might mean anything from a kind of allegorical narrative to metaphorical and enigmatic wisdom sayings—in their teaching.[2] Jesus, however,

1. A. S. Herbert, "The Parable (*Masal*) in the Old Testament," *Scottish Journal of Theology* 7 (1954): 180–96.
2. *Māšāl* in Hebrew, as well as in Aramaic and Arabic, signifies figurative discourse generally. See Jeremias 1963.

is the ultimate master of this art form, as Luke's Gospel shows. Here too is amply
borne out the succinct observation of Matthew, that in his teaching, "without a
parable he did not speak to them" (Matt. 13:34). It is by this means, even as the
"prophet" and poet long before foretold (Ps. 78:2), that Jesus would reveal "things
kept secret from the foundation of the world" (Matt. 13:35). That the revelation
of these secrets of foundational meaning was to be to poor men, simple and (by
comparison with the institutional masters of interpretation, the scribes and Pharisees) almost illiterate, was surely a source of aggravation to their sense of propriety
and pertinent merit. But this fact has critical significance for our understanding
of this next parable, as recorded here by Luke (cf. Mark 4:1–20; Matt. 13:1–23).

The first point to grasp about such a narrative as the parable of the sower and
the seed is that it is a simple fiction in the service of deepest truth. Early interpreters of this text realized the degree to which, in this parable, Jesus was delineating
his preferred method for obtaining breakthrough insight into the character of his
own teaching. While his method is distinctly literary, a kind of *poiēsis*, its purpose
is to draw his hearer into an encounter with philosophical truth. This indirect
means of engaging truth was to Jesus's hearers distinct from the more typically
narrow facticity, historicity, and especially legalism with which Jewish institutional
interpretation seems to have become preoccupied. As method, indirection has
always had its partisans in subsequent Christian culture. Such partisans—and
many of our greatest poets and fiction writers have been among them—include
the storytelling Franciscan preachers of the thirteenth century, Chaucer, the Pearl
poet, but also more recent writers such as Charles Dickens, Graham Greene, and
Wendell Berry. Origen was among the first intellectual observers to notice that
Jesus tends to use stories that fall within the realm of ordinary verifiability by
virtue of a commonsense, correspondence approach to moral or spiritual truth:
"Now a parable is a narration of an action as it may be done, yet not according to
the letter [reporting a specific historical action], though it might have been, but
representing certain things by means of others which are given in the parable"
(*Commentary on Proverbs* 1; cf. *Commentary on Matthew* 10:15–16). The "things"
represented, accordingly, are not merely literal or historical—having to do with
tangible realities only—but are a cue to the intelligible, spiritual realities that are
the inner substance of Jesus's teaching. Jesus's stories are notably commonplaces;
he elaborates no fantasy. Origen notes that the Old Testament contains at least
one kind of allegorical or parabolic narrative of the sort with which Hellenic and
Roman culture were much more familiar (by way of such works as Aesop's *Fables*
or Ovid's *Metamorphoses*, for example); he instances the account in Judg. 9:7–15
in which Gideon proposed to the men of Shechem the parable of the bramble,
when "the trees . . . went forth to anoint a king over them." Origen calls this kind
of tale an enigma, "a continuous narration of things that are spoken of as if done,
and yet have not been done, nor are possible to be done, but nevertheless [also]
contains a concealed meaning" (*Commentary on Proverbs* 1). (Regarding this
example, the modern reader may be forgiven for thinking of J. R. R. Tolkien's Ents,

the walking trees in *Lord of the Rings*.) But Jesus eschews alternative-universe narration or fantasy fiction. Each of his narrative parables corresponds to a mundane, homely reality rather than to political drama, otherworldliness, or even important legal precedents. Yet in his handling, homely analogies persistently reveal, almost sacramentally, a higher truth that cuts across all these spheres. Perhaps we need hardly add here that to minds oriented exclusively to political fact, history, and legal precept, a literary method such as is overwhelmingly preferred by Jesus can (and still to some does) seem hardly worth paying attention to; this will especially be so for those who want less to hear what he is really saying than to trip him up on a technicality. As Henry says, "Where the word of God is heard *carelessly* there is commonly *a contempt* put upon it too" (1728: 658). It is clear that there are always those in Jesus's audience who will look down upon the parables he tells as insufficiently intellectual to be taken seriously. This is a mistake, for the parables of Jesus, like so many rabbinic parables, are intellectually and theologically far richer than on first glance they may seem.

The Sower and the Seed (8:5–18)

The crowd has begun to gather (the Greek double genitive absolute suggests that they "were gathering together . . . and coming to him"), yet even before they have fully assembled, Jesus begins to speak. No preface, no funny story, no analytical framework: he just tells a story. Actually, it is more like a vignette. Hardly any (except possibly some of the women) would have failed to have seen out in the countryside a sower casting seed from a bag into the earth; it was the universal way of seeding grain in that culture—even as it was to be in our own for another nineteen hundred years. Fields were not 50-acre, let alone 640-acre rectangles in ancient Palestine; there was a lot of rocky outcropping here and there, and much of the soil was shallow, with limestone or tufa rock not far beneath the surface. Even a good hand cannot in such conditions get all of the seed to fall where the soil is best. And there were serious weeds that, as in all places, might spring up and choke out the crop. To some degree, therefore, the sower, to be successful, must be profligate. Some seed will inevitably fall where it will perish or produce poorly. Yet some seed does land where it can really thrive, and it "bore fruit a hundredfold" (KJV). So Jesus is just stating the obvious. That much said, he just stops talking—there is no internal conclusion to this descriptive story. After a pause he then cries out, "He that hath ears to hear, let him hear" (KJV). Luke makes it plain: that was it. Even the disciples are confounded. One can imagine them saying to themselves, "Hear what?" or "What was that about?" Had we been there to hear this parable, would we have thought differently?

Finally, perhaps embarrassed or even irritated that nothing more appears to be forthcoming, and sensing the bewilderment of the crowd, the disciples ask Jesus outright, "What might this parable be?" (8:9 KJV). The KJV seems better to capture the question here than many other translations: not simply "what does it mean?" but effectively, "what sort of talk is this?" Jesus tells them, "To you it has been given to know the mysteries of the kingdom of God"—which is to say, you understand the "things hidden"—"but to the rest it is given in parables, that 'seeing they may not see, and hearing they may not understand'" (8:10). To some modern readers, this reply has been taken as evidence that Jesus was "encoding" his message, as a Gnostic might, in effect excluding from comprehension all but those with the code.[3] For early Christian interpretation, this use of parable by Jesus was likewise seen as a means of distinguishing between hearers, though not quite in the sense Kermode has in mind. Bede is representative: he regards those *without* an understanding of what Jesus is doing as having "closed the sense of their heart, [caring] not to know the truth, and forgetful of what the Lord has told them already" (quoted in Aquinas, *Catena Aurea* 3.1.269); because the scribes and Pharisees have not responded to the much more straightforward teachings Jesus has already given in his sermon in Luke 6, they are obtuse to his now building on that teaching by analogy. For Bede, what is said here builds on the story about good and bad trees in 6:43–45, in which the application had been explicit.

Yet Jesus graciously lays out for his disciples the allegory in detail: there are those who receive the seed, or "word of God," only at the outer margins, as bystanders, and in their case the devil snatches the word out of their hearts lest it bring about their salvation without any real commitment on their part (8:12); the seed on rock is akin to those who have an immediately joyous, emotional response, but who fail to become rooted, so that in a time of temptation they "fall away" (8:13); the seed that falls among the thorns is like those who, having heard, have the very life of God's word choked out of them by their being encumbered with weeds—riches and worldly pleasure. Happily, there are also those who, with "an honest and good heart, having heard the word, keep it, and bring forth fruit with patience" (8:15 KJV). That is, there are hearers who have an integrity and desire for righteousness that makes of them good soil for the word. Luke is unique in capturing the seat of this fruitfulness as the "heart"; his word here is *kardia* (he uses it twenty-one other times), but the phrase has Hebraic overtones, suggesting that Jesus might have been evoking the Old Testament notion that "wise-heartedness" is necessary to pursue the wisdom of God and that one of Luke's informants has relayed the Hebraism as an echo of the "wise heart" (Job 9:4), "understanding heart" (Prov. 8:5), and "the heart of him who has understanding" (15:14) of the wisdom books. On the biblical view, it is a characteristic of such hearts that they are open to *māšālîm* ("the sayings of the wise"), which is another way of saying that they are "good soil."

But there is a warning, then, in what follows. The purpose of a light is to reveal things that are hidden in darkness, says Jesus. The candle that no sane person lights

---

3. Frank Kermode, *The Genesis of Secrecy: On the Interpretation of Narrative* (Cambridge: Harvard University Press, 1979).

and puts under a bushel is not a reference to the faith of a believer but to the light of Christ that comes into the world to reveal things long hidden. Even as Jesus's parables distinguish the preparation and intention of the hearts of those who hear him, and some choose to make dark and obscure what ought to an honest searcher be plain, so there is a context of judgment in which prepared readers are to appreciate that the light of Jesus's teaching penetrates into dark recesses of habitual self-deception. One hears here an echo of the prophet Jeremiah, recording the voice of God: "I, the LORD, search the heart . . . even to give every man according to his ways, according to the fruit of his doings" (Jer. 17:10). Nothing is secret that shall not be made known in *that* light, says Jesus, nor is there any dark business squirreled away that shall not be exposed widely (Luke 8:17). The conclusion of his explanation to his disciples accordingly takes on an eschatological as well as a morally prophetic tone, and the distinction between the disciples as rapidly progressing learners of God's truth and the essentially ossified institutional "keepers" of right interpretation is now becoming brutally evident as to final end: "Therefore take heed how you hear. For whoever has, to him more will be given; and whoever does not have, even what he seems to have will be taken from him" (8:18). This is *not* a "dark saying" of Jesus for anyone who has been paying attention; rather, it is as bright as lightning on a dark and stormy night, and far more frightening. Bede applies it especially to those who are called to the life of learning and exegesis; it is, says Bede, as if Jesus says, "Give heed with all your mind to the word which you hear, for to him who has a love of the word shall be given also the sense of understanding what he loves; but whoso hath no love of hearing the word, though he deems himself skillful either from natural genius or the exercise of learning, will have no delight in the sweetness of wisdom" (quoted in Aquinas, *Catena Aurea* 3.1.272).

Mothers and Brothers (8:19–21)

Commentators sometimes imagine that, when Jesus is interrupted by a message that "his mother and brothers" have come to see him but cannot get through the crowds (8:19–20), the message was a simple matter of information or a call to some obligation. One may suspect something more: Mark 3:21, 31–35 suggests that the family had doubts about his teaching, wondering even if Jesus was "beside himself" (3:21 KJV). Further, it may well be that the messenger here in Luke was implying, in his manner of interruption, a certain cynicism about whether Jesus might not need the sort of "reining-in" that such an unexpected family visit might imply. Jesus's answer—to the messenger, not to Mary and his brothers directly—is consistent with what he will say later on, as Ambrose puts it, about the "priority of heavenly ordinances to earthly affection" (*Exposition of Luke* 6.38–39). This is one of several passages in Luke, beginning with the account of Mary and Joseph finding Jesus in the temple with the elders discussing scripture, in which we see him teaching by example a new concept of family, namely the family of God. The point is not to denigrate natural family but rather to suggest that natural nurturing is, in the maturing disciple, to be succeeded by spiritual nourishing and a deeper sense of mature *koinōnia*. Basil the Great gets at what Jesus says about both hearing the word of God and doing it as the basis of this new, spiritual family: "Intimacy with the Lord is not explained as kinship according to the flesh, but it is achieved by a cheerful willingness in doing the will of God" (*Morals* 22). A second issue is more controversial; the preoccupation since the time of Eusebius (fourth century) over whether Mary had other children (partially summarized in Bock 1994–96: 1.752–53) turns on the range of inclusive meaning for *adelphoi*, a term that may be translated "brothers," "kinfolk," or "cousins" (Fitzmyer 1981–85: 1.724). Either reading is possible. But there is no ambiguity whatsoever about what Jesus says counts for membership in the family he is drawing together in the kingdom of God.

Peace in the Storm (8:22–26)

Those who balk at miracles that can have no purely psychological explanation (which is to deny, of course, their miraculous character) are often more troubled by this story and the first nature miracle that precedes it, the miraculous draught of fishes (5:1–11), than by the healing miracles. This particular skepticism is instructive regarding the significance of such doubts for the actual view of the doubters concerning who Jesus is; what is being rejected, in fact, is precisely the thing Luke is demonstrating, namely that Jesus is Lord over all creation.

Crossing Genessaret, in a "boat" (*ploion*) that must have been large enough to seat Jesus, the Twelve, and some other disciples (including perhaps the women), Jesus, weary, lies down to sleep. The group includes Peter, James, and John, veteran sailors and fishermen all. Yet when a sudden and severe storm springs up, the waves rise and the boat, presumably unmanageable by this point, begins to take on water (8:22–24), even they become frightened. Unaccountably, Jesus sleeps on. They feel they have to wake him: disaster is upon them. Jesus gets up and without so much as a prayer, "rebukes" the storm. Immediately a calm descends upon the lake (8:24). Imagine their awe. Jesus then rebukes *them*: "Where is your faith?" Cyril of Alexandria notes that Jesus is here rebuking their fearfulness especially, showing that it may sometimes be less an assault of carnal temptation than constitutional faint-heartedness that undermines our faith, and that fear is itself an evidence that faith is weak (1983: Homily 43). In this light Jesus's criticism is calling the integrity of their discipleship into question. Suddenly they become really afraid, yet this fear is better than the first, for it is a species now of that fear of the Lord that scripture says is necessary for the pursuit of wisdom. They ask the right question, at least among themselves: "What manner of man is this! For he commandeth even the winds and water, and they obey him" (8:25

KJV). Since Rembrandt's powerful painting of this scene (1633) and Doré's similar nineteenth-century etching, this dramatic moment, with Jesus standing at the prow of the reeling skiff, arm stretched over the waters, has been a popular subject with Protestant artists especially. Many of the depictions emphasize the terror of the storm; a recent depiction by Chinese artist He Qi (*Peace, Be Still*) captures rather the tranquil, untroubled command of the Lord as a moment of great beauty. The whole of this narrative is strikingly metonymic—a *māšāl*, perhaps, for the church in our own time also.

The Gadarene Swine (8:27–39)

When Jesus and his companions reach the other side, they are in a region called the Decapolis, a group of ten cities in which Hellenic influence has come to be more or less pervasive. People even raise swine—something hardly normative in a faithful Jewish culture. The particular spot is Gadara (cf. Matt. 8:28), "over against Galilee" (Luke 8:26 KJV), and it is probably not too much to call it (as does Bock 1994–96: 771) "Gentile territory." Here, outside the city, Jesus is met by a naked man who Luke describes as homeless and living among the dead, in a place of graves and tombs (8:27). John Chrysostom saw this location in Gentile (pagan) terms and thought that the madman's familiar haunt was because "evil spirits visit the tombs of the dead, to instill into men that dangerous notion, that the souls of the dead become evil spirits" (*Homilies on Matthew* 28). This, of course, is a nearly universal pagan notion.[4] Yet the naked man is clearly disordered in a radical way. While Hippocrates derived all forms of psychic disease from natural causes (*On the Sacred Disease*), Luke, though as a physician almost certainly familiar with Hippocrates, regards this man as in a different category, namely as a casualty of the cosmic battle between Christ and Satan. Among Reformed interpreters, Calvin prefers a more nuanced explanation of the haunt of the naked demoniac than that of Chrysostom: "Now, those who think that the man lived in the tombs because evil spirits enjoy the stench of corpses, or find sweetness in the savor of the offerings, or because they are after the souls which they seek to have close to their bodies—all this is quite insubstantial, foolish speculation. Rather, the unclean spirits kept the poor man at the tombs, to rend him with unending terror at the gloomy spectacle of death" (1972: 1.284).

The possessed man's symptoms are found in other accounts of demon-possessed persons. In his fits he exhibits strength sufficient to break chains and fetters, and he has in effect a multiple personality. Yet he flees when able "into the wilderness" (8:29). Oddly, he both approaches Jesus and is repulsed by him: "What have I to

---

4. Peter G. Bolt shows that many people in the Greco-Roman world assumed a connection between daimons and the spirits of the dead; "Jesus, the Daimons, and the Dead," in *The Unseen World: Christian Reflection on Angels, Demons, and the Heavenly Realm*, ed. A. N. S. Lane (Grand Rapids: Baker, 1996), 75–102.

do with you, Jesus, Son of the Most High God? I beg you, do not torment me!" (8:28). The following verse clarifies: Jesus had already "commanded the unclean spirit" to leave the man, and "it" was resisting. When Jesus asks the name of the spirit, the man replies, "Legion." We can hardly miss the military overtones here, strengthening the cosmic warfare motif that we have seen developing in Luke's narrative. Here it is intensified, for "many demons had entered into him" (8:30). We get a notion of just how many in what follows.

When the demons plead not to be sent out into the "deep" (*abyssos*), they seem to be referring to the place of the dead (Ps. 107:26), or the pagan Tartarus, or even to "the depths of the sea"—also occasionally referred to as *abyssos*. Whatever associations spring to mind, the number given by Mark 5:13 for what Luke calls here "a herd of many swine" is "about two thousand" pigs. The unclean spirits request permission from Jesus to enter the unclean beasts, and these run all together (like a legion?) down the steep slope, over a precipice, and into the sea, where they drown (Luke 8:31–33). In a moment of wildly dramatic irony, the demons thus go into "the abyss" anyway. For Calvin, this passage "also teaches us what stupid nonsense it is to say, with some ungodly folk, that devils are not real spirits, but only the depraved passions of men." Rather than being possessed by some sort of psychic manifestation of mere human vices, Calvin continues, "we should realize that unclean spirits (being doomed to destruction) are the foes of the human race, and aim to drag whom they may into the same pit as themselves" (1972: 1.287). The demonic spirits are certainly unified as to purpose: Canadian political philosopher George Grant once remarked upon a clamor by some among his countrymen for "unity at all costs" on a political matter, that for a "convincing demonstration of that kind of unity one ought to consider the example of the Gadarene swine." He was thinking, doubtless, of what logicians refer to as the Gadarene Fallacy, which is the fallacy of supposing that because a group is in the right formation and all headed in the same direction it is necessarily on a good course. Not a few readers have seen irony in this story and drawn on it. Perhaps the most direct sort of reading is exhibited in Dostoyevsky's novel *Demons*, in which the redemption of the radically disordered Verkhovensky comes by means of his "interpretation" of this very passage.

From a more mundane point of view, this was not a good day for the hog farmers. (That the price of pork bellies was bound to jump higher wouldn't much cheer those with no hogs left to sell.) The swineherds run to the city and surrounding countryside with the bad news (8:34), which in its turn brings a bigger crowd out "to see what had happened." Luke's repetition of this phrase in 8:34 and 8:35 strengthens the reader's sense of both the magnitude and the irreducibility of the event in his eyes. The crowd, many of whom must have previously observed the mad behavior of this poor man, now see him sitting at the feet of Jesus (a posture suggesting that he was calmly being taught in the fashion of a disciple), "clothed and in his right mind." To their shock is added another irony: now they are more afraid of him than ever they were in his violent insanity. Eyewitnesses quickly describe to the newcomers the whole process, but that fails to quiet their anxiety. The crowd's distress prompts a request that Jesus "depart from them, for they were seized with great fear" (8:37). Jesus, apparently heeding them, turns toward the ship, about to go back the way he came.

In one of the most intriguing touches of this whole sequence, the healed man wants to join the group following Jesus and to leave with them. But Jesus sends him away: "Return to your own house [i.e., not to the graveyard], and tell what great things God has done for you" (8:39). And the man obeys, staying behind in "Gentile country" as a witness. Indeed, Luke's language suggests that he becomes a kind of Gentile evangelist, for he "proclaimed" (*kēryssōn*) to the city. The apostolate to the Gentiles has in this conversion clearly begun, and in an astounding symbolic way. For Bede, whose own grandparents were pagans and who knew well enough about evil spirits and possession by demons, "he who had a devil is a figure for all the Gentile people" (although Ambrose makes the same connection in his *Exposition* 6.44). Likewise for Augustine long before him: "By the expression that there was in him a legion of devils, the nations are signified who served many devils" (*Questions on the Gospels* 1.2.1.13). Thus, the ministry to the "nations" to be continued by Paul has been here pioneered by the Lord himself.

Healing and Raising the Dead (8:40–56)

Back on the other side of the lake, yesterday's crowd is waiting for Jesus and "gladly" (KJV) welcomes him back (8:40). Hardly has he rejoined them when suddenly there appears a man who, well honored in the community, is nevertheless distraught. In a gesture of abject supplication, he falls down at the feet of Jesus and begs him to come to his house. This is no ordinary Galilean but a "ruler" (*archōn*) of the local synagogue; his name, Jairus, is given only in Luke's account. We may reasonably imagine this inclusion to be an indication of Luke's historical precision, perhaps especially in the light of the unusual behavior of such a man for some of Luke's readership, accustomed as they were by now to the skepticism of many in like positions. But it is likely also that Luke intends more than a precise historical marker for the sake of credibility. Jairus's name means "he will give light" or "may he enlighten," a philological suggestion perhaps that he may be regarded as not merely a politically prominent person but representatively as an "enlightened" or learned man. Luke's use of *archōn* suggests, in fact, that he may most probably be the chief ruler of the local synagogue. Jerome, Bede, and Bonaventure see this inclusion of his name by Luke as having the narrative function of highlighting his illustrious reputation (Bonaventure 2001–4: 1.8.74). The reason for the distress and abject supplication of Jairus is soon made clear: his only daughter, twelve years of age, lies at home dying (8:42). Jesus turns to go to the house at once.

The crowd follows, to see what he will do, and the press of human bodies is intense. Nevertheless, there is a woman in that throng who is on a mission of her own—and determined. She has been sick herself for twelve years, just precisely the age of the young girl. Bock opines (1994–96: 1.793) that her condition has the symptoms of a uterine hemorrhage, a condition that would be debilitating and embarrassing and that would also make her ritually unclean (cf. Lev. 15:25–31; Ezek. 36:17). If he is right, it is not much wonder that the physicians to whom she has had recourse over the years have used up all her financial resources and, as Mark 5:26 more astringently suggests, have only aggravated her condition. Luke, himself a physician, knows how untreatable this condition is in his time and is less harsh; he simply notes that none could heal her (Luke 8:43). Somehow, weakened as she is, she works her way up through the crowd from behind Jesus and reaches out just sufficiently to touch "the border of his garment." Immediately her bleeding stops (8:44). (The term *histēmi* means just that—"the blood stops"; it is a medical term found elsewhere in contemporary texts.)

Jesus is immediately aware that something has transpired: "Who touched me?" he asks. No one answers. Peter is incredulous; all kinds of people are pressing in, jostling about and pushing closer. Why does Jesus ask this apparently absurd question? But Jesus persists, "Somebody touched me, for I perceived power going out from me" (8:46). This is too much for the woman; she knew he knew. She now comes trembling before him, falls down, as did Jairus, and declares why she has indeed reached out to touch his robe and that as a result she has been instantly healed (8:47). There is a conflict between desire and conscience in the woman. Cyril of Alexandria understands that coupled with her faith is actually a legitimate fear of contaminating Jesus with her own impurity (1983: Homily 45). Jesus has sensed this too, of course. He then speaks softly to her (there is no rebuke for her breach of decorum) and says in an intimate, familiar voice, "Daughter, be of good cheer; your faith has made you well. Go in peace" (8:48). Three short utterances here comprise the deep significance of what has transpired: in a kind way he has said, "Don't be afraid; the reason you have been healed is because of your faith in me"; and "Do not be any longer distressed, either by your former disease or by a lingering sense of your impropriety." It is a remarkable encounter, discrete in its compressed power, yet inextricably tied to what follows.[5]

Even as Jesus is speaking these comforting words, assuring her, someone comes rushing from the house of Jairus to say to him, "Your daughter is dead. Do not trouble the Teacher" (8:49). It appears that the delay occasioned by the spontaneous healing of the histemic woman has been costly. But Jesus doesn't, as we would say, skip a beat. He speaks to all, presumably, but especially to Jairus: "Do not be afraid; only believe, and she will be made well" (8:50). We need to pause over all of Jesus's words carefully, and here is no exception. Much of what we have been

5. Tradition gives her the name Bernice (Latin Veronica). Eusebius writes in the fourth century that her fellow citizens in Paneas (Caesarea Philippi) created a bronze monument of a woman, her hands joined as if in prayer, opposite another statue, male, clothed in a stole and holding his hand out toward the woman. This bronze sculpture was set, says Eusebius, near her house but later destroyed by the emperor Maximinus (*Ecclesiastical History* 7.18).

seeing for several episodes is the face of fear: fear of the disciples in the boat for their safety, followed by a new fear occasioned by Jesus stilling the storm; the terror of the unclean spirits; the fear of the Gadarenes when they see the demoniac fully clothed and in his right mind; the general fear of the wider Gadarene community, as they in turn learn of these events; the gnawing anxiety of the woman with her issue of blood; and now the fear of Jairus that his daughter would die, apparently confirmed in fact. But into this series of fearful contexts now enters the definitive word of that one in whom we see exemplified "the peace . . . which surpasses all understanding" (Phil. 4:7), saying, as had the angelic voices to such as Daniel, Zacharias, the shepherds on the hillside, and Mary herself: "Fear not!" The disciples may not yet fully see that, as later it will be expressed (1 John 4:18), perfect love casts out fear. They certainly have by now already seen that the deed of the Lord is as good as his word, and that correspondence is the bedrock upon which their maturing faith is building.

When he enters the death room, Jesus takes only Peter, James, John, and the girl's parents as witnesses. There are mourners already there, ritually wailing the girl's death, as was the custom. These too he silences, as he did the waves: "Do not weep; she is not dead, but sleeping." To the mourners, this comment is ludicrous; they laugh at him in scorn (Luke 8:52–53). Their laughter is evidently that of unbelief; as Bonaventure says, "The person who is certain about something not only does not believe [another view], but also derides the person trying to persuade him to the contrary" (2001–4: 1.8.93). But within Luke's text there is an entirely contrary level of ironic resonance: "Woe to you who laugh now," the reader should be hearing, "for you shall mourn and weep" (6:25). So Jesus puts all of them out of the room, takes the girl by the hand (since she was dead, an "unclean" act), and calls to her, almost as her parents might in the morning: "Little girl, arise" (8:54). She does, and the Great Physician orders that she be given a meal (8:55). Her parents, Luke says matter-of-factly, were "astonished." Small wonder. They have just experienced a living demonstration of the sort of ironic reversal upon which the Lukan beatitudes are built (6:21). But Jesus commands them, as he had not commanded the Gadarene demoniac, to be silent about what has happened in that room. This is a curiosity sufficient to attract Luke's attention, but it is not explained.

Several things about Luke's account suggest either a different informer from Mark or that he has a particular eye for significant details that Mark has passed over in his own account. Luke early on mentions the girl's age as twelve (8:42); he mentions that she was an only child, a parallel to the only son of the widow of Nain (8:42; cf. 7:12); more sympathetically than Mark, he sees the physicians who have been unable to cure the woman with the hemorrhage (8:43); Peter is named as speaking to Jesus in his confusion about the question regarding who touched him (8:45); Luke gives an explanation for why the crowd laughed (8:53); and Luke gives more detail about the girl returning to normal health (8:55) (Fitzmyer 1981–85: 1.743–44). In such details we may appreciate how much Luke's perspective on these events is shaped by his physician's eye and ear.

LUKE 9

Whereas Jesus has already chosen from among his disciples twelve for particular apostolic duties, Luke tells us now that he is commissioning the Twelve for more than their education in his company. This particular commissioning, while not as global as the Great Commission to come, is nonetheless remarkable for what it includes. Luke says that Jesus called them together formally and conferred upon them "power and authority over all demons, and to cure diseases" (9:1). The term "authority" is used in the parallel accounts in Mark 6:7–13 and Matt. 10:1–15; Luke is unique in adding "power" (*dynamin kai exousian*), a term that seems more than appropriate given that Jesus is conferring upon the Twelve the ability to do what heretofore he alone has been able to do—namely to cast out "demons" (*ta daimonia*) as a prolegomena to curing disease.

Demonology in Luke

Luke's Hellenistic education and Gentile culture would have disposed him more than most to cast experience in terms of a clinically objective, rational analysis. This would have been for a physician a normative component of everyday verification and diagnosis. Yet his persistent observation of the role of demons and the necessity for effective reception of the gospel of the evil spirits being cast out is not, for many modern readers, all that easy to understand. Biblical critics since the eighteenth century have often betrayed their discomfort with these narratives, suggesting that the order of healing regularly represented there (casting out demons, forgiveness of sins, healing both mental and physical) is either something peculiar to the apostolic period or something for which we can provide a better (more clinical) diagnostic explanation. Yet it is intrinsic to Luke's Gospel that spiritual war against the forces of evil involves the reality of demonic possession that is vincible by the power of Christ alone. That this power is now conferred upon the apostles is of critical importance for the ministry of the gospel in every time and place.

Evading this aspect of the gospel is a characteristic impulse of much twentieth-century biblical criticism: Bultmann is not a solitary voice.[1] We should not be surprised at secular incredulity concerning miracles in this light, nor should we be surprised at the failure of anthropological and ethnographic study to grasp the reality of dark spirits as phenomenological. We should, however, recognize that condescension toward the demonology in biblical texts is not a universal view. An example of the tension between post-Enlightenment and biblical views may sharpen the point at issue: a 2010 American television report on shamanistic murder of young African boys for ritual use of their internal organs understandably reflected simultaneously horror and dismay at the barbarism. A "reformed" shaman was interviewed, who somberly said that shamans were directed in this practice by "evil spirits." The television news report concluded with an interview of the Ugandan Minister for Ethics and Integrity in which the interviewer said to this evidently university-educated minister, shown standing by his desk in a Western suit and tie, "Surely *you* do not believe in evil spirits yourself." The government representative, James Nsaba Butero, replied, "Yes, I do. And you have them too," he said, pointing his finger at the reporter, "only you do not wish to recognize it."[2] In reading Luke, I suggest that we need to think less like the television reporter and more like the Ugandan Minister for Ethics and Integrity.

If we consider early modern treatises on demonology, such as that by King James I, we will see that an obsession with fame and secret knowledge was then thought to make even a learned person vulnerable to "the devil's schoole and his rudiments" (1.3), because an addiction to the power of knowledge was seen, like all addictive behavior, as potentially entailing an enslavement of the will, ironically under the illusion of achieving unbounded freedom of the will.[3] Readers of Christopher Marlowe's dark but theologically astute *Tragical History of Doctor Faustus* will have seen a dramatic parable on this point, in which the illusion of unbounded "freedom" is a lie told by the victim of Satan to himself. But the issue for a biblical worldview is not only intellectual pride and self-deception. Here are some thought experiments we might make that could help us better to understand, say, Mary Magdalene. It is not too much subtlety to suggest that in a culture of many rampant addictions (including in our own case addiction to the gratifications of obsessive materialism, sexual licentiousness, pornography, alcohol, or drugs), one may perceive the shadow of an analogous dark entrapment. Under an illusion of achieving greater self-control or of some poor imagination of a

1. Rudolf Bultmann, *The New Testament and Mythology* (Minneapolis: Augsburg Fortress, 1984). He has allies in this regard in Fitzmyer 1981–85; and E. P. Sanders, *The Historical Figure of Jesus* (New York: Penguin, 1996), esp. chaps. 9–10.

2. BBC Newsnight, June 7, 2010, available online at news.bbc.co.uk.

3. King James VI of Scotland (King James I of England), *Daemonologie* (Edinburgh, 1597; repr., London, 1604).

gratified will to power, the rebel-victim thinks he or she is liberated by indulgence from conventional morality (mere boredom). And yet, even at the height of such experiences of autonomous self-gratification, a person customarily so deluded has actually become a slave of their preferred, now habitual escape mechanism; their condition, as wise observers from Solomon and Boethius to the present have regularly observed, entails not freedom but its opposite, a loss of freedom of the will, the chains drawn tighter the longer the addiction (whatever the addiction) persists. Yet characteristically, when presented with the reality of this enslavement, such victims vigorously reject the truth. Psychologically, we sometimes just call such protests "denial." But denial of the truth, especially truth about the self, is not compatible with accepting healing, especially the healing of that one who *is* truth; it is rather a function of the effective dominion of that one who is called in scripture "the father of lies." In extreme cases, profound neurosis ensues, which may degenerate into actual madness, whether clinically so described or not.[4]

Sugarman points out that what a nineteenth-century writer like Kierkegaard was not embarrassed to call "sin" in such matters, twentieth-century psychiatry has sought to describe rather by a clinical etiology, with no moral judgments visible in the nomenclature.[5] Yet the path to psychological disease that she describes is one that Christians have from biblical times recognized as a flight from truth. Sugarman's chapter headings fit well enough into a pattern fully described in spiritual terms by writers such as Gregory the Great, Maximus the Confessor, William of St. Thierry, and more recently Paul Tournier, Christopher Lasch, Walker Percy, and René Girard: "Sin: The Flight from the Self"; "The Divided Self"; "Sin and Madness: A Transformation of Consciousness."[6] Meanwhile, in many contemporary churches, even the word "sin" is now avoided. How then can we begin to understand why Christ and the apostles had to cast out demons before the sin-sick souls of men and women could be healed and receive the good news of the gospel?[7]

In his delightfully instructive *The Screwtape Letters*, C. S. Lewis includes a sober counsel with which much of Christian tradition would agree: "There are

4. Scott Peck, *People of the Lie: The Hope for Healing Human Evil* (New York: Touchstone, 1998).

5. Shirley Sugarman, *Sin and Madness: Studies in Narcissism* (Philadelphia: Westminster, 1976). This is reflected in secular attempts to analyze the vices. Gabriele Taylor wants to show that "to pronounce [vices] harmful to the agent is not to judge by some externally imposed standard based on what constitutes a good or flourishing life"; *Deadly Vices* (New York: Oxford University Press, 2008), 3. Even so stripped of a normative biblical basis, however, the basic point remains: there is such a thing as vice, and it entails self-destruction as well as damage to others.

6. Paul Tournier, *A Doctor's Casebook in Light of the Bible* (London: SCM, 1954); Christopher Lasch, *The Culture of Narcissism* (New York: Norton, 1978); Walker Percy, *Lost in the Cosmos: The Last Self-Help Book* (New York: Noonday, 1983); and Girard 2005.

7. *The Works of King James I* (London, 1616). The author, combating the rationalist dismissal of actual evil spirits by Reginald Scott (1585), suggests that "the Papists" may have a distinctive power to cure the possessed, "because Christ gave a commission and power to his apostles to cast out devils," not because of their rectitude in all matters theological, he goes on to say, but because of their willingness to follow strictly the formula given by Christ, the power of which he sees as a reality invested in those words (3.4.120–1).

two equal and opposite errors into which our race can fall about demons. One is to disbelieve in their existence. The other is to believe, and to feel an excessive interest in them."[8] If anything, both of these errors are more common in our time than when, in the dark days of World War II, Lewis wrote these words. But the forms that each error takes—academic formalism on the one hand and jejune fascination with vampirism and witchcraft on the other—are such as to cloud such situations as the Gospels, especially Luke, more realistically depict. In Jewish culture of the first century, the idea of possession by a demon was well established and associated with what today we would think of as insanity. Zoroastrian dualism in the postexilic period may have contributed to this; in Josephus (*Jewish War* 7.185; *Jewish Antiquities* 8.45), one can find remedies associated with the wisdom of Solomon for driving away demons such as the "night hag" Lilith (cf. Isa. 34:14). In later texts, the demons are seducers who lead into temptation, and they may be the personification of vices; these are sometimes called "the seven spirits of deceit" (*Testament of Reuben* 2.1; 3.2–6) or "demons of falsehood" (*Testament of Judah* 23.1; 20.1). In Gentile Greek texts, just as *eudaimonia* ("good fortune," conditions making for happiness) was the goal of the philosophical good life and dependent on a benevolent spirit, so *kakodaimonia* ("bad fortune," choices making for misery) was thought to be instigated by a dark, malicious spirit (Hesiod, *Works and Days* 253–55). The difference in the Jewish tradition is marked by an accentuation of the moral and spiritual element and by the implication of some more explicit order of moral transgression in the one possessed. While the familiar Greek term *daimōn* is used only once in the New Testament (Matt. 8:31), the parallel passage in Luke 8:27 uses *daimonion*, a term that overall will occur more than sixty times. When it occurs, it refers not to ordinary ailment or disease but to a deep spiritual (or mental) disorder for which physical manifestations are of a secondary, merely symptomatic order. When in the thirteenth century Thomas Aquinas considers the biblical passages in question, as he does extensively in his "Treatise on Angels" (*Summa Theologica* 1.50–64), he accordingly implicates the human will, not fate or fortune, in the condition of demon possession. He regards, as we should also in reading Luke, that such events as are described in scripture are real and that they represent a palpable presence of real evil. For Aquinas, it is evident that the demons act out of malice, with a depraved intention of corrupting innocence and destroying souls. Despite his whimsy, this is the sort of spiritual analysis that informs Lewis in *The Screwtape Letters*: what may begin as a temptation to small obfuscations of truth, love, and just action in time acquires a momentum by which the habitué is eventually enslaved, with hardly anything left resembling freedom of will, placing the person effectively "beyond reason." While, as Aquinas says, discursive reason can help in our rescue (and that is the point of Lewis writing his book), in hardened cases only a divine intervention can set the

8. C. S. Lewis, *The Screwtape Letters* (London: Bles, 1942), 9.

prisoner free. The authority Jesus grants to his apostles is thus not a charism for therapeutic discourse; it is divine authority to cast out demons.[9]

Apostolic Proclamation and Reaction (9:1–10)

With this new authority, Jesus now "sent them to preach the kingdom of God and to heal the sick" (9:2). The verb here (*apesteilen*) yields the noun—our English "apostle" simply means "one who has been sent." But here in Luke's account we see that the apostolic commission to deal with the demonic, heal the sick, and preach the gospel is, in effect, a unified work having three aspects or expressions. Moreover, though the apostles have power and authority over disease and demons, in their task they are not to have much more than that power: Jesus expressly forbids, as Calvin puts it, "luggage" (1972: 1.293). No extra staff, no bag to carry bread and money, no extra coat (9:3). The early church was much of a mind that the Lord had here "commanded them to lead a life of extreme poverty," as Eusebius puts it (quoted in Aquinas, *Catena Aurea* 3.1.300–301). They are to receive hospitality only from those who willingly offer it (9:4–5). Francis of Assisi and his followers will much later point to the same passages as warrant for their own call to itinerant poverty. Bonaventure, the leading Franciscan theologian, adds his view "that this verse prohibits all sustenance, so that it may be shown that the preacher must rely with deep hope on God alone" (2001–4: 2.802–3). Bonaventure does not interpret this passage as narrowly as one might expect of a Franciscan (he was resisting extremism in his own order), but he underscores a fundamental principle that "the preacher of truth must avoid above all else the vice of cupidity. Otherwise he will not be a preacher but a flatterer" (2001–4: 2.804). Calvin thinks the apostles might well have such things as bag and coat at home, for use on subsequent forays (1972: 1.293); Luke does not say it, if this is so. It is interesting to reflect that the "bag" (*pēran*) would not, of course, resemble luggage in our sense at all, but suggests the sort of over-the-shoulder bag that itinerant philosophers and later mendicant religious used to keep the food and money they received. Without even a bag the equipment Jesus permits is extremely spare, and though the Essenes had similar astringent instructions for travel (Josephus, *Jewish War* 2.124–27), the resulting appearance of the apostles as they came into a town would have clearly been that of poor and undistinguished men rather than philosophers. Calvin sees that this minimalist equipage and their divine authority and power are stunningly contrastive: "They were not outstandingly clever or fluent," he observes, "but the excellence and novelty of their mission demanded more than human gifts: they had to derive authority from elsewhere" (1972: 1.290). In all of this, what must strike Christian readers of scripture at this distance is that to such simple

---

9. One of the most remarkable recent treatments of demonic possession and release—far more realistic than that which typically comes out of Hollywood—occurs in the recent Russian film *Ostrov* (The Island), directed by Pavel Lungin (2006).

and briefly instructed men Jesus entrusts what is effectively a measure of his own power. His power is not to be confused with any sufficiency of their own. One may well imagine that Luke, trying to get this down comprehensively on his page, would have had similar thoughts about his own inadequacy and felt empathy for the refractory line in Jorge Luis Borges's poem "Juan 1,14," where Borges has Jesus say, "I have entrusted the writing of these words to a common man."[10] This is just a stunning fact about the gospel commission. Yet for the apostles, theirs is an authority that will become apparent only after they have begun to act in obedience to the Lord's explicit command.

Once the apostles had spread out and were "preaching the gospel and healing everywhere" (9:6), the news about Jesus and the disciples' own ministry comes to Herod Antipas the Tetrarch, and it seems to him like a kind of nightmare. Rumors abound: some think that Elijah has returned, some think it is a resurrected prophet other than Elijah, and some think that John the Baptist has been raised from the dead (9:7–8). Mark 6:20 presents Herod as having greatly feared John the Baptist while he was alive, "knowing that he was a just and holy man"; his fear now returns, redoubled. He is reported as having said, in effect, "But I beheaded John already!" Now he says, "Who is this, of whom I hear such things?" (Luke 9:9). One senses more than curiosity here, but rather something like a tyrant's paranoia. When Luke adds that Herod "desired to see him" (KJV), there is an echo for readers of Matthew of Herod's father, Herod the Great, who had expressed a similar ominous "curiosity" about Jesus when Jesus was still a babe in Mary's arms.

As for the apostles, Luke tells us, once they had returned from their mission, they told him "all that they had done" (9:10a). One would like to have a record of this—and not least an account of what was said by Judas. Yet the verb Luke uses here is *diēgēsanto* ("they recounted"), a verbal form of the noun Luke uses to describe the genre in which he himself has written (*diēgēsis*), further strengthening our sense of his Gospel as a gathering of oral reports from participants or eyewitnesses.

Loaves and Fishes (9:11–17)

The account in Mark 8:1–10 and Matt. 15:32–39 is the second such miracle recounted by them and seems to be a separate incident from that recorded here in Luke. Matthew 14:13–21, Mark 6:32–34, and John 6:1–15 are nonetheless closely similar in detail to the feeding of the multitude recounted here. Because the story is so well attested, it is among the best known of Jesus's miracles,[11] and visual references to it appear in the second century as far away as China in the earliest

10. Jorge Luis Borges, *In Praise of Darkness*, trans. Norman Thomas di Giovanni (New York: Dutton, 1974), 15–16.

11. François Bovon calls it a "gift miracle"; *Luke 1: A Commentary on the Gospel of Luke 1:1–9:50*, trans. C. M. Thomas, Hermeneia (Minneapolis: Augsburg Fortress, 1989), 469.

Christian missionary sites, as well as in the Roman catacombs.[12] In this instance, something on the order of five thousand men, not counting women and children, are nearing the end of a day of absorbed listening to the teaching of Jesus when the Twelve urge Jesus to send the crowd away for food and lodging before night-fall (Luke 9:11–12). One may imagine that the "deserted place" near Bethsaida (9:10, 12) might imply that for many this would simply involve going home; for others, however, having come from farther away, it would not be so simple. Jesus's response is in any case arresting: "Just feed them," he says. The apostles protest that they have between them only five loaves and two fish—scarcely enough, one imagines, for themselves—and one wonders whether Bethsaida could provide sufficient provisions even if they or their women companions had enough money to buy it (9:13). Jesus, undistracted by these practical considerations, gets them to divide the crowd into a hundred companies of fifty each and have them sit down, and then he blesses the meal, "looking up to heaven" (9:16), breaking the two elements into pieces and giving it (*edidou*, he "continued to give") to the disciples to distribute. Augustine's sense is that the morsels grew in the hands of the Lord; by whatever means the small meal was multiplied, the entire crowd was fed to satisfaction, and twelve baskets of fragments left over were then gathered (9:17).

Understandably, this miracle has occasioned an ingenious array of modern efforts to explain it away.[13] It should rather be admitted that no such attempt removes the central difficulty for this, as indeed all of Jesus's other miracles; either it happened or it didn't. From the early church, which accepted the reality of the miracle as entirely consistent with Jesus's divinity and the character of God's special providence already revealed in the Old Testament (e.g., the manna and the quail; see Cyril 1983: Homily 48) or in the additional sense of spiritual sign in the fathers and medieval commentators represented by the comment of Ambrose that "the bread which Jesus breaks is truly the mystical word of God" (*Exposition of Luke* 6.86), there has developed a sense of the miracle as a sacramental sign. This is given clearly eucharistic overtones in the medieval period and is a sense still preserved in the Methodist hymn by Mary A. Lathbury (1877), "Break Thou the Bread of Life, / Dear Lord to me," as well as in references in both Anglican and Catholic liturgies. The emphasis of early commentaries that this miracle was one of superabundance (like the wine at Cana) extends in Cyril of Alexandria to the observation that in the twelve baskets that remained we have "a manifest proof that a work of love to our neighbor will claim a rich reward from God," and in John Chrysostom to the observation that there is a deliberate fittingness in the number of baskets, namely "that there might be as many baskets as disciples" (*Homilies on*

12. Floor mosaics in Asia Minor, the Trinity sarcophagus in the Lateran Museum in Rome (ca. AD 315), the representation in the Catacombs of Domittila (ca. AD 375) are all later than the stone relief carvings of this miracle—clearly five loaves and two fishes—in Luoyang, only recently come to light, which are thought to date from the second century.

13. See the catalogue assembled by Heindrik Van der Loos, *The Miracles of Jesus* (Leiden: Brill, 1965), and his splendid comment at p. 630.

Matthew 49). The very fact of the miracle is thus a sign of the abundance of the Lord "beyond what we can ask or think." Ambrose captures this sense of mystery: "Blessed is he who can collect those which remain over and above—even to the learned" (*Exposition of Luke* 6.90).

Jesus's Identity and Its Consequences (9:18–27)

We have noticed before that Luke is struck (more than the other Gospel writers) by the recurrent reports to him that Jesus often withdrew to pray alone; it seems likely that knowledge of this habit of the Lord comes to Luke, as it does here, because the disciples were often not far away from Jesus during these times. Mark 8:27–30 and Matt. 16:13–20 omit reference to Jesus's prayer on this occasion; Luke omits to mention the place, Caesarea Philippi. Here we see an instance of significant difference in narrative focus in Luke; he is more closely attuned to the role of prayer, the work of the Holy Spirit, the spiritual element in bodily disease (including sometimes a demonic element), and the place of forgiveness in the healing work of Jesus. All of these elements of observation in Luke's account play a part in his narrative disclosure of the identity of Jesus. *Where* things happen is of less interest, it seems, for the kind of narrative he is writing.

There is an acute pedagogy evident to the reader, at least, in Luke's representation of Jesus's asking his disciples, "Who do the crowds say that I am?" (9:18). One can only assume that Jesus already knows the answer and that his question has a deeper purpose. The disciples reiterate common opinions already known to the reader: John the Baptist, Elijah, or "one of the old prophets has risen again" (9:19). When Jesus then asks them, "But who do you say that I am?" he is effectively raising the disciples' awareness that, to themselves, as with the parable of the sower and seed, much more has been revealed. Peter gives the answer. He is definitive: "The *Christos* of God" (9:20). The term *christos* ("Anointed One") has Davidic overtones (e.g., reminiscent of 1 Sam. 16:12; 1 Kgs. 1:34; Dan. 9:26; Ps. 2:2) thoroughly integrated already in Luke 1. As many commentators point out, *christos* will also be Jesus's title at his trial (Luke 22:67) and crucifixion (23:35). Peter's confession here is nonetheless pivotal for Luke's entire Gospel, for it declares unambiguously that one clear difference between the disciples and the people generally is that they now recognize Jesus's true identity. Yet Jesus asks them to keep this knowledge to themselves for the time being (9:21), and he gives them an important counsel about a crucial aspect of his identity: the Son of Man must be rejected by the guardians of religious "correctness" and suffer, be slain, and resurrected on the third day (9:22). This must have been a jolt to their expectations, a disturbing warning about what it means for Jesus to be the *christos*, the Anointed of God.

Moreover, he now makes clear that they will share in his rejection and suffering—indeed *must* share in his suffering if they are to continue in faithfulness to him. His identity is to become, in measure, their identity also. So he says to them all, "If anyone desires to come after me, let him deny himself, and take up his cross daily, and follow me" (9:23). Much has been written about this declaration of the Lord; taken at face value, it is a severely daunting requirement for membership in his *koinōnia*. Yet it is a challenge to authentic discipleship that untold thousands upon thousands would soon enough meet at the cost of their lives and that millions have since. Whatever we think the good news of the gospel means, it clearly doesn't mean here something like "let the good times roll."

It is in that light that we should consider what Jesus says next: "For what profit is it to a man if he gains the whole world, and is himself destroyed or lost?" (9:25). Basil the Great captures the gist of the difference between authentic discipleship and the way of the world here clarified as simply a function of the divergence between what the believer sees in Jesus and what the world sees: "Now self-denial," he writes, "involves the entire forgetfulness of the past and surrender of one's will—surrender which is very difficult, not to say quite impossible, while living in the promiscuity customary in the world" (*Long Rules* 9.246–47). The marks of authentic discipleship are summarized in Jesus's three conditionals of 9:23: *arnēsasthō* ("deny oneself"), *aratō* ("take up"), and *akoloutheitō* ("follow"); these aspects of commitment express the substance of what it means to "come after," to imitate Christ. Luke is singular among the Gospel writers in recording that Jesus makes taking up one's cross *daily* the imperative, a point not lost on those who made this the "year-verse" for a calendar illustration in the Chinese churches in 1998. Chinese Christians know better than many what Basil the Great took to be self-evident, namely that "readiness to die for Christ, the mortification of one's members on this earth, preparedness for every danger which might befall us on behalf of Christ's name, detachment from this life—this it is to take up one's cross" (*Long Rules* 9.246–7). Writing many centuries later, Bonaventure adds (2001–4: 2.9.37) that this is the *imitatio Christi* to which Paul refers when he speaks of being "crucified with Christ" (Gal. 2:20) or "carrying about in the body the dying of the Lord Jesus" (2 Cor. 4:10), and it is this marker that sets apart believers, "those who belong to Christ . . . those who have crucified their flesh with its vices and passions" (Gal. 5:24, author's translation from Vulgate). In short, the standard for "coming after" or imitating Christ, for being an authentic disciple, is exacting. Aversion, or being "ashamed" of Jesus and his words, will be sadly insufficient in the day when the Son of Man comes in judgment (Luke 9:26). A sermon entitled "Self-Denial" by John Wesley on this verse is one of the best addresses to the text in post-Reformation times, insisting that the call to "take up the cross" is not for those with formal apostolic responsibilities only but is "of the most universal nature, respecting all times and all persons." Wesley defines self-denial as an axiom of seeking the will of God, "refusing to follow our own will, from a conviction that the will of God is the only rule of action to us" (1895: no. 48 [pp. 678–90, esp. 682]). This seems indeed to be the plain sense of the text.

The concluding statement of Jesus, that some hearing him "shall not taste death till they see the kingdom of God" (9:27), has been an enigma for many. It may be that what Jesus signifies here is not the realized kingdom of the last days but the kingdom as presently being inaugurated in the faithful lives of his true disciples, those to whom he could say, "the kingdom of God is within you" (17:21): that sense of the kingdom we find in Matt. 12:28 and again in Luke 10–11. It does not, at least in this passage, seem to refer to an eschatological reward but to immanent participation in the shared life of Christ, suffering for his sake as a consequence of truly identifying with him.

The Transfiguration (9:28–36)

It is also evident that when Peter, James, and John awake to see the transfigured Christ conversing with Moses and Elijah they are seeing, in some fundamental sense, into the kingdom of God. As much as they have been warned by Jesus that to identify with him as the Suffering Servant long announced means that they too must suffer, so here these three are given a glimpse of that glory reserved for Jesus and to be shared by his faithful.

Luke's version of this event is briefer than the parallel passages in Mark 9:2–10 and Matt. 17:1–9, but Luke has interesting details that their accounts lack. Oddly, Luke makes it eight days after Peter's confession, whereas Matthew and Mark have six days, a discrepancy accounted for by John of Damascus and Augustine by divergent methods of reckoning the gap, the other evangelists not counting the days at either end as complete days. But this is only one of several indications that Luke has his account from a different source (cf. Marshall 1978: 380–82, 387). Only Luke notes that Jesus "went up on the mountain to pray" (9:28) and that while he was praying "the appearance of his face was altered, and his robe became white and glistening" (9:29), details found in the other accounts but not connected to Jesus's prayer. Luke seems to avoid the Greek word for "transfiguration" (*metamorphōthē*) used by Mark and Matthew, perhaps because he had scruples about using a word so much associated with Hellenistic pagan mystery cults; his meaning, however, is the same. Luke also is unique in speaking of the conversation of Moses and Elijah as concerning Jesus's exodus (*exodon*), "which he was about to accomplish at Jerusalem" (Luke 9:31). This word, in this particular context, should probably not be translated "decease" (KJV, NKJV) or "departure" (RSV) (pace, e.g., Henry 1728: 671) but rather, as befitting the presence of Moses and the memory of that great exodus inaugurating the Feast of the Passover, "deliverance," and as having a clearly typological resonance. Perhaps the most powerful visual representation of this juxtaposition in Western art is the *Exodus* of Jewish painter Marc Chagall, in which the crucified hangs over the multitude fleeing behind Moses (1952–56). As at the first Passover the blood of the lamb slain marked out for deliverance the families of the chosen people who Moses would lead out of bondage and into freedom, so here we are on the cusp of the greater deliverance of which that was the harbinger. Jesus, the Chosen, Suffering Servant, and Lamb of God, for sinners to be slain, is the fulfillment of all that the law (Moses) and the prophets (Elijah) have spoken.

Peter the spokesman, James the first martyr, and John the beloved are selected to receive thus a privileged insight into the meaning of their spiritual history and its culmination in Jesus. For them, what they see is a paradigm of Jewish identity in which God as revealed in Jesus is united with all that God has been doing in the history of redemption. The radiance of Jesus's face would have recalled that of Moses coming down from the presence of God on Mount Sinai—except, as John of Damascus noted, that whereas Moses bore a reflected glory, our Lord's radiated from within, "proceeding from the inherent brightness of the divine glory" (*Sermon on the Transfiguration* 13). This radiance is accordingly a further manifestation to the disciples of the divine identity of Jesus; as Cyril of Alexandria has it, they were having a preview of Christ's eschatological return in majesty (1983: Homily 5). In Bede's way of putting it (*Homilies on the Gospels* 1.24), "the transfigured Savior shows the glory of his own coming for our resurrection. . . . As he then appeared to his apostles, [he] shall in like manner appear to all the elect." And he quotes to the point a later scripture: "It doth not yet appear what we shall be: but we know that when he shall appear, we shall be like him" (1 John 3:2 KJV). Calvin, focusing on the main text, adds that he gave them such a taste of his infinite glory as they were able to receive" (1972: 2.198).

When Luke says, "But Peter and those with him were heavy with sleep" (Luke 9:32; cf. 22:45–46), he may be hinting that Peter was his primary source for this account. Peter's response—thinking perhaps of the Feast of Tabernacles (Booths)—a suggestion that a booth or tabernacle be erected for each of Jesus, Moses, and Elijah, shows perhaps just how sleepy he was, or that he had yet to perceive the enormity of the event to which he had been a witness. Moses and Elijah, however great, are not on a par with Jesus. Only Luke mentions that Peter blurts this idea out just as Moses and Elijah were departing (9:33). Both Luke 9:34 and Matt. 17:5 note that even as he was speaking these words, a cloud, likewise reminiscent of the exodus, came over them and they were afraid. The reader attuned to scripture will immediately think of the cloud that "covered the tabernacle of meeting" when "the glory of the LORD filled the tabernacle" (Exod. 40:34). At that time Moses could not enter the tabernacle "because [of] the cloud" (40:35); here too, when the cloud has lifted, Jesus alone is present. Theophylact, an eleventh-century commentator, sees this cloud as a kind of "tabernacle not made with hands" (quoted in Aquinas, *Catena Aurea* 3.1.324), a harbinger of the reference to Christ himself in Hebrews. And for Calvin it is a sign that even those special apostles are "not yet fit to contemplate the brilliance of the heavenly glory"; he adds that the cloud ought to be regarded as an admonition to us as well "to hold back our frisky curiosity" concerning what was seen (1972: 2.200). The echo of Jesus's baptism (Luke 3:22) in the divine voice from the cloud is to Luke unmistakable: "This is my beloved Son [literally, "this is the Son of me, having been chosen"]. Hear him" (9:35). The reference to Jesus having been "chosen" (*ho eklelegmenos*) is found only in Luke (cf. Isa. 42:1). Mark 9:7 and Matt. 17:5 appear to echo the divine pronouncement at Jesus's baptism more precisely. The point in each case is clear: the Father's distinctive identification with the Son. What Luke adds uniquely, Gentile though he was, is a characteristically Jewish way of hearing it, tying the identity of Jesus even more closely to the messianic prophecies now being fulfilled. Jesus is God's distinctive, ultimate, authoritative Word; he is also the Suffering Servant, the true Israel, the Chosen. As the transfiguration ends, the three see Jesus "alone," and this time, they apparently need no warning to "keep it close," not to disclose "in those days any of those things they had seen" (Luke 9:36). They had been standing on very holy ground, and they now understood the identity of Jesus in a far more profound way than ever before. As Calvin says, also framing his remarks with an eye to the Epistle to the Hebrews, "And this is why the Apostle says in Hebrews [1:1] 'God, who at sundry times and diverse manners spake in time past through the prophets, hath in these last days spoken by his Son'" (1972: 2.201).

Imperfect Identity (9:37–62)

The Feast of the Transfiguration (August 6) began in the Eastern church and, as many works of art, literature, and liturgical references will attest, is most important there. In the West, where it was adopted more slowly, the Feast of the Transfiguration was not made official until 1457 under Pope Callistus III. In Byzantine art, it tends to be reflected symbolically in a way that ties it to apostolic identity with Christ as the Lamb of God: the apse mosaic at Sant' Apollinaire in Classe, for example, shows the three disciples as sheep beneath the vision. Raphael's last major work (1518) is a painting in which the great scene of the transfiguration is shown above a representation of the healing of the "epileptic" boy that follows immediately in all three Synoptic Gospels (Matt. 17:14–21; Mark 9:14–29). Whereas the Eastern tradition thus typically allegorizes the identity of the apostles with Jesus (himself represented in the Apollinaire mosaic, *imitatio Christi*, by the saint), the work by Raphael provides us a solid link to the balance of the chapter, in which it is the inadequacy of the disciples' achieved identity with Jesus that predominates as subject. In fact, this section constitutes a significant criticism of the disciples, one that would hardly have been pictured were these episodes an invention of the disciples, as is sometimes claimed. Early church commentators are in fact uncomfortable with this apparent criticism of the disciples (e.g., Cyril, Chrysostom), but the text seems unambiguous. These events can be summarized briefly. In the crowd at the foot of the mountain is a man with his "only child," a boy who is possessed by a spirit that is throwing him about bodily in a destructive fashion, with symptoms resembling an extreme form of epilepsy. The man claims that he has asked the disciples (presumably some among the other nine) for a healing, and they have proved unsuccessful. The disciples have been effective before; why not now? Luke hints at the reason in what follows; Matt. 17:19–21 gives it more fully in recording Jesus as telling them, "because of your unbelief"; essentially their problem is weak faith. Jesus himself heals the boy, rebuking the unclean spirit, but not before decrying his own followers in terms reminiscent of Old Testament denunciations of faithless Israel: they are a "faithless and perverse generation" (cf. Deut. 32:5, 20; Isa. 59:8). This must have stung. Nonetheless, because of the transformation in the boy, everyone present, says Luke, was "amazed at the mighty power of God" (Luke 9:43 KJV). Jesus now turns to his disciples and in an emphatic Hebraism that means essentially "memorize this" ("let these words sink down into your ears"), he repeats the substance of what he has said earlier (9:22): "The Son of Man is about to be betrayed into the hands of men" (9:44). But Luke records that they did not understand him in this context either and that they were afraid to ask him for a further explanation (9:45).

Instead, they fall into a puerile conversation among themselves, which, as Luke's language shows, quickly turns into an argument (*dialogismos en autois*) about who among them would be the "greatest" (9:46). This occasions a moment of still more painful embarrassment, especially in the context. When Jesus sets a little child before them, saying, "Whoever receives this little child in my name receives me; and whoever receives me receives him who sent me," he stresses the primary ground of identity with himself that the whole chapter has been developing. When he adds that whoever is "least" in worldly terms is "great" in his terms, he reveals plainly a dissonance, a failure in their comprehension of what it means to fully identify with Christ. Calvin follows the fathers here in suggesting that "children are not yet aware what rivalry is" (1972: 2.214) and that it is a property of adult ambition to scrabble after "the sweetness of honors."

It seems that the disciples, understandably, want to change the subject; John reports that an outsider has been casting out demons in Jesus's name and that the disciples "forbade him because he does not follow with us" (9:49). Sadly, this gesture, defensively meant to show that the disciples really are zealous to protect their special identification with Jesus, backfires. "Do not forbid him," says Jesus, "for he who is not against us is on our side" (9:50). The outsider is being effective, after all, and accomplishing good in Jesus's name. The contemporary reader should sense an accumulation of ironies here in Luke's text; all work to show the limitations of the disciples. Further, Jesus is underscoring the deep spiritual struggle between all that the demons represent and what he and his faithful followers represent and that, in a fashion the disciples still have not anticipated, the battle is about to intensify.

But so also intensified is the evident desire of the disciples to find a way of demonstrating to Jesus their loyalty. When the people in a nearby Samaritan village, perceiving that he was heading toward Jerusalem (the city representing much of what they had chosen not to identify with their own pieties), they will not hear him (cf. John 4:9). This is clearly a rejection of Jesus based on established religious prejudice and party spirit. But the disciples now exhibit an aggrieved sense of party spirit and offense of their own, and much more extremely. Unlike Abraham in Gen. 18, who wanted to *delay* the judgment of the Lord, they want to use their powers to call down capital judgment on the Samaritans: "Lord, do you want us to command fire to come down from heaven and consume them, just as Elijah did?" (Luke 9:54). This ill-thought attempt to ingratiate themselves with the Lord is sadly misguided. Jesus, evidently exasperated, rebukes them yet again, ignoring the Samaritans. Most painfully now for the disciples, his rebuke takes the strong form of saying to them, in effect, "You have no sense of who you are," or perhaps, "You have no self-knowledge." Still worse, the phrase "you do not know what manner of spirit you are of" (9:55) soundly refutes the very case for loyalty and affinity they have been trying to make. Jesus's words following now add a final blow; the utter inadequacy in their understanding of their own calling derives from a basic misunderstanding of the character of the Lord himself: "The Son of Man did not come to destroy men's lives," says Jesus, "but to save them" (9:56). Could anything be more obvious? Yet they have been blinded to the obvious by ambition and envious jockeying to be regarded as important. Sadly, in this self-righteous impulse they have had too many successors.

As the now somber group is on the way to the next village, still en route to Jerusalem, they are tagged by a volunteer, a would-be disciple (9:57); Jesus's well-known reply to him serves to highlight part of the cost of discipleship: "Foxes have holes and birds of the air have nests, but the Son of Man has nowhere to lay his head" (9:58). The poignancy of this remark is surely a marker for the loneliness Jesus feels in relation to the persistent incomprehension of those who would follow him. When he invites another person to follow him, that person demurs, saying he needs first to bury his father—probably an idiom meaning "my father is ill and frail; once he has died I will come." Jesus's response, one of his hard sayings, is a figure of speech that here may mean something like, "Let those who are dead to the kingdom of God take care of themselves—you take care of the kingdom" (9:60). Another would-be follower says that he needs to go back first and say good-bye to his family. Jesus treats all of these as dodges, pretexts for holding back on a total commitment. His final remark in this chapter summarizes the challenge to all who would *really* follow him, identifying with him authentically: "No one, having put his hand to the plow, and looking back, is fit for the kingdom of God" (9:62). This, to confused, uncomprehending, and perhaps even double-minded seekers, is the darkest warning of all. Half measures will not do.

LUKE 10

Luke alone says that after these events the Lord appointed seventy (a few Greek manuscripts, followed by the Vulgate and many modern English translations, say seventy-two) additional disciples and sent them to announce his coming.[1] Since it is unlikely that Jesus visited all the places to which, "two by two" (10:1), they went, we may imagine this as a general proclamation to the people that the Chosen One, the Anointed, had appeared and was making his way toward Jerusalem (Marshall 1978: 416). There is reason to think that the time was close to the Feast of Tabernacles (Booths) (Lightfoot 1979: 3.97) and that Peter's suggestion of "booths" at the transfiguration was in part a reflex of his anticipation of this important feast, the general harvest festival still widely celebrated in the time of Jesus (Josephus, *Jewish Antiquities* 8.100; 15.50).

An appreciation for this feast is helpful for our understanding of this chapter. Established as the Feast of Ingathering at year-end (Exod. 23:16; 34:22), in the context of tabernacle worship it was known variously in the Torah as the Feast of Booths (Lev. 23:33–36; Deut. 16:13–15) or the Feast of Tabernacles (2 Chr. 8:13); it is called by the latter name in the New Testament (John 7:2). One of three major feasts to which Jewish males were obliged annually (the others being Passover and Pentecost), it began on the fifteenth day of the seventh month (Tishri), about mid-October, and five days after Yom Kippur, the Day of Atonement. It lasted for a week and was known as a "pilgrim" festival, celebrating God's provision for his people during their forty years of postexodus desert wanderings, looking forward to the promised land. During this feast, especially after the time of Ezra (Neh. 8:13–18) a time of rejoicing for divine blessings emblemized in the harvest, booths were constructed out of interlaced willow branches, simple shelters in which the family ate special meals for the week. (Nowadays the *sukkah* ["booth"]

---

1. Lightfoot 1979: 3.94–99 thinks seventy was original and corresponded to the number of elders in the Sanhedrin (Mishnah, tractate *Sanhedrin* 1.5–6) and with Moses (Exod. 24:1, 9).

is made from plywood or similar materials.) According to Zech. 14:16–21, in the messianic "day of the LORD," a mark of the worshipful recognition of all nations will be a keeping of the Feast of Tabernacles by "com[ing] up to Jerusalem to worship the King, the LORD of hosts." In the time of Jesus's ministry, it was the preeminent family feast, comparable in some respects to harvest-home in Britain or Thanksgiving in North America.

Apostolic Duty (10:1–16)

In this light, when Jesus says, "The harvest truly is great, but the laborers are few," there is a natural context; when he says, "Therefore pray the Lord of the harvest [*tou kyriou tou therismou*] to send out laborers into his harvest," a symbolic language for evangelization—"bringing in the sheaves"—and preparation for the eschatological final feast is established, language that continues into the present both in hymnody and liturgy. But the work of the harvesters themselves is not to be unhindered; they will be "as lambs among wolves" (10:3). Then Jesus repeats the instruction he had earlier given (9:3–5) to the apostles to travel light and focus on the mission. They are to give a blessing to those who offer hospitality, eat what is set before them (perhaps being not too particular about *kashrut* restrictions, though this is unclear), heal the sick in such households, and announce the kingdom (10:4–9).[2] Rejection, as before (9:5), invites judgment and separation; the kingdom of God will have come near such people, but their rejection of it makes their disbelief more to be condemned in the last judgment than even the orgiastic wickedness of Sodom (10:12); they have seen the miracles of Jesus and refused to repent. Such people will therefore, even in Capernaum, freshly "exalted to heaven" by all that Jesus and his Twelve have done there, be "brought down to Hades" (10:15). The reason? Rejection of Christ, for when they reject the apostles and messengers, they are in effect rejecting both Jesus and God the Father who sent him. In fact, Jesus raises the notion of rejection to a higher register, using the strong verb *athetōn* ("despisers") (10:16). This is very strong language: the distinction between those who receive (*dechontai*) and those who are rejecting (*athetōn*) is sharp and uncompromising, and it presages other such distinctions Jesus will make.

Results and Recognition (10:17–24)

Luke tells us that "the seventy returned with joy, saying, 'Lord, even the demons are subject to us in your name'" (10:17). Here the disciples clearly recognize that

---

2. Early commentators saw the relation of the Twelve and the additional messengers as prefiguring the relationship of bishops or primary pastoral teachers and local priests; e.g., Augustine, *Questions on the Gospels* 1.2.1.14.

their authority depends upon Jesus, on the name of him whom they now call Lord. Jesus's response produces one of the most remarkable of the Lord's sayings: "I saw Satan fall like lightning from heaven" (10:18). The utterance is arresting. What does it mean? It seems in the context that we should understand his statement as a clear indication that the effect of the apostolic ministry now established has been a severe blow to the power of the adversary. The advent of the Messiah was expected in late Judaism to bring about an end of Satan's dominance over the world; this idea is evidently reflected in Rev. 12:8–9. It is not that Satan now becomes inactive, but it is "rather the end of his false transcendence" (Girard 2005: 185). Thus far in Luke we have seen Jesus deal with devils, demons, and evil spirits, and the apostles clearly have also done so in his name. But now we have the archaccuser, the master among demons (introduced in Luke 4 simply as "the devil"), named by his Old Testament name (Job 1:6; Zech. 3:1–2; 1 Chr. 21:1). Basil the Great says that "he is called Satan because he is an enemy to God (for this is what the Hebrew word signifies), but he is called also the devil, because he assists us in doing evil, and is then an accuser" ("Why God Is Not the Author of Evil"). In effect, in the war between God and Satan since the work of the serpent in Eden, Satan has had much power; the ministry of Jesus and the disciples marks the beginning of the end for Satan.

Jesus clarifies by saying that he has given disciples power that has, until now, largely been vested in himself and the Father alone—power "to trample on serpents and scorpions, and over all the power of the enemy" (Luke 10:19). This language recalls not only Gen. 3:15, which says that the offspring (seed) of the woman shall crush the head of the serpent, but also Deut. 8:11–19, where Moses reminds the people that their deliverance from bondage in Egypt and passage through a wilderness full of "fiery serpents and scorpions" is not a testament to their own strength but to the power of God. The allusion to covenant history helps to clarify what follows, when Jesus tells the disciples that rejoicing is indeed appropriate, not primarily because "the spirits are subject to you, but rather . . . because your names are written in heaven" (Luke 10:20). This too is a correction, though more gentle, and it is congruent with what Jesus says elsewhere about the last judgment, namely that there will then be people who will say, "Lord, Lord," and who will even go so far as to claim, "Have we not prophesied in your name, and cast out demons in your name, and done many wonders in your name?" and yet the Lord will say to them, "I never knew you; depart from me, you who practice lawlessness!" (Matt. 7:22–23). Some things, the disciples are here reminded, vastly exceed in importance the casting out of demons, even when that is done in Jesus's name. The efficient power in such action, of course, *resides in Jesus* and is not a credit to some cleverness or virtue of the immediate agent of that power.

But Jesus is happy, too, with their first great apostolic success. He lifts up his heart in prayer, rejoicing in spirit, and thanks his "Father, Lord of heaven and earth," invoking the one who sent him, the omnipotent God of the Old Testament. He gives thanks that God has "hidden these things from the wise and prudent," the literati and religiously educated scribes and Pharisees, and "revealed them to babes," the simple and unlettered disciples. He acknowledges further that this order of disclosure has been something that God himself has judged to be "good" (Luke 10:21). The repetition of "father" (*pater*) in his prayer stresses the intimate relationship between Jesus and God (cf. 6:36; 9:26; 11:2). What follows is perhaps the strongest christological declaration so far in Luke's Gospel: "All things have been delivered to me by my Father, and no one knows who the Son is except the Father, and who the Father is except the Son, and the one to whom the Son wills to reveal him" (10:22). This is a high point in the theme of identity in respect to Jesus and, by derivation, the disciples, as Luke has been developing. It is a powerful narrative moment, and when Jesus now turns to his disciples "privately" for an intimate recollection, he confirms the unprecedented blessedness of what has been revealed to them more fully than to any previous mortals: "Blessed are the eyes which see the things you see; for I tell you that many prophets and kings have desired to see what you see, and have not seen it, and to hear what you hear, and have not heard it" (10:23–24). All of the yearning for the full disclosure of God's promised redemption, generation after generation, has been looking toward a moment, a presence, a "tabernacle not made with hands" (Heb. 8:2; 9:11). At the very threshold of this tabernacle, so to speak, the disciples now stand.

The Great Commandment with Midrash (10:25–37)

"And behold [*kai idou*]," writes Luke, "a certain lawyer stood up" to put Jesus to the test with a question designed to expose the degree of his Jewish orthodoxy. The term *nomikos* is distinctive in Luke, and while sometimes also translated "scribe," "lawyer" better captures the gist of the speaker's intent: he is one focused on the law and its "correct" interpretation. This particular *nomikos* now asks, "What shall I do to inherit eternal life?" (10:25). There are similar accounts in Matt. 22:34–40 and Mark 12:28–34, but they come later in the events recorded by those Gospels. Matthew's and Mark's accounts do involve a scribe (Mark has *grammateus*), and each involves a recitation of the base principles of the law from Deut. 6:5 and Lev. 19:18. But there are also real differences: the scribes in Matthew and Mark ask about the "greatest" commandment, as distinct from the scribe in Luke, who is interested in the normative Jewish issue of "eternal life." Also, as Talbert points out (2002: 120), in Luke's narrative there is an edge to the question of the scribe that immediately becomes evident as a matter of tone; this fellow is more clearly baiting Jesus, yet in a way that focuses on a fundamental issue, namely the life practices necessary to be numbered among those who, as the rabbis would say, share in the life of the blessed in the world to come. He does not imagine that any can be justified at the resurrection who are not righteous Jews. What the scribe professes to wish to know is, "What counts as righteousness?" Regardless of his motives, this for a serious Jew was the least trivial of questions (cf. *Genesis Rabbah* 28b; *Pirke Avot* 2.7; Babylonian Talmud, tractate *Sotah* 7b). In Luke, finally, it is not Jesus who quotes the texts from Deuteronomy but the lawyer, in what Jesus greets as the correct answer (10:28). "Do this, and you will live," says Jesus, echoing the Torah precisely. All of these differences suggest that we are dealing with discrete events, but also that this point about the summary of the law was a repeated theme in Jesus's teaching.[3] It is not surprising, then, that the parable of the good Samaritan that follows as a kind of midrash on the question asked by Luke's *nomikos* is found uniquely in Luke's Gospel. The story is occasioned, as often in Luke, by a moment of awkward embarrassment in the questioner (typically a disciple). So "he, wanting to justify himself," asks Jesus, "Who is my neighbor?" (10:29). It is this observation as to motive that clarifies a major point about theological questions both in scripture and beyond it: this particular question presents itself as an enquiry after the good, or justice, but is actually something else. It is not the commandment to love one's neighbor per se that is likely to be most problematic for the lawyer but rather the legal question about excluded groups (Philo, *Special Laws* 2.15).

Few parables of Jesus are so well known as this story of the good Samaritan. One reason for this must surely be the counterintuitive redefinition of what is meant by "neighbor." Normative Jewish views on this matter excluded the Samaritans specifically, since they were after all a proscribed group. Accordingly, they were among those to whom one owed no social obligation and with whom one could not so much as break bread without censure (Babylonian Talmud, tractate *Sanhedrin* 57a); they were in this sense like Gentiles or ritually unclean persons. The Samaritans heartily reciprocated the prejudice. But surely there are few of us who do not have our own versions of the resistance to the demands of neighborliness that Jesus proposes: hence the universal apropos of the story. As Jesus tells his parable there is much realism in it; highway robbery and attendant brutalizing of victims on the road from Jerusalem to Jericho were all too common. There is something of a pinch for the lawyer when Jesus says that the severely wounded victim, "half dead" (*hēmithanēs*), is bypassed successively by a priest and a Levite, two members of the religious class. The one who does stop to help is evidently a layman; worse, he is religiously opprobrious, a Samaritan. Worse still, this Samaritan is no legal minimalist: he takes careful prophylactic measures with the victim's wounds, takes him to an inn (a *pandocheion*, not a *katalyma* as in Luke 2), stays with him during the first night to ensure that he is responding to treatment, then leaves two pence with the innkeeper (at that time enough for a three-week stay), and says that any further expense (the victim has, after all, been robbed) he will repay on his return. The standard for who should be understood as one's neighbor is not the only thing shattered by Jesus's midrash on the law of love; in this story, authentic love for the neighbor is expressed in an extravagance of generosity. However uncomfortable he is with the narrative, the lawyer gets it:

3. T. W. Manson, *The Sayings of Jesus* (Grand Rapids: Eerdmans, 1979), 260.

when Jesus asks his rhetorical question about who acted as a neighbor to the man who fell among thieves, the response is unavoidable: "He who showed mercy on him" (10:37). When Jesus tells him to go and do likewise, we recognize that a question about an abstraction, "the neighbor," and about justice according to the law has been turned by Jesus into a personal commandment to show mercy. As philosopher Paul Ricoeur says in his excellent short essay on this parable, Jesus is not articulating a "sociology of the neighbor"; he is showing forcefully that "one does not *have* a neighbor. I make myself someone's neighbor." It is this element, for Ricoeur, that most trenchantly expresses a "radically anti-modern attitude." He goes so far as to say that "the Gospel would totally condemn the modern world ... denounce it as a world without the neighbor, the dehumanized world of abstract, anonymous and distant relationships."[4]

The theme of the conjoined commandment to love God in a total, all-encompassing way, and out of that to love the neighbor as oneself, was regarded by medieval writers as one single and basic rule for the Christian life. They referred to it as the law of love. There is much biblical warrant for this compression, and it is assembled in the short treatise of that title written by Richard Rolle, sometime before 1350.[5] The good Samaritan story casts a practical light on the love of God for the *kosmon* ("world") (John 3:16), which those who reciprocate his love are called to imitate at many levels. There is a polyvalent aspect to the good Samaritan, who reminds us by his action that on the biblical definition, "God is love" (1 John 4:16) in a wider sense than might occur to us. Since Jesus himself is the "image of the Father" (2 Cor. 4:4; Col. 1:15; 3:10; Heb. 1:3), what he is teaching in such passages is primary theology, intensifying what he has already told his disciples earlier, namely that to follow him is to walk in a moral way of life in which everything is verified or falsified in terms of actual godly behavior rather than formal or legal understanding. He is also showing them poetically that they are called to nothing less than to imitate, as *imago Dei*, the divine prototype (cf. 2 Cor. 3:18). Girard grasps this point well: Jesus "commits all his powers to imitating his Father. In inviting us to imitate him, he invites us to imitate his own imitation" (2005: 13). It need hardly be said that this standard entirely alters the perspective in which questions about obligation or justice may be raised and considered. The totalizing character of the commandment to love the Lord your God with all one's "heart" (*kardia*), "consciousness" (*psychē*), "will" (*ischys*), and "intelligence" (*dianoia*) (Luke 10:27) makes the radical character of the kind of neighbor-love the good Samaritan exhibits a necessarily corollary: neighbor love, too, must be total and unstinting (Fitzmyer 1981–85: 2.880). The familiar Calvinist distinction between faith and works in regard to eternal life is not at issue here. What is at issue is the "perfection" to which we are called, in imitation of

4. Paul Ricoeur, "The *Socius* and the Neighbor," in his *History and Truth*, trans. Charles A. Kelbley (Evanston, IL: Northwestern University Press, 1965), 98–109.

5. David Lyle Jeffrey, ed., *The Law of Love: English Spirituality in the Age of Wyclif* (Grand Rapids: Eerdmans, 1988; repr., Vancouver: Regent, 2006), 155–61.

Christ to present ourselves as "a living sacrifice" (Rom. 12:1) and so to conform to the "perfect will of God" (12:2). "Be ye therefore perfect, even as your Father which is in heaven is perfect" (Matt. 5:48 KJV; cf. Lev. 11:44; 19:2; 20:7; 1 Pet. 1:16). To follow Jesus will not only take us out of our comfort zone, as was suggested to would-be disciples in the latter part of Luke 9; when we put the totality of our personhood into loving God, we will find ourselves axiomatically living out *his* love in a self-sacrificial way toward others. This too is *imitatio Christi*, as perhaps Origen, Ambrose, Theophylact, and others also intended, when in their allegorical readings of the parable they identified the good Samaritan with Christ.

Thus, while most of the exegesis of this parable is moral theology, reflecting the tropological or moral force of the text (which indeed was its point in the immediate context), the allegorical sense of the text is an added dimension that struck early Christian interpreters as a characteristic register for further contemplation of the believer. On this level the parable reveals itself as essentially christological, broadly hinting at Christ's full soteriological identity, his own saving ministry to a sin-wounded world. For Origen, as for Ambrose and Augustine after him, we can see in the poor traveler, descending from Jerusalem, the *visio pacis*, toward Jericho, a city identified with the sin of the world, a kind of everyman figure, embodying in his descent from divine intention the universal journey into the fallen world of the first Adam. On this reading the robbers are the demonic assaults and depredations of sin, which indeed leave us bereft of substance and half dead. The priest and Levite are figures for the law and the prophets, or for the establishments of religiosity, which do not minister to our condition. Christ is the good Samaritan, the one regarded as outcast by these religiously proper persons and institutions but who actually seeks and saves the lost at his own expense. The *pandocheion* or inn is like the church, which receives the wounded first Adam for whom the Second Adam, Christ, alone has made saving provision. This Christ, moreover, will return to his church and restore all accounts one day (Origen, *Homilies on Luke* 34; Ambrose, *Exposition of Luke* 7.73–74; Augustine, Sermon 179A.7–8). At this level, the parable of the good Samaritan is not only an explicit guide to loving our neighbor as ourselves but also tacitly and more deeply an insight into the history of human salvation as the early church saw it revealed in scripture and fulfilled in the ministry of Christ. In Luke's schema for his Gospel, it comes near to the midpoint of his symmetrically organized narrative and is in the spiritual sense a synecdoche, a précis of the whole biblical story of salvation.

Mary and Martha (10:38–42)

If Luke 10 had ended with the parable of the good Samaritan, we might be justified in thinking that the proper end of the Christian life is generous service to others, exceeding in its abundance what the law alone might be thought to require. This brief pericope, however, balances our perspective in a crucial way. This is one case where the sometimes artificial thirteenth-century chapter divisions of Archbishop of Canterbury Stephen Langton have it just right: the true disciple of Jesus must surely love and serve his neighbors—even those not normally thought of as neighbors—but the Lord must be loved first and always. Communing with him, being in his presence and taking in his instruction, is accordingly fundamental nourishment for the balanced Christian life.[6]

This episode is recorded only by Luke, and it may be yet another indication that the women who followed Jesus were among his most important informants. If Lightfoot is right in connecting this event to the days immediately preceding in this chapter (1979: 3.110), then the time of this visit to the house of Mary and Martha is during the celebration of the Feast of Tabernacles, and Martha is doubtless preparing a festive meal. Much work in the kitchen would be involved, and we should not be entirely surprised that Martha was miffed that her sister, so far from helping with preparation of the meal to come, was sitting at the feet of Jesus, listening to him. The reflexive *parakathestheisa* ("she sat herself beside") indicates that Mary's gesture—and choice—was deliberate (Fitzmyer 1981–85: 2.893). It was also most unusual: women were not in Judaism permitted to sit at the feet of a rabbi, since discipleship in their context was reserved for men alone. Martha's accusation, that Mary "has left" her to do all the work by herself (Bock 1994–96: 2.1041), well enough suggests that she hopes that Jesus will send Mary back to the kitchen (10:40). But Jesus, in a loving double enunciation of Martha's name, commends and corrects her for being "troubled about many things" (10:41); what Martha is doing by way of service to the Lord is good, but what Mary is doing is actually better: "One thing is needful," Jesus says, "and Mary hath chosen that good part, which shall not be taken away from her" (10:42 KJV). The "good part" (*tēn agathēn merida*), the fathers suggest, is a figurative reference to a better meal, as Augustine puts it, the Bread of Life (Sermon 179.5). The point, Augustine says elsewhere (Sermon 108, cited in Aquinas, *Catena Aurea* 3.1.380), is not that we should imagine a stern disapprobation of the service of Martha, for that would undercut all that has previously been taught, but rather that Jesus here distinguishes between two kinds of duties incumbent upon the faithful disciple.

This distinction later will become symbolic of a choice of vocation between the active and contemplative life. Gregory the Great, following John Cassian, writes in *Moralia* 6.18 of the passage in this way, and many spiritual writers from medieval to modern times repeat him. It is probably to some degree true that, while medieval Christians were inclined to elevate the choice of the contemplative Mary over the active Martha, in Western Christianity since the Reformation the Martha model has become ascendant. Calvin, in fact, sets the Protestant emphasis when he strongly resists any interpretation of this episode that would seem to praise the contemplative over the active life, referring to the earlier view

6. An excellent digest of ancient as well as modern scholarship on this episode, focused on the elegant painting by Allesandro Allori, is provided by Hornik and Parsons 2003–7: 2.111–33.

of his medieval predecessors as "wickedly perverted" and assuring his readers that "Christ was far from intending that his disciples should devote themselves to idle and frigid speculations" (1972: 2.89). Graham argues persuasively that the "way of Mary" has continued to be regarded as the higher calling in Eastern Orthodoxy.[7] Here, as an epilogue to the main narrative thrust of this and the previous chapter, it seems that Luke intends us to perceive a complementarity: while active service of the Lord coupled with love of one's neighbor is a hallmark of the disciple's life, none can long practice it rightly without sitting at the feet of the Lord. Another way of putting this would be to say that the commandment to love our neighbor as ourselves is subsequent to and dependent upon our loving the Lord our God with all our heart, soul, strength, and mind. In the spirit of Ps. 119:57–64, drawing near to God and attending, undistracted, to his word is certainly essential to developing that kind of self-effacement: in the apt comment of twelfth-century Cistercian William of St. Thierry, *amor ipse intellectus est* ("love itself is understanding").

7. Stephen Graham, *The Way of Martha and the Way of Mary* (New York: Macmillan, 1917).

LUKE 11

In Luke's Gospel, we see Jesus praying so frequently that we recognize that our author intends not only a leitmotif but a major theme evident to him from the accounts of Christ's actions he has gathered. As a theme, it is here in this chapter drawn to a high moment; we see the disciples not only noticing but also wishing to imitate the Lord by learning from him how to pray. By this point they have been taught how to understand him as *kyrios* ("the Lord") and to strive for a totality of love for God and neighbor that bears fruit not only in the active life but also in the docility of heart necessary to learn at his feet. Understanding something of the character of his prayer is now most appropriate. That they refer to John having taught his disciples how to pray suggests that they are thinking perhaps of common prayer, the sort of prayer appropriate to them as a community of his disciples.

The Lord's Prayer (11:1–13)

What the early church called the *pater hēmon* in the East and *pater noster* ("Our Father") in the West quickly became a central part of Christian worship, as well as a pattern for understanding the appropriate general character of believers' prayer. Today most Protestant Christians who use common or liturgical prayer recite the version found in Matt. 6:9–13 (with its concluding doxology from 1 Chr. 29:11); it occurs there in a public setting as a prayer Jesus prays himself. The context for this prayer in Luke is more private and lacks the concluding doxology; it is the one favored in Catholic liturgy. Given the divergent contexts, the omitted lines in Luke are less likely to be omissions from a common source than reflections of a distinct occasion; in this second instance, it is, however, evidently a pattern of prayer that Jesus is concerned to teach. This text is the only place where a request for instruction in prayer occurs in the Gospels (Marshall 1978: 456), and it is important that we recognize it as coming from a group familiar with Jewish liturgical prayer—common prayer doubtless used by themselves as well as by Jesus in the synagogues. It may be an indication that the disciples are sensing that, somewhat like John the Baptist and his disciples, they have a community both Jewish and yet distinctive, one that needed now a form of common prayer more reflective of their knowledge of Jesus's identity.

There are familiar Jewish elements in the prayer model Jesus gives them, as well as distinct differences. It might be argued that more of the familiar is to be found in the Matthew version that ends with a benediction reflective of the Kaddish, a prayer with which the synagogue service ended: "Exalted and hallowed be his great name in the world which he created according to his will. May he permit his kingdom to rule in our days, and in the lifetime of the whole house of Israel, speedily and soon."[1]

A rabbinic prayer also has clearer parallels to the Matthew version: "Bring me not into the power of sin, nor into the power of guilt, nor into the power of temptation" (*Genesis Rabbah* 60b). When the congregation recites the Shema (from Deut. 6:4), "Hear, O Israel: the Lord our God is one Lord" (KJV), at the point they reach the word "one" (*'eḥād*), the leader says, "Blessed be the name of the glory of his kingdom forever and ever." Some in the early church accordingly wondered whether Jesus was indicating that his followers should pray specifically "only to the God and Father of all, to whom even our Savior himself prayed" and concluded that this is indeed the appropriate divine address, although it is through the name of Jesus that access is assured (Origen, *On Prayer* 15.1–2); this kept the form of prayer among early Christians closer to a Jewish pattern. Finally, there are echoes in both versions of the *Shemoneh Esreh* ("Eighteen Benedictions").

Other differences may be more a matter of nuance. The first of these, evident in both Matthew and Luke, is the comparative intimacy of address: the disciples are encouraged to address God as "Father" (Greek *pater*, Aramaic *abba*). Though this is certainly a divergence from normative Old Testament usage, it seems to have been a less sharp break in first-century contexts; in late (intertestamental) texts such as Sirach 23.1 and 51.10 and *Shemoneh Esreh* 4–6, "father" occurs alongside terms such as *kyrios* ("Lord") and *despotēs* ("master"). (This connection of "master" and "father" was well established also in pagan Roman culture at the domestic level, such as in the term *pater familias*.)

Regarding the following locution, often misunderstood, an excellent commentary on the Lord's Prayer by an anonymous fourteenth-century English cleric clarifies responsibly the now-archaic phrase "hallowed be thy name," in a manner suggested by Augustine (Sermon 56): "When we say 'hallowed be thy name,' we are actually praying that we who say this will be sanctified and brought to spiritual maturity [the original says "perfection"] by the holy name of God and his grace and mighty works, and that we will become sanctified by his grace—for our

1. C. W. Dugmore, *The Influence of the Synagogue upon the Divine Office* (Oxford: Oxford University Press, 1944).

Father is already holy in and of himself."[2] The next petition, "thy will be done," obtains an unusual application in Luther, who counsels that it should be prayed directly against the devils and demons.[3]

Here, as Jesus's subsequent stories will indicate, however, we are to think of the Father in his loving and provident role (Luke 11:5–13). The suggestion of loving intimacy is clearly enhanced by the language. There is also a greater sense of immediacy; whereas in the *Shemoneh Esreh* one prays for sustenance through the year, here it is for "daily bread"; the petition is not directed to securing a state of comfort but having needs met each day as they come. (The phrase seems also to imply an expectation of habitual, daily prayer.) But in 11:4 we sense the distinctive character of Jesus's instruction in the formula requesting divine forgiveness for sin: "And forgive us our sins, for we also forgive everyone who is indebted to us." This is the one clause that has no known origin in Jewish prayer. Matthew 6:12 used "debts" and "debtors," while Luke used both "sins" (*hamartia*) and "debt" (*opheilō*) here, and his version intensifies the conditional element in our request for forgiveness by requiring a precondition: "For we also forgive everyone who is indebted to us." As Origen puts it, Luke says essentially "the same thing as Matthew, but does not seem to leave room for the person who wishes to forgive debtors only if they repent" (*On Prayer* 28.7–8). The final clause may refer to the desire to be freed from the power of sin and possibly also to be protected from the powers of evil in the world, such as is manifest in the ongoing battle between Jesus and his followers and the forces of darkness in the world. Luther here again stresses that this prayer should be directed against demonic forces and "the dominion of Satan."[4]

In all respects, the Lord's Prayer as found in both Luke and Matthew is a "concise direction for the Godward life of the soul," as Evelyn Underhill puts it. In this prayer, she continues, "the soul opens its eyes upon Reality and discovers itself to be a child of the Eternal Perfect; and [that] the essence of worship is to be a total devotion to his interests, hallowing his name and cooperating in the action of his will."[5] The Lord's Prayer clearly invites, as Jan van Ruysbroeck wrote in the fifteenth century, "a turning of all things of the self into the freedom of the Will of God."[6] It is in this respect a summary of all that Jesus has been teaching, by his words and by his example, so that once again the disciples are invited by the very form of this prayer into an action of *imitatio Christi*, imitation of their Lord. As he prays to the Father, so also should we. With Underhill, we should recognize that "the Lord's prayer looks towards a goal in which every action shall

---

2. Quoted in David Lyle Jeffrey, ed., *The Law of Love: English Spirituality in the Age of Wyclif* (Grand Rapids: Eerdmans, 1988; repr., Vancouver: Regent, 2006), 102.

3. Martin Luther, *Ten Sermons on the Catechism*, Luther's Works 51 (St. Louis: Concordia, 1990), 175 ("Petitions of the Lord's Prayer").

4. Ibid., 179–80.

5. Evelyn Underhill, *Worship* (Cambridge, UK: Clark, 2010), 224.

6. Jan van Ruysbroeck, *The Twelve Béguines*, trans. John Francis (London: Dent, 1913), chap. 7.

be an act of worship; an utterance of the Name."[7] Indeed, given the double sense of the Hebrew word *ăbōdâ* to signify both "work" and "worship," Underhill's comment is an excellent summary.

The short illustrative narrative with which Jesus then continues his discourse on prayer underscores the desire of the heavenly Father to be generous toward his children. Jesus makes use of analogies. A friend will not refuse a friend who has an unexpected visitor and finds himself with an empty larder; even if he is asleep and the request is a nuisance, such a friend will certainly answer need, especially if the petitioner is persistent (11:5–8). The disciples are accordingly encouraged to beseech the heavenly Father with confidence in their own time of need: "Ask, and it will be given to you; seek, and you will find; knock, and it will be opened to you" (11:9). The parallel assurance of the next verse is explicit; the point, as Augustine says, is that "he would not so encourage us to ask were he not willing to give" (Sermon 108). In the rhetorical example that follows, Origen has seen an echo of the temptation of Jesus in Luke 4: "God does not in the place of bread offer a stone, which the devil wishes Christ to eat" (*On Prayer* 28.10). In his conclusion, Jesus shows that the function of the analogy is in part to show how much more generous and ready to give is God than we are, yet suddenly that which God is said to provide is not material needs or even forgiveness but something more: "If you then, being evil, know how to give good gifts to your children, how much more will your heavenly Father give the Holy Spirit to those who ask him" (11:13). This last is clearly a different order of gift. At this point, the entire discourse moves into a new register of meaning.

Of Signs and Skepticism (11:14–36)

When Jesus casts a devil out of a man long dumb (the parallel account in Matt. 12:22–30 suggests that he is also blind), the man then speaks. The crowd heard, but by now there was evident animosity in their response (less evident in Mark 3:22–27). It is this dissension, and the reasons for it, that occupy Luke's attention. The crowd taunts Jesus, some saying he casts out demons through Beelzebub. Others, not content with what they have seen, "testing him, sought from him a sign from heaven" (Luke 11:14–15). There is an echo here too of an earlier temptation, that by Satan in Luke 4, and it suggests rather strongly that the contest between Christ and Satan is coming out into the open in a nasty way. For early Christian cultures, this part of the Gospel has typically seemed immediately relevant. For example, the ninth-century Anglian poem *Christ and Satan* gets its name from the way in which it links the temptation of Jesus, the casting out of demons in his ministry, and this Lukan challenge to his divinity to the various deceptions by which Satan strives to turn the disciple likewise away from the word of God

---

7. Underhill, *Worship*, 226.

and toward counterfeit notions of authority; as the poet's elder countryman Bede, whose own grandparents were pagans, observes (in regard to 11:21–22), Satan's "arms . . . are the craft and wiles of spiritual wickedness, but his spoils are the men themselves, who have been deceived by him" (Commentary on 1 John 5:19).

The name "Beelzebub" for the devil requires explanation. Sometimes spelled Beelzebul in Jewish texts, it relates the pagan god Baal to the Hebrew word for excrement, *zĕbûl*, and, as Lightfoot notes, this creative etymology probably has its origins in impolite Jewish imprecations against the idolatrous worship of their pagan neighbors (1979: 3.114–16). The English form is derived from transliteration in Latin, and in early Christian commentaries the original meaning is sometimes softened to "lord of the flies," as in the title of the novel by William Golding (1954). It is one of a number of names for Satan in Judaism, such as Belial, Mastemah, Sammael, and Asmodeus (the discussion by Fitzmyer 1981–85: 2.921 is helpful). Paul uses Belial (2 Cor. 6:15), Asmodeus is found in Tobit 3.8, 17, and Sammael, which occurs frequently only in the Talmud, makes its way into Charles Williams's novel *Descent into Hell* (1937). The point here in Luke's account, given that the skeptics were Jews speaking Aramaic, is that the term "Beelzebub" applied to Jesus is not merely derogatory but the worst sort of insult possible, a real blasphemy.

When Jesus responds, it is with logic; his reply is a *reductio ad absurdum* of the charge of his opponents.[8] He knows what they are really thinking and not saying and exposes their fallacy straightforwardly: it is self-contradictory to assert that Satan works against himself in this way, for, as anyone with a sense of Israel's history knows, a house divided against itself cannot stand (Luke 11:17–18). The proverb stings. Jesus is not assuaging the crowd here but taking them on. Moreover, he implicates them more deeply when he refers to Jewish practices of exorcism, as Calvin suggests (1972: 2.421; see Acts 19:11–16): "If I cast out demons by Beelzebub, by whom do your sons cast them out? Therefore they will be your judges" (Luke 11:19). Bede makes a similar point (*Homilies on the Gospels* 2.6). Luther, in his treatise *On the Bondage of the Will*, makes this discourse central to his thesis that the human will cannot successfully be independent. For Luther, as for the popular musician Bob Dylan, "you've got to serve somebody"; the effect of Jesus's declaration is that Satan's forces remain potent and that one has to choose. Either the listener will be for Christ or, perforce, he or she will be with Satan. The will, says Luther, "is a captive, a slave, and servant to the will of God, or to the will of Satan."[9]

Others in the crowd have asked for "a sign from heaven" (11:16). It is hard to tell whether this request arises purely from skepticism or from a voyeuristic desire for spectacle. Cyril of Alexandria (1983: 80) is among those who have observed

---

8. Douglas Groothuis, *On Jesus*, Wadsworth Philosophers Series (Toronto: Wadsworth, 2002), 34–35.

9. Martin Luther, *The Bondage of the Will*, trans. J. I. Packer and O. R. Jonston (Old Tappan, NJ: Revell, 1957), §§25–26.

that the request indicates, in effect, an obtuse denial of the many signs they have already seen; Luke's text justifies this inference in his use of the imperfect verb *ezētoun*, they "were seeking" a sign, always and insatiably. In any case, Jesus indicates clearly by the manner of his reply that the skeptics are really cynics; they are not seeking to discover any truth, but in the habitual manner of those who refuse evidence in any time and place, they are really engaged in a mockery of inquiry, hence in intellectual dishonesty. When Jesus says, "But if I cast out demons with the finger of God, [then] surely the kingdom of God has come upon you" (11:20), the sense of eschatological judgment in the last phrase is obvious. When Jesus uses the Hebraism "finger of God," the Jewish hearer who has familiarity with the scriptures will remember that, after the miracles of Moses, Pharaoh's magicians exclaimed, "This is the finger of God" (Exod. 8:19), and perhaps yet more pertinently in this context, that in Dan. 5:5–6, 24–28 the doomed Belshazzar and his sacrilegious companions saw the hand and finger of God write their judgment upon the wall. The memories that Jesus appears to call to mind are not complimentary to the Jewish skeptics; in effect, Jesus is telling them that their attitude is both pagan and idolatrous, hence their blasphemous accusations. To conclude his rebuke of the skeptics Jesus now intensifies the contrast between himself and the adversary, referring to Satan as "a strong man . . . armed" by indicating that "a stronger than he comes upon him and overcomes him" (Luke 11:22). Here, John Chrysostom suggests, Jesus is referring to Satan's "ancient dominion" now to begin its sure demise (*Homilies on Matthew* 41). The imagery is of a battle, and Jesus makes it unmistakably clear to his interlocutors that they are going to have to pick a side: "He who is not with me is against me, and he who does not gather with me scatters" (11:23). Both those who are hostile to Jesus through envy, as Cyril says (1983: Homily 80), and those who try to avoid a choice are, in effect, already of the devil's party.

But Jesus is not finished with his critique of the opposition, here specifically of those who have been content with the Jewish exorcists. When an unclean spirit is cast out of someone, he says, it wanders restless until it finds someone to inhabit. Finding things cleaned up in his original abode and it still vacant, he sometimes moves right back in with "seven other spirits more wicked than himself," making the state of the repossessed person worse than ever it was (11:24–26). One thinks here of Mary Magdalene, out of whom Jesus had cast seven demons. These seven may, as Cyril suggests (1983: Homily 81), signify a plentitude of the vices, but the prayer surely indicates that if the powers of darkness that are driven out are not replaced by the kingdom of God within (see Calvin 1972: 2.44), things will only become much worse.

At this point an enthusiast in the crowd, unusually for the time a woman, blurts out, "Blessed is the womb that bore you" (11:27). Jesus's reply is less a rebuke of this woman than one of his classic and charitable redirections of a well-intentioned misperception: "Yea rather, blessed are they that hear the word of God, and keep it" (11:28 KJV). In the context of the ongoing contest between Christ and Satan that Luke has been recounting (Luke is the only evangelist to note this particular incident), Jesus's response is linked to the entire theme as it has unfolded through Luke's Gospel: true affiliation with him is a matter of obedience to God's word; God's word is the only sure means of combating Satan; and identification with Christ in doing the will of the God who sent him means choosing to side with Jesus in the great conflict.

By this time the crowd is getting noticeably larger; perhaps the word has spread that there has been something of a face-off brewing. Jesus, aware of his audience and of the presence of inhospitable motives, does not back down from his judgment. Now he takes aim at the predilection of those who are always seeking for a "sign"—some miraculous authentication or even just a mysterious phenomenon. "This is an evil generation. It seeks a sign, and no sign will be given to it except the sign of Jonah the prophet" (11:29). Now at first blush this remark would be enigmatic; when he clarifies by describing Jonah as a sign to the Ninevites, his Jewish audience would think of the repentance of the Gentiles whom Jonah actively disliked, and the analogy would strengthen the accumulation of suggestions in Jesus's remarks that his adversaries were more like the pagan *goyim* in their hearts than like the chosen people. Later readers of scripture would extend Jesus's analogy typologically, as Cyril does, to the whole of his "passion on the cross and resurrection from the dead" (1983: Homily 12). In the immediate context, the emphasis is surely on the implied rhetorical question: "If the Ninevites repented then, why not the skeptics now?" The analogy of the Queen of Sheba (here, "the queen of the South"), likewise a Gentile, coming to Solomon and recognizing his superior wisdom, accords: even Gentiles have repented, even Gentiles have recognized wisdom, and "a greater than Solomon is here" (11:31). As Bonaventure says, citing 1 Cor. 1:24, "Solomon was wise, but Christ *is* Wisdom" (2001–4: 2.11.1092). But when Jesus says that the men of Nineveh shall rise up in the judgment with this generation and condemn it, his Jewish audience is sure to be scandalized: the idea that Gentiles should judge Jews turns the normative Jewish prejudice inside out (Talbert 2002: 138–39).

At this point Jesus softens his tone somewhat, appealing perhaps to the faithful Jews in the crowd. His proverbs about the candle and bushel basket and about a healthy eye making external light into illumination for the whole body suggest plainly that health is possible when the "eye is good" (Luke 11:34). In these sayings Ambrose (*Exposition of Luke* 7.98) sees a reflection of Jesus's theme about the word of God being a light to lighten our path, citing Ps. 119:105; Origen (quoted in Aquinas, *Catena Aurea* 3.2.414) takes the eye to be metonymic for understanding generally. But there is perhaps an ironic barb here too, for surely "the evil eye" is what many in the crowd have been giving to Jesus. Bonaventure sees these sayings as speaking to the necessity, when we ourselves are coming to God's word, of having a "simplicity of right intention" and says that "an evil eye corrupts the will and makes it evil" (2001–4: 2.11.1096–1100, esp. §74). His point parallels that of the *Glossa Ordinaria* in the margins of medieval Bibles: "If

the intention that precedes an action [e.g., coming to Jesus] is perverse, an evil
deed will follow, even if it seems to some to be just." His comment applies well
enough to much of the chapter to this point.

Dining with the Pharisees (11:37–54)

Though there is debate about whether this event is the same as that referred to
in Matt. 23, Matt. 15, Mark 7, or Mark 12, it is likely that this dinner with Pharisees is distinct as to setting but similar in its topic and effect (see Bock 1994–96:
2.1105–10 for a good discussion of various views and conclusions on this point;
also Marshall 1978: 491). Here in Luke it seems that the invitation may have
been an act of simple hospitality on the part of the unnamed Pharisee to what
was probably a midday meal. The gathering is evidently large, including a number
of other Pharisees as well as scribes. Whether it was arranged by the host and his
friends as an opportunity to have an "inner-circle discussion" with Jesus, apart
from the "evil generation," the general crowd from whose rebuke they may have
seen themselves exempt, or whether it was something more malicious from the
outset, is impossible to say for certain. Yet malice aplenty is forthcoming, once
the lunchtime conversation is finished. This is clearly a gathering of the religious
elite, and as Jesus's remarks to them amply indicate, it is their own iniquity and
not that of the crowd in general that he has had principally in mind all along. The
moral of the story may be: one should count carefully the cost before inviting Jesus
to one's presbytery, consistory, synod, classis, chapter, or Knights of Columbus
lunch in the local Lions' Club hall. Neither ecumenical etiquette nor religious
"correctness" are evident in what follows.

It seems on Luke's account, in fact, that Jesus is quite deliberately going after
these lions, so to speak, in their own den. His first provocation is straightforwardly to recline himself at the table without washing his hands (Luke 11:37–38).
While such hand-washing is described in the Old Testament (Gen. 18:4; Judg.
19:21), it is not in the Torah itself required as a practice. It had become a ritual
observance, however, of the Pharisees (Jerusalem Talmud, tractate *Berakhot* 2.4).
In this gesture, Jesus is making a point on which he intends to elaborate. Thus,
he pursues their sense of his breach of protocol, probing the Pharisees' obsession
with rituals of purity in respect to cups and dishware; you make the outside clean,
he says, and leave the inside filthy (Luke 11:39). This remark is tantamount to
an invited guest lifting his empty plate or cup at the beginning of the meal and
saying, "This wasn't washed!" It is hardly the best way to ease into polite conversation. In fact, it is already apparent that Jesus is not in the least interested in polite
conversation. His rhetoric is fiery Jewish hyperbole, and he instantly turns his
observation about ritual purification of tableware into a comment on the whole
of the Pharisees' religious condition when he says, "Your inward part is full of

greed and wickedness."[10] Then he calls them fools, charging them with failing to reckon that the God who made human beings as vessels did not make them only for their external appearance but so that they might contain something pure and holy (11:40). This was the strongest possible order of challenge to the Pharisees' view of themselves as *the* guardians of Jewish purity. Why don't you, instead of being concerned with "just so" washing of the surfaces, asks Jesus by implication, repent of your sins and seek to be cleansed by giving alms? (11:41).

Alms—giving money, food, or aid to the poor—was regarded in Jewish culture already as a means of obtaining forgiveness (Mishnah, tractate *Bava Batra* 9–10; cf. Lightfoot 1979: 3.122). To the degree that sin is debt, as Anderson shows, giving generously to the poor was regarded in the Hebrew scriptures as a means of redeeming those sins (cf. Dan. 4:27; Luke 12:19–21).[11] Augustine ties this point back to the Lord's Prayer, saying that all acts of mercy may constitute alms if offered generously and that the person who forgives the trespasser "also gives alms" (*Enchiridion* 72). The Pharisees tithed scrupulously, right down to herbs (cf. Lev. 27:30), a biblical practice intensified in Pharisaic Judaism, and Jesus says, in effect, "keep it up." But with regard to the first principles of obedience, namely love and the pursuit of justice, they have not done well (Luke 11:42). They are more preoccupied with their own social standing—getting the front seats reserved for them in the synagogue, for example, and being recognized as notable persons out in the marketplace (11:43). Therefore (and this is Jesus's third "woe to you" imprecation here), the Pharisees live lives focused on appearances rather than on God. They have forgotten that while humans look upon the outward appearances, God looks on the heart (1 Sam. 16:7); inwardly they are like graves poorly marked, so that unsuspecting people can walk over the corpses and unwittingly become ritually unclean in a most serious way (Luke 11:44).

At this point a scribe leaps to the defense of the Pharisees: "Teacher, by saying these things you reproach us also" (11:45). In a grimly ironic vein, Jesus now turns on the scribes and offers three "woes" or castigations to them. You lawyers, he says, load people down with regulations you have no intention of keeping yourselves (11:46). You build tombs for the prophets Israel has murdered, yet your own fathers are the very ones who did the prophets in (11:47). It may be that this is a Lukan instance in which we can see that "the peoples of the world do not invent their gods. They deify their victims" (Girard 2005: 70). What is immediately clear as import in Jesus's rebuke is that the scribes' supposed veneration for the prophets is ritualized hypocrisy; actually, they much prefer their prophets safely dead. "Therefore the wisdom of God also said, 'I will send them prophets and apostles, and some of them they will kill and persecute,' that the blood of all the prophets which was shed from the foundation of the world may be required of

---

10. Ironically, this washing was to avoid what E. P. Sanders, *Jewish Law from Jesus to the Mishnah* (London: SCM, 1990), 29–42, calls "fly impurity."

11. Gary A. Anderson, *Sin: A History* (New Haven: Yale University Press, 2009), 144–48.

this generation, from the blood of Abel to the blood of Zechariah who perished between the altar and the temple. Yes, I say to you, it shall be required of this generation" (11:49–51). The phrase "from the foundation of the world" is peculiar to Luke and suggests that Jesus is describing a chain of violence against the righteous innocent that goes from the first murder by Cain to the passion itself (Girard 2005: 85). Given its consistency with the parable Jesus tells later (20:9–16) about the vineyard, the prophets, and the vineyard owner's son, we should assume that the judgment he is making on this occasion was a repeated message in his strong criticism of the perverse injustice in Jewish religious leadership. (This Zechariah, given the designation "son of Berechiah" in Matt. 23:35, has occasioned confusion, but there was a person of this name in 2 Chr. 24:20–25, murdered in the temple precincts, an act of sacrilege explicitly, and he was the last Old Testament prophet so murdered in the canonical books.)

The preeminent charge against the scribes is that they have "taken away the key of knowledge" (Luke 11:52). This would have been a terrible accusation for those who considered themselves the guardians of knowledge. Small wonder that an angry verbal fracas ensues, with the religious leaders intent on "interrogating" Jesus (*apostomatizō* is unique in the New Testament, as is *thēreuō* ["to hunt, stalk"] in 11:54). The collective determination of the Jewish leadership from this point is entrapment and accusation. In short, they have taken Satan's part.

DISCERNMENT
OF SPIRITS

LUKE 12

The seventy disciples who went ahead of Jesus to announce his coming were evidently effective. Luke 12 opens with Luke noting that the crowds were gathering in greater and greater numbers, to the point of "trampl[ing] one another," a phenomenon that virtually ensured that the mixed motives already encountered in the spectators following Jesus would intensify. Apprehending the dark purposes of some spectators must have occasioned understandable anxiety in the disciples; after all, it is a fine line that distinguishes a crowd from a mob in such circumstances. Jesus, sensing their uneasiness, here first addresses his disciples, presumably less volubly, beginning with a realistic appraisal of the animosity of their opponents. What Luke recounts here seems, once again, to be a number of Jesus's repeated themes and sayings.

Legitimate and Illegitimate Fears (12:1–12)

A public image, Jesus points out, does not necessarily correspond to private or personal reality. One's image can be phony, and religious hypocrisy is a particularly grievous instance of it. He is referring, of course, to the professionally pious and politically powerful men among the Pharisees, whose hypocrisy he likens to "leaven" (12:1). John Wyclif, in a sermon on 12:1–8 entitled "The Leaven of the Pharisees," makes the point that hypocrisy typically puffs up as with the air in a yeasted dough; it makes the loaf look more substantial, when in fact it is less nourishing and far more quickly grows stale and worthless (1975: 1–27 at 20). Wyclif was applying this text to his own fourteenth-century academic and religious culture, in which many he found "pharisaical" were fellow lecturers at the university, especially some in mendicant orders, such as the Franciscans and Dominicans. What Jesus says next Wyclif likewise addressed in a similarly angry tone to some of his colleagues, noting the clear warning of final judgment in Jesus's insistence that "there is nothing covered that will not be revealed, nor hidden that will not be known" (12:2); real shame will one day come to even the most skillful practitioners of a double standard (12:3). The point applies not only to universities and professors.

When Jesus turns to the disciples—with a shift to more intimate address: "my friends"—distinguishing between fear of political retribution and the more appropriate fear of the God himself, who cannot be deceived, his words hold both warning and comfort. Fear not the ones who can injure or kill your body, says Jesus, but rather "fear him who . . . has power to cast into hell" (12:5). This is the only time that Luke's text employs the term "Gehenna," not the place of dead bodies but the region to which the condemned are consigned after the last judgment. Here too are echoes of the war with Satan, for the only literal place with that name in Palestine was the burning garbage heap in the Valley of Hinnom that Israel's wicked kings had used in Baal worship, passing living infants "through the fire" to Moloch as sacrifice (2 Kgs. 16:3; 23:10; 2 Chr. 28:3; Jer. 7:31–32). It would be hard to imagine a more horrible kind of place than Gehenna—or a clearer indication that Jesus anticipates divine condemnation of the wicked.

Yet for all that, the God who in his omniscient love cares even for the sparrows sold in the marketplace and who numbers the hairs on the heads of his children will be their own defense on that day, confessing their fidelity before the angels as long as they have confessed him as Lord before the judgment of men. This saying invokes a "two courts" motif familiar from the Old Testament (e.g., 1 Kgs. 22); the phrase *homologēsē en emoi* ("confesses me") is a Semitism (Fitzmyer 1981–85: 2.960; Bock 1994–96: 2.1139) as, conceptually, is the notion of a trial before the angels of God in which one who has denied the Lord will also be denied. But it is clear that the either/or presented here is aimed at the disciples as well as the general throng and that it is designed to reorient their concerns from temporal to eternal security (Luke 12:8–9).

The next statement has occasioned much discussion in the history of Christian biblical exegesis and theology: "Anyone who speaks a word against the Son of Man, it will be forgiven him; but to him who blasphemes against the Holy Spirit, it will not be forgiven" (12:10). Among commentators in the early church, for whom Cyril of Alexandria can be our representative, these "blasphemers" can be either "those who in a time of persecution renounce the faith" or "heretical teachers and their disciples" (1983: Sermon 88). Later on, Bede focuses more on the preceding context, suggesting that Jesus is thinking of the denial of the scribes and Pharisees, who "say that the works of the Holy Spirit are those of Beelzebub" and that such blasphemy "shall not be forgiven either in the present world or that which is to come," but he imagines Jesus to have exempted those who say such a thing out of genuine ignorance (quoted in Aquinas, *Catena Aurea* 3.2.439). Augustine contextualized Jesus's saying by his observation that "the first blessing of believers is forgiveness of sins in the Holy Spirit," while "against this free gift the impenitent heart speaks"; hence "impenitence itself therefore is blasphemy against the Spirit" (Sermon 71, quoted in Aquinas, *Catena Aurea* 3.2.439). Calvin flatly rejects Augustine on this point and goes on to say that Christ and the Holy Spirit ought not to be cognitively dissociated here, that "it is not because the Spirit is superior to Christ that blasphemy against him surpasses all other sins. It is rather that once God's power has been revealed there is no longer any excuse on the grounds of ignorance for those who reject him." Calvin's long disquisition on this topic is worthy reading in its entirety, but it will suffice for our purpose to see where he will bring his argument in conclusion: "From all these things we can now gather that they sin against the Holy Spirit and are blasphemers who maliciously turn God's powers, revealed to them by the Spirit and in which his glory should be celebrated, to dishonor, and, with Satan as their leader, are the professed enemies of God's glory" (1972: 2.45–46). Calvin's point seems to be that, as Lightfoot put it (without explicit reference to Calvin), "apostasy cannot properly be charged on any but who have already professed Christianity: but blasphemy against the Holy Ghost was uttered by the scribes and Pharisees at the time they disowned and rejected Christ" (1979: 3.131). Obviously there has been a range of opinion on this question from learned and faithful expositors. It seems on balance, however, that Calvin's view has served to anticipate late modern commentators over quite a broad evangelical spectrum (cf. Nolland 1989–93: 2.679–80; Marshall 1978: 518–19; Bock 1994–96: 2.1140–43).

But the Holy Spirit is the real presence of God for faithful believers, and in their hour of persecution, another worry such believers need not to harbor is how they should answer their accusers in the best way: "The Holy Spirit will teach you in that very hour what you ought to say" (12:12). Many believers in a dark hour have found it to be just so, and Christian commentators down the centuries bear ample witness to the fact.

Narrative and Discernment (12:13–34)

This next pericope is unique to Luke, and since there is no mention of a context or temporal link, it may be that Luke has placed it here because thematically it connects to what precedes it. The parable that Jesus will tell is by way of response to a request (not in itself unusual to be brought before a rabbi) that he arbitrate in favor of a man who says his brother has wronged him concerning a shared inheritance (12:13). Jesus refuses to intervene (12:14); his rebuke is even harsh, perhaps, as the vocative "man" (*anthrōpe*) often suggests (cf. 22:58, 60). Instead of hearing him out, Jesus tells a story that goes to the heart of the underlying issue, presenting the supplicant's motive not as a simple matter of rights but as a matter of misdirected affection or covetousness (12:15). That this parable should come here in the text makes narrative sense, not least because of the evident insecurity of Jesus's disciples, who have become anxious about potential oppression from those who, like many of the Pharisees, were well off and able to use their wealth to advantage. Indeed, from the perspective of these poor itinerant disciples, it is possible both to envy the affluent religious rulers and to resent their injustice toward such as themselves—that is, to experience the same feelings that may have triggered the supplicant's complaint about his brother. (The problem is universal; one thinks here of Ps. 73.)

The story Jesus tells about the prudential "wisdom" of a rich man is as interesting for what is natural and legitimate in the action as for its stark denouement and judgment. For at first blush, the enviable farmer is responding to his bumper crop in what many would consider a sound, prudential fashion: he has more produce than his barns can store, so he will tear them down and build bigger ones (Luke 12:16–18). Many a farmer today would be advised by his agricultural agent to do just that—and then to hold on to his crop for higher prices. But what follows indicates a major problem of attitude and a failure to act responsibly toward others, given his blessings. Numerous passages in Isaiah and the Psalms reiterate an obligation toward the poor, especially of those who have been blessed with abundance, declaring that in God's perspective this is a simple matter of justice.[1] This farmer apparently has failed to take these texts to heart. His crops safely stored in his tidy new barns, the wealthy man congratulates himself (literally his *psychē*, "soul"), saying effectively, "Well, I have it made. I shall now retire in comfort, eat, drink, and be merry" (12:19). His position is one with many parallels in our own culture. When in the parable he is judged by God as a "fool" (*aphrōn*), the force of Jesus's derisive term turns the man's conventional wisdom upside down. There is ambiguity in the Greek phrase, which actually reads "this night they shall demand your soul from you" (12:20). Who are "they"? Perhaps thieves; perhaps, as some suggest, angelic servants of God; perhaps, as in previous texts, the "court of heaven" is being invoked as a witness against him. In any case, all that he has worked for will pass into other hands, for his treasure is not eternally portable (12:21).

The early fathers are still the best commentators on this parable. As Ambrose says, Jesus is here reminding his disciples that "the things we cannot take away with us are not even 'ours.' Only *virtue* is the companion of the dead. Compassion alone follows us" (*Exposition of Luke* 7.122). Augustine captures the context in which the wealthy farmer's worldly prudence is shown to be catastrophic spiritual imprudence:

> Obviously he was not redeeming his soul by giving relief to the poor. He was hoarding perishable crops. I repeat, he was hoarding perishable crops, while he was himself on the point of perishing because he handed out nothing to the Lord before whom he was now to appear. How will he know where to look, when at that trial he starts hearing the words, "I was hungry and you did not give me to eat"? . . . He did not realize that the bellies of the poor were much safer storerooms than his barns. (Sermon 36)

1. Dennis Tucker, "Democratization and the Language of the Poor in Psalms 2–89," *Horizons in Biblical Theology* 25 (2003): 161–78.

So also Basil describes the wealthy farmer's disposition of his goods as actually a form of robbery: "It is the bread of the famished which thou receivest, the garment of the naked which thou hoardest in thy chest, the shoes of the barefooted which rot in thy possession, the money of the penniless which thou hast buried in the earth" ("Homily on Avarice," quoted in Aquinas, *Catena Aurea* 3.2.442–45). Even while he is congratulating himself, adds Basil, "while he speaks in secret, his words are weighed in heaven, from whence the judgment comes upon him." In short, there is absolutely nothing to envy in the farmer's filled barns but rather something pitiable. A proper response to a superabundant harvest, on a biblical view, would have been for the wealthy farmer to distribute the surplus to the poor and stick with the barns he already had. His success is not in itself the problem, and it is not his success that is condemned. What is condemned is his self-indulgence, his neglect of a great opportunity to provide for others less successful than himself, and on top of that his self-congratulatory belief that he had made adequate provision for his own future. This farmer is no "Joseph the provider," laying up grain to sustain a population in a time of famine to come; rather, he is laying up treasure for himself and himself alone.

For the disciples, of course, being a good steward of material riches is hardly the issue; what Jesus has said to them, in effect, is that they should not only feel no twinge of envy for those with worldly power and wealth but also recognize how easily such possessions can corrupt appreciation of the "one thing most needful." Jesus nonetheless goes on to address their anxieties about being poor and their uncertainty about the future. "Therefore," Jesus continues, "I say unto you, take no thought for your life, what ye shall eat, neither for the body, what ye shall put on. The life is more than meat, and the body is more than raiment" (12:22–23 KJV). Luke's readers should remember here Jesus's reply, famished though he was in the desert, telling Satan that "man shall not live by bread alone, but by every word of God" (4:4). Everything that follows in his counsel to the disciples is of a piece with this principle: the ravens (an unclean animal; cf. Lev. 11:15) don't store up extra food, yet God provides for them; the lilies of the field can't fashion anything for themselves, and look how splendidly—with a glory exceeding Solomon's—God provides for them (Luke 12:24, 27–28). Who among you, asks Jesus rhetorically, by thinking ahead about it, can add one *hēlikan* to his stature? (The Greek term can mean an "hour" as well as the "height" of a person, and it may be that the double value is intended here.) We have the bodies we have been given, and our biological clock is set to stop at a point we cannot predict. The commentators have little to add, for Jesus's words are entirely perspicuous. What they come to as to purpose is well summarized by Cyril of Alexandria: "He makes them abandon unnecessary anxiety . . . a careworn and frenetic diligence that might make them wish to gather what exceeds their necessities" (1983: Homily 90). This is the sort of thing that the Gentiles are preoccupied with, says Jesus (the same sentiment is found in Matt. 6:31–32 in almost the same words), but your heavenly Father knows your needs and how to supply them. The bottom line is thus a general principle for the faithful Christian life: "Seek the kingdom of God, and all these things shall be added to you" (Luke 12:31; cf. Matt. 6:33).

There is great tenderness in Jesus's words here; he is comforting those he calls his "little flock." Their ultimate inheritance, in the "Father's good pleasure," is to be an inheritance rich beyond imagining in which the portion of any shall not diminish the portion of any other, namely the kingdom (Luke 12:32). Therefore, so far from preoccupying themselves with the normative prudential wisdom regarding bodily care, they should sell even the little that they have and give it as alms to the poor. This will obtain for them access to treasure in heaven that will neither diminish nor be vulnerable to moths or thieves (12:33). Such a choice for spiritual rather than material goods orders the affections rightly, "for where your treasure is, there your heart will be also" (12:34). The idea that giving alms to the poor here lays up treasure in heaven is presaged in Ps. 112:9; and Cyril, Augustine, John Chrysostom, and others strongly stress it. Gregory Nazianzus observes that before considering the scriptures carefully he had thought of such alms as voluntary but not necessary. On further reading, he says, he became "alarmed at the goats placed on the left hand [in Matt. 25], not because they robbed but because they did not minister unto Christ among the poor" (*Oration* 14). Bede adds a note of balance: almsgiving produces "a reward that abides forever" (*Homilies on the Gospels* 1.13), though he adds that Jesus's words ought not to be taken as a blanket order that the saints ought not to handle money at all, since the Lord himself permitted a purse for provision and for relief of the poor (cf. Luke 22:36; John 12:6). In sum, the principle stressed in Luke is that "righteousness should never be forsaken for fear of poverty."

Surprise and Final Judgment (12:35–48)

Jesus now heightens the force of his admonitions that the disciples should consider life less in terms of material security, more in terms of faithfulness to the kingdom of God. (What he says in this section of Luke's text is uniquely contextualized here, though the parable of the faithful and unfaithful servants itself is found in Matt. 24:42–51.) The ambience of this discourse is clearly eschatological; the call to "gird up" the loins and have lights burning suggests a time of immediate action and the need to be ready for it (Luke 12:35). Jesus counsels his followers to be like faithful servants of a lord who goes away to a wedding feat (these were multiday celebrations from which the time of return would be indeterminate). The returning lord could come home in the dead of night, but if the servants are ready to serve and the house is lit in anticipation, they will be blessed (12:36–38). The call to watchfulness is strengthened by a second example: preparation against thieves breaking in, also in the dead of night (12:39). The Lord makes an analogy to both: "Therefore, you also be ready, for the Son of Man is coming at an hour you do not expect" (12:40). Nothing here is obscure, and down through the centuries, reading into the role of the servants of the departed lord the apostolic stewardship of servants of the Lord, Lukan commentators have typically applied the text to themselves. Thus Cyril: "The girding of our loins signifies the readiness of the mind to work in anything praiseworthy . . . the lamp represents the wakefulness of the mind and intellectual cheerfulness" (1983: Homily 92); thus also Augustine, less inclined to intellectual laxity but with his own sense of frailty: "What does it mean to gird the loins? It is to restrain lustful appetite. This is about self-control. To have lamps burning is to shine and glow with good works. This is about justice" (*On Continence* 7). But the *Didache* stressed the need for attentive perseverance in awaiting the second coming of Christ, seeing in the text and context of Luke 12 a warning that "a lifetime of faith will be of no advantage unless you prove to be responsive to the very end. In the final days, many false prophets and seducers will appear. Sheep will turn into wolves and love into hatred. With the increase in iniquity, people will hate, persecute, and betray each other. Then the world deceiver will appear in the guise of God's Son" (*Didache* 16.2–4). Bede suggests, in another probative response to this text, that among the vices of the bad servant is diffidence, a belief that the Lord would be slow to return: "It is not numbered among the virtues of a good servant that he hoped it would come quickly, but only that he ministered faithfully." Bede here balances our reading: perseverance is crucial, but so also is steadfast faithfulness, since none can know "that which cannot be known," yet all can strive "to be found worthy" (quoted in Aquinas, *Catena Aurea* 3.2.463).

But to whom does this parable apply? asks Peter—"us" (e.g., the apostles) or "all" (12:41)? Jesus does not answer directly but, as is his wont, indirectly and with a rhetorical question that has the effect of asking who among the servants are real stewards, both "faithful and wise" (12:42); such a one, says Jesus, shall on the return of the Master be promoted in service and be "blessed" (*makarios*). The warning against unfaithful stewardship that follows shows us that the early interpreters were on track with those more recent (Fitzmyer 1981–85: 2.989; Nolland 1989–93: 2.702; Marshall 1978: 540; Bock 1994–96: 2.1177) in thinking that Jesus was addressing the whole group of those dedicated to following him, "who have been admitted into the rank of teachers," as Cyril puts it (1983: Sermon 92), rather than the general crowd. Once again the point seems to be (as in 9:23–27) that the disciples' obligation differs sharply from that of *hoi polloi*; the standard for them is very high. Jesus is careful to expand in such a way as to make evident the possibility that one who has the vocation of disciple can fail to do due diligence; the procrastination he attributes to the slothful servant, "My master is delaying his coming" (12:45), is echoed in 2 Pet. 3:4, even as the Lord's analogy of the "thief in the night" (Luke 12:39) is picked up in 2 Pet. 3:10. This explicit echo may suggest that the author of that epistle has been present on this occasion and possibly served as Luke's informer. It is clear that to know the Lord's will (Luke 12:47), that is, to be instructed, and to fail to do it is much worse than to be sloppy or even miscreant out of a genuine ignorance (12:48). The moral for disciples of the Lord is clear: "For everyone to whom much is given, from him much will be required." In a day of woeful clerical abuse in many Christian communions, these are dire words. Indeed, the apocalyptic context is still on the mind of the author in 2 Pet. 3:11–12: "Therefore, since all these things will be dissolved, [consider] what manner of persons ought you to be in holy conduct and godliness, looking for and hastening the coming of the day of God."

Signs of the Times (12:49–59)

Though there are partial parallels to what follows in the other two Synoptics (Matt. 10:34–36; Mark 10:38) there is little verbal overlap, indicating a probability that the eschatological element, particularly the notion of ultimate judgment, was a repeated theme in Jesus's teaching (cf. Matt. 24–25). The distinctive feature in this discourse is that the "fire" of the coming judgment, which is "already kindled" (Luke 12:49), is as much at the center of Jesus's divine purpose as is redemption. He expresses impatience to get to the climax of his ministry, his "baptism to be baptized with" (cf. Mark 10:38–39; Matt. 20:22–23)—a clear reference to his impending death (also Cyril 1983: Homily 94). It must have seemed counterintuitive to some (however gratifying to a Galilean Zealot like Judas) that Jesus's declared purpose in coming to earth is not yet to bring the peace for which all were in hope but rather "division" (*diamerismos*, a *hapax legomenon* in the New Testament but anticipated by the Greek text of Ezek. 48:29 and Mic. 7:12). There is to be a separating of family members from each other, of faithful from unfaithful servants, as even just now he has been saying (Talbert 2002: 144). There is no talk of general redemption here, or household salvation, or the redemption of all Israel. Clearly, as in Matthew, some will be saved and some will be lost. Echoes of the word of God from Ezek. 9–25 are in this speech (especially 12:22–28; 13:17; 18:2–25; 21:5); the father will not be held responsible for the sinfulness of the son, nor the son for his father, and so with mother and daughter: everyone's choice is his own responsibility, to obey or to disobey. These are not palliative words.

The conclusion to Jesus's denunciation is trenchant with the irony of God's voice as it is found in Jeremiah, Ezekiel, and other prophets. In fact, it is not too much to say of either those speeches or Jesus's words here that they are marked by sarcasm: his hearers—now clearly the general crowd—know well enough how to read the weather signs in the natural order and to predict the consequences that will follow as inevitable (Luke 12:54–55). Yet what is in its own way much more obvious—the presence of hypocrisy, willful disobedience, and their inexorable consequences (was this an oblique reference to the destruction of Jerusalem as well as the inevitable judgment of God?)—they entirely miss. As with Israel and the temple in the time of Ezekiel, denial had become a pervasive reflex. Few want to face reality. These are obvious signs of the "time" (*kairos* here, rather than *kronos*, suggesting a momentous time of divine disclosure): how can the people be so obtuse as to miss them? There is no Synoptic parallel to 12:57, where Jesus rubs it in, saying in effect, "How could you possibly miss this yourselves?"

The final analogy Jesus makes refers to people who are deep in debt and have not much time left to deal with it before time runs out. The bailiff is coming. A prudent person will go to the magistrate and do everything he can to renegotiate the debt or seek to have it forgiven; if he fails to do this, the judge will turn him over to the officer of the debtors' prison. This, for people of that time even more than for victims of debt in eighteenth- or nineteenth-century England, was a terrible fate. Typically, there was no way out unless the family could somehow raise what might prove to be an impossible sum. Moreover, Palestinian jailers typically beat the prisoners horribly to urge on the families to find a way to resolve the indebtedness. Most died in prison. When Jesus says, "you shall not depart from there till you have paid the very last mite [*lepton*]," he is, in effect, underscoring the hopelessness of the debtor.

We already have seen that "debt" is a synonym in Luke for sin. But who then is the judge? Origen says it is Christ (*Homilies on Luke* 35.10); Cyril makes Satan the "accuser, the enemy and exactor" of the penalty (1983: Homily 95), as does Ambrose. Almost all who see this parable in its eschatological context urge that the only sane response to an indebtedness of sin is to "seize the grace that is from Christ that frees us from all debt and penalty, delivering us from terror and torment" (Cyril 1983: Homily 95). Augustine has a nuanced reading of "the adversary with whom we should agree," saying that in this matter, our "adversary is the word of God," for it is by and out of God's word that all shall be judged (Sermon 109). The force of this warning, however, is as stark as anything in the prophets: now is the time, the *kairos*, the imperative moment before irrevocable judgment. Anyone who has heard Jesus give his warning knows well enough that something very like it has been given before in Israel's history and that to turn a deaf ear has stark, predictable consequences.

LUKE 13

Sometimes, when we don't quite know how to respond or what to say, we resort to comment upon the news, especially calamitous news, to fill in awkward silences while pretending to keep up a serious conversation. This may be all that is motivating those who report to Jesus the news of the Galileans "whose blood Pilate had mingled with their sacrifices." Perhaps it was a way of saying, in response to Jesus's eschatological warning (at the end of the previous chapter), something as innocuous as "yes—things are bad all over." But given Jesus's reply it is perhaps more likely that this was another form of test—a protest to the effect of saying, "If God is about to restore the kingdom to Israel, and really cares about us, why does he permit horror and sacrilege of the kind that fell upon the poor Galileans?" That Jesus takes their report in the latter sense is indicated by his reference to the accidental death of eighteen people when the water tower at Siloam suddenly fell on them, by no human hand. The topic is theodicy, the question of unmerited suffering and evil (13:1–2).

Suffering and Consolation (13:1–17)

The question about evil and its causes—or about evil and its relation to justice—can of course be asked in many ways. The epitome in biblical literature for theodicy examined from the perspective of unjust suffering is surely the book of Job; looked at from the other end, as a question about why the practitioners of evil seem to prosper as their victims suffer, it takes theological form in Ps. 73. Here it is the first perspective in which the question is raised, though the second hovers over it, since the Roman oppression was on everybody's mind. In order to address the issue more fundamentally, Jesus adds to it the fate of some people killed in an accidental manner, perhaps through a flaw in engineering long unnoticed. Talbert suggests that the issue might well have been raised because some in the audience took absence of tragedy as a sign of God's blessing, while thinking that "trouble is God's punishment for sin"; the effect would be as much as to say, "Our lives are tranquil . . . why should we repent?" (2002: 145). Whatever the motives of "some" in the crowd for turning to this subject, Jesus has an astringent answer: "Do you suppose that these Galileans were worse sinners than all other Galileans, because they suffered such things? I tell you, no." The idea of a *necessary* causal connection between personal sin and the experience of suffering is here dismissed in a word. But there is a more pressing, more universal question, and that is the question of the human sinfulness, from which no one is free, and its deeper consequences, from which no unredeemed person is exempt. Accordingly, "Unless you repent you will all likewise perish" (Luke 13:3). In the context of Jesus's immediately preceding eschatological remarks, this almost certainly means "perish eternally."

The fig tree parable (13:6–9), as Cyril of Alexandria observed sixteen hundred years ago, is such that "the literal sense . . . does not need a single word of explanation" (1983: Homily 96). The fig tree has captured the attention of many an allegorist, however, and in the spiritual sense it has been associated with Israel, the synagogue, and even all humanity. Perhaps (as Bock 1994–96: 2.1208 and others suggest) it involves an allusion to Mic. 7:1–6, a passage already invoked in Luke 12:53. Regardless, the net interpretation is unmistakable: God's judgment regarding fruitfulness is imminent. This seems to weigh in favor of it being in its context a parable primarily about Israel.

Like the preceding section of this chapter, the healing of the bent-over woman is an event unique to Luke. There is a gap of time between this and the parable of the fig tree, and we are told that this miracle takes place in the context of Jesus's "teaching in one of the synagogues on the Sabbath" (13:10). This factor, and the connection of the healing to Jesus's discussion of suffering and its causes, doubtless contributes to Luke's placement. It will be the last time in Luke's Gospel that we find Jesus in the synagogue on the Sabbath, and much of what has been building thematically concerning the Sabbath (we might represent this as an unfolding answer to the question, "What is the purpose of the Sabbath?") is here brought to a point theologically. A number of possibilities have been suggested to account for the woman's disease, including *skoliasis hysterica* (a muscular paralysis occasioned by psychic or neurological disorder). Whatever the etiology, her bent-over, disfigured posture, robbing her of both health and dignity, is the feature to which we should pay attention. Like so many of the miracles of Jesus, as Augustine noted, both her condition and her healing function like a "visible word," for in her painful, earthward orientation she is a physical sign for the spiritual condition of all humanity outside of Christ, juxtaposing sinful reality and the higher good to which we are called. In his homily on this passage, Augustine asks his hearers to see themselves in this woman, for "the whole human race was bent double . . . weighed down by earthly lusts." Her healing is thus a miracle that speaks powerfully of God's grace by which his image in us is restored and we are made ready for the "kingdom of heaven":

There is another life . . . a home country where no violence, no enemy is to be feared; there is a home country walled around by the will of God, encircled with the shield of God's goodwill, where no foe is ever allowed in and no friend perishes; there is a home country where nobody leaves dependents behind, nobody is succeeded by heirs. That country is called Jerusalem, "vision of peace." Straighten yourself up from your doubled up posture! . . . "you have risen with Christ" [Col. 3:1]; he is in heaven; stretch up toward him and you will no longer be bent double. (New Sermon 110A)

It may be, in fact, that this is one of those miracles that the spiritual theology of the fathers and the Middle Ages gets at in a fashion consistent with modern psychological analysis; for Anselm of Canterbury, as for Peter Lombard in his standard theological textbook a century later, a willing acceptance of the truth presages obedience to the Lord of truth and is called *rectitude* ("uprightness"). Because the devil, "the father of lies," and all his minions have abandoned truth, their condition is "bent," twisted away from their intended upright posture and from the possibility of an openness to the fullness of God's intention (Anselm, *De Veritate* 4; *Dialogues* 8–9). This creates the context, according to Lombard, in which we can better understand Peter's question to Ananias in Acts 5:3, "Why has Satan filled your heart?" Thus, "possession" by Satan is not mechanical, "by stepping into him and his sense," but rather an effect of drawing the soul, by cunning and fraudulent deception, into malice toward other persons and/or God. The bentness of the woman, on this reading, would be the outward sign of an inward disposition that, covertly or not, included malice and resistance, rather than an open disposition to the real, which is truth, and thus to obedience—which is "uprightness," *rectitude*. This is one way to think about such a condition, as emblematic of a spiritual disposition.

Yet we can hardly avoid compassion. In this bent-over woman, the beauty and dignity of her created humanity have been defaced for eighteen years. The proximate cause is described by Luke as "a spirit of infirmity" (Luke 13:11), a term that can cover considerable territory. Jesus looks at her, calls her to come to him, simply says, "Woman, you are loosed from your infirmity" (13:12), lays hands on her, and "immediately" (*parachrēma*), as Luke likes to say, she straightens up and, now erect, gives glory to God (13:13). There is here no address to sin and forgiveness—just a compassionate, instant healing. It must have been stunning for those present.

But not for one, namely the ruler of the synagogue. He is angry; perhaps, as Cyril says, "He condemns the miracle that he might appear jealous for the Sabbath." Of his sympathy for the woman in her suffering, gratitude for her healing, or empathy with her giving praise to God, there is not a hint. So we see here that the synagogue ruler's reaction silently frames another question: "How do we respond to others who suffer?" Also, "How do we respond to others who are 'loosed' from their infirmity?" What this sad fellow does is to rattle off some perfectly valid precepts of the law concerning Sabbath observance (13:14), entirely oblivious that in healing the woman Jesus has done no labor and violated no Sabbath regulation whatsoever. This man is one of those who has "added to the burdens" of the law and has not even a full command of that law that he has made, in effect, an idol. So when Jesus calls him a "hypocrite," he does so by pointing out that the law provides for such labor as may be involved in providing food and drink for one's animals—something that doubtless the ruler of the synagogue practices—and yet he cannot have comparable care for another human being, "a daughter of Abraham," as Jesus says (13:15–16). But now Jesus adds something about her condition that rounds out what he has said about suffering and its causes earlier. There may or may not be a direct personal cause in her own life, but there cannot help but be a cause of evil and suffering to which she is heir as a member of the human race: she is one "whom Satan has bound . . . for eighteen years." Now she is "loosed" on the Sabbath, symbolically the day of rest for creation that returns it to God's intended šālôm, his health and peace (13:16). There are here echoes of the deep meaning of the Sabbath that had become lost, it seems, to such as this synagogue ruler; the Sabbath spirit of Exod. 20:8–11—which suggests a renewal of and delight in God's creation, its beauty and fruitfulness (Isa. 58:13–14)—should have set the tone for his response to what he saw.

Perhaps the meaning of the Sabbath in relation to suffering and its causes lies deeper still; one thinks here of the requirement for Sabbath rest for the land every seven years and the provision for the year of Jubilee, with its remission of debt and bondage, both of which had long been forgotten in Israel, despite the warning in the law that to fail to keep these elements of Sabbath law would leave Israel itself in suffering, without rest, pining away in its iniquity (Lev. 26:36–39; Deut. 28:65–67). If this is the case (and it seems that it is), then Augustine is surely right to say that the synagogue leader's refusal to observe the Sabbath *spiritually* is at the heart of his blindness: "Since they entirely failed to understand the very things God had commanded [i.e., the law], they regarded them with earthbound hearts. They used to celebrate the sacrament of the Sabbath in a literal, material manner, and failed to notice its spiritual meaning" (Sermon 162).

Augustine's allegorical or spiritual reading of the woman herself in this light is most appropriate. At one level, she symbolizes Israel, bowed down with the burden of its iniquities. But at another, he suggests, "the whole human race is like this woman, bent over and bowed down to the ground" (Sermon 162). At the personal or immediate level, it makes little difference, as Cyril says, whether she suffered "because of her own crimes or for the transgression of Adam"; Satan often, as Cyril notes, receives authority over certain persons because of their sins, and, as Augustine has it, this certainly applies to the human race as a whole—even to the very creation itself, which, in Paul's words, "groans and labors with birth pangs together until now . . . waiting for the adoption, the redemption of our body" (Rom. 8:22–23). In this added light we can see the healing of the bent-over woman anagogically, as a sign of the ultimate Sabbath rest, the final redemption of those for whom Christ died.

The congregation gathered in the synagogue seems increasingly to be split. "All his adversaries," Luke says, were ashamed, while "all the multitude" (suggesting those who were not religious leaders) "rejoiced for all the glorious things that were done by him" (Luke 13:17).

The Coming Kingdom (13:18–21)

Jewish expectations had long been that in the messianic age, restoration of the kingdom would be, as we might say today, "a big deal"—sudden, dramatic, and definitive. The comparisons Jesus makes here (overlapping with sayings in Matt. 13:31–33 and Mark 4:30–32) are thus incongruous for many of his hearers. A mustard seed? That grows into a shrub maybe even ten feet tall at maturity? A pinch of yeast in the dough before baking? These examples suggest not only a miniscule beginning but also a nearly invisible beginning. Yet they also suggest a surprisingly large development from an apparently inauspicious starting point. This seems to be just what Jesus has in mind (cf. Ezek. 17:22–24). His kingdom at first scarcely attracts the attention of Israel's political oppressors, but it is a growing, living organism that will in time surprise everyone. Writing seven centuries later, Bede comments on the "three measures" of flour, seeing the woman as emblematic of the nascent church, which in the end imparts the bread of life "to parts of Asia Minor, to Europe, and to Africa" (*Homilies on the Gospels* 2.13). Who then, he implies, could have seen *that* harvest coming?

Onward to Jerusalem (13:22–30)

As Jesus combines his journey to Jerusalem with teaching along the way, a sense of urgency is increasing for him and his hearers, as Luke tells it. Some of his teaching has parallels elsewhere (Bock 1994–96: 2.1230), but what marks this narrative most is a sense that Jesus is "on the move" (*diaporeuetō*) and that the crowd has begun to be apprehensive (13:22). Understanding at least one implication of the previous parables, someone asks him, "Lord, are there few who are saved?" (13:23). This is not, we may be sure, a disinterested question. Jesus's answer is, as so often, not the prescriptive or statistical declarative that we or the questioner might expect. What he says is a confirmation, nonetheless, that the question is perceptive: whereas most Jews expected a universal salvation for Israel (Isa. 60:21; cf. Mishnah, tractate *Sanhedrin* 10.1), Jesus offers no comfort on this point whatsoever: "Strive to enter through the narrow gate, for many, I say to you, will seek to enter and will not be able" (Luke 13:24). And now he makes it worse, dramatizing a situation in which people who have spent time with Jesus, eating and drinking in his presence, and who remind him that he has "taught in [their] streets," will hear the terrible words, "I do not know you, where you are from. Depart from me, all you workers of iniquity" (13:25–27). He goes on to say, in Hebrew idiom, that "there will be weeping and gnashing of teeth, when you see Abraham and Isaac and Jacob and all the prophets in the kingdom of God, and yourselves thrust out" (13:28). Obviously, this is not a very inclusive or ecumenical speech. What follows, however, is inclusive in a way that many Jews found inimical to their notion of entitlement as members of the chosen people. Unthinkably, the despised *goyim*, the Gentile nations, from east, west, north, and south, shall be represented in those who "sit down in the kingdom of God" (13:29), even as many among the "chosen" will be shut out. For, as Jesus says, there are those among the last to receive the word who shall be first at the messianic banquet table, while some of those first called will be last. Jesus is not talking about universal salvation here: as the absence of definite articles on the grammatical subjects "last" and "first" indicate, only some of both are included. There is consequently in Jesus's remarks on this occasion a distinct affront to the Jewish sense of "special position" and especially their belief that *they*, universally, would be saved, while the *goyim* would be condemned to outer darkness.

It would be possible for Gentiles to respond to Jesus's remarks with a kind of smug satisfaction, just as it has always been possible for Jews to respond to the covenant promise with an equivalent smugness. But both groups among Luke's readers should be careful, even as Jesus was urging his questioner to be careful. The issue to be concerned with is not so much, "Will only a few be saved?" What Jesus has done in his answer, as Bock notes (1994–96: 2.1241), is tacitly to turn that question on every listener: "Will *you* be among the saved?"

Lament for a Nation (13:31–35)

There is no Synoptic parallel for this next important prophetic passage. It is uncertain if the Pharisees who came to warn Jesus ("Herod wants to kill you") were intent on keeping him from harm or just taunting him about his anticipated terminal collision with political power. Jesus's response, however, makes it evident that he understands these particular Pharisees as of Herod's party, and his reply is curt: "Go tell that fox: 'Behold, I cast out demons and perform cures today and tomorrow, and the third day I shall be perfected [i.e., "complete my work"].'" "Fox" was a rabbinic term of derision for someone known to be habitually deceptive, a creature of low cunning,[1] and this connotation would probably have been familiar to an educated Greek like Luke, for it appears with this same sense in Plutarch (*Life of Solon* 30.2). What Jesus is saying, essentially, is that his ministry is now drawing rapidly to a close (the phrase "today, tomorrow, and the third day" should be taken figuratively to suggest rapid culmination rather than a literal three-day period) and that, as in the historical pattern for prophets, he will come to the end of his earthly road in Jerusalem.

1. David Daube, *The New Testament and Rabbinic Judaism*, Jordan Lectures 1952 (London: University of London Press/Athlone, 1956), 191.

It is in fact Jerusalem that is now weighing heavily on Jesus's mind. His lament for Jerusalem is a synecdoche—a lament in which the city stands for all of Israel—which, as in his parables, has killed the prophets and stoned the messengers sent to them rather than repent. His figure of a hen trying to gather her chicks under her wings to spare them from the ravages of fire will have special poignancy for anyone who has seen after a grassfire the burned carcass of a prairie chicken or pheasant that has sheltered and saved perhaps one or two, though seldom all, of her chicks. There is deep foreboding here, as well as parental sorrow. The image of a desolated house anticipates the house of David ravaged, the house of Jacob a wasteland. When Jesus adds that "Jerusalem" shall not see him "until the time comes when you say, 'Blessed is he who comes in the name of the Lord!'" (13:35), it is a way of warning that until messengers of God are received by his chosen with gracious blessing and hospitality, Jesus himself will not again appear. Those in his immediate audience would have heard an echo of Ps. 118:26: "Blessed is he who comes in the name of the LORD! We have blessed you from the house of the LORD." The familiar words of this psalm were sung in the "Great Hallel," a recitation of Ps. 113–18 on every feast, in every family (Lightfoot 1979: 3.146). The latter part, including 118:26, would have been the hymn that the Lord and the apostles sang at the end of the paschal meal on the Thursday before his crucifixion. It was called the "Great Hallel" because the head of the family or leader of the group would sing the whole, with the others singing after him the first line only of each psalm; after every verse they would respond antiphonally, singing "Hallelujah!" No one in Jesus's immediate audience could fail to get the deep layering of messianic portent in what Jesus is saying; it may be that later readers of Luke's account are getting here also a literary foreshadowing of the sudden recognition of the Lord at the occasion of two disciples' postresurrection hospitality to him, as to a stranger, at his blessing of the bread (Luke 24:13–35). The breaking of bread and blessing, a major theme in Luke, is headed toward its climactic sequence.

LUKE 14

But not just yet—though the breaking of bread and hospitality is our immediate topic in Luke's next chapter. We begin with another reiteration—the last of a series of Sabbath healings—and the setting reminds us further of the symposium setting in Luke 7 (*comissatio* or *afikomen*), here perhaps also a midday meal. This time, more obviously, what appears on the surface as hospitality is quite obviously a trap, and by now the reader expects it. The particular incident, distinctive in Luke, may be included by him because it reveals that the die has been cast; Jesus is consistent in what he does and says, and there is consistency also in the Pharisees' animosity and predatory motives, like unto those of Herod.

Sabbath Observance (14:1–6)

Cyril of Jerusalem observes that although Jesus "knew their bad intentions," he accepted the invitation from some of the Pharisees to dine with them (1983: Sermon 101). He is noticing here the periphrastic form *hēsan paratēroumenoi* ("they were watching him, lurking"), as a fox ready to pounce (cf. 11:54). Their distracting bait is in plain view, a man who is *hydrōpikos*, a condition we call hydrops or dropsy (the medical term, doubtless familiar to Luke, is a *hapax legomenon* in the New Testament). The condition, typically symptomatic of a serious underlying disorder, produces extreme puffiness or swelling all over the body because of fluid retention. Rabbinic tradition associated the condition (falsely) with sexually transmitted disease (Bock 1994–96: 2.1256); perhaps with a sense of double offense, then, the Pharisees put the ill man right in front of Jesus so that in the grotesque character of his misery he could not be missed. Luke brings us in in midconversation, for Jesus, he says, "replied" (*apokritheis*) or "answered" the lawyers and Pharisees (perhaps seeing the man before him as, in effect, the pawn he has become, really a silent, symbolic provocation to debate). As so often he does, Jesus turns the tables on his foes, responding to their indirect, implicit question with one directed at their obdurate legalism: "Is it lawful to heal on the Sabbath?" Suddenly, in their dance around honest dialogue, it is the Pharisees who are trapped: they will not answer (14:4). So Jesus "embraces" (*epilabomenos*) the man, singularly treating him as a real person and not an object for argument, heals him, and lets him leave the room and get away from what must have been, for the poor fellow, an extremely awkward situation (14:4).

Now Jesus will press the discussion forward, renewing his focus on the *purpose* of the Sabbath and, indeed, of the law itself. His question to his accusers (for that is what they have become) is one the reader by now recognizes: the repetition (from 13:15) adds "ass" to "ox," not perhaps only as an intensification but so that the mishnaic provisions for looking after the needs of domestic animals on the Sabbath can be adduced (Mishnah, tractate *Shabbat* 5.2; cf. 10.5; tractate *Eruvin* 2.1–4) more forcefully. Augustine connects the plight of the sick man visually to the plight of animals in need, perhaps recalling Jesus's earlier rebuttal of the Pharisees (Matt. 15:12–14); as one who knows something about "an animal which has fallen into a ditch," Augustine envisions the bloat that follows when an ox or ass cannot get its legs under itself to rise, and sees an analogy with the bloating, dropsaic man (*Questions on the Gospels* 2.29). But this phrase also recalls a taunt in the opening words of Isaiah's prologue (Isa. 1:1–20), a text that has in its rhetorical structure a pertinent and proleptic argument representing God's effort to get reprobate Israel to "reason together" and, as a result, repent. God's lament to both earth and heavens is that he has "nourished and brought up children, and [yet] they have rebelled against me." "The ox knows its owner," says the divine voice with heavy irony, "and the donkey its master's crib; but Israel does not know, my people do not consider" (1:2–3).[1] The issue in Isaiah is not only the meaning of the Sabbath but also acceptance of the divine purpose in all of creation, of which the Sabbath is both the celebration and the culmination as to purpose. As in Isa. 1:5–6, so in Luke: the consequence of rejecting obedience includes disease of both body and soul; the unwell brought to Jesus are a visible sign of a more widespread, systemic condition. As in Isa. 1:10–15, so in Luke: ritual observances of the law count for nothing when accompanied by continued willful sin. As in Isa. 1:16–17, so in Luke: what is needed is authentic repentance—a complete transformation of life. As with the voice of God in Isa. 1:18–20, so with the voice of the Lord in Luke: people are called into a serious conversation to reorder perspective, to "reason together" honestly, then make a choice. Either way, there are consequences. It seems certainly the case that the rhetorical pattern of Isaiah's prologue is being reiterated in Jesus's teaching and debate with the scribes and Pharisees; it is also the case that their strategy of going silent (Luke 14:6) when

1. I have discussed this and related passages at length in "How to Read the Hebrew Prophets," in *Mappings of the Biblical Terrain: The Bible as Text*, ed. Vincent Tollers and John Maeir (Lehigh, PA: Bucknell University Press, 1990), 282–98.

asked a probative question about the purport of either the Law or the Prophets with regard to a righteous response reflects a pattern familiar in the writings of the prophets. Repentance is far from the hearers' minds. Yet failing to give an answer—failing to choose—is itself, as in Isaiah, a real choice. And Luke's readers at this point are fully aware of it. The silence of the group mocks any pretense of honest dialogue. It has been the prejudice of the Pharisees that they refuse to see the law itself as a sign of God's desire for honest dialogue and thus of his ultimate redemptive purpose, for, as Cyril of Alexandria says, "the law was a shadow and a type, waiting for the full truth . . . Christ" (1983: Homily 101).

Hospitable Intentions (14:7–24)

Hospitality, as we have seen, can actually mask inhospitable intentions. Appearing to be generous, it can be disingenuous. In the view of Jesus, no hospitality driven by political motives, or employed as a stratagem for social positioning, is virtuous. As he has watched the guests scramble for preferred seats, positions they imagine to be indicative of their status (14:7), he has noticed this further mark of inauthenticity in the *afikomen* of the Pharisees. As the parable he tells makes clear enough, the virtue of self-effacement is a corollary of the practice of hospitality. The parable and its context, unique to Luke, call for a reflection of the divine principle laid down in scripture (e.g., Lev. 19:15; Num. 16:15) and given by Luke as Peter's summary of Christ's teaching concerning the gracious outreach of God to "all the world": "Of a truth I perceive that God is no respecter of persons" (Acts 10:34 KJV). Peter then tells of the ministry and teaching of Jesus (10:35–43), following which immediately the Holy Spirit falls on all who hear the word, Gentiles included (cf. Jas. 2:1–5).

Both the Old Testament remembrances and the later account in the book of Acts of Peter's sermon following the conversion of Cornelius help us to understand Luke's persistence in underscoring this aspect of Jesus's message. It is not just that the poor matter to God and must be served but also clearly that "worth" as measured in human eyes does not correspond to the way God sees things. Scrabbling after the "seats of honor" (*prōtoklisiai*) is not only unseemly; it is imprudent. The "parable" (*parabolē*) Jesus gives here is a counsel of wisdom concerning the virtue of humility. In pursuing ambition for the place of honor, or fame, overreaching may result in profound embarrassment, even shame (Luke 14:9). Accordingly, humility is also a form of prudential wisdom; by sitting in the lowest seat the wise person avoids both offense and embarrassment (cf. Prov. 25:6–7). Jesus offers out of his treasure here "something old," but that has by his present company been forgotten (Luke 14:10). The principle that one day the last shall be first and the first last is, in 14:11, given in words that recall the Magnificat of Mary, but they also echo Jesus's earlier warning that in the eschaton the judgment of God and God alone pertains, and accordingly a lot of people are due for a surprise (Matt. 19:30; 20:16; Mark 10:31; Luke 13:30). This repeated warning transforms the idea of social prudence into something "new," grounding it in an eschatological principle (but cf. Ezek. 21:25–26). As the word "humility" suggests (from Latin *humus*), this virtue is no more than a candid recognition of the limitations appropriate to the human being as a creature of the Creator. Yet, as citation of this verse in *The Rule of Benedict* 7 and as the schema in Bernard of Clairvaux's *Steps of Humility* demonstrate, a careful practice of humility in our relationship with others is essential to our coming to an authentic knowledge of God.

It is altogether a new and higher standard of hospitality to which Jesus calls us. John Newton, the former British slave trader so powerfully converted in the eighteenth century, once wrote to one of his affluent correspondents, urging him to spend at least as much on the poor as he does on himself, in the process addressing the teaching of Jesus in Luke in briskly straightforward terms:

> Let your friends who are in good circumstances be plainly told, that, though you love them, prudence ... will not permit you to entertain them, no, not for a night. What! Say you, shut my door against my friends? Yes, by all means, rather than against Christ ... [who] says of the poor, "Inasmuch as ye did it unto one of the least of these my brethren, ye did it unto me. ..." The poor need relief. One would almost think that the passage [in] Luke 14:12–14 was not considered as a part of God's word; at least I believe there is no one passage so generally neglected by his own people. (Newton 1995: 1.136)

The old evangelical seems here to be as faithful a reader of the passage as any in the history of exegesis, and more candid than most. He sees that the "amazing" graciousness of God toward us in Christ calls for a reciprocal graciousness toward those who have no obvious claim to it. Hospitality in the light of Christ is not part of social obligation or reciprocity: rather, it is, like our very forgiveness, part of our identification with his love for the unlovely and those who can never hope socially to reciprocate. For authentic hospitality there will be, however, both present blessing and future reward (14:12–14) in the "resurrection of the just" (cf. Josephus, *Jewish Antiquities* 18.14).

At the sound of the word "blessed," someone at the table, perhaps out of piety or a prick of conscience, or possibly out of religious sanctimony at mention of the familiar Jewish concept of the resurrection of the just, blurts out, "Blessed is he who shall eat bread in the kingdom of God!" (14:15). He may well be reflexively making a claim, or voicing the expectation, that people just such as himself will be honorably seated at the banqueting table in the world to come (cf. Isa. 25:6; Ps. 22:26; *1 Enoch* 62.14). The parable that Jesus tells in response would have unsettled those expectations. It may unsettle our own.

"A certain man gave a great supper [*deipnon*] and invited many" (Luke 14:16). Once all things were prepared, the man sent his servant to rouse the invitees to the table (14:17). Astonishingly, "they all with one accord began to make excuses"

(14:18). The excuses were both disingenuous and lame (14:18–20), though commonplace enough that the guests around the table with Jesus on this occasion must have thought them reasonable. When the servant in the parable returned with the dismal news, the master was angry; having such a bountiful table adorned and spread, he refused to have the meal go to waste. The servant was sent first to the suburbs of the city (then and for long afterward suburbs were the least desirable places to live) to ask those from "the streets and lanes," the homeless and destitute, "the poor and the maimed and the lame and the blind," to come (14:21). Yet still there was room (14:22), so the servant was sent out a second time to "the highways and hedges" to compel even wayfarers to come, until the house was filled (14:23). Ambrose sees in this reference an allusion to Prov. 1:20, where Wisdom "calls aloud in the streets" or, as he puts it, "sings aloud in the alleyways" (*Exposition of Luke* 7.202–3). Certainly, it was folly to refuse, for the master then, as it were, barred the door: "None of those men who were invited shall taste my supper" (Luke 14:24). By this point those present could probably sense that Jesus was suggesting that even some among the despised Gentiles were included in the master's feast. This thought would have been received by the Pharisees (all scriptures about strangers and sojourners notwithstanding) as a formal insult; even in less adversarial times a little poem sometimes attributed to Ogden Nash[2] captures the religious prejudice of both Gentile and Jew succinctly: "How odd / Of God / To choose / The Jews. // Not so odd / (him being God). / The Goyim / annoy 'im."

The point that is essential to grasp here is that, unlike many of us, God is "no respecter of persons" and that while "man looks at the outward appearances [including racial or religious labels], the LORD looks at the heart" (1 Sam. 16:7). Jesus's parable is a universal call to an examination of conscience (cf. 2 Cor. 10:7). It exempts nobody. Hospitality and humility are complementary virtues; both are requisite for obedience to the commandment that we should love our neighbor as ourselves.

The Cost of Discipleship (14:25–35)

Bonhoeffer stresses very strongly the believer's obligation to *nachfolgen*, following after Christ. Referring specifically to 14:26, he says, "We must face up to the truth that the call of Christ *does* set up a barrier between man and his natural life."[3] It may be that Bonhoeffer's strongly Protestant emphasis on individual choice and stance pushes this text too far in the direction of individualism (e.g., his remark that "it is Christ's will that [the follower] should be thus isolated, and that he

2. This first part of the witticism may originate, rather, with William Norman Ewer, *The Week-end Book* (1924); the rejoinder is sometimes attributed to Leo Rosten.

3. Dietrich Bonhoeffer, *The Cost of Discipleship*, trans. R. H. Fuller (London: SCM, 1963), 106 (emphasis original).

should fix his eyes solely upon him"),[4] but he draws our attention to an inescapable expectation in Jesus's words about the ordering of loyalties.

What does it mean when Jesus says that following him will require a disciple to "hate" father, mother, wife, and children (14:26)? A big crowd is now gathered around him: is he rejecting the commandment to honor one's father and mother, the first commandment "with promise"? He has said in Matthew's version of the Sermon on the Mount that one who calls his brother a fool "shall be in danger of hell fire" (Matt. 5:22). The extreme language here is an example of Jewish hyperbole; Jesus is making a rhetorical, not a literal, point designed to show that following him is a radical choice, requiring a clear priority in allegiance (Bonaventure 2001–4: 2.53). What this means is best understood if we imagine that to follow Jesus in that time put one at distinct odds with the claims of one's Jewish family, almost in the way that can be true of a Christian convert from a Muslim family or in some Hindu or Marxist communities today. Family solidarity and honor in some cultures can be thought of as the highest good. But no such priority outweighs the claims of Christ for a disciple's undivided loyalty. Does this sometimes lead to painful choices? Certainly. As Basil the Great puts it, this is "a severe decree" (*Concerning Baptism* 1.1), and early church catechumens often paid a severe price accordingly. The word "disciple" Jesus uses here is *mathētēs* ("learner"): one cannot learn at the feet of Jesus without coming to be like Mary of Bethany, undistracted by many of the claims of family. Yet such a focus is "the one thing most needful," even if it comes at a high cost. Family members are to be honored and loved but are not to be used as an excuse, as we may remember some did in sending their regrets to the master's feast to which they had been the first invited (Luke 14:20).

This is why Jesus now repeats what he has said before (9:23), that *unless* one bears his cross and thus comes after him, that person cannot be his disciple. For many early church, Franciscan, and later commentators, the costly discipleship of *imitatio Christi*, the imitation of Christ, is understood in just this way. Their warrant for this sense of discipleship was confirmed also by Paul, who describes the "normal Christian life" (cf. Watchman Nee) as "always carrying about in the body the dying of the Lord Jesus, that the life of Jesus also may be manifested in our body" (2 Cor. 4:10). Bonaventure (2001–4: 2.55.1377) connects this passage directly to Luke 14:27 and adds also that "those who are Christ's have crucified the flesh with its passions and desires" (Gal. 5:24). Basil applies to this text Gal. 6:14, in which Paul writes, "The world has been crucified to me, and I to the world" (*Concerning Baptism* 1.1; cf. Gregory the Great, Homily 37). A loss of this biblical sense of relation to the world—the practice of seeing oneself as in it but certainly not *of* it—has disabling effects upon authentic Christian life in any time. More generally the absence of salt and light has enervated the proclamation of the gospel to the point at which what was given for healing has in many

4. Ibid., 105.

cases become merely palliative care, the "sickness unto death" that Kierkegaard famously denounced as the woeful state of "Christendom" (this passage from Luke is quoted many times in his writings). In the light of the demise of Western "Christendom" in our time, we ought to appreciate how in considerable part the collapse has occurred because, as Guorian puts it, the church "endeavored to be not what it *is*, but what it is not."[5] As Harvey and others point out, when Christians fail to be radically clear about the absolute claims of Jesus as to discipleship, then authentic Christian life has already ceased.[6]

Counting the cost is therefore a critical part of the decision to follow Jesus. One ought to eschew the folly and embarrassment of someone who sets out to build a tower without determining if he has the resources to complete the job (Luke 14:28–30). A king going into battle, if he is at all prudent, takes an inventory of his troops and field strength so as to determine whether he can win the day (14:31–32). Counting the cost for a would-be disciple, however, involves something more than such measures of normative prudence. Rather than just assessing resources needed to complete the job, the true disciple will get rid of everything he has in the way of such material resources! For Basil, Jesus's examples are organized rhetorically in this way "to show the impossibility of pleasing God amid those things that distract the soul" and to show that our bonds of attachment to the comforts of this life must be broken if we are to be true to Christ: "This is done," he says, "through complete separation from and forgetfulness of old habits. It is impossible for us to achieve our goal of pleasing God unless we snatch ourselves away from fleshly ties and worldly society. We are then transported to another world, another manner of living, discovering with the Apostle, that our citizenship is in heaven [cf. Phil. 3:20]" (*Long Rules* 5).

Jesus concludes this discourse with another saying we may remember from Matthew's account of the Sermon on the Mount (Matt. 5:13). In this culture salt was used by bakers of bread to cover the floors of their ovens, because it had a catalytic (not to mention antiseptic) effect when cattle dung was burned as fuel (Bock 1994–96: 2.1290; Marshall 1978: 596). After a time the salt burned off its "saltiness" and hence lost the required properties. For the modern reader, who might have been just as happy not to have learned of the practical, earthy aspect of Jesus's concluding point in this discourse, the spiritual exegesis of medieval commentators (who most likely would not have known of the ancient Palestinian practice either) may be more welcome. For Bede, "It is as if he says, 'should a man who has once been enlightened by the seasonings of truth fall back into apostasy, by what other teacher shall he be corrected, seeing that the savor of wisdom that he tasted, he has cast away, merely because he was either alarmed by the troubles or allured by the attractions of the world?'" (quoted in Aquinas, *Catena Aurea*

---

5. Vigen Guroian, *Ethics after Christendom: Toward an Ecclesial Christian Ethics* (Grand Rapids: Eerdmans, 1994), 122.

6. Barry Harvey, *Can These Bones Live? A Catholic-Baptist Engagement with Ecclesiology, Hermeneutics, and Social Theory* (Grand Rapids: Brazos, 2008).

3.2.521). In another colloquial but pertinent allusion, Bonaventure connects this to Paul's admonition that the disciple should use "discretion in conversation." Paul's injunction is: "Let your speech, while always gracious, be seasoned with salt" (Col. 4:6). All of these understandings are helpful, but there is another point that remains and that is instanced in Jesus's answer to his own rhetorical question about the spent salt: "It is neither fit for the land nor for the dunghill, but men throw it out. He who has ears to hear, let him hear!" (Luke 14:35). As with the prophets before him, notably when relaying the word of God, Jesus's own speech is very often salty. It can sting. But his words cleanse, purify, and bring a transformative savor to everything in life. What Bonhoeffer grasps is that the teaching of Jesus concerning discipleship is not in the least ambiguous, nor do his imperatives blur at the edge; as with the voice of God in Isaiah, the force of the divine voice in argument carries us to a clear point of decision: either/or (cf. Isa. 1:19–20). It is in the obfuscation of some modern commentators that the "hard sayings" of Jesus are made to die the death of a thousand qualifications. The honest reader needs to read the text straightforwardly and beware of such commentators as may be guilty of what Kierkegaard, one of Bonhoeffer's worthy predecessors, calls an "abolition of the principle of contradiction" or, to use the phrase of one of his modern editors, "betrayal by an interpretation."[7] It is a sobering reflection for any disciple of Jesus, especially one who seeks to comment on a Gospel text, that any form of defense or apologetic for Christianity that fails to honor scrupulously the stark judgments and "salty" speech of Jesus in just such terms as he himself gives can, in effect, betray the Lord with a kiss.[8] And so, gentle reader, this saying is both for me and for thee: "He who has ears to hear, let him hear."

7. Søren Kierkegaard, *The Present Age*, trans. Alexander Drû (New York: Harper & Row, 1962), 68; also Walter Kaufmann in the introduction, p. 12.
8. Søren Kierkegaard, *The Sickness unto Death*, trans. Walter Lowrie (New York: Doubleday, 1954), 218.

LUKE 15

Parables of Redemption (15:1–3)

Among the most widely known of Jesus's parables are those found in Luke 15. All three parables are unique to Luke's Gospel, and each has to do with a common subject: redemption of the lost. What occasions this string of stories is a particular setting; a large crowd has gathered to hear Jesus, but pressing closest to the front, of all the crowd most eager, are "the tax collectors and the sinners" (15:1). Seeing this, the Pharisees and scribes, as is their wont, are reported as standing off at some distance, yet just close enough to monitor what Jesus is saying. They "complained, saying, 'This Man receives sinners and eats with them'" (15:2). We may from our own perspective too easily fail to grant them the measure of rectitude from which they judge; if hospitality to Gentiles was, for observant Jews, an offense, so especially was table fellowship (5:30; 7:39) and, as here, even standing in close proximity with those that Jews considered reprobate by the Pharisees' strict standards. It was regarded in the Mishnah as an offense to ritual purity. These scruples have also a certain biblical warrant, perhaps most memorably in Ps. 1 (also Deut. 21:20–21; Prov. 2:11–15; Isa. 52:11; cf. Talbert 2002: 148). Where the text says Jesus "receives" (*prosdechetai*) such people, the force of the verb is such as to suggest that he has, in fact, "goodwill toward" these sinful folk (Nolland 1989–93: 2.770). In fact, this verb becomes a key to the whole chapter. Yet there is much about Jesus's receptivity to suggest to the more strictly religious that he is himself insufficiently scrupulous in regard to injunctions found in all of the Law, Prophets, and Wisdom books, in their injunctions about separation from such people. It is altogether clear to the observantly religious that Jesus does not "stand off" as he should (and as they do) by these standards and that, to this degree, in their eyes he lacks the comportment of one who is "righteous." All three of the parables that follow are spoken to them by way of declaring, as Jesus does elsewhere, that his mission is not primarily to people of a strict observance—that he has come not to call the righteous, but sinners, to repentance. Christian interpretation here is well represented by Gregory the Great, who draws from the contrast between Jesus's standard of righteousness and that of the scribes and Pharisees the observation that a new standard of justice is being exhibited, by which we see that "true justice feels compassion, false justice scorn" (*Homily on the Gospel* 34).

The Lost Sheep (15:4–7)

Since the work of Jeremias, interpretation tends either to localize a reading at the literal level or, in the fashion of medieval interpreters, to provide for an allegorical understanding. At the level of historical context it appears here that the shepherd is one of modest means (his flock is not large) and that he looks after it himself. The parable is otherwise self-interpreting, which is, after all, its purpose pedagogically. The early interpreters (e.g., Cyril, Augustine, Gregory the Great) are surely right to see the numbers, however, as there more for spiritual than literal reasons; one hundred, they observe, is a perfect number, and this makes the urgency of the shepherd to recover his lost sheep, leaving the ninety-nine in the fold, more significant at the symbolic level. Gregory of Nyssa draws on the moral (or tropological) level of exegesis to find in the action of the shepherd a model for pastors dealing with penitent sinners: "But when the shepherd had found the sheep, he did not punish it, nor did he get it back to the flock by driving it, but rather by placing it upon his shoulder and carrying it gently he united it to his flock" (quoted in Aquinas, *Catena Aurea* 3.2.525). Literarily, governing all these elements is the note of "joy" or "rejoicing" (*chairōn*) in 15:5 that characterizes the finding and return of the lost in all three parables in this chapter. Following each, as we shall see, the joyful protagonist "calls together" (*synkaleō*) his neighbors and friends for a celebration (Jeremias 1963: 134); as in the wonderful story of the water turned to wine at Cana, so here: each parable suggests that the one who seeks and finds then throws a big party. It is interesting that in early church writings this parable was used (sparingly) to accommodate the reconciliation of lapsed Christians (*Apostolic Constitutions* 2.12–14) as well as the restoration of those who lapsed during the Diocletian persecution (Cyprian, Epistle 46, 51).[1] Later, in Protestant hymnody, the parable became a standard figure for Christ's seeking out the wayward or backslidden nominal Christian, as in Ira Sankey's hymn "The Ninety and Nine," a musical setting composed while he was on an evangelistic tour in Scotland with Dwight L. Moody. The message in every application is the same: the one who is lost may be restored to the flock,

---

1. Though dealing with a wider range of good shepherd parables, Matthew Levering, better than anyone, shows how the exegetical tradition regarding these texts developed through to the Middle Ages. See his "Augustine and Aquinas on the Good Shepherd: The Value of an Exegetical Tradition," in *Aquinas the Augustinian*, ed. Michael Dauphinais, Barry David, and Matthew Levering (Washington: Catholic University of America Press, 2007), 205–42.

as has been shown by the Great Shepherd of the sheep. Exclusion of the lost is not the divine intention.

The Lost Coin (15:8–10)

Here a woman has lost one of ten coins. In symbolic terms this number mirrors the tension between imperfection and perfection in the ninety-nine and hundred sheep. It is thought that a drachma (a noncircular coin) was then about the equivalent of a day's wage for an ordinary workman. Chrysostom is typical of early commentators in observing that such a coin would typically bear the image of the emperor, suggesting to him that we, even when lost, "were made according to the royal likeness and image, that is to say, of the most high God" (on Ps. 5:7). There are parables like this in mishnaic literature (cf. Lightfoot 1979: 3.157), and there too the focus is on the necessity of seeking, and joy in finding, the lost, a note echoed by Augustine (*On the Merits and Remission of Sins* 1.40) and others.

The Prodigal Son (15:11–32)

To say that this is one of the best known of all parables would be an understatement; almost every major English and American fiction writer and dramatist makes reference to it. From Chaucer to Edward Arlington Robinson's dramatic monologue "The Prodigal Son," this story becomes, in its various treatments, a kind of touchstone for literary consciousness. Shakespeare alludes to it more often than any other parable, and the prodigal's return figures in the denouement of plays as divergent as *Comedy of Errors* 4.3.18–19 and *Winter's Tale* 4.3.103. But here is an important clue to the way in which both comedy and romance in Christian culture draw on this parable as a metonymic story of sin and salvation, casting it as the good news or *euangelion* in microcosm: the parable of the prodigal son is a magnificent example of the happy ending, closure expressed as a return after calamitous miscreance and dismal wanderings—home at last. Such a story is of particular interest in contexts where spiritual separation anxiety is profound; it is no accident, I think, that widespread literary interest in this story begins in the sixteenth century, both in Germany and in England, spreading from Burkart Waldis's vernacular drama *De Parabell vam verlorn Szohn* (1527), in myriad treatments by German and English playwrights, including such interesting texts as Thomas Ingelond's *The Disobedient Child* (ca. 1560) and the anonymous *London Prodigal* (1604) to Lope de Vega's striking *El hio prodigo* (1604). It becomes a major theme also in American literature.[2] Here too the focus tends to be on the wayward son as

---

2. Manfred Siebald, *Der verlorene Sohn in der amerikanischen Literatur* (Heidelberg: Winter, 2003); and Manfred Siebald and Leland Ryken, "Prodigal Son," in *A Dictionary of Biblical Tradition in English Literature*, ed. David Lyle Jeffrey (Grand Rapids: Eerdmans, 1992), 640–44.

protagonist. In our own time, Henri Nouwen's beautiful meditation *The Return of the Prodigal Son* (1994) adds to eloquent insights in Luke's text a refraction from Rembrandt's remarkable painting of the same title, also an artistic work of Reformation-era culture. Nouwen makes a case that the meaning of the parable for us today is entirely congruent with the meaning Jesus intended for the scribes and Pharisees, namely its challenge to "older brothers" to love as the father in the parable loves and to accept, as does the repentant son, that love amid the ignominy of all of our wayward sinfulness, as the means of our own homecoming, reconciliation with the father. On such a view, it is the father who is the ultimate protagonist.

In light of the evocative power of this story for literature over the past five centuries, it is interesting to observe that in the early church the parable was seen less individually and more in its Lukan context of literary unity with the two preceding parables. The three together inscribe a context that stresses their role in both Christology and ecclesiology. Ambrose represents it in this way: "Luke did not idly present three parables in a row. By the parables of the sheep that strayed and was found, the coin which was lost and was found, and the son who was dead and came to life, we may cure our wounds, being encouraged by a threefold remedy. 'A threefold cord will not be broken.' Who are the father, the shepherd, and the woman? They are God the Father, Christ, and the church" (*Exposition of Luke* 7.207–8). The emphatic unity of purpose Ambrose identifies here is to be discovered, of course, on another horizon (that of the Christian reader), rather than the perspective of the scribes and Pharisees at whom it was originally aimed. In their own case, natural identification was with the elder brother, whom they saw as wronged by the father's impetuous forgiveness and generosity. Among Christian interpreters who hold firmly to the original horizon of meaning, Calvin is the clearest expositor: "For what gave rise to this parable," he observes, "was the grumbling of the scribes, who could not bear Christ's humanity toward the wretched and men of doubtful lives" (1972: 2.225). Calvin goes on quite sympathetically to describe the scribes as "obedient sons, who throughout their lives have patiently borne their father's government," and he ascribes to Jesus a generous if tactical concession to the residue of virtue in their "feigned holiness" in his analogy. We see thus that the parable invites reflection from several perspectives and from a point of identification with each of the three main characters. The modern reader will benefit from considering each perspective thoughtfully in turn; there is theological richness that will escape a singular reading.

One or two final examples will underscore early ecclesiological interpretation. John Chrysostom notes how the parable provides an important insight into the relationship between human freedom and God's providence: "The freedom of will," he observes, "is shown in that the father neither kept back the son who wished to depart nor forced the other to go that desired to remain" ("Homily on the Father and Two Sons," quoted in Aquinas, *Catena Aurea* 3.2.533). Ambrose sees the younger son's exercise of freedom as producing a loss of freedom, and both in terms of relationship to the church: "For what is more afar-off than to depart from one's self, to be separate not by country but by habits. For he who severs himself from Christ is an exile from his [true] country and a citizen [only] of this world." But Ambrose keeps his eye on the moral understanding of the original context: "Let us not look down on those who return from a distant land, as Isaiah [9:2] teaches" (*Exposition of Luke* 7.213–14). Closely echoing Ambrose, Augustine, thinking in terms of the citizenship question, reflects these ideas also in his discussion of conversion. Speaking of the prodigal, Augustine addressed God feelingly, confessing that "to be in the realm of lustful passion is the same as to be in the realm of darkness, and that is the same as to be far away from your face" (*Confessions* 1.18). In the "far country" in which, through a rebellious use of freedom, the son has utterly lost his freedom, it must at a deeper level be the agency of the father that speaks in the recesses of his memory and calls him home. In his own case, "far from God in the region of dissimilarity" (7.10), as he puts it poignantly, Augustine hears, as it were, a call to return as an invitation to the eucharistic feast.

I have paused longer on the reading of this parable down through the centuries in part because I believe that the familiarity of this version of "the old, old story" should not cause the modern reader too lightly to overlook an important reason for its perdurable pedagogical power: it is a précis of the central thesis of the gospel, an emblem of the literary power of Jesus's teaching, and as much as anything it reveals our need to read and reread scripture in company with the faithful of all ages. The parable also shows well how at its deepest reach the teaching of Jesus is a species of poetics; its concession to our woodenmindedness is by way of a story that draws us out, teases us into interpretation, only to find that we will need to reinterpret it again and again if we are to approach so much as a semblance of its larger truth and power. Whether we read it literally, morally, allegorically, or indeed as anagogy or eschatology that sees the divine plan for human salvation in terms of redemption of the lost, calling them to the heavenly banqueting table through the unimaginable mercy and grace of the Father, we are reading through partial understanding a text that nonetheless will always yield truth—as long as we do not reduce it to our own partiality.

The reader of this parable should endeavor to get inside its Jewish context, to imagine the discomfort among the members of Jesus's audience to which a Jew would be reduced not just by working for a Gentile but by feeding swine (cf. Lev. 11:7; Deut. 14:8; Isa. 66:17). This might well have been more horrific for them than the prodigal's debauched life, though even there Luke has to reach into his pagan Greek vocabulary to find a word (*asōtōs*—a New Testament *hapax legomenon*) coarse enough to capture whatever Aramaic term Jesus may have used. For Spurgeon the plight of any such prodigal recalled the story of Circe, "the enchantress who turned men into swine," a story from Homer that Luke surely would also have known.[3] We must try to grasp the profundity of the prodigal's

---

3. C. H. Spurgeon, *Spurgeon's Sermons* (New York: Carter, 1883; repr., Grand Rapids: Baker, n.d.), 9.17.284–5. Spurgeon preached on this parable at least four times, in two of which he used it to steer a course between the Arminians and a strict Calvinist view of God (4.9.145–60; 6.3.47–60).

alienation: "no one" (*oudeis*) will help him; he is utterly deprived of the home and community he has so crassly disregarded. We must also appreciate the disparity between the desperation of the son's determination to ask his father for the lowly status of a *misthios*, a "day laborer" (less secure than a household slave), and the father's astonishing munificence, clothing him in a regal *stolē*, giving him a ring (signifying full sonship), and putting on a feast with the fatted calf, a festive banquet such as otherwise might have occurred only once a year or so on a major religious holiday—such as the Day of Atonement (Bock 1994–96: 2.1315). Only when we can imaginatively enter into the first horizon of the story in something like this fashion will we be able to appreciate the sense of joy, the rejoicing that Jesus is speaking about in all three of these parables. And only by careful meditation on all of these elements will we be better able to appreciate the furious resentment of the elder brother.

What first catches the attention of the elder brother as he returns home from a weary day in the field is the sound of music; Luke's term here, yet another *hapax legomenon*, is *symphōnia*, which meant in the first century something of what it means to us—namely not only that people were singing but also that there was a band of musicians playing. By *symphōnia* we should not imagine anything like Mahler's No. 2, the "Resurrection Symphony" (though the point of this unspecified music is doubtless pretty much the same), but something much more boisterous, even rowdy. Augustine likens this singing and dancing to "men filled with the Holy Spirit, with harmonious voices proclaiming the gospel" (*Questions on the Gospels* 1.2.33). The songs were clearly festive dance songs; here again the New Testament *hapax legomenon* is a term as familiar to us as to Luke's Greek audience: *choros* (15:25). Who can fail to sympathize with the elder brother's enquiry of the servant: "What is going on here?" (15:26). It is not an unreasonable question. But when he learns, he wants no part of the party, no reconciliation, not even to go into the house. He who had been the "insider," having become so infuriated that the "outsider" has been readmitted, now becomes the outsider himself. Much heavy irony hangs over the text.

Hearing of the elder brother's refusal, the father goes out to him also (this echoes his going out to the prodigal brother) and, as the Greek verb *parekalei* makes clear, *repeatedly* entreats the elder brother to come in. The elder brother's tone is denunciatory of both his brother and his father (15:28–30), but the father's tone is tender nonetheless; he calls him *teknon* ("child"), a vocative that, as Jeremias notes (1963: 131), should be understood as "my child," assuring him that all that he owns is still destined for the elder brother. It is fitting, says the father, that "we should make merry and be glad, for your brother was dead and is alive again, and was lost and is found" (15:32).

The story leaves questions unanswered and, as is often the case with Jesus, the elements omitted also invite a response from his hearers. Who will they identify with? Will they, if their sympathy is with the elder brother, enter in? Ambrose and Augustine are typical of early and medieval commentators who see the elder brother representing the people of Israel, the younger son the sons of adoption, namely Gentile converts. Jeremias regards the story as dominantly about the father's love (1963: 128), as after him does Henri Nouwen, while Green thinks that the prodigal himself is the protagonist.[4] But almost all Christian commentators recognize that this allegory, however it may seem to be supported by the historical context and immediate application of the story, reaches much farther into the realm of spiritual and moral life, inviting plainly an examination of conscience on the part of every Christian. In the words of Ambrose, "Let us not envy those who return from a distant country, seeing that we ourselves also were afar off" (*Exposition of Luke* 7.214). Above all, perhaps, it is appropriate to say that the parable continues to speak to prodigals of many descriptions. John Chrysostom does no violence to any voice in the great conversation when he writes that "this parable was written to the end that sinners should not despair of returning, knowing that they shall obtain great things" (*Homilies on Matthew* 64). In this sense, too, Luke 15 is at the very heart of the gospel message. It has seemed to preachers in all times that the parable answers one question definitively, and that is through its depiction of God as a father who "wills not that any should perish" but that all should come to repentance. In Spurgeon's hallmark one thousandth sermon, the parable of the prodigal "puts plainly before every sinner . . . the exceeding abundance of the grace of God in Christ Jesus." Surely it has very often been preached, as Spurgeon puts it, in the hope "that the Lord will find out those who are his sons, and that . . . as they hear of the abundance of bread in the father's house, [they] may say, 'I will arise and go to my Father.'"[5] That is the spiritual level of understanding in this parable that opens the door to all separated brothers everywhere.

---

4. Joel B. Green, *The Gospel of Luke*, New International Commentary on the New Testament (Grand Rapids: Eerdmans, 1997), 578.

5. Spurgeon, *Spurgeon's Sermons*, 9.17.287.

LUKE 16

In this chapter, we again are almost entirely in territory covered by Luke exclusively (16:16–17 is the sole exception). Two parables dominate the chapter, the first of which, on stewardship, is followed by evident contestation from the Pharisees and Jesus's sharp response to it, and the second is a parable of warning concerning the danger of riches—indeed, of the consequences of failing to distinguish appropriately between the service of mammon and what is, in fact, due to God alone.

The Unjust Steward (16:1–13)

This is a difficult story to understand, and not least because in it there seems to be praise for someone whose actions are, to say the least, ethically murky. If, as seems possible, it followed in delivery close upon the heels of the forgiveness parables in Luke 15, then perhaps it is providing a perspective on worldly forgiveness for wrongdoing that has, in its own context, some rationale and plausibility, even if the "forgiveness" of the rich man falls far short of the divine standard suggested in the parable of the prodigal. But there is more likely something more than that at issue. Here the offender is not a son but a kind of estate manager, and the sin appears less to be a matter of completely profligate abandon (although some of that is suggested) than of bad management, a lazy neglect of duty and responsibility by which the "steward" (*oikonomos*) had "wasted" the goods of his master. Whatever the case, having been a bad steward, when called to give a full "account" (the term is *logos*, meaning in this context a "rational account") prior to dismissal from his post, the manager proves to be an unjust as well as ineffective steward.

Augustine reasonably thinks that no one should imagine that the Lord set this parable before us haphazardly or that he wished in any way to condone the cheating of the steward. Rather, it is because "he exercised foresight for the future," and he finds the lesson lies in comparison: "When even a cheat is praised for his ingenuity, Christians who make no provision blush" (Sermon 539A.10). Other early commentators have seen an application to the Pharisees who were rich, but not as solicitous as they might be toward the poor (Cyril of Alexandria, Bede), and these tend to regard this Lukan theme as the point. On this view, the theological teaching concerns appropriate stewardship for those who are rich. Consistently with the parable of Lazarus and the rich man that follows, another address to almsgiving as repentance and forgiveness, it is also a warning to the rich by use of an ironic example. Augustine accords with this view in his *Questions on the Gospels* 1.2.34, as do Ambrose and Chrysostom. Whatever we think about seeing the parable thus as a link between the forgiveness parables in Luke 15 and the "unforgiveness" parable of the rich man and Lazarus, the Lord's narrative arguably shifts the focus from forgiveness to a hasty effort at prudential avoidance of judgment by someone who really needs forgiveness.

The story describes a large estate with very substantial tenant debts, and the secretive reductions in debt represent a formidable loss of revenue for the owner. It may be that the amounts represent accrued interest on the outstanding debt (in which case usury of some sort may be a complicating factor).[1] A critical point in the story is the owner's response to the manner in which he has yet again been cheated, just as the unjust steward is headed out the door. Rather than being furious, as we would expect, he surprisingly commends the man for his "shrewdness," a better and more precise translation of *phronimos* than "done wisely." In two of his sermons on this parable, John Wesley sees the story as a call to prudent stewardship on the part of the Christian believer who "considered as a sinner . . . is there represented as a debtor to his Creator."[2] On this line of thinking, the parable has also an eschatological application; after death we all have to give an account of our stewardship.[3] In another sermon, however, Wesley stresses the element of *phronimos* in more material terms: "An excellent branch of Christian wisdom is here inculcated by our Lord on all his followers, namely the right use of money."[4] In a twist on the idea of the use of money for alms or charitable purposes, he argues for the moral neutrality of money and says that "it is an excellent gift of God, answering the noblest ends."[5] Consequently, "all who are engaged in worldly business [ought] to observe that first and great rule of Christian wisdom with respect to money, 'Gain all you can.' Gain all you can by honest industry. Use all possible diligence in your calling. Lose no time."[6] Yet whatever the general merits of Wesley's often repeated argument concerning industry and monetary stewardship, it is surely problematic in view of Luke's text at this point.

---

1. J. D. M. Derrett, *Law in the New Testament* (London: Darton, Longman & Todd, 1970), 65–72.
2. John Wesley, *Fifty-Three Sermons* (Nashville: Abingdon, 1983), no. 51 (p. 715).
3. Ibid., no. 51 (p. 724).
4. Ibid., no. 50 (p. 703).
5. Ibid., no. 50 (p. 704).
6. Ibid., no. 50 (p. 708).

Prudential wisdom of this order is not, it seems to me, compelling as the principal lesson to be drawn. Once again, the Lord's distinction (or comparison) is a key: "For the children of this world are in their generation wiser than the children of light" (16:8 KJV). That is, worldly people use mammon pragmatically in a self-interested way, and given their materialistic preoccupations, that makes a certain prudential sense. But "the children of light," who have every reason by virtue of scriptural instruction to know that for them worldly profits are mere dross compared with "laying up treasure in heaven, where moth and rust do not corrupt," have too often in practice a fundamental confusion of mind and method in their habits of life. One can too easily gain the whole world and lose one's own soul, as Jesus says elsewhere (Matt. 16:26; Mark 8:37).

What ought his hearers do with "unrighteous mammon" (Luke 16:9) (ill-gotten gains, perhaps), given that one has done the deeds and gathered the cash? The story of Zacchaeus (Luke 19) suggests one obvious answer, namely to repent of the deeds and disperse the money in generosity to others. Almsgiving, as noted earlier, had long been seen as a means of concretizing one's repentance, paying against one's indebtedness to God as incurred by sin. This, as the parable of the rich man and Lazarus will make perfectly clear, is one way to be "receive[d] . . . into everlasting habitations" (16:9 KJV). Stewardship in such comparatively insignificant material matters, Jesus says, is directly related to how people respond to true riches, the kingdom of heaven (16:10–12). If people cannot be faithful to the law in regard to their use of transient material wealth, who will commit to their trust the "true riches" (cf. Prov. 22:3–5)? In this light the problem of divided loyalties (and stewardship) makes apt if unsettling sense: mammon can be nothing more than an instrumental good, and it is folly to allow it to conflict with service to God: "No servant can serve two masters"; only one can be Lord, and only one good can be intrinsic to the rightly ordered mind of an ethical Jew.

Response to the Pharisees (16:14–18)

There is little in Jesus's teaching anywhere to warrant the self-affirming culture of the prosperity gospel. It is no accident that such teaching, in our time enormously popular, has negligible reference to sin and repentance and very little in the way of reference to Jesus. There are similarities in such viewpoints to the affluent among the Pharisees, who seem to have thought their wealth a kind of irrefragable evidence of God's blessing on their lives.

Unsurprisingly, there would thus be a sharp sting in this parable for some. Some among the Pharisees could have easily seen themselves as openly targeted (Marshall 1978: 625). In this case, their covetousness, as Luke says, gets the better of them, and they begin to "deride" Jesus (16:14), a certain indication that the barb has found its mark. Luke does not record any of their doubtless harsh remarks, but he does show us plainly that Jesus responds to their derision with trenchant criticism. He does so simply by quoting from the scriptures, the Torah they claim to cherish, and the wisdom texts they claim to honor. "You are those," he says, "who justify yourselves before men, but God knows your hearts" (16:15). They must have heard in these words echoes of Prov. 21:2: "Every way of a man is right in his own eyes, but the LORD weighs the hearts" (cf. Deut. 12:8; Judg. 17:6; Job 32:1).

"Man looks at the outward appearances, but the LORD looks at the heart" (1 Sam. 16:7) echoes there too, and in the light of it one wonders if Jesus was thinking of another passage in Prov. 30:12–14: "There is a generation that is pure in its own eyes, yet is not washed from its filthiness. There is a generation—oh, how lofty are their eyes! And their eyelids are lifted up. There is a generation whose teeth are like swords, and whose fangs are like knives, to devour the poor from off the earth, and the needy from among men." "Woe to those who are wise in their own eyes," Jesus seems to say, "and prudent in their own sight" (Isa. 5:21). For theirs is a foolish prudence. In this one remark by Jesus, the whole Tanak seems at his disposal—Law, Prophets, and Writings together.

Thus he summarizes: "The law and the prophets were until John. Since that time, the kingdom of God has been preached, and everyone is pressing into it" (Luke 16:16). On this view John the Baptist is seen, as elsewhere, as a transitional figure between the authority of the Hebrew scriptures and a new authoritative presence (Luke 1–2; 3:1–6, 15–20; 7:18–35), Jesus himself as the embodied and eternal Torah of God. What does he mean when he says of the kingdom of God that everybody is "pressing into it"? Matthew's parallel says famously that "the violent bear it away" (Matt. 11:12–13 Douay). Luke's verb, *biazetai*, certainly suggests a forcible entry, as if people were trying to force their way into the kingdom on their own terms. Was Jesus referring to those, like the Zealots, who sought to bring in the messianic age through a political and military revolution? If so, the text is too cryptic for readers to be sure. Moreover, Jesus did not critique the Zealots anywhere else. For all that a great transition has occurred in his coming and message, Jesus insists that the law is in some sense still valid: the smallest pen stroke on the page is more likely to endure than the cosmos itself (Luke 16:17). This makes perfect sense rhetorically in the context, for he has scrupulously adduced the law in his immediate criticism of the Pharisees and scribes.

The last verse in this sequence may seem at first to be out of place: what is a rebuke of "divorce" (*apolyō*) doing in this context? It seems that Jesus intends a point of insistence upon the law as it stands, and indeed, mishnaic tractates, especially *Sotah*, suggest that the practice even of religious Jews had wandered quite a distance from the prescriptions of the law of Moses regarding fidelity in marriage. Further, if we are to take the nuptial imagery of Luke seriously, to reflect on its appearance earlier specifically in relation to John the Baptist as friend of the bridegroom and to remember the characterization of sinful Israel as a bride degenerated to the status of harlot (Jeremiah, Hosea), then we may imagine that here too Jesus is going after the issue of Israel's representative infidelity. He may also know something about the character and life choices of some of those to whom he is talking. Infidelity had become a universal blight, to the degree that it had been normalized in the culture of the religious themselves. The surfaces may have looked nominally clean, but the practices on both the personal and national levels could reasonably be regarded as grossly negligent of covenant responsibilities to marital fidelity.

There is thus, as Jesus himself elsewhere says plainly, a sword at work in his hand, dividing the crowd not along the usual lines of Jew and Gentile, disciple and onlooker, but spiritually down the middle of each conscience. No one present could escape this; all were challenged. The kingdom of God proclaimed by Jesus has real rules, and these rules often intensify, not merely uphold, the law by which Israel was to live. And yet we may say with Cyril of Alexandria that the whole force of Jesus's teaching is to say also that there is something really new by means of which fidelity may be regained: "The kingdom of heaven here means justification by faith, the washing away of sin by holy baptism, and sanctification by the Spirit. It also means worshiping in the Spirit, the service that is superior to shadows and types, the honor of the adoption of children, and the hope of glory about to be given to the saints" (1983: Homily 110). Everything the Pharisees thus found repugnant in the teaching of Jesus, his disciples could accordingly receive as a welcome liberation, "good news of great joy to all people."

Lazarus and the Rich Man (16:19–31)

Not many parables are much illustrated in Christian art, but along with Jesus's story of the good Samaritan (and later, the lost sheep), this is one that may be found in medieval manuscript illustration (including the *Bible moralisée*) through the fifteenth century; it appears also in Jacopo Bassano's mid-sixteenth-century painting (ca. 1550), now found in the Cleveland Museum of Art (Hornik and Parsons 2003–7: 2.98–102). A mid-fifteenth-century prose treatise, *Dives et Pauper*, which reflects the typical Latin translation of "rich person" (Greek *plousios* = Latin *dives*), is a dialogue in which the parable provides a framework both for a discussion of poverty and a catechetical exposition of the Decalogue.[7] But this text, and in general the use of the story of the rich man and Lazarus in medieval preaching and moral literature, introduces an element regarding genre that is illuminating for contemporary scholarship, in which the status of this narrative as a parable has sometimes been questioned. The objection attends to rhetorical framing of the story. Luke does not call it a parable, unusually, nor is it introduced with a comparative ("the kingdom of heaven is like unto . . ."); moreover, this would be the only parable in which a character is given a name, Lazarus. Ambrose, one of the first to notice these features, said simply, "This seems rather a narrative than

7. H. G. Pfander, "Dives et Pauper," *Library* 4, ser. 14 (1933): 299–312, analyzes the content of this text, which survives in six manuscripts and three early printed editions.

a parable" (*Exposition of Luke* 8.13). Medieval sources typically follow him in referring to this story as an "exemplum," a category typically defined as a moral anecdote used to illustrate a theological or ethical point. That certainly applies here, but it hardly contradicts the category "parable" in doing so. The name "Lazarus" (*Lazaros*), interestingly, is a form of the name "Eleazar," which means "God helps"; given that Abraham features in this story, some might associate him with Abraham's faithful servant (in Gen. 15), himself a kind of Jewish exemplum for loyalty and covenant service. It is highly unlikely, however, that the purpose of the name is to point to any real person, living or dead.

Lazarus surely does emblemize the plight of the very "poor" (*ptōchos*, the term used by Jesus in his beatitude discourse in Luke 6). Perhaps too sick to move on his own, he has been reduced to begging near the ornate "entrance" (*pylōn*) to the rich man's mansion. While there is perhaps a hidden mercy in the dogs licking his suppurating sores, the dog was considered in Jewish law an unclean animal, and the scene so powerfully sketched in two verses—of Lazarus, prostrate, licked by dogs, all the while yearning for crumbs from the sumptuous table of the rich man as if he were himself a dog—is one of palpable anguish. It seems a mercy also, therefore, when he dies, and indeed that is precisely to the heart of Jesus's exemplum. The poor beggar is carried into "Abraham's bosom" immediately; meanwhile, the rich man has also died and gone on a one-way ticket straight to Hades (16:22–23). Suddenly, the tables are turned. This is a story of complete reversal. The once comfortable man, now bereft of his fine garments and gourmet fare, is in torment more acute than the erstwhile sufferings of poor Lazarus. It is Lazarus who is now rich; the worldly rich man has been "sent empty away," not into some oblivion but rather into an acute and tortured consciousness of the vastly better situation of the once-wretched man he had so studiously ignored—even though he lay in misery right on his doorstep and even though he had abundant means to alleviate his suffering. It is therefore not only his own immediate torment that anguishes the poor rich man; as is common in Jewish views of the afterlife (*2 Esdras* 7.85, 93; *2 Baruch* 51.5–6), he is acutely conscious of the sublime happiness of the "blessed." That point is amplified immediately by the phrase "Abraham's bosom," for in stunning contradiction of his doubtless expectation, the "true son of Abraham" turns out not to be himself but the poor beggar. Though he pretended not to notice Lazarus in life, now he can hardly notice anything else.

One significant theological point suggested in the parable is that not all "sons of Abraham" will have a blessed "life to come." For some there will be no Sabbath rest (the Greek word for the rich man's suffering is *odynaomai*, which implies not only pain but also profound restlessness; it is at the root of Odysseus's name and identity in Homer). This is the pained discomfort of one who is not, and in this case cannot be ever, "at home." For Lazarus, by contrast, now is the very first time, perhaps, that he has been at home; in his consciousness there is a profound sense of "comfort" (*parakaleō*), closure, and completion. It makes psychological sense—however surprised we may be to imagine such a communication—that the rich man calls out to "father Abraham" for relief in the flames. But there is such poignant irony in his request; reflexively, he is in his own mind still master. He wants Lazarus, like a slave, to bring him a drop or two of water to cool his tongue (Luke 16:23–24). The answer he gets only increases his torment. Abraham underscores not only the reversal of circumstances but also its unchangeable character. As if to acknowledge his privileged (but now futile) status, Abraham refers to him as "son," even as he explicates the justice in the reversal the rich man has suffered. Lazarus has been comforted at last; the rich man, though born a son of Abraham, failed to live up to his sonship and will never be comforted again (16:25). This story is very far from making a case for universal salvation; it is plainly aimed in the opposite direction, making a case consistently with what scripture says in many places about God's judgment on poor stewardship of wealth in the face of the poverty for others. Here too the issue is not wealth or poverty as such but ethical and spiritual stewardship: as Ambrose so eloquently summarized it: "Not all poverty is holy, or all riches criminal, but as luxury disgraces riches, so does holiness commend poverty" (*Exposition of Luke* 8.13). The point is broadly applicable, I think, but we must not press it too hard on this story, where we are not given by Jesus any reason to regard Lazarus as particularly holy. But the issue of the rich man's poor stewardship is visible enough. As Jerome puts it, "The rich man, in purple splendor, is not accused of being greedy or of carrying off the property of another, or of committing adultery, or in fact of any [obvious] wrongdoing" (*On Lazarus and Dives*). His sins are those of omission: he has neglected the poor and needy. In this story of Jesus, that is all that is necessary for damnation.

Abraham also says plainly that neither Lazarus nor he can cross the unbridgeable "chasm" (*chasma* is another *hapax legomenon*). The rich man must continue to suffer in a fully conscious separation from what might have been. When the rich man cries out that Lazarus might be sent to his family, to testify to his "five brothers . . . lest they also come to this place of torment" (16:28), it just gets worse for him—and more especially for some of the already angry among Jesus's hearers. Abraham says, "They have Moses and the prophets; let them hear them" (16:29). In the context, in which Jesus has just been demonstrating to the scribes and Pharisees that they have the Law and the Prophets and yet have not paid attention to them, this comment cuts deeply into their hearts. It is a brilliant rhetorical move.

The rich man makes one last effort. Now he is really thinking of somebody besides himself: "No, father Abraham; but if one goes to them from the dead, they will repent" (16:30). Not so, says Abraham, in a voice that not only calls to mind his character in the medieval *Dives et Pauper* but is also anticipatory of a slightly more optimistic C. S. Lewis in *The Great Divorce*:[8] "If they do not hear Moses and the prophets, neither will they be persuaded though one rise from the dead" (16:31). (There may be in these words a tacit prophecy of Jesus's own resurrection and of the persistent obduracy in unbelief on the part of many who,

8. C. S. Lewis, *The Great Divorce* (London: Bles, 1946).

having neglected Moses and the Prophets, will be unmoved by even the most extraordinary signs.) In Jesus's story, the "great gulf fixed" had been prepared long before the rich man's moment of tragic perception. This is not a story to encourage unfocused hope, as Augustine put it long ago; here "it is shown by the unchangeableness of the divine sentence that no aid or mercy can be rendered to men by the righteous, even though they should wish to give it" (*Questions on the Gospels* 2.88).

This implication of this uncompromising narrative makes modern readers distinctly uncomfortable. It may be easier to read it as we would a passage from Dante's *Inferno* or *Purgatorio*, though there is no suggestion here that the rich man is in any transitional state. *Gaudium et spes*, a product of Vatican II, shifts the emphasis in this parable to Lazarus and "the innate dignity of every human, independent of his social, financial, cultural, or religious position" (Vatican II, *Gaudium et spes* §27). This view is certainly an entailment of the parable's meaning, but it does not capture the eschatological portent of which Jesus's hearers were as acutely aware as any medieval or modern evangelistic preacher. More recently, Wright distances the parable (which he rightly sees as a species of Mediterranean folk tale) from an eschatological context: "The parable is not, as often supposed, a description of the afterlife, warning people to be sure of their ultimate destination" (1996: 255). While surely "eye has not seen, nor ear heard," as Paul says (1 Cor. 2:9), I am not so sure that we can say that it is not a warning regarding "ultimate destination." In a way, the evident stress on the abuse of wealth, while ignoring the poor, consistent in the Law, the Prophets, the Psalms, and in Jesus's own explicit teaching, is given its full weight here only if we can admit that this is a story about truth and consequences, suggesting that a focus on treasure on earth can lead inexorably to eternal poverty.

On the other hand, I do accord with Wright's reading that "the welcome of Lazarus by Abraham evokes the welcome of the prodigal by his father, and with much the same point" (1996: 255). This seems to me to be precisely right, and also that "the five brothers at home correspond quite closely to the older brother in the [story of] the prodigal son" (1996: 256). This echo develops a strong theme running through all of these parables, even in the midst of their evident function as a warning to the Pharisees and scribes. The story of Lazarus and the rich man is not only a story about judgment but also a story about the boundless mercy of God upon those who in no obvious way deserve it. It is thus yet another polyvalent story filled with hope for those who "have eyes to see and ears to hear," and yet again a proclamation of "good news to the poor."

LUKE 17

Luke 17 divides into three discrete sections, dealing respectively with (a) counsel to Jesus's disciples concerning sound pastoral principles and appropriate attitudes; (b) an apparently unrelated incident of healing for ten lepers; and (c) Jesus's response to a (possibly mocking) question from the Pharisees about when the kingdom of God would begin. This is one of these situations in which the medieval chapter divisions suit the topical distinctions less well than might three more pronounced divisions.

Pastoral Wisdom (17:1–10)

The first six verses are not unique to Luke (cf. Matt. 18:6–7, 15; 17:19–21; Mark 9:28–29, 42), while Luke 17:7–10 is unparalleled. The entire unit, however, contains guidelines for what we might think of as pastoral care. Jesus begins with a warning: inevitably, he warns the disciples, misrepresentation of the gospel, or "offenses" (*skandala*), will come. Cyril of Alexandria is typical of those who read this as a reminder of human infirmity, namely that "all of us stumble in many things" (1983: Sermons 113–16, citing Jas. 3:2). Peter Chrysologus (Sermon 27) represents those who think that the Lord is here warning about Judas in particular, especially when he says, "But woe to him through whom they come!" (Luke 17:1). Matthew's parallel, however, seems more focused on the disciples generally (Matt. 18:6–7), and this is where the emphasis in exegesis should probably fall. The most serious aspect of such offenses seems to be the potential of pastors or teachers to "confuse" or "mislead" (*skandalisē*, the verbal form repeats the opening noun) "one of these little ones" (Luke 17:2). Jesus may be referring to children in the crowd, or he may be talking about recent and still immature converts. In either case, it is very clear that the offense is serious, since he says that it would be "advantageous" (*lysiteleō*) to the health of the community if such a one were drowned in the deep blue sea, to put it in modern idiom. His phrase about the millstone around the offender's neck is itself proverbial; one finds it used precisely in this way in Aristophanes (*Equites* 1361, quoted in Lightfoot 1979: 3.177). It seems on the plain sense of this passage to be unambiguously a bad idea to be the occasion of such a scandal, for it invites a capital offense penalty. This is clearly not the same sense of the term that Paul uses when he says that, to the Jews who rejected him, Christ is a "stumbling block" (1 Cor. 1:23); it is, however, analogous to his warning to the Corinthian believers that they should "beware lest . . . this liberty of yours become a stumbling block to those who are weak" (8:9), only here the warning is much more dire in respect to consequences.

At the same time, Jesus is turning the point for pastoral-care purposes in quite a different direction: if a brother trespasses against you, he says to his disciples, the appropriate response is to "rebuke him; and if he repent, forgive him" (Luke 17:3). There is no warrant here for taking divine judgment into one's own hands. It is the duty of the community first to correct: Cyril has it that "it is our duty, having a common feeling for our mutual infirmities, to bear one another's burdens, and so fulfill the law of Christ" (1983: Homily 113.6, citing Gal. 6:2). There is a long exegetical tradition that, seeing correction as a mutual responsibility to be exercised for the sake of the health of the whole body, regards the correction itself as an act of mercy that "must not issue from anger," as Bonaventure puts it (2001–4: 3.8.1630), citing Gregory the Great's *Moralia* 32.21.44 to the effect that "if we are to love our neighbor as ourselves, it follows that we be angry with their sins just as we are with our own." Nor is there any invitation here to feelings of superiority; just the opposite (cf. Calvin 1972: 2.216). This leads Bonaventure to a discussion of church discipline based on Matt. 18:15–17 as well as Paul (Gal. 6:1), emphasizing that "first the sinner must be brought back *by love*, which is expressed when the sinner is admonished in secret" (3.18.1630). Bede marks the important distinction in Luke 17:3 when he observes that "he does not bid us forgive every one who sins, but only him who repents of his sins" (*Homilies on the Gospels* 2.22), a point reiterated by Bonaventure (2001–4: 3.10.1362; 3.10.1635) and others. Even if someone "sins against you seven times in a day" (the number is symbolic for "again and again"), according to Jesus the appropriate response, as long as the sinner indicates his repentance, is for the offended one to forgive him (17:4). The verb here is imperative (*aphēseis*): "You *shall forgive* him." Especially in a Mediterranean culture at that time, so attuned to retributive justice and the expectation of revenge, this must have seemed a hard saying. Perhaps it is not much easier for us.

In that light, we should hardly be surprised that the disciples find themselves near the limit of their understanding of how such forgiveness may be possible. "Increase our faith," they plead (17:5). They have faith, but surely not enough for living up to such a standard. Fortunately, their request is to the Lord himself. "Faith depends partly on us," says Cyril of Alexandria (in the passage already cited), "and in part it is the gift of divine grace." Virtually the whole of Christian tradition sees this question, and the response of Jesus, as marking the dependency of the believer on a faith that transcends human capability and *must* therefore be given by the Lord as a gift (Bonaventure, Thomas Aquinas, Luther, Calvin). The medieval *Glossa Ordinaria* adds that even to understand this commandment of the Lord requires that our faith be increased. Jesus responds with a comparison that indicates at once how powerful even a modicum of faith, faith as miniscule "as a grain of mustard seed" (KJV), could cause a tree (KJV's "sycamine" is probably a long-lived, deeply rooted species of mulberry) to uproot itself and fly out to the ocean and plant itself there (17:6). At the very least the disciples would have heard this as an invitation to enter imaginatively into the enormity of what may be possible to them compared to the mere wisp of faith they now have.

Now Jesus turns to another issue. Calvin (1972: 2.216), like John Chrysostom (*Homilies on Genesis* 31.4), infers that one occasion of the "offense" that will come is the tendency to ambition, competitiveness, and ego-centeredness generally—even in the midst of the vocation of the disciple. As Chrysostom puts it plainly, one of the greatest enemies of a truly faithful discipleship is the pursuit of human glory. Jesus sets all such ambition in perspective by his example of what really the lot of the servant (his word here is *doulos*, "slave") is in relationship to the master: the work of the *doulos* is never finished, nor is it immediately rewarded. When one task is finished, another awaits. The *doulos* may not expect some immediate honor, such as being now served by his master. Such a servant does not reasonably expect accolades, applause, or even to be thanked(!) for doing what after all is his duty. Rather, Jesus says emphatically, than having aspirations to temporal praise, his servants should exhibit a marked humility, saying in deliberate self-effacement, "We are unprofitable servants. We have done what was our duty to do" (17:10). Here then, suggests Bede, "is the perfect faith of men, when having done all things which were commanded them, they still acknowledge themselves to be imperfect" (quoted in Aquinas, *Catena Aurea* 3.2.584)—and are thus open to correction and further growth. Spiritual maturity requires this. Good pastors, according to Gregory the Great, do not rejoice immoderately in any earthly benefits that happen to be bestowed on them (*Book of Pastoral Rule* 20.21); rather, they await benefits that are bestowed by God alone when their earthly service has been brought to its mortal conclusion. Bonaventure summarizes the tradition usefully: "The person who humbles himself in this way is the one who disposes himself for perfect and eternal glory" (2001–4: 3.21.1647).

One Thankful Leper (17:11–19)

The incident that follows has the teaching force of a parable and in its theme—gratitude—underscores an indispensable condition for one who would live life toward God. It happened, Luke says, as Jesus continued on his way toward Jerusalem, somewhere in the adjacency of Samaria and Galilee. It is clear that Jesus is not journeying to Jerusalem by the straightest route, whether because he wishes to avoid capture by Herod's agents before he arrives on his own schedule or because he has other errands in mind, we are not told. There is a geographical ambiguity about his route, but Marshall clarifies this in pointing out that Perea had by this point been subsumed under Galilee as a jurisdiction (1978: 650), an observation that follows from Pliny (*Natural History* 5.15), Tacitus (*Annals* 12.54), and others. In any case, his route, indirect like his manner of teaching, takes Jesus and the disciples into a region where Samaritans and Jews live in proximity.

At the outskirts of an unnamed village, ten lepers are found in a group, having heard of Jesus's approach. From a distance (as was by law required of their condition), they call out to him, addressing him as *epistatēs* ("master"), a term found in Luke only, who uses the term where exclusively the other Synoptics have *didaskalos* ("teacher, rabbi") or *kyrios* ("lord"); perhaps "master" is a more natural term in this context. Jesus's response is noteworthy: he does not lay hands on them, but in a fashion reminiscent of Elijah's messenger's direction to the Syrian general Naaman (2 Kgs. 5:10–15), he sends them to show themselves to the priests, as the law required (Lev. 13:19; 14:1–11). It is helpful for the modern reader to recall that for Jews, the quarantined group were by their disease exiled from the temple and from all forms of full communal worship, though it happens that together, had they all been Jews, they would constitute the minimum for a *minyan* (Wright 1996: 191–92). By definition, the lepers are ritually unclean, unholy, outcasts from the people of God.

Luke's narrative suggests that it will be in the process of their faithful obedience to Jesus's command that the ten will suddenly recognize that they have been healed. This is indeed what happens. We must imagine the sudden, joyous discovery, as they pick up their pace en route to the priests. One, only one, stops himself and returns to the source of his deliverance, the true physician. With a "loud voice" he "glorified God." Healed, he may now come close to the Lord; he falls down at Jesus's feet and gives him thanks (Luke 17:12–16). And now Luke adds his skillfully withheld point: "And *he* [*autos* is emphatic] was a Samaritan" (17:16). That, in this narrative, is the real kicker.

Were the other nine Jews? Luke does not say; his point is that the only one who expresses gratitude for his deliverance is not a Jew. (If the others are, there is poignancy on several levels, one of which is that in the extremity of their disease they are forced to form a community of sorts with the Samaritan, a man with whom, in normal circumstances, they would have nothing to do. Luke sees but understates the irony.) Jesus's rhetorical questions are not to the healed man but to his disciples and are designed to heighten the contrast between gratitude for God's mercy from a "stranger" and the oblivion of the rest to their great gift and its giver. This indirection also points to a deeper truth. Marshall is on the mark, I think, to point out (1978: 652) that the term "stranger" (*allogenēs*), while a New Testament *hapax legomenon*, was precisely the term used on signs prohibiting foreigners from passing the inner barrier of the temple (Josephus, *Jewish*

Antiquities 15.418). Thus, the one who could never have worshiped in the temple, here overcome with gratitude, worships Jesus. And gratitude is critical to what follows, for it indicates a further crucial distinction. To the grateful man Jesus says, "Arise, go your way. Your faith has made you well" (17:19). All ten have been physically healed, but only one, having established right relationship with Jesus, is now fully reconciled to God.

Signs of the Coming Kingdom (17:20–37)

Two distinct audiences are addressed by Jesus in this important teaching. The first, Luke makes clear, is the Pharisees, who have asked Jesus, perhaps in a tone of skeptical mockery, when the kingdom of God should come. His answer to them seems to be conditioned both by the bias of their enquiry and also by the clichéd character of the age-old Jewish preoccupation with apocalyptic "signs of the times." His point is that they are missing—or indeed have consistently missed—the main point, and their question shows it: "The kingdom of God does not come with observation" (17:20). At one level, this is like a proverbial saying such as "the watched pot never boils." But given the contemporary and recent preoccupation with apocalyptic signs (as reflected in *1 Enoch* 91, 93; *2 Baruch* 53–74; and some documents found at Qumran), it is likely that Jesus sees their question in that context, and essentially as probing him for his views on these matters. He declines to answer them in those terms. Rather, he diffuses this preoccupation with gentle sarcasm: "Nor will they say, 'See here!' or 'See there!'" (Luke 17:21). Competing theories are also beside the point. "Look," says Jesus emphatically, "the kingdom of God in the midst of you *is*." Bock makes the helpful point that when the syntax of *entos hymōn estin* is rendered literally we see at once what Jesus is saying to the Pharisees: "The kingdom of God in the midst of you *is*"—right under your noses. That is as much as to say that the ultimate sign of the kingdom is precisely the one they have overlooked in asking their leading question—the one of whom they have asked it (1994–96: 2.1424–25).[1] Jesus's response is, accordingly, no mere rhetorical dismissal of the Pharisees' disingenuous query. Rather, it underscores a dialectical relationship in Luke's text between the present, in which the kingdom has appeared (though some cannot see what should most plainly be visible), and the future, final, and definitive revelation of the kingdom of God as a judgment on all those who have had "eyes to see" but have not seen. The English translation often given, for example, NKJV's "the kingdom of God is within you" (rather than "among you" or "in your midst"), misses the point because it misses the syntax. It also misses the target of Jesus's comment; it is clearly the Pharisees, not the disciples, to whom Jesus is really speaking.

---

1. Cf. J. P. Meier, *A Marginal Jew: Rethinking the Historical Jesus*, vol. 2, *Mentor, Message, and Miracles*, Anchor Bible Reference Library (New York: Doubleday, 1994), 428–30.

Jesus turns his attention to the disciples in 17:22, addressing them as his "true companions," as Cyril puts it, because "he wants them ready to endure patiently so that approved they may enter the kingdom of God" (1983: Homily 117). To this end he will give them a picture of the future, and do so in the context of a counsel to future hope in the face of their intervening trials and tribulation. What Jesus says to them, in effect, is that there are going to be times ahead for them in which, for good reason, they will long for the fullness and final triumph of God (17:22). But they ought, no more than the Pharisees, to be taken up with various fevered human attempts to make claims upon having discovered it (17:23). There will be sensationalists and apocalyptic "prophets," but the disciples are to ignore all that sort of excitement. When the real "Day of the Lord" comes, it will be unambiguously and instantaneously evident to all, as much as is a powerful flash of heat lightning illuminating the whole dark sky (17:24). That will be the real thing, and it will need nobody to point it out or "interpret" the signs. As did most Christians for many centuries, Cyril sees these words as clearly referring to the second coming of Christ (1983: Sermon 117): "At the end time of the world, he will not descend from heaven obscurely or secretly, but with godlike glory and as dwelling in the light which no one can approach."

This section of Luke's text has occasioned a great deal of debate among textual critics. This is not on account of Luke's narration itself being in any way problematic, but because, while Matt. 24–25 and Mark 13 each contain only one eschatological discourse, Luke has two, here and in Luke 21:5–36. While there are a number of obvious similarities between Luke 17 and Matt. 24 especially, there is no overlap between what Jesus is recorded as saying here in Luke 17 and what he says later in Luke 21. The closest Lukan parallels to Matt. 24–25, moreover, are back in Luke 12:35–48. How should we understand these disparities? Bock gives a detailed table of comparison and analyzes various theories that have been put forth to account for various aspects of this textual disjunction (1994–96: 2.1420–25), and the interested reader will find much there to enlighten the variance; his own view is that Luke had at least three separate eschatological discourses available to him and that he chose to use two. Wenham's suggestion of a single, pre-Synoptic, pre-Pauline source is interesting also,[2] but neither view can be conclusively demonstrated at this point. What can be surmised is that what we have reflects discrete eyewitnesses reporting to Luke. Although textual criticism per se is not our brief in this commentary, the eschatological discourses in Luke provide an occasion for seeing how some textual questions remain unsolved and that more work will have to be done for us to resolve them completely. But since eschatological references abound in the remainder of Luke's Gospel and have everything to do with his characterization of events and the words of Jesus as to ultimate meaning, we need to be closely attuned to eschatology as a theme.

2. David Wenham, *The Rediscovery of Jesus' Eschatological Discourse*, Gospel Perspectives 4 (Sheffield: JSOT Press, 1984).

Luke 17:25 contains the only prediction of his passion given in Jesus's eschatological discourses. What he says is cryptic but unambiguous: the Son of Man must suffer and be rejected by "this generation" before he can return in judgment in another generation. There is an implicit question for his hearers in all of this: if there is to be suffering for the disciples and suffering for the Lord in coming days, how are we to think about the final Day of the Lord? Jesus does not address this question, but he does make analogies between the experience of God's judgment in generations past and the coming day of final judgment: "And as it was in the days of Noah, so it will be also in the days of the Son of Man" (17:26). One may readily sense how this analogy follows from what Jesus has already said: while the ark was being built, Augustine says, even though its building was a kind of visual preaching to them, the people of that day did not believe. They just carried on carrying on (17:27), and so do their "imitators," as Augustine calls them, today (Letter 164). Then the ark was filled, its doors shut, and the lightning struck across the sky as the clouds began to pour their torrents of incessant rain. So also with Sodom; it was business as usual and party time as usual, and as suddenly the fire and brimstone fell and all were destroyed except for part of one family. "Even so will it be in the day when the Son of Man is revealed" (17:30). Signs of the end times are, in the face of such unanticipated and instant cataclysm, more or less nugatory by comparison with the task of making oneself ready.

Above all, Jesus says by his qualifying examples two things. The first is that God's action in final judgment is discriminating: "One will be taken, and the other will be left" (17:34). The other point is that escape from the wrath to come will be dependent on a cultivated disposition to forget material possessions (17:31) and to have no second thoughts or even nostalgia for the old world that is passing violently away: "Remember Lot's wife." That which is "left behind" is precisely that which has no value in such an hour. These injunctions prepare for the adage that follows: "Whoever seeks to save his life will lose it, and whoever loses his life will preserve it" (17:33; cf. John 12:25; Matt. 10:39; Luke 9:24)—a saying that Jesus has uttered many times, itself a paradox. What does he mean here? Cyril of Alexandria connects the paradox to the actual experience of the early martyrs, "enduring conflicts even to the loss of blood and life" for the sake of their love of Christ, exemplifying in this dramatic fashion a loss of physical life that leads to life eternal (1983: Homily 118). The two examples that follow are unique to Luke; one will be taken, the other left behind, male and female alike (17:35–36). As Bede puts it, one is either inside the ark or out of it (*On the Tabernacle* 1.25.32); there is no moderate position in these examples. Eusebius likens the division to the separating of tares from the good wheat in Jesus's parable (Matt. 13:24–30, 36–43); now we live in a condition of conflict and uncertain identity, but "at the end of the world, the consummation shall not come before all the just are separated from the wicked." That is, these examples are consistent with all of Jesus's teaching on the life after death, whether personal (as in the case of the rich man and Lazarus) or concerning the chosen people of God (as in the parable of the wheat and the tares). "Where, Lord?" Where will the Son of Man be revealed? Jesus's answer here too is foreboding: one will know the place by the gathering of vultures over the corpses of the wicked (Luke 17:37). This is a dark saying and troubling still to many.

LUKE 18

Despite the traditional chapter break, what follows here is really part of the same eschatological discourse as in Luke 17.

Prayer and Perseverance (18:1–8)

The parable of the importunate widow and the unjust judge is unique to Luke (though Sirach 35.18–19 offers a thematic precedent). The judge in this story is irreligious and haughty, almost above the law. On established Jewish principles judges are to defend widows, especially against an unjust adversary (Exod. 22:22–24; Deut. 24:17–18; Pss. 68:5; 82:2–7), but because this judge had no fear of God, he has been notably indifferent to his obligations. It is well to recall here that in those times widows without visible means of support were sexually vulnerable as well as poor; doubtless she wants not only justice (*ekdikeō*) against the "adversary" who stands in the way of her receiving what her husband has left for her (as often as not such adversaries were members of the husband's family, which may imply a refusal of levirate marriage as well) but also a means of protection from abuse. Perhaps the judge finds it inconvenient to aggravate a politically powerful family; perhaps he is just too preoccupied or in other ways indifferent to the plight of the destitute. It really doesn't matter. His refusal to act confirms the adjective "unjust" (*adikia*) in Luke 18:6. But the woman persists, asking again and again for "vindication" (*ekdikēsin*), a further wordplay on *dikē* ("justice").

Eventually she begins to get to the judge. His reasoning does not suggest that he considers the justice of the matter she brings to him at all but rather the political cost, public shame, or irritation that might be occasioned by her persistence. "In the end [*eis telos*]," he says, "she may wear me out" (18:5). Here again, the Greek contains a subtle eschatological hint ("in the end") that English translations typically obscure, and it prepares for what Jesus says next: "Hear what the unjust judge said. And shall God not avenge his own elect who cry out day and night to him, though he bears long with them?" (18:6–7). The idea of God's "being patient" (*makrothymon*) has occasioned difficulties; God's patience clearly represents a contrast rather than a parallel with the unjust judge's loss of patience and consequent vindication of the widow. With whom is God showing patience, and why? It may be that the focus here is on God's long-suffering patience with Israel, permitting time for a greater number to repent (cf. 2 Pet. 3:9). Yet the prayers of the faithful would seem to be for "vindication" that the Lord promises will come "speedily" or "soon" (*en tachei*)—which may mean that this action will happen suddenly when finally it happens. The following verse with its rhetorical question seems to make the eschatological connection explicit: "Nevertheless, when the Son of Man comes, will he find faith on the earth?" (Luke 18:8). Will there be perseverance in faith that God will answer prayers, that his promises will be fulfilled, or that his final vindication will come to pass? Even though the answer seems to be delayed, will the Lord on that day find his faithful ones at prayer?

It is obvious that, as Augustine says, we are not to read the parable as an allegory (*Sermon on the Mount* 15). Rather, it is a form of argument from the lesser to the greater, which is characteristically Jewish in its form and its tone of ironic hyperbole (we have seen already such an argument in 11:11–13: "If you then, being evil, know how to give good gifts . . . how much more will your heavenly Father . . ."). The term for this in Hebrew is *qal wahomer*; it is a device found frequently in rabbinic texts. We learn something about the qualitatively superior character of God's benevolence and mercy through an analogy that elevates the divine standard far above human practice. Jesus's point is not that the disciples should pray long prayers but that they should pray without ceasing (Augustine, Letter 130). Bede suggests that one who is praying the canonical hours exhibits one kind or example of prayer without ceasing, but that another is an attitude of heart in which "all things which the righteous person does and says toward God are to be counted as praying" (quoted in Aquinas, *Catena Aurea* 3.2.600). Deeds may be prayers, if offered up in that spirit. The Lord seems to be suggesting, says Augustine, that "when faith fails, prayer dies" (Sermon 115). It is interesting to consider Augustine's rhetorical order: persistence in prayer is evidence of persistence in faith. The question Jesus asks finally is rhetorical because pedagogical, and it clearly bears an eschatological warning. Cyril of Alexandria understands it in the light of a failure of many to persist in the authentic gospel: "People sell the word of righteousness, and make many abandon sound faith [doctrine]. They involve them instead in the inventions of devilish error. As scripture says, they belch things out of their own hearts rather than speak words from the mouth of the Lord." Cyril makes an explicit connection of this passage to 1 Tim. 4:1–2, referring to an apostasy in which "the love of many will grow cold." In the end times, some will "depart from a correct and blameless faith, instead going after seducing spirits and listening to the false words of people whose conscience is seared" (1983: Homily 119). Read in this way, we are led straightforwardly into a discourse on the distinction between phony and real prayer, a distinction that itself has eschatological implications.

The Pharisee and the Tax Collector (18:9–14)

This very Jewish parable, also distinctive to Luke, has entered deeply into the consciousness of Christian exegetical tradition. Also about prayer, it continues the theme of vindication. Augustine relates it to 18:8, especially the Lord's question about whether, on his return, Christ will find faith on the earth. "Knowing that some would arrogantly attribute this faith to themselves, he immediately said 'To some who seemed to themselves to be just and despised others,' he spoke this parable" (Letter 89). We have had already occasion to reflect on the way in which Jesus's stories distinguish sharply between human self-esteem and the all-seeing perspective of God; this is a theme that bears particularly on any consideration of what constitutes authentic repentance. This particular parable sharpens a central distinction in many biblical narratives, namely that between unrepentant and repentant or between hard-hearted and brokenhearted hearers of Jesus's word.[1] The Pharisee in this parable is one of the "some" (*tinas*) who have, in effect, self-justified, asserting their notion of vindication before God; this "stage" Pharisee is not one of those who, like Nicodemus or Gamaliel, have some humility about their standing before God and who refrain from presumptuous judgment over others accordingly. In this respect, the Pharisee in Jesus's story is an exemplar of a type; those who have earlier made self-confident judgments about Jesus are doubtless the immediate targets of his parable (Marshall 1978: 678). The attitude this Pharisee represents was in fact also criticized by Jewish writers of the period (Josephus, *Jewish War* 1.110; Babylonian Talmud, tractates *Sanhedrin* 101a and *Sukkah* 45b), so it is likely the case that Jesus's condemnation would not have been seen by most in the audience as unwarranted (Jeremias 1963: 142–43; cf. Tosefta, tractate *Berakhot* 6.18). The problem is not the religious man's rectitude concerning the law, or even his going beyond some of its requirements, such as fasting two days each week. His problem is self-righteousness, out of which he "despised" others. In short, he is a kind of paragon of spiritual pride.

The "tax collector" (*telōnēs*) is equally a type, in his case already a general object of contempt because of his profession. Tax collectors in general had earned the reputation of being toadies to the occupying Roman power by serving as Herod's bagmen, and thus were as a class often seen as traitors to their own people. Tax collectors often used their power to overcharge. As such they were social outcasts, the "moral equivalent of lepers" (Wright 1996: 267), and while it may not have been strictly necessary for this tax collector to make his prayer for God's mercy from the outer court, or Court of the Gentiles, the way the narrative is framed

---

1. David Lyle Jeffrey, *People of the Book: Christian Identity and Literary Culture* (Grand Rapids: Eerdmans, 1996), 362–63.

makes it seem that he goes no farther before stopping to make his prayer. Though this is a parable, there could be no doubt in the listeners' minds that Jesus's story described a real and painful social reality.

The prayers of the two men are even more a contrast than their social station. The Pharisee has gone with full confidence straight into the inner court; there he begins to "pray with himself," probably after depositing his tithe in one of the thirteen chests for tithes and offerings found there. Tellingly, "the Pharisee manages to refer to himself in the first person five times in two verses," speaking of himself in his prayer in the active voice (Bock 1994–96: 2.1458). To whom is he really speaking? The phrase Jesus uses to introduce his prayer is already damning: he is talking not to God but rather as one curved back in upon himself, as Basil puts it, not feeling any need to ask for forgiveness or to pray "forgive us our debts as we forgive our debtors" (*Commentary on Isaiah* 2). Nor, as Augustine points out, does he ask anything of God (Sermon 115). Rather, he has the audacity to thank God that he is "not as other men are, extortioners, unjust, adulterers, or even as [*kai hōs*] this publican" (18:11 KJV)—the unnamed tax collector, whom he regards at the very least as an extortioner. As Martyrius trenchantly puts it, this prayer is an unmistakable sign of counterfeit spirituality of the sort by which Satan traps the religious: "He makes you drunk on pride in the lovely and sweet sound of your own voice, the beauty of your phrases that are sweeter than honey and the honeycomb" (*Book of Perfection* 78). For Walter Hilton in the fourteenth century, such a prayer betrays fake spiritual knowledge, discoverable by the dual evidence of presumption on one's own part and the "putting down and undercutting of one's fellow Christian" (*Ladder of Perfection* 114–15). It matters little after that whether the Pharisee fasts and tithes (18:12); as Ephraem the Syrian sees it, the claims of the Pharisee were doubtless true (*Commentary on Tatian's Diatessaron* 15.24). What he utterly failed to understand, as Cyril puts it, is that pride is "foreign to the mind that fears God" (1983: Homily 120) and that, as Augustine notes, "God resists the proud, but gives grace to the humble" (Sermon 351.1; cf. 1 Pet. 5:5; Jas. 4:6). The Pharisee proves to be as devoid of a spirit of repentance, and as hard-hearted about it, as Pharaoh; the law is unable to call him to repentance because he is after all a master of the law, not one mastered by it.

What a contrast is the prayer of the wretched tax collector. A man without community, without acceptance, without self-respect, and even perhaps without love—what should he do but cry out for mercy? He pleads, as he should, for pardon. (The term *hilasthēti* implies atonement and relates in the Septuagint to the Hebrew word *kipper* ["to cover"], as in Yom Kippur, the Day of Atonement.) And on the explicit interpretation of Jesus it is this poor outcast who goes "down [from the temple] to his house justified rather than the other" (Luke 18:14). We are reminded that Jesus came to call sinners, not the righteous, to repentance (5:32; cf. Mark 2:17; Matt. 9:13). Who then, though sinful, is brokenhearted? Such a one is capable of repentance. Who is condescending, full of self-justification, confusing institutional status with personal righteousness so completely that he can no longer even conceive of a reason for repentance? The hard-hearted man of religion. These are not difficult questions to answer—just discomfiting. As with so many of Jesus's stories of reversal, it turns out to be the case that here too "the proud" are "scattered . . . in the imagination of their hearts," "the mighty" are "put down . . . from their thrones," and "the lowly" are "exalted," even as "the rich" are "sent away empty" (Luke 1:51–53).

The Heart of a Child (18:15–17)

As social beings, we develop hierarchies of importance based upon majority or fashionable perception. These categories are often better attuned to obvious, external appearances than to deeper, less visible realities. In this way, there is a bit of the Pharisee in most of us; depending on our social position we tend to condescend to those we regard as lower or less equipped than ourselves, whether these be "sinners," the poor, the disadvantaged, or in many cases children. In a variety of ways, sometimes in our culture expressed through babying and the retardation of maturity by coddling, we express our prejudices regarding those we consider less able than ourselves. As adults, we often consider ourselves to be smarter than children. Yet anyone who spends much time actually listening to small children and hearing the often astonishing penetration of their observations and questions knows that this is a preposterous adult illusion. Great novelists understand this; occasionally, a narrative genius such as Charles Dickens, Mark Twain, Harper Lee, or Leif Enger will be able to expose the pretensions of an adult world to itself through a narrative voice that reports reality with almost painful precision, as it sees the world through the eyes of an intelligent child.

In the narrative that immediately follows here, some parents, presumably mothers, want Jesus to "touch" their children in a blessing. The mothers' impulse is somewhat awkwardly expressed, but what is sought is profoundly admirable. This episode is not distinctive to Luke; it is found in Mark 10:13–16 and Matt. 19:13–15 as well. Among the distinctives in Luke are his omission of the indignation Jesus expresses at the disciples' forbidding the children to come to him, found in the Mark account especially, and his singular use of the term *brephos*, which indicates that these are very young children—preschoolers, as we might say (Luke 18:15). Sometimes this Greek word is more appropriately translated "babes" or "infants."

The church historically has accordingly connected the bringing of children to Jesus with familial commitment to salvation and to the baptism of infants (e.g., Augustine, Letter 182; cf. Calvin 1972: 2.251). The disciples resist this act out of a sense of protectiveness of Jesus or, perhaps, propriety: toddlers should be seen and not heard. In fact, they might better be not seen. "They placed much value on order," Cyril says of the disciples, implying that their good intention was to spare Jesus undue fatigue (1983: Homily 121). But Jesus presses the point of his acceptance of the children much farther than they might have imagined: "Suffer little children to come unto me, and forbid them not: for of such is the kingdom of God" (18:16 KJV). What does this mean? Well surely innocence is implied here, and also a guileless transparency of trust that experience in the world will soon enough strip away. Jesus goes so far as to say that no one, adult or not, who cannot "receive the kingdom of God as a little child" can hope to enter it (18:17). Now we see how this incident connects to the previous parable: a strong sense of socially constructed decorum and a hierarchy of what counts based upon a view of the world according to norms created to cope with guile and social duplicity prove to be inimical to the openness of trust necessary to one who would receive the Christ—either as Christ-child or as God's Chosen One, the Anointed King.

The Rich Young Ruler (18:18–30)

All three Synoptic Gospels contain this story (cf. Matt. 19:16–30; Mark 10:17–31); each follows the vignette of Jesus with the children. The dialogue between Jesus and the prominent young nobleman (Matt. 19:20, 22) provides dynamic instruction in a fashion reminiscent of a Socratic dialogue; as Talbert points out (2002: 172), the young man learns something about himself as he speaks with Jesus. After the young "ruler" (Luke alone calls him an *archōn*, suggesting, given his age, a prominent civic rather than religious leader), there is an exchange between Peter, the disciples, and Jesus that likewise produces a moment of greater self-understanding or "recognition," this time not only for the disciples but also for Luke's readers.

The first element in the dialogue with the *archōn* is the way he phrases his question to Jesus: "Good Teacher, what shall I do to inherit eternal life?" (Luke 18:18). The question about how to inherit eternal life is not in itself unusual (cf. Pss. 37:9; 15:1; Dan. 12:2; *1 Enoch* 37.4); it is a very Jewish sort of question, and it is anticipated almost verbatim by the question asked by the lawyer that earlier had prompted Jesus's parable about the good Samaritan (Luke 10:25). There the answer had to do with loving the neighbor consistently with loving God; so also here.

But there is a most unusual element in this young man's form of address, and it is this that produces a new element in Jesus's response. The young man (kneeling, according to Mark 10:17, and breathless from running to catch up to him) refers to him as "Good Teacher" (*didaskale agathe*), a title with no known precedent in either the Septuagint or Talmud when referring to a rabbi who is alive and present. Accordingly, the adjective has received a great deal of comment, both ancient and modern. Luke himself treats the adjective as if it was an equivalent of Hebrew *ṭôb*, and Hebrew seems most likely to have been the language this pious young man and Jesus were speaking, as well as the language in which the conversation was reported to Luke. *Agathe* in Greek is fully consistent with the noun *agathos* and the predicate *ta agathon*, just as it would be in Hebrew. To say that Jesus is "good" in this way is to imply something different from the Hellenistic concept of excellence with which Luke would have been long familiar (Plato, *Cratylus* 412c) or "the good" for which the wise philosopher seeks and which implies not only a certain kind of life goal but also a certain morality (*Republic* 7.517b–c)—though it does not exclude either. In Hebrew "the good" used in this way has messianic, eschatological overtones, as in the promise "I will bring on them all the good" (Jer. 32:42) or Isaiah's reference to the messianic "good messenger" to come—perhaps the closest parallel to the title for Jesus used by the young ruler (Isa. 52:7). What Jesus does, it seems, is to consider the adjective in the young man's address as if implying the noun—that is, as an acknowledgment of the messianic overtones of Isa. 52:7: "Why do you call me good [*agathon*]? No one is [in that sense] good [*agathos*], but one, that is, God" (Luke 18:19). In his beautiful commentary on this story, Pope John Paul II draws the point powerfully: "Only God can answer the question about what is good, because he is the Good itself. To ask about the good, in fact, ultimately means to turn toward God, the fullness of goodness" (*Veritatis Splendor* 16). Here, I think we must remember again that the conversation is taking place in Hebrew (or possibly in Aramaic, which is closely parallel on these points). When Jesus says "but one," we should think of the one of whom one prays in the Shema: *Yhwh ʾĕlōhênû yhwh ʾeḥād* ("the LORD our LORD is one"). In this Lukan transposition, the good Lord (adjective) becomes effectively Yhwh the Good (substantive). The response Jesus makes to the man acknowledges that "there is nothing in this world that deserves the predicate [*agathon*], and that there is no one who has the predicate [*agathos*]" (W. Grundmann in *TDNT* 1.16). Neither Greek nor Hebrew works here lexically and phonetically quite like medieval English, in which aurally "Gode" the adjective and "Gode" the divine name sounded identically. The net effect, however, is not dissimilar, just achieved in a different way. Jesus is not then commenting upon himself or his own sinlessness; regarding that matter, he does not bear witness to himself but probes deeply for the young man's understanding of the words he has just spoken (cf. Calvin 1972: 2.254). Augustine thinks that Jesus explicitly forbears saying "no one is good save the Father alone," but says "the one God," a silent Trinitarian reference that includes himself, and he may well be right (*Trinity* 8).

This part of the dialogic exchange is accordingly rich with philological and theological implication. Jesus is, in effect, showing the man that his form of address implies to some degree his recognition of the identity of the one to whom he speaks, the same who gave to Moses the commandments, including here specifically those directed toward interpersonal relations—love of one's neighbor as oneself (18:20). "All these things," says the young ruler, "I have kept from my youth" (18:21). The question of his love of God is not raised because it seems not to be at issue, and in Mark 10:21 we read immediately, "Then Jesus beholding him loved him" (KJV). For these reasons, I think a reader looking at the Luke account in conjunction with Mark and Matthew, and in the light of the pertinent philological considerations, must be careful about following Cyril of Alexandria on this point ("observe how he [the young man] mixes flattery with deceit"; Sermon 122) or Jerome ("the young man speaks false"; *Commentary on Matthew* 19:19) and those who have seen him as too much like the Pharisee in the temple of the parable preceding (Danker 1988: 249). Rather, we should see him as a genuinely pious Jew who really does have an inkling of who Jesus is and is drawn to him authentically. (Bede [quoted in Aquinas, *Catena Aurea* 3.2.612] anticipates this view, pointing, as I have here, to Mark's account.)

But not completely. For Jesus, he "still lack[s] one thing"; he is too much attached to his comfortable material life. "Sell all that you have," commands the Lord, "and distribute [the proceeds] to the poor, and you will have treasure in heaven," where it really counts (Luke 18:22). Here we are once again in the dialectic of poverty and riches that marks Luke from beginning to end. The young man would like to go further in his relationship with Jesus, but he just cannot imagine a life for himself like that which Jesus models. But when Jesus says, as the Koine Greek implies, "You can do this! Make a clean break. Follow me," he cannot bring himself to do it. Seeing him torn inwardly and downcast, Jesus then says some memorable words: "How hard it is for those who have riches to enter the kingdom of God!" (18:24). Here the commentaries of the ages struggle to find a way of justifying a compromise between the extremes of poverty and wealth (Bede, Bonaventure) and attempt to show that the principle is, as in Acts, distribution and sharing (Basil, Chrysostom, Calvin). Calvin says that what Jesus was doing in this evidently extreme command to the ruler was "testing his latent vice" (1972: 2.258). The poor young rich man sadly fails this test, and, as Mark 10:22 puts it, "his countenance fell," and he walked sorrowfully away.

In the silence afterward, alone with the disciples, Jesus makes a hyperbolic comparison: "It is easier for a camel to go through the eye of a needle than for a rich man to enter the kingdom of God" (Luke 18:25). Because "camel" (*kamēlos*) sounds like "rope" or "ship's cable" (*kamilos*) in Greek, some (e.g., Cyril, Calvin) have thought that is how the word should be translated. In either case, as Theophylact long ago observed, "impossibility is implied" (quoted in Aquinas, *Catena Aurea* 3.2.614). The disciples clearly saw it this way themselves and were alarmed. "Who then can be saved?" (18:26), they ask, to which Jesus's reply is enigmatic: "Things which are impossible with men are possible with God" (18:27). Again, Pope John Paul II:

> But if God alone is good, no human effort, not even the most rigorous observance of the commandments, succeeds in "fulfilling" the law, that is, acknowledging the Lord as God and rendering the worship due to him alone (cf. Matt. 4:10). This *"fulfillment" can only come from a gift of God*: the offer of a share in the divine Goodness revealed and communicated in Jesus the one whom the rich young ruler addresses with the words, "Good Teacher" (Mark 10:17; Luke 18:18). What the young man now perhaps only dimly perceives will in the end be fully revealed by Jesus himself in the invitation, "Come, follow me" (Matt. 19:21). (*Veritatis Splendor* 19)

John Paul II goes on to make the point that "to imitate and live out the love of Christ is not possible for man by his own strength alone. He becomes capable of this love only by virtue of a gift received" (*Veritatis Splendor* 37). At some level the young man evaluates the call of Jesus in terms of "his own strength alone." He is afraid to receive the very gift that would make obedience possible, namely the gift of grace that invites him to open his hand and "let go," renouncing an over-wrought love of this world (a species of what Augustine was to call a "disordered affection") for an uncluttered love of God and neighbor. This is the one choice of life that would permit him to experience the liberty, the freedom for which Christ would set him free—not merely a freedom of conscience but a freedom to love in a hearty and holy way. As Clement of Alexandria summarizes it, this is his opportunity to realize that the one who is "truly and rightly rich . . . is rich in virtue, and so capable of making a holy and faithful use of any fortune" (*Who Is the Rich Man That Shall Be Saved?* 19). This is an extremely poignant moment in all of Luke's narrative, and coming as it does here it epitomizes how the very best in Israel might, right on the cusp of their possible salvation, refuse, albeit sorrowing, to become the true Israel to which Jesus is calling them. The story is thus a powerful theological propaedeutic for the narratives about healing, gratitude, and joyous repentance that follow in this and the next chapter.

Peter's response to all of this is clearly anxious; he seeks assurance: "See, we have left all and followed you" (Luke 18:28). Lest we think that the sacrifice of the disciples in leaving everything behind is small potatoes in comparison with what the rich young ruler was possessed with, it is important to go deeper than the question of net worth. Calvin gets this point well, I think, when he observes that in reality "simple men, used to a quiet and modest life, take it harder to be separated from wife and children than do those who are ruled by ambition or whom the breeze of prosperity blows hither and thither" (1972: 2.261). This is a point that J. R. R. Tolkien gets at in a comparable fashion with his hobbits in *The Lord of the Rings*, as they are faced with leaving their beloved shire. The disciples really *do* feel their loss, and Jesus knows it: "There is no one who has left house or parents or brothers or wife or children, for the sake of the kingdom of God, who shall not receive many times more in this present time, and in the age to come eternal life" (18:29–30). This is one of the most homely and touching things Jesus says to the disciples; he loves them too, even more, for their choice of obedience, than he loved the rich young ruler who was in so many ways attractive to him. The question of the rich young ruler about what must be done to "inherit eternal life" is answered in the choice of unqualified obedience made by the disciples. Now Peter has the answer to his own implicit question. The comment on this passage by Cyril of Alexandria defines the general way in which the church has, in the light of this passage, come to understand the present and future rewards of Christian vocation:

> If a man has left his home, he shall receive an abiding place above. If his father, he shall have a father in heaven. If he has forsaken his kindred, Christ shall take him

for a brother. If he has given up a wife, he shall find divine wisdom, from which he shall beget spiritual offspring. If a mother, he shall find the Heavenly Jerusalem, which is our mother. From brethren and sisters already united together with him by the spiritual bond of his will, he shall receive even in this life far more kindly affections. (quoted in *Catena Aurea* 3.2.617)

The Prediction (18:31–34)

Jesus now draws the Twelve aside as they are approaching Jerusalem and in the most direct way tells them that "all things that are written by the prophets concerning the Son of Man will be accomplished" when they get there. This includes some very specific detail—being turned over to the Gentiles (Romans), being mocked, insulted, spat upon, whipped ("scourged"), and executed. And he adds plainly that on "the third day he will rise again" (18:32–33). What seems astonishing to the reader is Luke's observation that the Twelve "understood none of these things" (18:34) any more than they had earlier (9:22–23, 44–45). We, of course, have hindsight of the events that to them were still in the future. It may well be that so great was their expectation of a glorious welcome of Jesus as the Chosen One that they could not imagine such events as he spoke of being a *literal* outcome; after all, he spoke to them and to others in figurative, parabolic speech all the time. This is the view of Bede, who imagines the Twelve to be puzzling over these words as if they were an allegory rather than literal portent and to sense the meaning was "hid from them" (quoted in Aquinas, *Catena Aurea* 3.2.618). It is remarkable, nonetheless, that on neither of these two occasions does even one disciple ask what Jesus meant; it may be that here also they were afraid to ask him about it (cf. 9:45), perhaps because they did not wish to appear as obtuse as they felt.

Eyes to See (18:35–43)

The disciples have learned much, but there are some things, even very plain things, to which they remain blind; so remarks Gregory the Great in his second homily on the Gospel. The miracle that here follows is a physical mirror to their spiritual circumstance, perhaps. Of course, it is much more than that, some of it also to be understood by way of contrast with immediately preceding events. A blind beggar, who cries out to Jesus, calling him "Son of David," expresses in his use of this clearly messianic title a kind of recognition of Jesus's identity that at least parallels that of the rich young ruler. When Jesus enables him to see, he immediately follows Jesus, "glorifying God. And all the people, when they saw it [the wordplay reinforces the point], gave praise to God" (18:43). The rich young ruler also saw, spiritually, but unable to ask for mercy, walked sorrowfully away. The blind beggar has nothing to lose. In his urgent plea for mercy (18:38), he echoes the plea of the tax collector in Jesus's parable (18:13), and like him is rewarded. Like Lazarus in the earlier parable, he is among those who, though poor, are "blessed" (16:22, 25; cf. 6:20). Meanwhile, many are the rich who have been sent empty away (1:53).

Matthew's parallel account (Matt. 20:29–34) has two beggars rather than one, and, as in Mark 10:46–52, the miracle takes place as Jesus goes out of Jericho rather than, as in Luke 18:35, as Jesus was drawing near to Jericho. This discrepancy has occasioned much discussion, from the time of Augustine's *Harmony of the Gospels* to the present. Augustine's conclusion is that two healing events must have been involved, one on each side of the city (2.48). Calvin's view is similar; he posits that a two-stage healing was condensed by Luke into a single account (1972: 2.278–79). In fact, there were two Jericho cities, the ancient ruins then still quite visible and "new Jericho," a little more than two kilometers apart. This probably accounts for the divergence, though why Luke and Mark record only one blind beggar remains unclear. What is clear in Luke's narrative is that the next event, with Zacchaeus, occurs during the entry of Jesus and his by now ample cohort of celebratory followers into the new, inhabited city (Luke 19:1). Mark gives the blind man's name as Bartimaeus, and both he and Matthew indicate that the crowd following Jesus was by now very large, perhaps swollen by pilgrims heading up to Jerusalem for the Passover celebrations (Mark 10:46; Matt. 20:29).

The crowd has explained to blind Bartimaeus that "Jesus of Nazareth" is passing by, and it seems to have been enough to let him put the large and doubtless noisy throng together with stories he has heard. It may have been a reinforcing coincidence to his sensitive ears that Hebrew and Aramaic *nāzîr* was a term used to denote someone consecrated to God, as in "Nazirite." Whatever the case, the dots are connected for him, and he cries out, "Jesus, Son of David, have mercy on me" (18:38). Perhaps it is the messianic title, perhaps just irritation at the clamoring of one more beggar, but some in the crowd "rebuke" (*epitimaō*) him, attempting to shut him up. This moment anticipates another shortly to come (19:40). Jesus stops and commands rather that the blind man be led to him, whereupon he speaks to him in as kindly a tone as he had to the rich young ruler: "What do you want me to do for you?" Then follow the famous words: "Lord, that I may receive my sight" (18:41). And Jesus says to him, "Receive your sight; your faith has made you well" (18:42). As Ephraem the Syrian writes, "The Light came into the world to give sight to the blind" (*Commentary on Tatian's Diatessaron* 15.22), and for Cyril of Alexandria, "The word was light to him that was blind, because it was the word of him who is the true Light" (1983: Homily 126). The symbolism here needs no further explication, for as Gregory the Great said wisely enough, "Blindness is a symbol of the human race" (Homily 2). In this blind beggar are we all figured, even though already disciples. Longfellow's macaronic poem (one line Greek, one English, alternating), titled "Blind Bartimaeus," and poems by John Newton (1779) and George Macdonald on this passage all concur in Gregory the Great's reading.

This is the last miracle recorded by Luke in his Gospel, and it is an epitome.

✠ # EXPECTATION
AND REVERSAL ✠

LUKE 19

Zacchaeus (19:1–10)

The road up from the Jordan River to Jerusalem passed by the ruins of old Jericho and seems to have gone straight through the new city (19:1). The crowd following Jesus by this time must have seemed very like a parade, and as it grew it attracted a throng of spectators. One of these, a "wee little man," as the children's song has it, wanted badly to get a look at Jesus but could not see over the other spectators (19:3). This little fellow was in some other ways, as we say, a "big man," for he was the head of the local tax collectors, doubtless collecting a percentage of all their gains, ill-gotten or otherwise. Luke puts it simply: "He was rich" (19:2). This episode is yet another uniquely found in Luke, and it is remarkable in several ways—also, in effect, an epitome, or metonymic story.

Running ahead of the procession, Zacchaeus "climbed up into a sycamore tree" on the main thoroughfare, eager to gain a view (19:4). When Jesus came to that point, he looked up, saw him, and said something that Zacchaeus could not have anticipated in any way: "Make haste, and come down," Jesus commands, "for today I must stay at your house" (19:5). Zacchaeus immediately obeyed and clambered down, and Luke says simply that he received Jesus "joyfully" (19:6). The crowd, however, was loath to share in this happiness. A man such as Zacchaeus, a notorious "sinner"? It would hardly be too much to say that they were scandalized. How did a rabbi of the holiness attributed to Jesus know to call such an inveterate rascal as Zacchaeus by name? Luke does not know either; it seems that Jesus is here displaying his divine insight. It is certainly clear from Luke's narrative that Jesus is in control of the hugely ironic reversal of expectations taking place among the residents of Jericho.

Zacchaeus is the Greek form of the Jewish name "Zakkai," which derives from Hebrew *zakkay* ("righteous one") (Ezra 2:9; Neh. 7:14)—a ludicrously incongruous name to begin with, given his occupation. He is the very opposite of righteous by any cultural reckoning. For all that, he has been so keen to see Jesus, and so overcome that Jesus greets him and even enters into fellowship with him just as he is, that he spontaneously undertakes a radical redirection of his entire life. From Luke's compressed narrative we cannot tell whether his enthusiastic speech to Jesus is more or less immediate, but it seems so: "Look Lord, I give half my goods to the poor; and if I have taken anything from anyone by false accusation, I restore it fourfold" (Luke 19:8). In Judaism, legal restitution for having been guilty of extortion was twenty percent (Lev. 5:16; Num. 5:7), but Zacchaeus assumes the harsher penalty imposed on people who stole livestock (Exod. 22:1; Bock 1994–96: 2.1520). Something truly profound has happened, and in the joy of his acceptance by the Lord he goes much farther than anything the law requires. His exuberant restitution indicates a genuine repentance; as Augustine notes, restitution is not enough for full forgiveness; by giving generously out of his acquired wealth beyond the normal requirements he takes his action to a higher level (*Sermons on the New Testament Lessons* 63.3). Augustine here grasps something basic about repentance in the Jewish context.

It can be understood here comparatively. When the rich young ruler walked sorrowfully away, he surely had a broken heart, but not a heart open to repentance. He had sought to be assured by Jesus that in his effort to be obedient to the law he had *kapparah*, acquittal from sin, or atonement. But he was not yet willing to follow through with what Rabbi Joseph Soloveitchik calls the necessary purification or catharsis that a true "restoration of spiritual viability" requires in Judaism, and without which one could not regain full legal status.[1] This second step, *taharah*, involves a deliberate removal of the self from the path of sin. In Zacchaeus, though his sin has been active rather than a matter of omission (as with the rich young ruler), this is precisely what occurs. Remorse is not required for such restitution but rather simple performance, an ethical action. By committing himself to restoration fourfold and to giving half of his goods to the poor, Zacchaeus demonstrated a genuine conversion from his sinful path of life and, in so doing, in a Jewish context, acquired again his full ethical status as a Jew under the law. This is what Jesus, as a rabbi, is formally recognizing when he says, "Today salvation has come to this house, because he also is a son of Abraham" (Luke 19:9). The public promise of restoration to his victims by Zacchaeus in the presence of Jesus and the joy of his being accepted by the Lord show that he has now come to terms with the law in the only way that ultimately matters—performatively. How had this so suddenly happened to him, after a life of "walking in the way

1. *Soloveitchik on Repentance: The Thought and Oral Discourses of Rabbi Joseph B. Soloveitchik*, transcribed by Pinchas H. Peli (New York: Paulist Press, 1984), esp. 49–52. Soloveitchik provides an especially good context for understanding this episode, not least because he observes that such a restitution to the covenant by repentance is made possible by the persistence of *hesed*, God's covenant love: "Through repentance of purification a man is reborn and he gains a new heart, a renewed spirit, another outlook of life and different horizons. One man enters the bath of ritual immersion, and another emerges from the water. The sinful person emerges as a pure one" (59).

of sinners"? The answer surely is the call and acceptance (reconciliation) offered him by Jesus. He has been bowled over by love, a love that will not let him go without a mimetic response. His story is thus a paradigm, for Luke an example of the lost soul found and rescued from inevitably dire consequences. And that is the point of it, Jesus seems to say: "For the Son of Man has come to seek and to save that which was lost" (19:10).

Later sources record that Peter appointed Zacchaeus bishop of Caesarea, though against his will (Pseudo-Clement, *Homilies* 3.63; *Apostolic Constitutions* 7.46). This is more than likely a pious fancy, but if actual, then it would be one more irony to crown the ironies already found in Luke's dramatic account of the surprising conversion of Zacchaeus. Transformed by grace, in his new calling he can for the first time in his life live up to the meaning of the name his parents gave him.

Investing in the Kingdom (19:11–28)

The tempo of Luke's narrative, like the movement of the crowd, is picking up noticeably now as Jesus and the disciples draw "nigh to Jerusalem." It is clear that the excitement is directly connected to their expectation: "They thought," writes Luke, that "the kingdom of God would immediately appear" (19:11). It is all too easy for us to regard the disciples as obtuse, oblivious to the warnings that Jesus has already given them concerning the sufferings he was about to undergo there. Calvin, for one, accuses them of a "brutish stupor" (1972: 2.286). Perhaps we should be more empathetic. Long attuned to an expectation and hope of Israel's deliverance, for the "consolation" (2:25) foretold in Isaiah, and flush with the unparalleled excitement of the miracles they had seen, and their conviction that they were going up to Jerusalem with the very Chosen One himself for a climactic self-disclosure of the purpose of God in redemption of his people, how easy it must have been to be carried along by euphoria and to be psychologically unprepared for the horrible events that were to occur.

It is clear that Jesus told this next parable to bring them down to earth, to make them aware that the events to which they looked forward so eagerly involved also the judgment of God upon Israel for persistent unfaithfulness. They were not wrong to sense that they had drawn nigh to the kingdom; they were, after all, in the company and presence of Christ. But they were not so nigh to the full disclosure of the kingdom in order of time.

Jesus does not make an analogy in this parable of the sort that would cause them to understand it easily, interpreting it in the light of the Hebrew prophets, such as Isaiah. His story about a "nobleman" who goes away to arrange to receive his kingdom and then to return (19:12) recalls, as several commentators note, a much more recent secular event. In about 4 BC, Archelaus, son of Herod the Great, traveled to Rome to petition Augustus Caesar that his father's kingdom (Judea, Samaria, Idumea) now pass to him. Unfortunately, he was so unpopular with the people that they sent a delegation to Augustus with a contrary petition (cf. 19:14). The result was a compromise: Augustus gave him only half the kingdom and with the reduced status of ethnarch (Josephus, *Jewish War* 2.1–38, 80–100; *Jewish Antiquities* 17.219–49, 299–320). Archelaus was understandably much irritated and on his return killed as many as three thousand of his fellow Jews in reprisal (cf. Luke 19:27). Luke 19:14 and 19:27 thus introduce a powerful element from recent political memory entirely missing from the similar parable in Matt. 25:14–30, indicating, among other elements, that these are two distinct parable events (cf. Bock 1994–96: 2.1526–29; Wright 1996: 632–39).

The parable here has each of ten servants receiving the same sum, a *mina* (translated "pound" in the KJV), which each was to put to work. Only three of the ten are commented upon, and they prove to have had various success; one has earned ten times the principle and another five, and they are handsomely rewarded. The other has hidden his *mina* in a napkin—not even a very safe place—and has no profit whatsoever to show. A *mina* represents much less money than the "talent" of Matthew's parable, which was equivalent to about four years' labor for a working man; a *mina* might be worth about four months' wages by contrast. But the issue of stewardship is the same in both cases, at least on the surface. Here, when the nobleman returns, he opens the books to evaluate his profits; the commercial term used by Luke here is *diapragmateuomai*, a New Testament *hapax legomenon*. This is a reference to accounting; there are no spiritual overtones to this term.

The unprofitable servant excuses his temerity on the grounds that he has feared the rapacious character of his boss and wanted to minimize his risk (Luke 19:21). The judgment on him is swift; he loses the *mina* he has to the one who has already ten, despite the protestation of others at the apparent unfairness of this (19:24–25). Then follows a "hard saying" of Jesus: "To everyone who has will be given; and from him who does not have, even what he has will be taken away from him" (19:26). This too, of course, is in the strict context of stewardship.

Theologically, many have taken the parable to be a lesson on appropriate stewardship between the first and second comings of Jesus (Bock 1994–96: 2.1535; Marshall 1978: 702; Calvin 1972: 2.286). Augustine also read the parable in this way (as did many in the early church), and the supposition is present in Cyril, Ambrose, and others.[2] Bonaventure sees the final reckoning of the nobleman in this way also, citing Dan. 7:10 to the point (2001–4: 3.1819). Wright is prominent among those who reject any view that Jesus is here speaking of the parousia. Rather, he argues that it was then and should be now regarded as a parable of the return of God to Zion, especially as that was understood in "Second Temple Jewish eschatology" (1996: 634). The emphasis in such a view is likewise that the kingdom is coming but that it entails judgment, not blessing or consolation for Israel (1996: 636). According to Wright, Jesus's journey to Jerusalem is "the

2. Stephen L. Wailes, *Medieval Allegories of Jesus' Parables* (Berkeley: University of California Press, 1987), 184–94.

symbol and embodiment of YHWH's return to Zion" and "Israel's rejection of Jesus" (1996: 639). Either way, with the traditional prophetic eschatological view or seeing it as a warning of impending judgment, the parable changes the mood and heightens the suspense as they continue on their way, ascending up to Jerusalem (Luke 19:28).

The moral focus has drawn attention to another theological issue. The unprofitable servant's punishment was taken by Gregory the Great and John Wyclif, among others, as misappropriation of a spiritual gift for worldly purposes; in this context, the *mina* becomes an important part of the symbolism of faithful as distinct from unfaithful obedience in fulfilling one's calling. In both Catholic and Protestant tradition, such a moral or tropological reading often eclipses any species of eschatological understanding. Thus, for Thomas More, the slothful servant's fearfulness is the result of succumbing, as in a charming medieval idiom he puts it, to the "devilles dryft," permitting ourselves to lose our trust in God's faithfulness to his servants (*Dialogue of Comfort against Tribulation* 2.13). John Milton, in his famous "Sonnet 19," worries that his physical blindness may impede his exercise of "that one Talent which is death to hide," but he is able to come at last to a trust that in the eyes of God his willingness to serve, though blind, will suffice to satisfy a gracious and loving God.

He Who Comes in the Name of the Lord (19:29–48)

At the foot of the Mount of Olives Jesus sends two of his disciples on a curious mission, and though the point of it is later on to become clearer, the disciples must have been initially puzzled: they are to go into the nearby little village, find a colt tied (Matt. 21:2 says the colt is tied up beside a donkey; John 12:14–15 describes the colt as a "donkey's colt"), and, after untying it, bring it back to Jesus. Jesus tells them to anticipate being asked what they are up to; they are to reply, "The Lord has need of him," and to expect that the owners will be satisfied with this. All of this happens just as Jesus says it will (Luke 19:30–35). This odd event, one of the few recorded in all four Gospels, may be explained at least in part by the ancient Levantine custom of *angaria*, whereby a civic leader or rabbi might request use of an animal for a specific purpose, later to return it. Recalling this custom may help us understand the otherwise surprising acquiescence of the owners. But it explains neither Jesus's prescience about where it will be found nor indeed why, so improbably, this young untrained animal, upon which "yet never man sat" (19:30 KJV), is not only docile to the disciples' leading (it may well have been halter-broken) but even in the midst of flapping cloaks laid on his back and on the path before him (19:35–36) does not buck off his rider or even balk on the road. Anyone familiar with the breaking and training of riding stock will know how remarkable this episode is, purely from a naturalistic point of view. There may also be here an echo of Jacob's ancient blessing upon Judah (Gen. 49:10–11), itself seen by some ancient interpreters in an eschatological light and as reflected in the text cited by John from Isa. 40:9 and Zech. 9:9 (e.g., Chrysostom, Homily 66.1).

For a clue as to the significance of the event, we have only to consider what many in the crowd (not only the scribes and Pharisees) would suddenly think about when confronted with this unusual scene. Jesus, who has trekked hill and dale over all Israel for several years, would not suddenly have mounted any kind of beast for the last kilometer or two because he is suddenly too tired to walk in through the city gate. This is a symbolic action. As Wright puts it, "His riding on a donkey over the Mount of Olives, across Kidron, and up to the Temple Mount spoke more powerfully than words could have done of a royal claim" (1996: 490). Wright notices, as have others (Danker 1988: 312; Marshall 1978: 712; Bock 1994–96: 2.1556), that this event recalls Zech. 9:9:

> Rejoice greatly, O daughter of Zion!
> Shout, O daughter of Jerusalem!
> Behold, your king is coming to you;
> He is just and having salvation,
> Lowly and riding on a donkey,
> A colt, the foal of a donkey.

This text is actually cited in the parallel passage in John, as just noted. There are hints also of Isa. 1:3 in the quiescence of the beast—"the ox knows his owner"—as well as to other regal moments in Israel's history (e.g., 2 Sam. 15:23–32). The "entry into Jerusalem" is called "triumphal" because to a knowledgeable Jew it was unmistakably messianic. To a Roman soldier it might initially have meant nothing at all, merely one more incomprehensible local phenomenon.

This image of Jesus on the foal, when reinforced by the "multitude of the disciples," is already in its Jewish symbolic context impressive. (Luke is distinctive in talking about a large number here, not just the Twelve or even, it seems, the seventy others, but all of those now in the band of followers.) When the disciples begin to chant, "rejoic[ing] and prais[ing] God with a loud voice for all the mighty works they had seen, saying: 'Blessed is the King who comes in the name of the Lord!'" (cf. Luke 13:35) and, like the angels to the shepherds, "peace in heaven and glory in the highest" (19:37–38)—no one, Jew or Gentile, could fail to see the magnitude of the claim. The quotation of Ps. 118:26, associated with Israel's eschatological hope and, pertinently here, the Feast of Tabernacles, makes it too clear a sign to miss. Consequently, the Pharisees demand that Jesus rebuke his disciples for such untoward exuberance. He refuses and, in words that echo down the centuries, replies, "I tell you that if these should keep silent, the stones would immediately cry out" (Luke 19:40). An aural pun here in the Hebrew may have added piquancy to Jesus's rebuke for the Pharisees, in that the Hebrew word for "stone" ('eben) is close to the word for "son" (ben), leading to many puns in rabbinic literature. In the plural ('ebenîm), as here, the suggestiveness is even stronger.

In the next chapter, this pun will move to center stage in Jesus's parable of the wicked tenants (20:6, 9–18). It is suggested that perhaps the Pharisees were primarily worried that the political dimension—a royal procession, the crowd's use of the words *ho basileus* ("the king"), and the casting down of garments—might well attract Roman anger (Marshall 1978: 716; Danker 1988: 313). But it seems likely that more overt rejection on their own part was also present. Whatever their motive, their demand for censoring is not a request with which Jesus will comply.

Now, in a striking change of tone, Luke (again uniquely) records that, as if the music and the hullabaloo had suddenly ceased, Jesus stopped and looked down across the Kidron Valley at Jerusalem. Jerusalem the Golden, the locus and symbol of so much he loved, so much of the good of Israel, and of all manner of blasphemy, idolatry, and soul-sucking violence—it must have been at once for him a beautiful and a most painful scene. In a moment recalling his earlier lament for Jerusalem (13:33–35), he begins to weep over the city: "If thou hadst known, even thou, at least in this thy day, the things which belong unto thy peace!" (19:42 KJV). Eyes to see and not seeing, the people are blind to what Jesus sees. The collective weight of the prophets' warnings to Zion are here summarized, and since Jesus would have been speaking in Hebrew or Aramaic, they are brought to a fine point by wordplay on the city's very name: *Yěrûšālayim/Yěrûšālēm* ("city of health and peace"). All things pertinent to Jerusalem's health and peace were laid out in the Law and the Prophets and echoed in the Psalms, but as in so much of Israel's history, so even now all these things are "hidden from [the] eyes" of its inhabitants. The dramatic irony for Luke's reader continues to build, for the reader knows that this terrible occlusion in their consciousness cannot prevent them from soon enough seeing firsthand the horror of divine wrath, witnessing the judgment to fall upon the city because of its rejection of the prophets and, indeed, of Jesus himself. In stark, terse words, sounding precisely like an Old Testament prophet, Jesus now describes the coming judgment of God upon the city to be effected, as of old, by the very enemies from whom they wish to be delivered; the description of the siege, the slaughter, and the razing of the city so that not one stone is left upon another (19:43–44) accords only too well with the devastation wrought upon them by the Roman army under Titus in AD 70 (cf. Josephus, *Jewish War* 5.466–72, 502–11). Soon, in quite another way, "every stone shall cry / for stony hearts of men" (Richard Wilbur, "A Christmas Hymn").

The inclination to a spiritual interpretation of the symbols and terms literally embodied in the entry to Jerusalem is theologically warranted, for each element gathers in a host of precedents in the Old Testament scriptures and focuses them on their ultimate significance, namely, as Paul says, on "that spiritual Rock that followed them [Israel], and that Rock was Christ" (1 Cor. 10:4). Such connections lead the spiritual exegetes to see Jerusalem as a sign, allegorically, for the church. Origen, for example, warns that in a very similar way Christ may weep over our "spiritual Jerusalem," the church, and for comparable reasons. As an example of that sort of sin that occasions the judgment of God on such a church, he instances "especially when a man, after long continency, after years of chastity, is overcome, and enticed by the blandishments of the flesh, has lost his fortitude and his modesty. They will not leave on him one stone upon another; according to Ezekiel [18:24], 'his former righteousness will I not remember'" (quoted in Aquinas, *Catena Aurea* 3.2.647). These are words of scripture some readers today, naturally enough, would prefer *not* to remember. But they are there in the prophets, and there in Jesus, and faithful interpreters cannot escape the connection.

This episode thus ends not with a weeping Jesus but with an angry Lord, come to the place of worship, there to drive out those who had turned the holiness of the temple into a mere opportunity for making money. As Ambrose put it, thinking of the perennial tendency of some in this direction, it is evident in Jesus's action that "God does not want his temple to be a trader's lodge, but the home of sanctity" (*Exposition of Luke* 9.17–18). The contrast between "house of prayer" and "den of thieves" (Luke 19:46) could hardly be stronger—and we can in our day provide our own analogies.

Now Jesus settles down to teach in the temple the precise contrary of business as usual, namely the way of holiness. The chief priests, scribes, and the civic magistrate all want to stop him, but they cannot immediately do so, because "all the people were very attentive to hear him" (19:48). The stone that the builders rejected (Ps. 118:22; Luke 20:17; Acts 4:11; 1 Pet. 2:7), the stone of stumbling to many (Isa. 8:14; Rom. 9:33; 1 Pet. 2:8), yet the very Rock of Ages nonetheless, was preparing to lay himself down as the chief cornerstone (Isa. 28:16), the foundation for another Jerusalem and for a tabernacle not made with hands (Heb. 9:11).

LUKE 20

This is one of those chapters for which the medieval chapter divisions we still employ actually make good thematic sense. The governing theme is authority, and each challenge Jesus faces from his adversaries in the temple is designed as a provocation intended to undermine and delegitimize him, both in his specific teaching, as Luke distinctly says, and above all to debunk his now increasingly explicit claim to be the Messiah of God. Rhetorically, it is as though Jesus and the various factions of his adversaries are engaged in a verbal chess match in which, for all parties, the stakes are very high.

Authority to Preach (20:1–8)

It is doubtful if many denominational seminaries today would grant Jesus a license to preach. I mean that not as a flippant remark, or to say merely that he was not an ordained rabbi, which of course he wasn't (Danker 1988: 316), but to point to something beyond today's required seminary courses or ordination procedures. Jesus was not only resistant to the theological clichés and political correctness of any of the religious parties in his era; he actually took them on directly, each in their turn (cf. the parallel accounts in Matt. 21:23–27 and Mark 11:27–33). By none of their standards was he orthodox.

The Sanhedrin in the first century was no longer composed of chief priests and, representatively, of the lower orders of Levitical priests, owing to an insufficient number of men sufficiently educated to serve (Maimonides, on Babylonian Talmud, tractate *Sanhedrin* 2). "Elders of the laity" were called to serve in their place, and such a one, namely Gamaliel (of the tribe of Judah), was at this time president of the council (Lightfoot 1979: 3.196). Gamaliel is not named in this incident, and because he was certainly prominent and known to Luke (cf. Acts 5:33–39), it is more likely that the Pharisees who came to trap Jesus were of the more rigidly conservative Shammai sect. There were also scribes (Luke 20:1). What they ask him, in effect, is, "Who gave you permission to come in here and teach like that?" Their formulation, however, implies more than the content of his teaching itself, for Luke has "these things" (*tauta*), suggesting that they are including actions, such as what he has just done to the money changers. "By what [kind of] authority" (*en poia exousia*) also has the force of asking about genre or category of mandate, tempting Jesus perhaps to answer straightforwardly: "the authority of God." But Jesus does not so readily give them what they are looking for—an opportunity to declare him a blasphemer on the spot. So he uses a standard rabbinical parry: "I also will ask you one thing [first], and [you will] answer me" (20:3). His tone is certainly authoritative; one hears the voice of God in Job 38:3 echoing in Jesus's challenge.

Jesus's own question about the baptism of John and its "authority" (whether divine or human) puts his interrogators back on their heels. Luke gives the reason; as they huddle, they realize that on either option Jesus has them trapped: if they say John's authority was from heaven, then he was de facto a true prophet and they should have believed him; if they say he was merely a human phenomenon, then the people, who by now hold John in high regard, will stone them. Luke alone mentions the religious leaders' fear of being "stoned to death" (*katalithazō*), the penalty under the law for declaiming that a true prophet is false (Exod. 17:4; Num. 14:10). Their discomfort here is not merely with their rhetorical disadvantage when trying to match wits with Jesus; they are clearly afraid of losing their institutional control. So they punt—saying they do not know the answer (Luke 20:4–7). Jesus replies that, accordingly, he will not answer concerning his own source of authority.

Wright draws attention to the earlier occasion (7:18–35) when Jesus had been asked by John's disciples whether he was indeed the Messiah and similarly refused to give a direct answer but with an allusion to Isaiah asked them to confirm for themselves whether messianic works were being performed. Here too, one subject of discussion is proxy for another (this also, of course, is a species of irony). As Wright puts it, "Jesus' riddle says, as clearly as a riddle can, that the reason he has the authority to act as he has in the temple is because, as the one to whom John pointed, he is in fact the Messiah" (1996: 497).

The Leased-Out Vineyard (20:9–19)

Now Jesus tells a parable, ostensibly to press further in response to their query about authority but more deeply to speak of Israel's history and his own place in it. Since the time of the early church this parable has been seen as an allegory for salvation history (Cyril, Eusebius, Theophylact): the one who plants the vineyard is God; the tenant farmers who are given stewardship over the favorable land represent Israel; the servants whom the vineyard owner sends to collect the rent due him are the prophets. The vineyard owner becomes exasperated: Luke has him saying, "What shall I do?" (20:13), heightening the dramatic tension. Now finally, he sends his "beloved son" (*ton huion mou ton agapēton*)—recalling the words spoken by God from heaven at Jesus's baptism (3:22) and again at the transfiguration (9:35)—believing that surely the authority vested in his son will compel obedience to the established covenant agreement (cf. Deuteronomy). It appears that the immediate audience caught well enough the general gist of this parable as a historical/political allegory. Even if they miss the dramatic irony present in the murder of the vineyard owner's son, an irony all too apparent to readers after the events now about to transpire, they do not miss the sting in Jesus's question: "Therefore what will the owner of the vineyard do to them?" (20:15). One imagines a moment of tongue-tied silence before Jesus provides an answer they dare not give: "He will come and destroy those vinedressers and give the vineyard to others" (20:16). This reference to the hated Gentiles is altogether too much for them to bear, and they blurt out *Mē genoito*! ("No way!").[1] Their sense of ownership is so deeply reflexive that they do not begin to see that their exclamation merely confirms how utterly implicated they are in the illegal usurpation of the wicked tenants in the parable. They are covenant-breakers, and to cover their tracks and defend what they wish to be their sole dominion, they have shot all previous messengers. Already they are looking at Jesus and saying, "This is the heir. Come, let us kill him, that the inheritance may be ours" (20:14). For the false Israel to vindicate its rejection of God, they will need to kill the "true Israel," God's Chosen One and "beloved son."

Now Jesus looks out at the whole crowd, and persisting with the Aramaic and Hebrew pun previously established (*ben/ 'eben*, "son"/"stone"), asks, "What do you make then of that scripture which says, 'The stone which the builders rejected has become the chief cornerstone?'" (20:17, author's translation). This is a reference to Ps. 118:22–23, a psalm sung by pilgrims going up to Jerusalem and the temple for the Feast of Tabernacles and the Passover (Wright 1996: 498). There may be an implied reference also to Isa. 28:16, which has God "lay[ing] in Zion a stone for a foundation, . . . a precious cornerstone, a sure foundation." Cyril of Alexandria sees the cornerstone as an image for "the gathering together and joining of the two people . . . Israel and the Gentiles in unity of feeling and faith" (1983: Homily 134). But the use Jesus makes of this messianic image is immediately linked by him to the judgment of God his parable has had in mind: "Whoever falls [stumbles] on that stone will be broken; but on whomever it falls, it will grind him to powder" (Luke 20:18). It is hard not to hear the image from Dan. 2:31–35, in which the coming of the messianic Day of the Lord is likened to a great stone rolling down from the mountain upon the mixed-iron-and-clay feet of the last great empire, Rome, and crashing it to pieces. Wright suggests that these allusions are themselves

---

1. KJV's "God forbid" is too formal and pious for the Greek here, and NKJV's "Certainly not!" is not much better. The exclamation of the leaders is found only in Luke.

a kind of riddle within a riddle (1996: 498), in which "the prophetic story of the rejected servants climaxes in the rejected son ... [who] is the messianic stone, which, rejected by the builders, takes the chief place in the building."[2] On this understanding of Jesus's allegory (with which I accord), "those who oppose him will find their regime (and their Temple) destroyed, while his kingdom will be established" (1996: 501). This is certainly how the parable looks from our side of Luke's narrative, and we can see not only how it portended the coming destruction of the historical temple and all Jerusalem in AD 70, but also why it could be that the early church would see in Jesus's allegory of salvation history also a hint of anagogical meaning for the church and for the expected second advent of the Lord for the final judgment. Thus, while in its given context the target of judgment is unfaithful Israel, Ambrose sees here also an implied warning for the church: "The vineyard prefigures us" (*Exposition of Luke* 9.30). With regard to the three servants who proceed the son, Bede adds to this spiritual exegesis a rather delightful liturgical allegory, by which he compares the three to the reading of the Law, the Psalms, and the Prophets; the Son is of course the gospel, and woe betide those who trample the saving witness of the word of God underfoot (*Commentary on Mark* 12 in Patrologia latina 92.192–93).

But we are here clearly grounded in the historical event and its own status as a summation of Israel's history "of all the Law and the Prophets have spoken." What on its given horizon that day in Jerusalem is a summing up of salvation history to that point—and a prediction of both the death of the Son and the judgment of the Father—in the light of experience of the expectant church still awaiting the parousia becomes a kind of historiographic theodicy: the church lives now in an interregnum between the death of the vineyard owner's son and the coming again in judgment of the lord of the vineyard. We may live now buffeted by disobedient overlords or powers, but there is a day of reckoning coming, when the owner will return to claim his own and set things right.

The chief priests and scribes now see the evidence of blasphemy they have been looking for and have every reason to believe that Jesus means them real harm. They nevertheless are conflicted about what to do, fearing that Jesus has too much popular support for them to act openly. But they are certainly in no doubt that "he had spoken this parable against them" (20:19).

Traps and Entrapment (20:20–47)

The Roman poll tax was hated by the Jews. It was not only a financial burden but, as "tribute," also a regular reminder of their subservience to the Roman imperium. It is thus a politically loaded conundrum that the dissembling spies of the chief

2. "Stone" became an early church code word for Jesus, as in Justin Martyr's *Dialogue with Trypho* 100, 126. In Eusebius (quoted in Aquinas, *Catena Aurea* 3.2.658), "Christ is called a stone on account of his earthly body *cut out without hands*, as in the vision of Daniel, because of his birth of the Virgin."

priests and scribes put to Jesus, clearly with the intent of getting him to offend the "governor," namely Pontius Pilate. Their insincere flattery of Jesus (20:21) is a clumsy attempt to put him off-guard for the question: "Is it lawful for us to pay taxes to Caesar or not?" (20:22). Jesus, however, perceives their "deceit" (*panourgian*) immediately: if he says yes, as Augustine puts it (Sermon 308: A.7), he is acknowledging the authority of the Roman state rather than that of God, and this would be seen by Jews as reinforcing or condoning their subjugated condition; if he says no, then he is chargeable as a rebel against the emperor. He says, "Show me a denarius" (20:24). Such a coin represents an average day's wage, and it is evident that upon the coin is an image of Caesar. Jesus's question about this image looks merely rhetorical, but it is not. The Jews found a human image on such a coin inherently unsavory, but in this instance there was something worse, an inscription proclaiming Tiberius Caesar to be a god, "son of the divine Augustus" (Wright 1996: 503; Marshall 1978: 735–36; Fitzmyer 1981–85: 2.1296; Bock 1994–96: 2.1612). This adversarial question is doubly loaded therefore, and it may be that Wright is correct in thinking that even by saying "render to Caesar what belongs to him" Jesus may have intended—and some of his hearers may have understood—a double entendre: "Render to Caesar what he deserves!" (1996: 504), or even that Jesus intends to protest Jewish compromise with the pagan cult of the emperor (1996: 506). Whatever the merits of those views, Jesus's reply deftly dismembers a false dichotomy: "Render therefore to Caesar the things that are Caesar's, and to God the things that are God's" (20:25).[3] "This amounts to saying," says Augustine, "if Caesar can require his image in a coin, cannot God require his image in a human being?" (Sermon 308A.7). The point about paying taxes to the civil authority is renewed by Paul (Rom. 13:7) and Justin Martyr (*Apology* 1.17.1).

Jesus no sooner deals with the deceivers of the party of Herod ("Herodians" in Mark 12:13) than on come the Sadducees. The Sadducees, as Bede correctly observed long ago, derived their name from Zadok, the name of the Davidic priest, meaning "righteous" (cf. Hebrew *ṣaddîk*). Luke delineates the doctrines that most distinguished them from others, such as the Pharisees (Luke 20:27; Acts 4:1–2): superficially they were Torah conservatives; they rejected the oral tradition (hence their conflict with the Pharisees). But they denied the resurrection, even perhaps the immortality of the soul, and they rejected belief in angels. Except for the first point they might be seen as a species of latter-day rationalists.

The absurdity of their question is a function of their rationalism taken to an extreme. The issue that they parody legalistically is one that we have already seen to be important in Luke, namely levirate marriage. In the *reductio ad absurdum* of a woman who has the sufficient bad fortune (or black widow magic) to have seven

---

3. For Oliver O'Donovan, "'Render to Caesar . . .' was not a means of Jesus acknowledging a two-fold authority. The crowds admired his clever answer—he did not deny their claim, but brushed it aside"; *Desire of the Nations: Rediscovering the Roots of Political Theology* (Cambridge: Harvard University Press, 1999), 93.

husbands, six of them levirate "kinsman redeemers," all die without producing children, leaving her to die eventually herself in her oft-widowed state. In their problematic scenario, the Sadducees hope to show the absurdity of belief in the resurrection: "In the resurrection, whose wife does she become? For all seven had her as wife" (Luke 20:33). Jesus's reply (was he wearied? did he laugh?) is that they have made a silly category mistake in formulating their trick question. The next world and this are qualitatively different (20:34–35). People don't marry there, since because they no longer face death, there is no need to provide for progeny (20:36). They are like angels (*isangeloi*), beyond the need for sex or food. Clement of Alexandria draws a point here: "The Lord is not rejecting marriage but is purging the anticipation of physical desire after the resurrection" (*Stromateis* 3.87.2–3). (There were some who, like Cyprian, would try to use this passage as a support for a life of virginity; *Dress of Virgins* 22.) Augustine follows Cyril here, stating the obvious: "Where there is no death, there are no marriages" (*Questions on the Gospels* 1.2.49). But there are other important theological issues on which this answer of Jesus bears directly, and the implicit support for the doctrine of the resurrection of the body is certainly central. Calvin, observing that some pagans differed from the Sadducees by a doctrine of immortality of the soul, sees the distinction between these doctrines, yet observes that, logically, "whoever destroys the resurrection is also depriving souls of immortality" (1972: 3.29). The Sadducees are, in effect, annihilationists. Jesus, referring to Abraham, Isaac, and Jacob in the present tense (20:37), seems to imply both views concerning the afterlife, for he adds that God "is not the God of the dead but of the living, for all live to him" (20:38). The scribes, who accord with the Pharisees in their belief in the resurrection, like the answer that Jesus gives to the Sadducees; he scores a point, they think, for them (20:39). At the same time, nobody wants any longer to tangle with Jesus in this game of entrapment. "After that," says Luke, "they dared not question him anymore" (20:40).

But Jesus does not, as victor in these debates, simply walk away. Rather, going after the would-be intellectuals, the scribes, once again he puts a question to them. It proves to be one they cannot handle, because it invokes a categorical relationship between time and eternity they have not begun to comprehend. He asks how the interpreters they know deal with Ps. 110:1–2: "The LORD said to my Lord, 'Sit at my right hand, till I make your enemies your footstool.'" Luke alone directs his readers' attention to the Psalms as location; he clearly knows the scriptures very well. Psalm 110 was seen in the first century as Davidic; the Septuagint superscription notes this, so that conventional debates about whether this psalm is or is not by David seem moot. Jesus says so, and he was doubtless aware that it was regarded by everyone as a royal psalm, even a coronation anthem (Bock 1994–96: 2.1636–37). Before Jesus there is no evidence that Ps. 110 had been seen as a messianic psalm; however, after this point, it is regarded as certainly messianic. The reference to "a priest forever according to the order of Melchizedek" (110:4) ensures this; this allusion becomes a topos in Heb. 5–7.

Considered chronologically, Jesus tells the doubtless bewildered scribes, these verses make no sense. We are reminded that Melchizedek in Gen. 14:18–20 was a mysterious figure and that Jewish tradition, reflected in Heb. 7:3, regarded him as "without father, without mother, without genealogy, having neither beginning of days nor end of life." If David calls him "Lord," how can he be his descendent?

Again, we must imagine a stunned silence and profound uneasiness. The scribes and the other antagonists have set out, at the least, to undermine the authority of Jesus and ideally to trap him into destructive self-condemnation. But it is they themselves who have been checked, thereby losing credibility and authority. "Beware of the scribes," Jesus tells his disciples "in the hearing of all the people" (Luke 20:45), for they are full of pompous solemnity, going about in long robes, seeking to be greeted formally in the marketplace, seated prominently at the front of the assembly and in the choicest places at feasts (20:46), yet this is just so much academic posturing. Josephus (*Jewish Antiquities* 3.151; 11.80) confirms this assessment of the scribes from his own point of view. They may "drag about their pompous dignity," as Cyril puts it, trying "to catch the praises of those who saw them," but their "solemn ways were not based on reality" (1983: Homily 137). Sadly, what must count as reality was far different, for in the shadows well beyond their long and ostentatious public prayers could be heard the plaintive cries of the widows and orphans who these miserable frauds preyed upon (Luke 20:47). It is evident that Jesus was not returning to the scribes the favor of their compliment in his earlier answer to the Sadducees.

LUKE 21

The Widow Who Gave All (21:1–6)

The brief interlude between Jesus's teaching in the temple and what is variously referred to as the "Olivet discourse" or "signs of the end" needs little explanation. Observing wealthy people in the outer court putting offerings into one of the thirteen receptacles placed there for that purpose (Neh. 12:44; Josephus, *Jewish War* 5.200), Jesus stops as an extremely "poor" (*penichros*) widow approaches and casts in two "mites" (*lepta*), coins with the value of about a hundredth of a denarius. Hers is a very modest contribution. But Jesus makes the profound judgment that, relevant to ability, she has "put in more than all" the affluent folks who have been putting their gifts into the "treasury" (*dōra tou theo*), perhaps making their much larger offerings a kind of public statement (Luke 21:3). The rich men have given such as costs them little (cf. 2 Sam. 24:24—King David's contrary remark as he purchased the threshing floor that was to become the site of Solomon's Temple); the widow, out of her near destitute penury, has given essentially what she had to live on (Luke 21:4). Her gift cost her not less than all she had. The vignette is a metonym, a glimpse of a much larger theme in scripture concerning what one offers to God (cf. Rom. 12:1–2). The most important of gifts, however, is not easily monetized.

The disciples, meanwhile, are discussing the magnificence of the temple structure itself. Well might they have done so, for if Roman historian Tacitus is to be believed, it was an "immensely opulent" edifice (*Annals* 5.8). Josephus records that Herod, in rebuilding Solomon's Temple, used slabs of white marble as much as sixty feet in length and eighteen feet in width. The gates were plated with gold and silver; doors were covered with pure gold that flashed in the sun. The sumptuous gifts that made these features possible, including the Babylonian tapestries, blue, scarlet, and purple, that formed a veil at the entrance, would themselves have been impressive to anyone; the art and architecture they supported was much more so (*Jewish War* 5.184–227; *Jewish Antiquities* 15.391–402). There were bejeweled, carved grapevine clusters also, perhaps implied in Luke's phrase "the jewels and consecrated gifts [*anathēmasin*]" (author's translation), with which the temple was also adorned (Luke 21:5). It is evident that the disciples were bedazzled by the opulence. But Jesus admonishes them immediately, commencing what will be a far more difficult teaching for them and, in fact, for all of the subsequent church: "These things which you see—the days will come in which not one stone shall be left upon another that shall not be thrown down" (21:6; cf. 19:44). In short, the glories of the temple, which perhaps symbolized for them with aesthetic splendor the coming kingdom, are to be destroyed. The shock of this pronouncement must have been wrenching, but it certainly focused their attention. Ambrose, writing three centuries later, makes this comment: "It was spoken then of the temple made with hands, that it should be overthrown . . . [but] there is also a temple in everyone which [likewise] falls when faith is lacking" (*Exposition of Luke* 10.6.393). Here is one example of many in which the spiritual interpretation of the church superbly reflects where Jesus is going with his counsel to the disciples. That it was attacked by Julian the Apostate, who perversely wanted to rebuild the temple, laying "one stone on another" again so as to refute the Christians, was an occasion of much of the deeper reflection on this passage in the interpretation of the early church. John Chrysostom included Julian's charges in his *Orations against the Judaizers* (Christians who maintained syncretistically Jewish practices).[1]

Signs of the Judgment to Come (21:7–26)

"Teacher [*didaskale*], but when will these things be? And what sign will there be when these things are about to take place?" (21:7). (In Matt. 24:3, the disciples add, "And what will be the sign of your coming, and of the end of the age?") Jesus has much to say about the second question, but he makes no direct response to the first. He begins by first warning them to "not be deceived" by people who "come in my name," proclaiming themselves to be the Christ (Luke 21:8). There were such people before the fall of Jerusalem, and afterward too (cf. Josephus, *Jewish Antiquities* 18.85–87; 20.97–99). Nor should anyone pay attention to such imposters who say "the time [*ho kairos* has eschatological portent] has drawn near" (21:8). There are to be bona fide signals: political unrest and wars, earthquakes in various places, famines, plagues, and frightening signs in the heavens overhead (21:9–10). Yet the disciples are not to be "terrified," "for these things must come to pass first, but the end will not come immediately." There is to be an interval, an interregnum of some kind, between these events that are coming quite soon and some as yet more distant event. Luke uses "first" (*prōton*) to indicate that a sequence of events is intended; "the end" (*to telos*) is an eschatological term that reinforces the idea of a sequence.

1. Robert Wilken, *John Chrysostom and the Jews: Rhetoric and Reality in the Late Fourth Century* (Berkeley: University of California Press, 1983).

Alas, before that, the disciples are to suffer at the hands of various authorities, who will persecute them, turn them over to the synagogue as well as civic rulers, and cause them to be imprisoned (21:12). This will be an opportunity for them to bear witness (21:13). But they should "settle it" in their hearts not to shore up their defenses against the day of their trials with "prepared speeches" (*promeletaō* in 21:14 is a New Testament *hapax legomenon*, a technical term for rehearsing a speech or part in a play; see Aristophanes, *Parliament of Women* 117). The Lord himself will give them a "mouth and wisdom" (21:15; Mark 13:11 says that it will not be them speaking but rather the Holy Spirit), and their adversaries will not be able to gainsay what they then shall utter. (That is, something like the ripostes of the Lord himself to his adversaries so recently in the temple will come to them also in their hour of need.) No more than for their Lord will this grant them a pass; they will be betrayed by family and friends, and some shall be put to death (Luke 21:16). Summarily, they shall be universally hated because they bear the name of Christ (21:17). Yet "not a hair of your head will perish," says Jesus, even in the context of the torture and martyrdom he has just predicted; this proverbial phrase apparently refers to their spiritual security and ultimate wholeness (Marshall 1978: 769; cf. Acts 27:34; 1 Sam. 14:45; 2 Sam. 14:11).

"By your patience possess your souls" (Luke 21:19) seems to underscore the previous words. Gregory the Great interprets this adage in the context of the virtue recommended by the Apostle James (Jas. 1:2–4, 12): "He who preserves patience in adversity is thereby rendered proof against all affliction, and so by conquering himself he gains government of himself" (*Moralia* 5.16). To which he adds (in a fashion reminiscent of Boethius, a Roman Christian intellectual executed by the Arian emperor Theodoric, in his classic *Consolation of Philosophy*): "Now patience is to endure calmly the evils which are inflicted by others, and also to have no feeling of indignation against him who inflicts them" (Homily 35). James, who was doubtless there when the Lord spoke these words about the coming trials and tribulations of his apostles, seems to have gathered that perseverance in faith required an extraordinary patience in the face of adversity, and this now seems undeniably to be a quality in which the early church excelled.

But the more immediate event to which Jesus refers is made clear in Luke 21:20, and it carries back to 21:6. The description he gives of the coming fall of Jerusalem is vivid and terrible; the methods of siege and treatment of the conquered city accord with the retrospective account by Josephus in brutal detail; more than a million people were killed, nearly one hundred thousand taken captive, and in the long months of the siege children were cooked and eaten by desperate adults, even their parents (*Jewish War* 6.201–13). Small wonder that Jesus warns them to flee when they see that the city is compassed about with armies (21:20–21); many Christians took his advice, with a large contingent fleeing to the Transjordanian city of Pella (Eusebius, *Ecclesiastical History* 3.5.3). These are to be "days of vengeance," Jesus says, and he doesn't mean by Rome, though Roman armies will be the agent, even as the Assyrians and others were before them, but by God himself, "that all things which are written may be fulfilled" (21:22). To what writings does Jesus refer? Many passages in the prophets apply here (e.g., Isa. 1:20–24; 34:8; Jer. 6:1–8; 27:1–9; Dan. 9:26; Zech. 8:1–8), all of which promise such punishment for persistent unfaithfulness to the covenant. These prophecies had a near application to events proximate to the time of warning but evidently also a far application, and it would seem that the second horizon of these prophecies may be what Jesus refers to here as the coming vengeance to "be fulfilled."

There are terrible days coming for pregnant women and those with nursing infants (Josephus amply confirms this); many shall fall by the edge of the sword, others will be led captive, and "Jerusalem will be trampled by Gentiles until the times of the Gentiles are fulfilled" (Luke 21:24). This too has happened before (cf. Isa. 10:5–14; 16:1–19:10) when other Gentile powers had run their course and incurred the wrath of God. But here there seems to be a more universal sense; the "time of the Gentiles [being] fulfilled" suggests an ultimate destiny, for *kairoi* ("times") has here again an eschatological flavor. When the disciples ask Jesus after his resurrection if now is the time for the kingdom—"Lord, will you at this time [*en tō chronō toutō*] restore the kingdom to Israel?" (Acts 1:6)—his reply is that "it is not for [them] to know times or seasons [*chronous ē kairous*] which the Father has put in his own authority" (1:7). Bock notes (1994–96: 2.1682) this usage carefully, and while he allows that it is possible that these terms are used synonymously, in a kind of hendiadys, he points out that 17:26 refers to "preappointed times" (*prostetagmenous kairous*) in the same eschatological sense.

The times of the Gentiles, who will have trodden down Jerusalem, will come to an end some day. The church has generally seen this sense of interval between the destruction of Jerusalem in AD 70 and the end of the Gentile domination as being heralded by the cosmic signs that now follow, including the distress of nations as well as their sense of impotence in the face of nature itself breaking all normative patterns (Luke 21:25–26). Cyril of Alexandria represents this general understanding: "Now he explains what will happen at the consummation of the world and warns them." Cyril writes further that Christ's second advent from heaven "will not happen secretly, as did his coming at first, but it will be spectacular and terrifying" (1983: Homily 139). Ambrose (*Exposition of Luke* 10.15–18), Augustine (Letters 198, 199), Bede (in Aquinas, *Catena Aurea* 3.2.681), and Calvin (1972: 3.83–94) are representative of the tradition in seeing the second advent of Christ here foretold.

"Then [*kai tote*] they will see the Son of Man coming in a cloud with power and great glory" (21:27). This cosmic spectacle is reflective of imagery found in Dan. 7 (cf. Zech. 12:10; Rev. 1:7; 19:11–16), and it has been taken by the church historically that this prediction refers to the triumphant return of the king to claim his own and to inaugurate his kingdom finally. In the *Didache*, a first-century manual of Christian instruction and practice, believers are warned that in the whole passage (Luke 21:20–28) Jesus is conveying to his disciples a message to be passed down to the future church. This message sees the Olivet warning of future perils to come when "the world deceiver will appear in the guise of God's Son. He will work 'signs and wonders' and the earth will fall into his hands. He will commit outrages such as have never occurred before, and many will fall away and perish." But then, says the *Didache*, echoing the phrases of Luke, "there will appear the signs of the truth: first, the sign of stretched out hands in heaven, then the sign of a trumpet's blast [Matt. 24:31], and third, the resurrection of the dead—but not all the dead." The *Didache* then quotes Zech. 14:5 (cf. 1 Thess. 3:13; Matt. 24:30): "The Lord will come and all his saints with him. Then the world will see the Lord coming on the clouds of the sky" (*Didache* 16). The *Didache* synthesized, dependent more on Matthew's account than Luke's, and thereby established the pattern for understanding the destruction of Jerusalem as the definitive end of the old kingdom as prolegomena to an interregnum in which the faithful would seek to persevere through trials and tribulations, waiting and watching for the Lord to "come again in glory, to judge both the living and the dead" (Apostles Creed). The *Didache* is the earliest of a series of church orders, and it forms the core of the seventh book of the *Apostolic Constitutions*, a fourth-century Syrian work that became a vehicle for further transmission of Christian teaching about the "end times." But we can see this general pattern also in Augustine (e.g., Letter 199) as well as in Cyril of Alexandria, Gregory the Great, the Venerable Bede, Calvin, and later commentators. In the East, the eleventh-century commentator Theophylact of Ohrid, an unusually adept close reader of the New Testament text, shows that the same understanding of the text has prevailed in the Byzantine tradition. On Luke 21:27 he writes, "Both believers and unbelievers shall see him, for he himself as well as his cross shall glisten brighter than the sun, and so shall be observed by all" (Patrologia graecae 123:1056b). Aquinas quotes Theophylact on this throughout his *Catena Aurea* (e.g., 3.2.687), indicating thereby the essential unanimity of the church on these points to the late Middle Ages. Moreover, as we have seen, Calvin does not depart from this understanding, nor does Theodore Beza, nor do the run of Protestant commentators after the seventeenth century (e.g., Matthew Poole, Matthew Henry) down to the present.

It is appropriate that we should remind ourselves of the consistency in Christian understanding regarding the Olivet discourse, both East and West, Catholic and Protestant, which has prevailed more or less intact to the end of the twentieth century. The broad lineaments of interpretation treated here in brief formed the nexus of Christian expectation for the end of history and the return of the Lord in judgment for two millennia. But they need to be reconsidered now, if for no other reason than that there has developed a significant challenge to all of this in the biblical scholarship of N. T. Wright, until recently bishop of Durham.[2]

2. Wright is a scholar of enormous intelligence, erudition, and fluency. In his knowledge of talmudic and mishnaic literature, as well as of ancient Greek writings that have a bearing on the New Testament, he has few modern peers, and indeed he bids to rival John Lightfoot, the great Puritan scholar of the seventeenth century, whose observations on the New Testament are still invaluable. Wright's major works on the Gospels are frequently cited here.

For Wright, "the 'kingdom of God' has nothing to do with the world itself coming to an end."[3] It is not "a timeless truth . . . not the ending of the space-time universe."[4] Wright thinks that we should see Jesus here and in the parallel passages in Matthew and Mark as drawing on Jewish apocalyptic metaphors to describe a picture of the coming destruction of Jerusalem as God's judgment on Israel, and nothing more. "There is not much evidence," he writes, "for a direct connection between the symbol 'kingdom of God' and the coming of a Messiah."[5] He thinks that the church has misunderstood Jesus on this point for two millennia because "in a good deal of Christian theology the fall of Jerusalem has no theological significance" (1996: 343). From a Jewish point of view, however, the destruction of Jerusalem was seen as both literally catastrophic and theologically devastating. Everything was changed. The gospel language Jesus uses, Wright argues, is "a well-known Jewish story retold" (359) of God's inevitable judgment on his disobedient people. Accordingly, "the 'coming of the son of man' does not refer to the 'parousia' in the modern scholarly, and popular, sense of a human figure travelling downwards toward the earth on actual clouds. Nor does the phrase 'son of man' of itself refer to a 'superhuman' figure" (361). Rather, "the 'coming of the son of man' is . . . [simply] good first-century metaphorical language for two things: the defeat of the enemies of the true people of god[6] and the vindication of the true people themselves" (362). On this view, Wright continues, "the reference to heaven and earth passing away must not, of course, be taken as an indication that the [Olivet] discourse has after all been about the end of the space-time universe, but as another typical Jewish metaphor such as those in Isaiah or Jeremiah" (364). Anything else is "crass literalism" (361). Therefore, "there is no need for the common understanding to remain in place a minute longer" (365). On Wright's view, while Jesus has achieved a decisive victory over sin and death, it is the church that now is entrusted with the ongoing task of implementing this achievement.[7]

As may be evident, Wright's argument on these points is at odds not only with a large segment of broadly evangelical eschatological thought, which he addresses specifically, but also with the broad sweep of historic Catholic eschatology, on which he largely remains silent. In addition, he critiques the liberal Protestant traditions from Albert Schweitzer forward, who see the purposes of Jesus's discourse much as do evangelicals but come to opposite conclusions, thinking that Jesus was himself deluded concerning the eschaton. Wright's position, though it has attracted many followers among Anglo-American evangelicals particularly,[8]

3. N. T. Wright, *The New Testament and the People of God* (Minneapolis: Fortress, 1992), 285.
4. Ibid., 307.
5. Ibid.
6. Wright uses lowercase "god" throughout.
7. N. T. Wright, *The Way of the Lord* (Grand Rapids: Eerdmans, 1999) and *The Lord and His Prayer* (Grand Rapids: Eerdmans, 1997).
8. Travis Tamerius, "Sounding the Alarm: N. T. Wright and Evangelical Theology," *Reformation and Revival Journal* 11.2 (2002): 11–32.

is thus more or less distinctive in the history of biblical exegesis. Evans, who takes up some of these questions in a more philosophical way, is troubled by this emphasis on self-conscious novelty in Wright's work: "It must be said," Evans demurs, "that to the degree that Wright's reading of the narrative is absolutely original, it seems less probable that it could be true, insofar as the reading is seen as an attempt to describe the significance of Jesus' life in a way that is useful for Christian theology."[9] I take Evans's point to be consistent with cautions that have been given by Christian exegetes down through the centuries: if one's interpretation, however interestingly argued, is fundamentally out of step with received interpretation, perhaps it should be presented somewhat cautiously. In the case of Wright there is, particularly in regard to eschatological discourse in the New Testament, a tendency to present his own work as fundamentally original, in part by representing the language and teachings of Jesus as unoriginal. Among the several consequent dangers, the view of Jesus that emerges can come across as reductive; by so exclusively characterizing Jesus in normatively Jewish prophetic and rabbinic terms, the universality as well as the uniqueness of his gospel can be diminished. In the gospel words of God the Father from heaven at Jesus's baptism and again at the transfiguration, in the terrible recognition of Satan and the demons, in his own works and words such as "I am the way, the truth, and the life. No one comes to the Father, except through me" (John 14:6), and in the words of angels at the tomb and after his ascension (Acts 1:11), it seems to me that we have elements without precedent or successor and that their purpose and significance, transcending all mere acculturation, can yet be grasped by a child.

As acknowledged earlier, Wright is nevertheless now the dominant Protestant voice in these matters, and I am among those who have great respect for him as a scholar and reader of texts. Regarding the Olivet discourse, however, and related issues such as the new Jerusalem and heaven, I am unable to be persuaded that two millennia of careful Christian exegetes and theologians have gotten so much wrong.[10] Accordingly, I present Luke 21 in pretty much the traditional way, mindful of the principle expressed by Cardinal Joseph Ratzinger: "The understanding which elevates the Scripture to the status of 'revelation' is not to be taken as an affair of the individual reader, but is realized only in the living understanding of Scripture in the Church."[11] Nowhere does this counsel seem more apt than in regard to the words of Jesus recorded in scripture, and nowhere more necessarily

9. C. Stephen Evans, "Methodological Naturalism in Historical Biblical Scholarship," in *Jesus and the Restoration of Israel: A Critical Assessment of N. T. Wright's Jesus and the Victory of God*, ed. Carey Newman (Downers Grove, IL: InterVarsity, 1999), 203. See also C. Stephen Evans, *The Historical Christ and the Jesus of Faith: The Incarnational Narratives as History* (Oxford: Clarendon, 1996).

10. David Lyle Jeffrey, "Masterplot and Meaning: Interpretation and Grand Narrative in Hebrews 11 and Galatians 4," in *History and Biblical Interpretation*, ed. Craig Bartholomew and Murray Rae (Carlisle: Paternoster, 2003), repr. in my *Houses of the Interpreter: Reading Scripture, Reading Culture* (Waco: Baylor University Press, 2003), 15–38, 242–47.

11. Joseph Ratzinger, *The Theology of History in St. Bonaventure*, trans. Zachary Hayes (Chicago: Franciscan Herald, 1989), 67.

so than in regard to those matters concerning what he describes as the return of the Son of Man—especially since there has recently—indeed perennially—been much speculative interpretation. All such reflection, it seems to me, needs to be subtended by recognition of two things: (a) that Jesus taught plainly that he *was* the Son of Man, that he *would* return, and this was attested to right up to the moment following his resurrection, when he ascended into heaven and the angels gave their assurance; and (b) that he chose *not* to address the first part of the disciples' question concerning the *time* of his return (21:7). On these two factors depend much of that which the church with confidence believes, and also much that in self-constraint it leaves aside as a mystery Christ chose not to disclose in more than a cryptic, figural way.

Perseverance, Vigilance, and Future Hope (21:28–38)

What the unrepentant will see with terror, Jesus says, will be for those who love him and are attentive to his bidding a sign of hope in the imminence of their redemption; while others cower, they should "lift up [their] heads" (21:28). This bifurcation of all humanity presages the final judgment and is to be a moment of terrible discernment for all. Bonaventure reflects the tradition of the church well when he connects the returning Son of Man in these verses to the words of John in Rev. 1:7: "Behold, he is coming with clouds, and every eye will see him, even they who pierced him." He also cites as perspective Daniel's vision: "I was watching in the night visions, and behold, one like the Son of Man, coming with the clouds of heaven! He came to the Ancient of Days, and they brought him before him.... His kingdom ... shall not be destroyed" (Dan. 7:13–14). Bonaventure adds other full quotations, such as Isa. 2:17–21, and in such a way as to conclude that the second advent of the Lord will be both terrifying and visible to many (Bonaventure 2001–4: 3.21.46).

Bonaventure's comfortable sense of the ultimate *kairos* in all these passages is reflective of the *sensus plenior* the church typically has understood in such anagogical passages as Luke 21, and it helps us, I think, to understand how to situate ourselves in respect of the temporality of which Jesus speaks. John in Rev. 1:7 was writing long after the decease of most who had literally "pierced" Jesus— perhaps as much as sixty years after the crucifixion, and certainly two decades later than the destruction of Jerusalem in AD 70. By "every eye shall see him" he clearly means something more than the eyes of every one still living at that moment. When Daniel, writing centuries earlier, describes the Son of Man coming in clouds and going before the Ancient of Days to receive his kingdom, he writes in the present tense of a far distant future horizon, yet his words clearly describe the ultimate closure on the history of human kingdoms, as they are succeeded by a kingdom that shall last forever. The events to which Jesus points are clearly the end of something we have known and the beginning of something new, the long-hoped-for kingdom of God in itself fully appearing. For the apostles, Jesus was certainly coming again, as Peter in his great sermon declared, when the Lord shall bring about the consummation of his purposes (Acts 3:19–21). Peter's sense of the interregnum in which we live is that it should, in its trials and tribulations, admit no dissuasion from the confident hope expressed by the prophets, of the "restoration of all things" (3:21) at the Lord's return. The language recorded by Luke is more modest than the same account in Matt. 24:31, which mentions the blast of a great trumpet and angels being sent out to gather the elect from "the four winds, from one end of heaven to the other." But this too is a suggestion that the text is unmistakably about final closure in the divine plan of salvation history.

The parable of the fig tree is also an encouragement to future hope. Anyone who lives close to an agricultural way of life has here an advantage in grasping the power of Jesus's example: when human life depends directly upon the springtime renewal of creation, the heart leaps up at the first signs of spring, and the imagination races joyously toward the summer. "So you also," Jesus says, "when you see these things happening, know that the kingdom of God is near" (Luke 21:31). The subsequent promise has occasioned in this light more perplexity than it ought: when Jesus says, "this generation will by no means pass away till all things take place" (21:32), it seems that he means that when all the signs subsequent to the fulfilling of "the times of the Gentiles" are apparent (21:24–26) then that generation that sees these things will not pass away before the end.[12] The generation that sees these last signs sees the consummation in their lifetime. In Bonaventure's understanding, this means that "the resurrection will not occur before the consummation of the things predicted" (2001–4: 3.21.52). Bede thinks that Jesus means "either the whole human race, or perhaps especially the Jews" (quoted in Aquinas, *Catena Aurea* 3.2.691). It has always seemed obvious to the tradition that Jesus did not mean the literal, chronological generation of the disciples to whom he spoke these words, for otherwise the early church in apostolic times would have had reason to elide or attempt to explain away this saying—and so, perhaps, to have abandoned their own sense of future hope. Bock is right to say that this overall view of the passage, which he as an evangelical at the end of the second millennium shares with most of the Catholic and Reformation tradition that preceded him, needs to be tempered by the hermeneutical weight of what Jesus does not say; "It is hard to be dogmatic about the meaning of this difficult text," he wisely concludes (1994–96: 2.1692). The point of this teaching of Jesus is *that* the Son of Man will return to establish his kingdom forever; neither Luke nor the other Synoptics show him establishing a template for *how* it shall all unfold, or *when*. What we are given is signs—and grounds for hope.

The parallel statement of Jesus anchors this expectation in the promise of the Lord of creation (and therefore of time) himself: "Heaven and earth shall

---

12. Fitzmyer 1981–85: 2.1353; E. Earle Ellis, *The Gospel of Luke*, 2nd ed., New Century Bible (Grand Rapids: Eerdmans; London: Marshall, Morgan & Scott, 1974), 246–47; and Bock 1994–96: 2.1691.

pass away, but my words shall not pass away" (21:33 KJV). This is the strongest possible anchor to future hope. How then should we live in the light of this assurance and call to follow the Lord of history? Well, by prudent watchfulness over our own tendency to grow impatient, careless of the future he has promised (21:34). Anesthetizing ourselves against what we cannot know with certitude is no option, whether that be by drink, diversionary entertainment, or workaholic preoccupations. Repeating the warning he has made elsewhere about the Day of the Lord coming like a "thief in the night" (12:39–40), as surprising as the gathering storm around Jerusalem was not (21:20–24), Jesus urges watchfulness and perseverance in prayer, that "you may be counted worthy to escape all these things . . . and to stand before the Son of Man" (21:35–36). There is no parallel to this text in Matthew or Mark. Luke's version lays a crisp emphasis upon the believers' need for endurance in faithfulness and hope. The call to pray is found only in Luke and is indicative of his special attention to this persistent characteristic in Jesus's example and teaching.

Luke concludes his recounting of the Olivet discourse by saying that Jesus continued by day to teach in the temple, staying by night at or within the precinct of the Mount of Olives. The people came in the morning to hear him in the temple (21:37–38), though the storm was clearly gathering ominously all the while.

PASSOVER
AND ATONEMENT

LUKE 22

The story of Jesus's anointing by a woman in Matt. 26:6–13 and Mark 14:3–9 serves in those texts to make it almost the prompting motive for Judas in his betrayal—so irritated is he in those accounts at the waste of money that he feels ought to have gone into the purse for benefit to the poor. This is an important reminder in those contexts that it is entirely possible to identify with a central element in Jesus's teaching but, out of an inability to respond fully to his undergirding first principle of love (so crucial also to worship), to then seize almost exclusively upon that central element with unholy motives. This reflex betrays—which is to say that it presages further betrayal. Luke omits that narrative here and goes straight into the betrayal sequence.

The Last Passover (22:1–6)

The Feast of Unleavened Bread (synonym for the Passover) being about to begin, it is not an auspicious time for the chief priests and scribes to effect their purpose to kill Jesus. Jerusalem is thronged with Passover pilgrims, many of whom have been hearing about Jesus or have already listened to him teach; the religious leaders are afraid that they may already have waited too long. Suddenly, as the Slavic saying has it, it seems "the devil helps." Luke says pointedly that "Satan entered Judas, surnamed Iscariot, who," he reminds us, "was numbered among the twelve" (22:3). This horrible moment recalls the confrontation when Jesus is tempted in the desert (4:1–13) by its repetition of the name of the great adversary (Hebrew *śātān*) for only the second time in Luke's Gospel. Luke is unique among the Synoptics in this regard. That Judas "strategizes" (*stratēgois*), probably with the temple guards, suggests that he has been thinking about his dark deed for some time and that he also sees an "opportunity to betray him" while the crowds are not present to intervene (22:4–6). Commentators through the centuries have seen two motives for Judas's betrayal. The first of these is "envy . . . which always leads to the guilt of murder," as Cyril of Alexandria puts it (1983: Homily 140); this motive has been examined most extensively in recent times by Girard, who argues that mimetic desire for the charism of a leader to whom one is drawn powerfully can metamorphose into a hatred based in resentment that one does not himself possess the aura to which he is magnetically attracted (2005: 121–36). The second motive, of much less weight, is possibly greed. It may be that Judas, as keeper of the purse, was already siphoning away funds for himself. Matthew 26:15 specifies the amount of the blood money; Luke does not.

The Passover Meal (22:7–20)

Luke is careful in recounting the preparations for Passover, and he shows us that Jesus has been arranging for this last feast with his disciples in some less than obvious ways. In sending in Peter and John to "prepare the Passover," an effort that requires purchasing and slaughtering the Passover lamb (22:7–8), he provides mysterious directions. They are to meet a man with a pitcher of water, whom they will follow to a house where Jesus has apparently prearranged an "upper room" (*anagaion*) for himself and his disciples. The city is crowded, so perhaps Jesus has done this some time ago. But his method of directing Peter and John prevents Judas, if he was within earshot, from overhearing and planning to have the temple guards arrest Jesus in the midst of the meal (22:9–13).

The day of the beginning of the feast was 14 Nisan, in the evening. When all—bitter herbs (*měrôrîm*), unleavened bread (*maṣâ*), and the lamb—had been prepared, everything would have been in accord with the normal Passover meal preparation. Jesus and the apostles "sat down," Luke says (22:14). Jesus makes clear to the Twelve that having this Passover with them before he suffers has been something he has deeply desired (he uses a Hebraism that Luke renders as *epithymia epethymēsa*, "with fervent desire I have desired"), and he adds that this will be his last Passover (indeed his last meal) until "it is fulfilled [*plērōthē*] in the kingdom of God" (22:15–16). The desire of which Jesus here speaks, doubled for intensity, is an important key to the very character of his love. It is too easy for us to accept a view of Jesus that sees him strictly in terms of his equanimity in the face of adverse circumstance, or intelligence in the context of his teaching and dialectical verbal exchanges, or worst of all, to imagine him as socially indifferent, preoccupied only with his divine mission, an ancient sage whose words from the mountain imply tacitly that he himself is "above it all." No one who reads the Gospels, perhaps especially Luke's, can think of this as an accurate picture of Jesus. Jesus was above all characterized by a passionate love, a desire more profound than any who knew him had ever seen. At any number of places the intensity of his love is so strong that the tears come to his eyes unbidden (for example, at the tomb of Lazarus and again just as he was about to enter Jerusalem). We may still speak of his passion not merely because of his agony in the garden and his suffering on the cross (Latin *passio* is cognate with Greek *paschō*, "to suffer") but also because of such scenes of compassion as that forthcoming in his rejoinder to the women on his way to the cross that they should rather weep for themselves. His heart goes out to them.

His desire for the holiness of the Lord, moreover, is so great that he hates every perversion of it, from the sterile hypocrisy of the Pharisees to the professional arrogance of the scribes, and it infuriates him in a way no Socrates or Aristotle could understand that money changers have perverted the whole meaning of what "the sacrifice of a clean heart" really amounts to, and his zeal for the house of the Lord is so great he resorts to a kind of violence in expelling the commercializers. To him the political sellout by Herod, "that fox," is an occasion of his pronounced disdain. Meanwhile, his affection for sinners of all kinds, especially for those who are themselves of a passionate, immediate, and exuberant heart is as characteristic of him as all of these expressions of his desire for purity of relationship in gratitude to God. Thus, though his desire is notably restrained in respect of what must have often been the tacit if not explicit erotic desire in some of the women, he is nonetheless, despite his chastity, passionately committed to them as authentic persons. Luke reveals Jesus to be much more receptive, even in awkward moments such as the anointing of his feet by a woman of ill-repute, to exuberance of affection and gratefulness of heart than he is inclined to be patient with the prudish but prurient piety of the presumptuously religious hosts of that meal. When he performs a miracle so the wedding guests can continue to make merry, the wine that miraculously appears is of a superlative quality, and he provides it in extravagant abundance.

Jesus, as Luke has learned from many witnesses, is the farthest thing from a dispassionate sage or cool-medium rabbi. He is as passionate as the God of the prophets, as passionate as his predecessor the poet David, and we cannot, unlike Michal in her famous disdainful scorn, begin to imagine Jesus being anything other than immensely pleased with the *heart* of that true lover of God when he danced naked before the ark. His desire is real; a passionate heart loves a passionate heart. When he says just at the beginning of the Passover meal that, in effect, he has long been yearning toward this moment, this feast of love with his cherished friends and the students who must carry on his work, only such an intensified expression makes sense, and it is a Hebraism entirely consistent with everything we have learned about the love of Jesus. It also makes sense, or begins to make sense, of the astonishing and utterly extravagant language he is now about to use with respect to his own self-giving and their sharing in it, now and forever.

It is at this point that the reader begins to see, as did the Twelve themselves, that in relation to fulfillment Jesus is here speaking of the ultimate redemption of which the Passover has been a sign. The Passover ritual is now about to take on a future as well as past significance. The Lord will not participate again in this high festival meal, he says, until some future date. Yet there is, in the ritual meal, a sense of sacramental transposition that the apostles will later recognize retrospectively, in the words of the ancient liturgy: "Christ, our Passover, is sacrificed for us." It is absolutely clear that considered, thoughtful retrospect is crucial to the realized theological understanding of the disciples, and Luke's narrative is full of evidence that he as narrator had been all along actively participating in this sort of remembering—putting events back together in such a way that their fullness of expression gathers in a proper register of abiding theological significance for all subsequent Christian history. *Anamnēsis* ("remembering") is thus the heart of Christian celebration of the Eucharist and serves for us to make Christ eternally present to us and us to him, in what he has done and still does for us as we live in him and he in us. It also is propaedeutic, "until he comes" in glory, to take unto himself his faithful and beloved for the final, everlasting eucharistic feast in the celestial Jerusalem that will have no end.

When the Lord takes the first cup, something more is being revealed (22:17). This verse is unique to Luke (the other Synoptics refer only to the cup that here is second). Whereas the traditional Passover meal had four cups (Fitzmyer 1981–85: 2.1390; Marshall 1978: 797–98), it is probable that the cup here referred to is the first cup of blessing over the meal, since it says he "gave thanks" (*eucharisteō*). The prayer may have been a version of the thanksgiving still in use: "*Baruch atah adonai elohenu, melech ha 'olam, boreh peri hagofen.*" "Fruit of the vine" (*peri hagofen*) is a Hebraism for "wine," and while Jesus has asked each of the apostles "to divide it among [them]selves" (22:17), he indicates that he will not himself taste this wine "until the kingdom of God comes" (22:18). When Jesus now takes the bread, gives thanks and breaks it, and gives it to them with the words "this is my body which is given for you; this do in remembrance of me" (22:19), we have entered fully into transposition of the Passover into the meal Christians everywhere celebrate as the Eucharist, the divine liturgy, the Lord's Table, holy communion, or "breaking of the bread." Evelyn Underhill observes that "no devout Jew, reflecting on the incidents of that night could fail to understand" what Jesus intended.[1] Yet Jesus himself is clearly instituting a new understanding; as Bede puts it: "He himself breaks the bread which he holds forth, to show that the breaking of his body, that is, his passion, will not be without his will" (quoted in Aquinas, *Catena Aurea* 3.2.705). When he raises "the cup after supper" (perhaps the traditional third Passover cup), he makes a similar equation: "This cup is the new covenant in my blood, which is shed for you" (22:20). The analogy between the lamb slain for the Passover and Jesus in his coming suffering is now explicit. Luke is the only Synoptic writer to mention the "new covenant," much as does his friend Paul in 1 Cor. 11:25. There are other slight variations in the wording found in each Synoptic account, which most likely owe to Jesus's praying in Hebrew and perhaps speaking Aramaic, so that transposition to Greek would produce slight differences.

1. Evelyn Underhill, *Worship* (Cambridge, UK: Clark, 2010), 143.

No Christian who participates knowledgably in the eucharistic *anamnēsis* ("remembering" the Lord's passion, resurrection, and ascension into heaven—the high point of the eucharistic remembering enjoined upon his followers by the Lord) is in disagreement with Basil the Great that "we should eat the body and drink the blood of the Lord as a commemoration of the Lord's obedience unto death" (*Morals* 21). This "memorial offering" (*'azkârâ*) was also a familiar element in temple worship, and the idea of a memorial "thanksgiving" (*eucharistia*) appears with these connotations as well in the *Didache*. In this way, as Underhill puts it, "in all liturgies the history of redemption, God's loving operation on the stage of history, is set forth as an essential feature of the Eucharist."[2]

Differing understandings about the precise meaning of his words in this passage have nevertheless led, especially since the Reformation, to divergent accounts of how they should be understood theologically. For our purposes, it seems wise to begin, as does the early church, with the plain if mysterious and demanding words of the text itself. With Cyril of Alexandria, for example, we are to recognize in this account that the mystery of our participation in the body and blood of Christ is likewise necessarily communicated by physical signs, even as his truth has been communicated by verbal signs: "Humbling himself to our infirmities, God infuses into the things set before us the power of life. He transforms them into the effectiveness of his flesh, that we may have them for a life-giving participation, that the body of life thus might be found in us a life-producing seed. Do not doubt that this is true. Christ plainly says, 'This is my body. This is my blood.' In faith, receive the Savior's word. Since he is the truth, he cannot lie" (1983: Homily 142).

There is more. The body and blood of the Lord are signified by the signs of bread and wine in a mystery instituted by his word. One cannot begin to penetrate this mystery except by faith, as Bonaventure puts it, not least because while "there is no difficulty about Christ being present in the sacrament as a sign, there is real difficulty in understanding him as being as truly in the sacrament as he is in heaven" (*Commentaria in quattuor libros sententiarum* d.10 q.1 a.1). The magnificent hymn of Thomas Aquinas, "Pange Lingua Gloriosi," perhaps the finest on this topic of the eucharistic mystery, is still sung in Catholic parishes at the Feast of Corpus Christi. John Donne, the seventeenth-century dean of St. Paul's and metaphysical poet, in his sermon on 1 Cor. 13:12 makes an analogy that shows the persistence of these ideas in some Protestant contexts under the species of vision: "If we see [God] *sicuti manifestatur*, as he looks in his Word and the Sacraments, in his Kingdom of Grace, we have begun to see him, *sicuti est*, as he is, in his essence, in the Kingdom of Glory" (*Collected Sermons* 4.73). This conception is formally analogous to our finding Jesus "present in his word" when the scriptures are read as *lectio divina* or to Paul's way of speaking of the presence of the living Christ within himself (e.g., Gal. 2:20), and it is reflected in the phrase

2. Ibid., 146.

of the evangelical hymn: "He Lives within My Heart." But perhaps some further historical reflection, particular to the Eucharist, may be helpful.

A point worth recollecting here is the strong association in the mind of early Christians between the presence of Christ in the elements of bread and wine and the underlying concept of the incarnation. It was customary in the life of the early church to recite or sing the prologue to John's Gospel (1:1–14) as the last element in the eucharistic service. That is, the transmutation was understood in a fundamentally spiritual sense, as in Augustine's phrase "believe and you have eaten" (Sermon 131; cf. Sermon 112.4–5; Hugh of St. Victor, *On the Sacraments* 2.8.5). The idea of the Eucharist as spiritual sustenance for the faithful appears very early and is reflected already in second-century catacomb art showing a basket of bread containing a cup of wine resting on a fish.[3] Justin Martyr reflects this sense when he refers to "the food which is blessed by the prayer of his word, and by which our blood and flesh by transmutation are nourished by . . . the flesh and blood of that Jesus which was made flesh" (*Apology* 1.66–67).

The doctrine we know as transubstantiation was not fully developed until Thomas Aquinas; the doctrine in its essentials was, however, already declared in the Fourth Lateran Council (1215). Much of the early modern (especially Protestant) doctrinal resistance to it may relate in part to semantic difficulties. Latin *substantia* meant for Aquinas "spiritual" substance; that is, he understood it in the sense in which it is used in the creed, where Christ is said to be "of one substance with the Father" before his incarnation. After the sixteenth century the term, as in John Locke's use of the English word "substance," refers almost exclusively to material rather than spiritual realities. Luther came just at the time of this semantic shift and drew on the conciliarist Pierre d'Ailly to suggest that in the sacrament of the altar there was not a physical change in the elements (transubstantiation) yet there was nonetheless a radically objective presence ("this is my body") of Christ in the sacrament, a position that came to be called "consubstantiation." It is not necessary to review here all the permutations of understanding the theological meaning of the words Luke records Jesus saying; it may suffice to say that in a hymn such as "Adoro te devote" by Thomas Aquinas (and in the lovely translation by Gerald Manley Hopkins), there is reflected a Catholic tradition of taking Jesus's words literally, while in some Protestant formulations these are words that (like "wine") are taken figuratively in such a way as to remove the mystery of transmutation (cf. Aquinas, *Summa Theologica* 3.75.1). It is also necessary to add, however, that among the most beautiful hymns on the "real presence" of Christ in the sacrament are two penned by that most eminent of evangelical hymnists, Charles Wesley. In a fashion that puts him in harmonious company with all of Catholic tradition, he acknowledges in "The Eucharistic Mystery" that there is here in Luke's text an irreducible mystery:

---

3. W. Lowrie, *Art in the Early Church* (New York: Harper, 1965), pl. 13b, c.15.

> Who shall say how bread and wine
>   God into man convey!
> How the bread his flesh imparts,
>   How the wine transmits his blood,
> Fill his faithful people's hearts
>   With all the life of God!

In regard to the "Father's wisdom," he continues, even "angels round our altars bow / To search it out in vain." In "Communion Hymn," he describes the sacrament as "the real sign, / A sure and effectual means of grace," and prays that Jesus will prepare his heart, "To find thy real presence there, / And all thy fullness gain." This attitude, it seems, puts the eighteenth-century evangelical and Thomas Aquinas pretty much on the same page with the early church and gives us a satisfactory sense that the mystery in which, by the Eucharist, we participate has apostolic warrant for understanding and practice thoroughly rooted in the first event as Luke describes it.

Temptation in the Ranks (22:21–34)

Yet there was overt betrayal, right in the midst of the mystery. And when Jesus says so, and with his acknowledgment that this was "determined," he warns of "woe" on the betrayer (22:21–22). The apostles begin at once to ask among themselves who would do such a thing (22:23). Sadly, this leads both to strife and to posturing. In a passage extremely uncomplimentary to the apostles, Luke records that they begin to rank themselves, so to speak, concerning who among them would be regarded as "greatest" (22:24). It is a shameful moment. Jesus's correction seems, given the context, to be extraordinarily patient and restrained. Only Gentiles talk like that, he says; rather, they should count as greatest who most is a servant (22:25–26). Cyril of Alexandria observes trenchantly that in this sad moment of dissension (unfortunately to recur again and again in the historic church), "the net of sin is spread everywhere, and Satan makes us his prey in different ways" (1983: Homily 143). He is reflecting upon the vulnerability of the faithful, not of Judas or even of Peter (Homily 144). Pride is such a venom; Jesus is the model for all in being always a servant (22:27). Yet who can be humble, even as he is humble? Humility is not simply a matter of according due respect. As Ambrose says, "Not every kind of respect and deference to others betokens humility, for you may defer to a person for the world's sake, for fear of someone's power, or mere regard to your own interest. In that case you seek to build up yourself, not to honor another" (quoted in Aquinas, *Catena Aurea* 3.2.710).

Jesus commends them for continuing with him in his own "trials," promising them that they will eat and drink with him at a better feast, in his kingdom, from whence they will judge the tribes of Israel (22:29–30). But their own present temptation is more real than they think. He now tells Simon Peter, no less, that Satan has "desired to have you, that he may sift you as wheat" (22:31 KJV). He has prayed for Peter, that his "faith should not fail," and that when Peter has "converted" (so KJV; NKJV has "returned to me" for *epistrephsas*) he would strengthen the brothers (22:32). This must have been a shocking thing for Peter to hear; he has no imagination of failure at this point, and he protests his willingness to go to prison or death for his Lord (22:33). Peter is a passionate man, and this claim is characteristically passionate. Yet Jesus most soberly tells him that the cock will not crow in the morning before Peter—loyal Peter—has three times denied that he even knows Jesus (22:34). What a somber statement this is, at the end of so intimate and cherishable a shared Passover supper.

Preparation for Darkness (22:35–53)

There are no parallels for the next several verses in Luke's account, where Jesus both reminds his disciples of his previous instructions concerning minimal provision for their apostolic work and says, in effect, "This time it is different." He tells them that if they have a purse they should take it, likewise with a traveling bag, and that if they don't have a sword they should get one, even if they have to sell their outer coat to do it. He makes it clear once again that he is going to suffer as a criminal, citing specifically Isa. 53:12, hewing to the Masoretic Text rather than the Septuagint in so doing. It turns out that there are two swords present, and Jesus says, "It is enough" (Luke 22:38). What accounts for this apparent reversal of his earlier injunctions (9:3; 10:3–4)? One possibility may be that Jesus does not wish a mass arrest of his followers with him and so foresees that a sword or two may forestall such a move on the part of the temple guard, who likely hope to avoid any confrontation that would blow the cover of their stealth operation. In any case, the apostles are ready to go back to the Mount of Olives, where Judas, who has slipped away already in the darkness, knows he will be able to find them when he returns with the temple guards, priests, and elders. Jesus, of course, is aware of this, and he has made no effort to evade the outcome. He prepares in quite another way.

When he asks the disciples to pray, it is specifically for themselves, that they "may not enter into temptation," like Judas (22:40). When he withdraws from them a short distance, one of Luke's informants saw him "kneel down" to pray, something unique not only in Luke's account but in all of the New Testament, and especially noteworthy because it was not then the usual posture for Jewish (and early Christian) prayer, which was usually standing with palms raised (the *orans* posture in early Christian art). Luke neither calls the place Gethsemane (Mark 14:32; Matt. 26:36) nor singles out Peter, James, and John (Mark 14:33; Matt. 26:37). What he does have uniquely is a more dramatic sense of the agony of Jesus as he prays that, if the Father is willing, "this cup" be removed (Luke 22:42); in

Luke alone does he sweat so profusely that it falls from him like "drops of blood" (22:44); and in Luke's account alone do we learn that an angel has appeared, standing by to "strengthen him" (22:43). The *agōnia* (a Greek word related to *agōn*, "struggle") is a New Testament *hapax legomenon* that serves to refract in Classical Greek terms the *agōn* of Christ and Satan from the beginning of Luke's account. The agony in the garden is intense, yet Jesus yields himself to the will of his Father. His decisive words are, "Nevertheless not my will, but yours, be done" (22:42). These are among the most important words in the New Testament, and indeed all of Christian theology. That they come of an intense struggle was a demonstration to the early church of Christ's humanity in the incarnation (Athanasius, *Orations against the Arians* 3.29). But beyond that, in his decision he exemplified the attitude of heart appropriate to his followers: "In the second part of his prayer," writes John Chrysostom, "he demonstrates his virtue and self-control, teaching us even when [our] nature pulls us back, to follow God" (*Homilies on Matthew* 83). In the thirteenth-century *Meditations on the Life of Christ*, where the attending angel is identified as Michael, the angelic commentator connects the obedience of Christ in Gethsemane to the disobedience of Adam in Eden, reflecting a typology regarding the garden and disobedience/obedience that has persisted to the present in Christian homiletics, poetry, and hymnody (Pseudo-Bonaventure 1961: 320–24).

Yet when Jesus "rose up from prayer," he came back to his disciples to find them sleeping. Disappointed, he rouses them to pray, "lest you enter into temptation" (22:46). Perhaps we should imagine the disciples less as slothful than depressed, psychologically exhausted at the prospect that Jesus has indicated now faces him and that has dampened their joyous hope for a triumphant beginning of his kingdom. Whatever their state of mind, they are immediately aware of a mob coming up to them, led by Judas, who—Luke reiterates to underscore the ignominy of it—was "one of the twelve" (22:47). The kiss—a normative Mediterranean form of greeting among friends and confederates—just makes it worse. Luke is distinctive in the way he recounts this sad gesture, which obtains a heavy rejoinder from Jesus: "Judas, are you betraying the Son of Man with a kiss?" (22:48). As we have seen earlier, the willingness of Jesus to treat Judas so equitably, while knowing all along that he was a betrayer, is one of the mysteries of the whole Gospel narrative. Thomas More, who knew better than most what such betrayal was like, notes moreover that

> even to Judas, God gave many opportunities of coming to his senses. He did not deny him companionship. He did not take away from him the dignity of his apostleship. He did not even take the purse strings from him, even though he was a thief. He admitted the traitor to the fellowship of the beloved disciples at the last supper. He deigned to stoop down at the feet of the betrayer and to wash with his most innocent and sacred hands Judas' dirty feet. . . . [Therefore] there is no reason why, in this life, anyone should despair of any imitator of Judas. (*De tristitia Christi*)

The annals of Christian saints' lives indicate amply that if, like the saints, one is willing to imitate Jesus in the circumstance of betrayal, a truer discipleship will be exemplified, a sacrifice pleasing unto God (Rom. 12:1).

There is a pathetic quality to the motley crew of disciples as it begins to dawn on them what is happening. They are unprepared mentally, and so ask Jesus, "Shall we strike with the sword?" (Luke 22:49). Before Jesus can answer, the impetuous Peter (John 18:10) has struck—rather ineffectually, it seems, managing to lop off only the ear of a servant of the high priest whom subsequent tradition will call Malchus. But that is just enough in another sense; the Lord reaches out and heals his ear, restoring it (Luke 22:51)—simultaneously performing his last miracle in just such a fashion as to bless his enemies, while restraining violence on both sides. While the sword-blow is inept, the healing is a masterstroke. Jesus does not lose opportunity, however, to let his adversaries know he has seen their cowardice for what it is—coming against him as if he were a brigand under cover of darkness, while they had plenty of opportunities to seize him while he was teaching in the temple but did not, for fear of the then still attentive and appreciative crowds (22:52–53). Without further ado, they lead him off. Because the Sabbath is coming, there is another reason to make haste.

Trial and Dissimilation (22:54–71)

"But Peter followed at a distance" (22:54). Already the image we have of Peter is that of one who, full of passionate intensity, clearly loves the Lord yet has nevertheless profound unsteadiness and ungoverned fear in his heart. As Jesus is being led to "the high priest's house," Peter is clearly conflicted and under temptation. In the courtyard, a fire has been lit and the men are gathered around it, waiting for the dawn when proceedings could begin. A servant girl, probably of the high priest (whether Annas or Caiaphas, Luke does not specify), spots Peter and identifies him to the others as one who "was also with him" (22:56). The conflicted state of Peter's heart, torn between loyalty and disloyalty, love and fear, is a fit subject for the chiaroscuro paintings of Caravaggio and Georges de la Tour of this scene. Accusation, denial, honesty, dishonesty, light, and darkness. Peter denies (*arneomai*) what the girl says, insisting that he does not know Jesus (22:57). By the time someone else renews the accusation and Peter again denies, employing language that recalls the ban formula used in synagogue dismissals (Bock 1994–96: 2.1783–84), the darkness has deepened. An hour later comes a third accusation, bolstered by recognition of Peter's Galilean accent, and again Peter denies emphatically. Just then "the rooster crowed" (22:59–60). The moment is poignant with grief and remorse: Jesus turns and looks at Peter. Peter is stricken; suddenly now he remembers what the Lord had said to him only hours before and turns away, out of the courtyard, weeping bitterly (22:61–62). For what follows, Luke clearly has unnamed sources; what they have witnessed must have been painful to behold.

Medieval and early Renaissance artists are more willing than most later painters to depict the "mocking," "scourging," and "buffeting" of Jesus, but it is hard to believe that even these grotesqueries (perhaps best instanced by the violent engravings of Albrecht Dürer) capture the physical torment and the laconically demonic attitude of Jesus's tormenters. Blasphemy is what Luke sees (22:65), not only in the blows and mockery (22:63) but especially in the blindfolding and demands for "prophecy" (22:64) that were part of it. The author of the *Meditations on the Life of Christ* describes this in excruciating detail, connecting the sufferings of Christ to Isa. 53:2–4, inviting the reader to imagine how "again and again, repeatedly, closer and closer it is done, bruise upon bruise and cut upon cut, until not only the torturers but the spectators are tired; then he is ordered untied" (Pseudo-Bonaventure 1961: 328–29). Cyril's comment captures something of the gross injustice of the scene: "He, who in nature and glory transcended the limits of our understanding and our powers of speech, patiently endured those officers when they not only mocked but also hit him." He adds, apropos the mock question about his identity that now follows, "sacred Scripture says, 'God is not mocked'" (1983: Homily 150). "As soon as it was day," the elders, chief priests, and scribes can legally bring him before the council (Sanhedrin), for night trials had no legal status by Jewish law. Now they can put him before witnesses to interrogate him (Luke 22:66). They demand, "If you are the Christ, tell us." Jesus's reply is irenic but damning of their pretense to justice: "If I tell you, you will by no means believe. And if I also ask you, you will by no means answer me or let me go" (22:67–68).

What he says next proves to be better for their dark purpose than anything they had hoped by their torture to wring out of him: "Hereafter the Son of Man will sit on the right hand of the power of God," says Jesus (22:69). But in Jewish literature only God sits in heaven. The image of God enthroned is of the Shekinah glory of the judge and ruler of all; by saying this Jesus puts himself on a par with the supreme judge and, in effect, when he answers "you rightly say that I am" to the natural follow-up question ("are you then the Son of God?"), Jesus is really indicating that he will one day judge *them*. In this way, Jesus has chosen to go to the cross by uttering words that the Jewish leaders could not but have taken as the most egregious and, indeed, aggressive blasphemy. In their view, though the theological irony lies heavy over Luke's narrative at this point, Jesus has convicted himself. They could hardly be happier (22:71).

LUKE 23

The passion sequence of the Gospels has provided for numerous magnificent settings in Western music; among them, those of Bach and Schütz for Matthew and Bach's "Passion according to St. John" are among the greatest settings for any biblical text in the history of music.[1] No comparable setting has been attempted for Luke's text. This is in one respect a surprise, since Luke's Gospel more than any other in the New Testament has yielded up prayers and responses for the liturgy itself, as we have seen. Part of the reason may be Luke's focus on details of the trials before Pilate and Herod, and part of it may owe to the greater complexity of his account of the crucifixion itself. But that we can speak accurately of Luke's narrative as the "Passion according to St. Luke" is, as we shall see, beyond question.

The term "passion" (*pathēma*) itself deserves further reflection here theologically. The anglicized form of Latin *passio* has been used since early Christian times to refer to the narratives of Christ's suffering and death as found in all four Gospels (Matt. 26–27; Mark 14–15; John 18–19; Luke 22–23). The Latin term, as we have seen, translated Greek *paschō*/*pathos*; in New Testament accounts with one exception (Heb. 2:9) *pathēma* occurs in the plural, *pathēmata* ("sufferings"). Metonymically, "the cross" (*stauros*) comes in Christian texts to be an equivalent term (e.g., 1 Cor. 1:18). The emphasis on the Suffering Servant analogy (Isa. 52:13–53:12) in Heb. 5, 7, 9 and Rev. 5:6, 12; 7:14; 12:11; 13:8 tended to strengthen the focus on Christ's suffering as substitutionary and as a redemptive sacrifice for the sins of the world, and all subsequent Christian reflection sees the Calvary event in this way. The cross is at once the most terrible event in human history and the most to be cherished, because without it redemption would be impossible. This paradox—the ugly and ignominious death of the innocent Son of God being

---

1. An excellent account of Bach's treatment is given by Jaroslav Pelikan, *Bach among the Theologians* (Minneapolis: Fortress, 1986), esp. 74–115.

also an object of devotion and reverence, even (as in Franciscan spirituality) the height of beauty—is the source of much of the rich language and ideation in both theology and poetry. After the vision of Constantine (Eusebius, *Life of Constantine* 1.28–32; 3.26) it even became possible to proclaim the most obvious symbol of ignominious defeat in the Roman Empire as a sign of transcendent victory. In the passion hymn of Fortunatus, "Pange Lingua Gloriosi," as well as almost a century later, in the Pseudo-Bonaventuran "Arbor Vitae Crucifixis Jesu" of Bartholomew of Pisa, the cross is represented as the "tree of life." Legendary association of Golgotha as the place of Adam's temptation, and thus of the original tree of life, fits naturally in such typological thinking with the Lukan and Pauline (1 Cor. 15:45) idea of Christ Jesus as the Second Adam, whose obedience unto death (Phil. 2:8) reversed the disobedience of the first Adam.

Other elements, more closely linking passion to its association with powerful emotion, even the emotions we associate with human love, as well as pathos and empathy, are also connotatively enriched by biblical typology. This is evident in Clement of Alexandria's view that Isaac carrying the wood for his own sacrifice is a type of Christ carrying the instrument of his own death to Calvary (*Instructor* 1.5). Likewise Irenaeus (*Epidiexis* 1.34) refers to the mystery of which Paul speaks (in Eph. 3:3, 18) as the figuration in the cross of the love of Christ in all its "breadth, length, depth, and height" that accordingly "passes knowledge" (Eph. 3:19), and Paul's analogy of human marriage with Christ's self-offering on the cross simply deepens the resonances of passion for subsequent tradition (Augustine, *On Christian Doctrine* 2.41.62; Letter 55; *Commentary on the Gospel of John* 118.5). Finally, because the central memory of the church is God's redemptive act in sending Jesus to die on the cross as the atonement for sin, and because this is recollected in every eucharistic worship, the dominant image of Christ's passion in Christian tradition over the centuries is the crucifix itself.[2] This is accordingly the focal point for Christian identity, the source of our memory and identity as Christians, and the means of our remembering in his body. No Christian reader can come to Luke's account of the passion—or that of any other evangelist—except as to the "old, old, story," and therefore as to a narrative already deeply known and charged with layers of meaning and powerful emotion. In the hymns of the church, from the Victorine sequences "Laudus Crucis" and "Salve, Crux" (attributed to Adam of St. Victor in the twelfth century) through the intense Franciscan identification with the "suffered Christ," vividly imaged in the stigmata of Francis himself on Mount Verna and the subject of almost innumerable Franciscan hymns and poems

2. This was not true until after the third century in Roman church art, in part because of the associations with shameful death in the culture generally. The crucifix would have seemed to many comparable to an image of a gallows or electric chair in our own culture. Visually, however, the cross lends itself, in its crossed members, to being seen as an icon of reconciliation vertically between God and humanity and horizontally between individuals formerly estranged from one another—a fact about which there has been much Christian commentary.

(e.g., Jacopone da Todi's "Stabat Mater" and Bonaventure's "Laudisimus de Santa Cruce"), the poet-persona will ask to experience with Christ his passion, often in strong and what may appear to us as erotically charged language. Mostly, however, Franciscan contemplation on the passion of our Lord is seen as a principal means of entering into and maintaining an authentic spirit of discipleship. Thus, contemplation of the passion is in the fullest sense of the term "spiritual exercise," as the following passage from the *Meditations on the Life of Christ* makes clear:

> We must now treat of the Passion of our Lord Jesus. He who wishes to glory in the cross and the Passion must dwell with continued meditation on the mysteries and events that occurred. If they were considered with complete regard of mind, they would, I think, lead the meditator to a new spiritual state. To him who searches for it from the bottom of the heart and with the marrow of his being, many un-hoped-for steps would take place by which he would receive new compassion, new love, new solace, and then a new condition of sweetness that would seem to him a promise of glory. (Pseudo-Bonaventure 1961: 317)

For such purposes, Luke's account may be the most useful of Gospel narratives of the passion. As we shall see, he includes details lacking in the others, and they are such as to prompt meditative reflection on what it means to be willing to take up one's own cross and follow Jesus (Luke 9:23–24). That is, his account invites a strong participatory identification. If such intensity of emotion and meditative discipline tends to fade in many Protestant treatments of the passion after the eighteenth century, it is certainly still resonant in Isaac Watts's "When I Survey the Wondrous Cross" (1707), in which echoes of the Franciscan contemplation of the passion are apparent. The third and fourth stanzas thus unite this hymn of the great Dissenter poet and scholar with its pre-Reformation predecessors:

> See, from his head, his hands, his feet,
>   Sorrow and love flow mingled down:
> Did e'er such love and sorrow meet,
>   Or thorns compose so rich a crown.
>
> His dying crimson, like a robe,
>   Spreads o'er his body on the tree:
> Then am I dead to all the globe,
>   And all the globe to me.

Watts's fourth stanza is, however, typically omitted from nineteenth- and twentieth-century Protestant hymnals, perhaps as good an indication as any of an unfortunate tendency in modernist Protestantism to wish to move as quickly as possible to the resurrection, even if it means bypassing Calvary or averting the eyes to do so. The seventeenth-century Anglican divine and metaphysical poet John Donne, less squeamish, puts the question just so:

> Since Christ embrac'd the Crosse itselfe, dare I
> His image, th'image of his Crosse deny?
> Would I have profit by the sacrifice,
> And dare the chosen Altar to despise?
> It bore all other sinnes, but is it fit
> That it should bear the sinne of scorning it?
> Who from the picture would avert his eye,
> How would he fly his paines, who there did dye?

Donne goes on to make a point that seems, now as ever, crucial to a faithful claim to the name: "No Crosse is so extreme, as to have none."[3]

The First Trial before Pilate (23:1–7)

The death penalty was a Roman prerogative (Josephus, *Jewish War* 2.117), so the crowd follows the council elders to seek an arraignment of Jesus before Pilate (23:1). Their accusations, uniquely specified by Luke (23:2), are in the one instance false (Jesus has certainly *not* forbidden taxes to Caesar, as is clear in 20:25). Another is really a charge of sedition, namely that he was "perverting" (*diastrephō*) or misleading the nation. This also is to depict him as an insurrectionist against Rome, a political charge of dubious substance. The third charge, which they wrongly present as a political claim, is nevertheless substantially true: "king" (*basileus*) is probably what a Gentile translation of "Anointed One" or Christos/Messiah came closest to. It is thus the third charge to which Pilate directs his attention. "Are you the King of the Jews?" he asks, perhaps in a slightly mocking tone. Jesus answers him elliptically: "You say so," or "You have said so" (23:3 RSV).

It is clear enough to Pilate that whatever Jesus or his followers may claim about him, he is not, as his accusers assert, a claimant to political power of a sort to trouble the Roman purview, and so he turns to the chief priests and people and says, in effect, "There is nothing here that warrants your charge." The reply Luke records is even stronger: "I find no fault in this Man" (23:4). Normally, this would end the hearing; the charges have been declared unsubstantiated. But the adversaries become "more fierce," insisting on their first charge, namely that he has stirred up all Jewry from Galilee to Jerusalem with his teaching (23:5). When Pilate hears the name "Galilee," he glimpses a way to dodge some unpleasantness; Galilee is Herod's jurisdiction, Herod is bound to be in town at his Jerusalem residence for the Passover, and so he says, "Let Herod deal with it" (23:6–7).

3. H. J. C. Grierson, ed., *The Poems of John Donne* (London: Oxford University Press, 1933), 302.

The Trial before Herod (23:8–12)

Herod had long wanted to see Jesus (9:9), and this is reiterated here in such a way as to reveal the shallow as well as the malevolent character of the man. The Hasmonean palace was only about a ten minutes' walk from Pilate (Marshall 1978: 855; Bock 1994–96: 2.1819), so arranging for the interview was apparently easy. Herod hoped he could get Jesus to entertain him, to perform a miracle of the sort he had heard so much about (23:8). He is disappointed in his hope for entertainment. Herod then asks many questions but is disappointed in this regard also, for he gets no answers (23:9). All the while the chief priests and scribes are haranguing Jesus, and finally, lacking any gratification of the sort he wanted, Herod and his guards join in arraying Jesus in a stately robe (*lampros*, "shining" or possibly "white") as part of the mockery. The self-control Jesus exhibits in the face of all this abuse has often been remarked upon by commentators; Ambrose is representative of many: "By remaining silent, he does not confirm the accusation. By not refuting it, he despises it. A special attribute of Christ is that among wicked judges he seemed to be unwilling rather than unable to defend himself" (*Exposition of Luke* 10.97–99). For Christians attuned to the book of Isaiah, the silence of the Suffering Servant (Isa. 53:7) has come often to mind in this context, but not so to Herod and his supporters quite obviously. Eventually frustrated in his attempt to wring something of interest to him out of Jesus, Herod is obliged to send the now most palpably Suffering Servant back to Pilate.

And yet there was some gratification for the despot, for Luke observes that the animosity between Pilate and Herod was relieved by this exchange. They "became friends" over it (Luke 23:12). For Girard, following the ancient commentator Theophylact, "It is their common participation in the death of Jesus that brings Herod and Pilate together." These two imperious and rival representatives of Rome's colonial power are by now, on Girard's compelling view, merely agents in the spirit of mob violence that has taken over all the proceedings and made the formal trappings of justice a complete sham, so that "their reconciliation is one of those cathartic effects that benefit the participants in a collective murder" (2005: 132). Luke, however, recognizes in writing about it later what Herod and Pilate do not at the time, namely that this is no true reconciliation but merely the momentary gratification of shared complicity in the service of ulterior motives, motives that have nothing to do with justice at all.

Pilate's Second Hearing (23:13–25)

The form of justice, of course, is scrupulously observed, as Luke narrates it. The second trial therefore conforms to standard Roman procedure:[4] notation of the

---

4. J. H. Neyrey, *The Passion according to Luke: A Study of Luke's Soteriology* (Mahwah, NJ: Paulist Press, 1985), 81.

arrest (23:14a), charges (23:14b), determination (or *cogitio*: "having examined him in your presence, I have found no fault in this Man concerning those things of which you accuse him"; 23:14c). To this is added the supporting verdict of Herod ("neither did Herod"; 23:15a) and a formal acquittal: "And indeed nothing deserving of death has been done" by Jesus (23:15b). Accordingly, Pilate will "chastise" Jesus and "release" him (23:16). Luke adds here parenthetically a reference to a standing custom to release a criminal at the time of the Passover, a detail incorporated more directly in Matt. 27:15 and Mark 15:6. He omits, however, the symbolic washing of hands by Pilate at the end of this episode found in Matt. 27:24.

On Luke's account it seems that Pilate would clearly have preferred not to condemn Jesus (23:20). The whipping that ensues is no small "chastisement"; we know from contemporary accounts that it could kill by itself and certainly left its victim's back a bloody pulp (Suetonius, *Domitian* 11; Josephus, *Jewish War* 2.306–8). But the angry mob is by no means assuaged: they demand that Jesus now be executed (Pilate's verdict notwithstanding) and that a genuine political rebel and murderer, one Barabbas, be released instead (Luke 23:17–19). There is heavy circumstantial irony here; the name "Barabbas," as Ambrose noted long ago, means literally "son of the father." From this etymological fact Ambrose draws out a further irony (*Exposition of Luke* 10.101–2), once again in the vein of Theophylact and Girard: "Those then to whom it is said, 'Ye are of your father the devil,' are represented as preferring to the true Son of God the son of their [own] father, that is, Antichrist." For Origen, as for Girard, the irony in this exchange extends to the ritual of the "scapegoat," in which the second goat, "offered to God as an offering to atone for sins," is for those who believe in Christ the "true atonement" (*Homilies on Leviticus* 10.2.2). The repeated chant, "Crucify him, crucify him!" (23:21), elicits a third appeal to reason from Pilate, and with it a restatement of his original "not guilty" verdict (23:22). But the yelling goes on, and in one of the most ignominious observations in all biblical narrative, Luke records that "the voices of these men and of the chief priests prevailed" (23:23). Mob violence here trumps justice, denies truth, and makes a mockery of the legal sanction and due process it claimed to have sought. Pilate's ignominy is yet worse, for in capitulation to the mob he "gave sentence that it should be as they requested" (23:24). Barabbas, who actually did the things (and more) of which Jesus was most falsely accused, is released. Luke repeats the charges that got him into prison so that we who are his readers do not miss the perversity of it. Now Jesus, the condemned though innocent, is "delivered" into the frenzy of the mob (23:25). It is a terrible moment and clearly presages a terrible nemesis later to come. Ambrose, who is one of the most searching of all early fathers in his commentary on these events, asks rhetorically a question often rather more shallowly debated by subsequent commentators, usually in the form of apportioning blame to the Jewish leaders, the Romans, or the mob: "What kind of people crucified the Lord of glory? Those that violently demand the death of an innocent man fittingly seek the release of a murderer. Wickedness has just such laws as to hate innocence and love guilt" (*Exposition of Luke* 10.101–2). This observation applies to us in our own time, alas, as much as to anyone in first-century Palestine. Everyone—every kind of person and every species of self-interest—has become guilty of the death of Jesus. No single party escapes the shame and the blame for it.

The Crucifixion (23:26–49)

Luke does not, as do Matthew and Mark, record Jesus first carrying the crossbeam for his execution, as was the horrible practice in a Roman crucifixion. Jesus was to undergo a tortuous and especially degrading form of death reserved by Rome for slaves and foreigners, and this miserable ritual was part of it. Whoever was Luke's informant seems only to have conveyed that an innocent bystander, one Simon of Cyrene (from the region now known as Tripoli, which oddly enough could mean that this man was a Gentile), was forced by the soldiers to take up the crossbeam when it was evident that Jesus was too far damaged by his torture to carry it. The image of Jesus attempting to bear up this burden, like a brutal yoke, but failing for loss of blood and exhaustion to be able for it, recalls a saying of Jesus in Matt. 11:28–30, but here with heavily ironic overtones. This yoke is not easy; this burden is not light. Since Mark tells us that Simon of Cyrene was the father of Rufus and Alexander, it may well be that Simon was, or would later become, a follower of Jesus, thus later on of his own free will living out in a spiritual and less graphic fashion, perhaps, the imitation of Christ he now so horribly pantomimed in the hour of Christ's own passion. The slow, grim pilgrimage to Golgotha (Luke omits the name) has given rise to the Franciscan inspired stations of the cross (*Via Crucis* or *Via Dolorosa*), of which this moment is the fifth station of the medieval version, and the eighth of the "scriptural" stations revised by Pope John Paul II (1991) to accord more strictly to the biblical account. En route we come to another station (eighth in the traditional numbering, ninth in Pope John Paul II's), Jesus responding to the weeping women who were singing or chanting a threnody (*thrēneō*) of grief, a grief that Jesus, in a fairly lengthy response, says would be better saved for themselves and for their children. A terrible day is coming, he warns (Luke 23:27–31), one to which his death is, at one level, the prolegomena. It seems clear that he is speaking again of the coming destruction of Jerusalem, a time in which, as Theophylact notes, the women in the besieged city of Jerusalem, starving, "shall cruelly roast their own children, and the belly which had produced shall miserably again receive that which it bore" (quoted in Aquinas, *Catena Aurea* 3.2.747). Jesus foresees, as the bystanders do not, that the physical horrors of his own crucifixion will in a generation be exceeded by several orders of magnitude when God, in his judgment, allows the Jerusalem vacated of his holy presence to be destroyed, root and branch, by the Roman armies. The form of Jesus's reply to the women would have been orally memorable, as a simple chiasmus:

weep not
>   for me
>   for yourselves
weep

For readers after AD 70, those would have been unmistakably ominous words, recollected by some of those survivors who had heeded Jesus's warning to flee Jerusalem when the sign of siege drew near (21:20–24).

But for now, the cruel march to Golgotha continues, with a melee of mocking as well as moans on both sides of the road, as two common criminals are in the ugly procession, also being led to their death (23:32). Soon enough they are at the place of death. Luke is minimalist in his description of the crucifixion at this point, omitting the effort to get Jesus (as well, presumably, as the others) to drink some drugged wine vinegar, a typical amelioration of executions by crucifixion by the Roman military (cf. Matt. 27:34; Mark 15:23; Lightfoot 1979: 3.211). Beyond this gesture comes the final phase of the torture. Here in Luke is just the bare fact of it: from contemporary accounts of such executions we can all too readily fill in some of the gaps. Three men, in the agonies of torment, having been nailed or roped to their respective crossbeams, are hoisted up by poles and dropped with an agonizing thud into sockets at the top of the poles already fixed in the ground, so that the feet of the condemned cannot touch the earth. Luke uniquely records that Jesus prayed, "Father, forgive them, for they do not know what they do" (23:34), modeling in a most striking way his teaching: "Bless those who curse you, and pray for those who spitefully use you" (6:28). They take away his garment and cast lots for it (all the evangelists allude to Ps. 22:7 here, but there is an echo also of Luke 6:29). The rulers taunt Jesus, effectively saying, "If he is the Christ, the Chosen One of God, let him save himself"—a mockery aimed at his identity directly and echoing the temptation by Satan in the wilderness (4:5–12). The soldiers also mock him, even as they offer him the customary vinegar, taunting the agonized victim, "If you are the King of the Jews, save yourself" (23:37), ridiculing what they take to be his political pretensions. Luke does not mention that it was Pilate who caused the sign to be placed over his head, alluding to the ostensible capital crime of sedition, but this feature too was normal. The sign is trilingual—Greek, Latin, and Hebrew—in each saying, "This is the King of the Jews," as much as to say also, in a grim jest, "This is what comes to such folly as to claim to be a king" (23:38). Even the two criminals mock him, or at least Matt. 27:44 and Mark 15:32 say so. Luke, however, mentions only the one criminal, his foreshortened account highlighting the condemned man who evidently has bethought himself, with an account unique to him of conversation between Jesus and the others crucified (evidently Luke's informer in this matter was not one of those "who stood afar off"). Whereas the one malefactor mimics the taunt of the elders (23:39), the other is suddenly stricken: "We indeed justly" suffer, he says, "the due reward of our deeds; but this Man has done nothing wrong"

(23:41). Even as he is declaring something truthful about Jesus's identity, he is moved to a plea: "Lord, remember me when you come into your kingdom" (23:42). This plea is also, of course, a confession of belief in Jesus's true identity, and Jesus immediately responds, in a voice audible to those close to the foot of the cross but not to those at a distance, in words that have intrigued theologians and laypersons alike for centuries: "Assuredly I say to you, today you will be with me in Paradise" (23:43).

The promise of the Lord to the repentant criminal,[5] taken, as it should be, at face value here, raises questions about "paradise." Is it the same thing as heaven? Early Christian commentators paused over this uniquely Lukan statement by Jesus, wondering how the idea of paradise, apparently to be instantly entered by a repentant criminal, squared with the doctrine of the last-day resurrection of all justified sinners. One way they reflected on this passage was in relation to the Jewish equation "paradise = Eden" (Lightfoot 1979: 3.213; but cf. Paul's being "caught up into paradise" in 2 Cor. 12). Bypassing the Pauline reference, some writers imagined Golgotha, the "place of the skull," as the place of Adam's burial; the typology of "old Adam/New Adam" applied, and the motif is recurrent in painterly iconography for Calvary in the Middle Ages and Renaissance. Athanasius, for example, in his "Homily on the Passion of the Lord," speaks of the connection in this way: "He who for our sakes took upon him all our conditions, put on our garments, the signs of Adam's death, that he might put them off, and in their stead clothe us with life and incorruption" (quoted in Aquinas, *Catena Aurea* 3.2.753). Ambrose makes the "very place of the cross . . . above the grave of Adam" (*Exposition of Luke* 10.114), and the same typology leads a similar context for Cyril of Jerusalem (1983: Homily 153): "The tree of life brought ruin to Adam. It will bring you to paradise" (*Catechetical Lectures* 13.31). The typology is summarized memorably in John Donne's poem "Hymn to God, My God, in My Sickness" as an expression, at death's door, of his confidence in the resurrection:

> We thinke that Paradise and Calvarie,
>   Christ's Crosse and Adams tree, stood in one place;
> Looke Lord, and find both Adams met in me;
>   As the first Adams sweat surrounds my face,
>   May the last Adams blood my soul embrace.[6]

All of these reflections may have been innocent of the Hebrew/Aramaic phrase that grounds the relation philologically; Jesus is the Son of Man—*ben-ʾādām*. All, that is, except for Donne, who, because he certainly made use of Theodore Beza's commentary on the Gospels in his sermon preparation, would have found it there, and there most richly commented on.

5. The traditional shorthand designation of "thief" for the two malefactors is not justified by the Greek term *kakourgos*, which simply means "criminal."
6. Grierson, *Poems of John Donne*, 337.

In a sermon on this text, Spurgeon noted in 1885 that the use of the "dying thief" account to support confidence in last-minute conversion is not a false, but rather an incomplete, appreciation of the text. His question, prompted by the popular hymn of eighteenth-century evangelical poet William Cowper ("There Is a Fountain") concerns what "the dying thief rejoiced to see." He suggests that the criminal had been watching attentively all along and listening to Jesus's address to the mourning women, his prayer for forgiveness of his executioners, and his meekness in the midst of the taunting mockery of his tormenters.[7] For Spurgeon, the desire to be with the Lord in paradise is the natural longing of the believer for Sabbath rest.

But this leads to another theological question: are the saints who have departed now in paradise? Origen thinks so, and that the assurance to the dying criminal was to all the faithful (*Homilies on Genesis* 15.5). Ambrose hedges along the axis of spiritual interpretation, apropos Jesus's words: "For life is to be with Christ, because where Christ is, there is the kingdom" (*Exposition of Luke* 10.121). This answer may have been intended to forestall literal questions such as, "Was the repentant criminal also with Jesus when he descended into hell?" In one of Giotto's predella panels, *Christ in Limbo*, we see that Christ in his descent is represented as indeed accompanied by the repentant convict, who is bearing the sign of the cross (Hornik and Parsons 2003–7: 3.109). Aquinas held to this view of the matter. But such a view then must be reconciled with the doctrine of the final resurrection. Chrysostom captures the dilemma in this way: "But if the reward of the good has already taken place, surely a resurrection will be superfluous. For if he introduced the thief into paradise while his body remained in corruption without, it is clear there is no resurrection of the body" (*Homilies on Matthew* 81).

One way to approach this conundrum was articulated by Lutheran theologian Oscar Cullmann in his highly controversial pamphlet *Immortality of the Soul or Resurrection of the Dead?* (1956). Cullmann argued persuasively that immortality of the soul is essentially a Hellenistic conception, that it relates to the doctrine of Plato (in the *Phaedo*) and is thus incompatible with the biblical doctrine of resurrection of the body, which for Paul (1 Cor. 15:13–15) was the sine qua non of Christian faith. For Cullman, in short, the two doctrines are opposed and mutually canceling; nothing could be more different in this regard, he suggests, than the death of Socrates and the death of Jesus. It is of some interest, as we have seen, that there was a first-century debate between these two positions, essentially between the Sadducees, who denied the resurrection, and the Pharisees, who upheld it; meanwhile, late Hellenistic apocryphal Jewish writings such as the Wisdom of Solomon nod in the direction of the immortality of souls (even though this immortality is available only at the discretion of God). The division between the Sadducees and Pharisees is maintained by Cullmann, especially on the authority

7. C. H. Spurgeon, Sermon 1881: "The Dying Thief in a New Light," available online at spurgeon gems.org.

of one eminent Pharisee, namely Paul. The early fathers of the church, however, partly because of this same verse in Luke, found it more difficult to hold one view to the exclusion of the other; unless the soul persists, some reasoned, there can be no beatific vision of God in the life to come; on the other hand, without the resurrection of the body spoken of in the New Testament, one is obliged to trope away the reality of the body of Jesus so emphatically stressed in the resurrection account. Augustine reflects this "both/and" approach in his *City of God* 22.11–29.

Varieties of this approach by the fathers—some by way of spiritual or allegorical readings of paradise—have persisted for centuries. John Chrysostom, in the passage earlier quoted, tells us that some punctuate the Greek of Luke's text so that it reads, "I say unto you, on this day, that you shall [one day] be with me in paradise." Another strategy is illustrated by Henry (1728: 829), who identifies this paradise with "the Paradise of God" spoken of in Rev. 2:7, as alluding to Eden, recollecting the first Adam/Second Adam typology in such a way that paradise "is the happiness of heaven, to see Christ, and it with him, and share his glory." Henry goes on to say that "it is immediate on death," applying the promise to the dying criminal to all the faithful, in the manner of Origen. More recently, Wright, who steadfastly maintains that "dying and going to heaven" is not a New Testament doctrine, suggests that Jesus's words to the dying man about paradise must be taken in the sense of the beginning of a journey that none beside Christ himself will complete until the final resurrection. For Wright, paradise "is not the final destination; it is a beautiful resting place on the way there."[8] Wright goes on to make the point, essentially, that if the dying criminal doesn't go to purgatory, nobody does; the text here in Luke becomes a witness for him against that doctrine. Pope Paul VI articulates the Catholic view in contrastive terms: "We believe that the souls of those who die in the grace of Christ—whether they must still make expiation in the fires of purgatory, or whether from the moment they leave their bodies they are received by Jesus Christ into Paradise like the good thief—go to form that people of God which succeeds death, death which will be totally destroyed on that day when these souls are reunited with their bodies" (*Creed of the People of God* 28).

Later New Testament teaching, such as that of Paul in 2 Corinthians, contrasts earthly bodies with a body "eternal in the heavens" (5:1) and speaks of the aspiration of the faithful believer "to be absent from the body and to be present to the Lord" (5:8), yet Paul goes on to suggest that at "the judgment seat of Christ" we will all be judged according to "things done in the body" (5:10). These passages tend in Christian doctrines of the afterlife to be incorporated synthetically with the word to the penitent convict here in Luke, so that paradise is thought of in the way suggested by the story Jesus tells about Lazarus being delivered by angels into the bosom of Abraham after his death—conscious and happy in a way he has never been in the body but without yet a mention of the final resurrection (Luke

8. N. T. Wright, *For All the Saints? Remembering the Christian Departed* (London: SPCK, 2003), 24.

16:19–31). Perhaps, as Wright suggests, an intermediate state is implied, but it seems impossible to say much more than that on the authority of the text itself.

At about the sixth hour (or noon; Mark 15:25 tells us that the crucifixion itself began about nine in the morning), a sudden darkness fell "over all the earth until the ninth hour" (Luke 23:44). Luke does not speak of an eclipse but rather of the sun being darkened—by what we do not know. About this same time, mysteriously, the veil in the temple was torn down the middle (23:45). This was an evident shock to all, and the commentators see it as a divine intervention, exposing the sanctuary in such a way as to suggest the departure of the divine presence from the holy of holies (e.g., Ephraem the Syrian, *Commentary on Tatian's Diatessaron* 21.6). Theophylact comments, "By this our Lord showed that the holy of holies should be no longer inaccessible, but being given over into the hands of the Romans, should be defiled" (quoted in Aquinas, *Catena Aurea* 3.2.759). Ambrose sets another trajectory for spiritual interpretation in his observation that "the old veil is rent that the church may hang up new veils of faith" (*Exposition of Luke* 10.127). Luke here omits what must have been at least as terrifying, namely that this event was the result of a great earthquake, in which "graves were opened; and many bodies of the saints who had fallen asleep were raised," and that they went into the city "and appeared to many" (Matt. 27:51–53); this is perhaps the most striking of his omissions in the narrative.

Jesus's last words erupt on the page with a voluble utterance Luke does not include ("My God, my God, why have you forsaken me?"; Matt. 27:46), as well as one he alone records: "Father, into your hands I commit my spirit" (Luke 23:46), at which Jesus expires. Only John's account adds to Jesus's final utterances: "It is finished!" (*tetelestai*) (John 19:30). Again, one senses that Luke's primary informant is standing much closer to the cross than the disciples, whom he notes "stood at a distance" (Luke 23:49). The Roman centurion in charge of the crucifixion was moved by all that he had seen and, seeing Jesus die, "glorified God, saying, 'Certainly this was a righteous Man!'" (23:47). At this point the bystanders smite their breasts in grief at the "spectacle" (oddly to our sense of the Greek term *theōria*) and turn toward home, even while the disciples and "the women who followed him" look on the desolate crucifixion scene, "watching these things" (23:48–49).

Recension B of a text called *The Acts of Pilate* (a text partially written in the late second century but in this version mostly of the late fourth century) gives the name "Longinus" to the soldier who pierces Jesus's side to determine death (John 19:34), a feature often conflated with John's account of the centurion's concluding observations. Thus, at the last moment, yet another Gentile also bears witness to Jesus.

The Burial (23:50–56)

Joseph of Arimathea was a "counselor" in the Sanhedrin, the very council of elders that had condemned Jesus to death. Luke makes it clear that Joseph of Arimathea had not consented to this judgment (23:51); he must therefore have been absent, since the members present are recorded as giving a unanimous verdict (Mark 14:64). For Luke he is an exception of the sort that proves a rule; he is rich, yet faithful. Although a member of the Sanhedrin that condemns the Lord, he is nonetheless, like many of the faithful remnant before him, one of those who "wait[ed] for the kingdom of God"—a just man (Luke 23:50–51). More than that, though one of the council of elders, he was also a disciple of the Lord (John 19:38; Matt. 27:57). He was able, as Augustine puts it, by "confidence in his rank" to enter "familiarly into Pilate's presence" (*Harmony of the Gospels* 3.22). In this respect, he must have been closely connected to Nicodemus, whom John 19:39 records as cooperating with Joseph, bringing a hundred pounds of myrrh and aloes with which to surround the body. But it is Joseph of Arimathea upon whom Luke focused his attention, perhaps because he was the negotiator. As a member of the council he is in a position to do what none of the immediate disciples can do in this circumstance, requesting of Pilate, in person, the body of Jesus (Luke 23:52). Pilate accepts his request, and Joseph takes down the body, prepares it for burial, and puts it in a new tomb, hewn out of the tufa rock nearby, "where no one had ever lain before" (23:53). This leads Maximus of Turin to say, "A new womb conceived him and a new grave enclosed him . . . the womb is virginal; the tomb is virginal." Maximus goes on to note the obvious conclusion to his analogy: "The last birth is more glorious than the first. The first conceived a mortal body, but the last an immortal one" (Sermon 78.2). All of this burial preparation had at the time to be effected quickly, for the Sabbath was almost at hand (23:54). The women follow, marking the tomb, so that after the Sabbath they can return and anoint the body in spices and ointments (23:55–56). Bede has a moving comment that ties the death of the Lord and the death of those who died "in him" to the Sabbath, and especially to Sabbath rest: "Now, that the Lord is crucified on the sixth day and rests on the seventh, signifies that in the sixth age of the world we must of necessity suffer for Christ, and, as it were, be crucified to the world. But in the seventh age, that is, after death, our bodies indeed rest in the tombs, but our souls with the Lord" (*Homilies on the Gospels* 2.7). As in so many other aspects of the typological reading of the Christians of an earlier age, a pattern is reiterated. As in creation, so in re-creation; the redeemer of all creation renews his creation by restoring it to the spiritual Sabbath so long misunderstood.

RESURRECTION
AND RECOGNITION

LUKE 24

Sometimes it is necessary to see—to imaginatively engage as with the eye and not merely the ear. It is not likely an accident that the early modern painter whose depiction of the crucifixion is among the most memorably gruesome and yet empathetic, Matthias Grunewald (1475–1528), also called Mathis Gothart, is also the one whose representation of the resurrection is most evidently joyous. As with all of his extant crucifixion images, that in the famous *Isenheim Altar-piece* (1515) is dark with a terrible realism, yet at the same time iconic.[1] The cross is depicted more accurately (about seven feet high) as to historical type, and the death agony of Christ, with his contorted fingers and mashed feet, is much more akin to reality than many a more tranquil description, whether medieval or modern. But at the foot of the cross, opposite from a swooning Virgin Mary, comforted by the Apostle John, and the weeping Mary Magdalene, bent down in sorrow next to her alabaster jar (Luke 7:37–48; cf. Matt. 26:12–13), is the commanding figure of John the Baptist, here anachronistically, pointing viewers to the crucified Christ and saying (the words are painted by his head), "He must increase, but I must decrease" (John 3:30). Before him is the symbolic Lamb of God "who takes away the sin of the world" (1:29), repeated also in early liturgy. The breast of the lamb has been opened in the sacrificial cut, on its shoulder it is bearing a cross, and its lifeblood pours into the eucharistic chalice. This painting is an almost perfect example of the late medieval altarpiece, at once an object of contemplative devotion and, in the sense given by Thomas Aquinas, a theological symbol. Visual theology can be powerful; this painting is most certainly that.

When the altarpiece wings are opened, it reveals perhaps the most stunning representation of the resurrection in all Christian art, altogether eclipsing both in its dramatic power and its theological fidelity such well-known representations

1. A convenient and reliable explication along with color reproduction is found in Wendy Beckett's *The Story of Painting* (New York: DK, 1994), 75–77.

as those by Piero della Francesca and Mantegna. It is not the sprawling Roman soldiers at his feet that capture the viewer's eye but the stunning white body and radiant face of the risen and transfigured Lord, behind whose body is a magnificent red-gold orb, not a nimbus but the rising sun. Graphically, we are at the dawn of an utterly new day; as Jaroslav Pelikan says in the title of his essay on depictions of the resurrection, Grunewald's magnificent image depicts nothing less than "the turning point of history."[2] The German vernacular of the painter (as in English) permits the verbal pun (*Sohn/sonne*) that his radiant image makes visual. The resurrected Christ is here the "Son of Righteousness," which Mal. 4:2 had promised would "arise with healing in his wings"; here is the risen Christ who "reflects the glory of God and bears the very stamp of his nature, upholding the universe by his word of power" (Heb. 1:3 RSV). The painting says succinctly what all of the Gospels and the rest of the New Testament are saying: nothing can ever be the same again.

Euchatastrophe and Wonder (24:1–12)

But as Luke's last chapter opens, the sorrowing women do not yet know that. Stricken with grief over an immeasurable loss, yet united in their devotion, they have been up all night, waiting for the dawn that ends the Sabbath, preparing the spices and ointments for Jesus's body (24:1). To their dismay, when they arrive at the tomb they see that the stone has been rolled away from its entrance (24:2). How could this have happened? (Matt. 28:2 speaks of an earthquake when the angel rolls away the stone.) As they stand there, wondering (Luke says "perplexed"—*aporeō*, which we might also translate "stymied" or "confounded"), they become aware of "two men" in "shining garments." Luke withholds the term "angels" until 24:23, but the women are "afraid and bowed their faces to the earth" (24:5). When the angelic witnesses speak, it is in the form of a mild rebuke to the evidently disconsolate purpose that has brought the women to the tomb: "Why do you seek the living among the dead? He is not here, but is risen! Remember how he spoke to you when he was still in Galilee, saying, 'The Son of Man must be delivered into the hands of sinful men, and be crucified, and the third day rise again'" (24:5–7). Luke's narrative here again reveals a powerful symmetry in the divine design. As Cyril puts it, "Angels brought the joyful tidings of the nativity to the shepherds in Bethlehem; now they tell of his resurrection" (1983: 24).

"They remembered his words," Luke puts it tersely (24:8; cf. 9:22; 18:32–33). In these last remarks, found only in Luke's account, we have just a hint that one of his own sources has been one of these women. But their understanding—or lack of it—Luke will show to be representative. As John Chrysostom summarizes it: "Such was the understanding they had. They expected that the kingdom

2. Jaroslav Pelikan, *The Illustrated Jesus through the Centuries* (New Haven: Yale University Press, 1997), 22–23.

would come to him immediately in Jerusalem because they had no better grasp of what the kingdom of heaven really is. They thought of it as a human kingdom, as another Evangelist suggests. They were expecting him to enter into it, but not to go to the cross and death" (*Against the Anomoeans* 8.29–30). How could the human imagination before the resurrection have begun to conjure with the scope of it? asks Chrysostom. The triumph of the resurrection is far more glorious than anything that had ever entered the human mind, even the mind of faithful Jews who had "long awaited the coming of the kingdom." This is the essential point of Heinrich Schütz's magnificent Easter oratorio of 1623: "Historia der frölichen und siegreichen Aufferstehung" ("History of the Joyful and Triumphant Resurrection") and his later "Musikalische Exequien" (1636), as the words of Job 19:25 lift that music from lamentation to jubilant affirmation: "Ich weiss das mein Eerlöser libt!" ("I know that my Redeemer lives"). And still, the profoundest of Christian mysteries remains to mere exegesis an irreducible wonder. None of the evangelists shows *how* it happened; *that* it happened they are able to show quite effectively after the event. But the difficulty of conveying such a momentous thing as the resurrection verbally is instanced by Luke in his depiction of the women's own immediate frustration, even as they become the first to proclaim the very essence of the good news. Mary Magdalene, Joanna, Mary the mother of James, and all the others have returned breathless to "the eleven" (24:9–10), yet their words seem to the grieving men as "idle tales" (Luke's term is *lēros*, a graphic *hapax legomenon* apparently used by physicians to describe the delirious babblings of very ill persons; Josephus, *Jewish War* 3.405; cf. Bock 1994–96: 2.1898). Thus, in sharing this most important news imaginable, the women are disbelieved and ignored (24:11).

These women are soon, of course, to be vindicated. Peter will be troubled and eventually leap up and run to the tomb to see for himself. John will record that he also, having been approached by Mary Magdalene, then runs toward the tomb, where he and Peter likewise find it empty (John 20:1–10) and that meanwhile, Mary Magdalene, having returned to the area to search, queries one she takes to be the gardener about the body of Jesus and discovers herself to be both seeing and speaking with the risen Lord (20:11–18). So it is the women who first learn of the resurrection, and Mary Magdalene among them who first sees and speaks with the Lord before he has "risen to the Father." There is just no getting around this, as Augustine says: "So in this fact we have to reflect on the goodness of the Lord's arrangements, because this, of course, was the doing of the Lord Jesus Christ, that it should be the female sex which would be the first to report that he had risen again." Augustine goes on to emphasize this fact too, in the narrative symmetry reflected in Luke's Gospel especially, that though "humanity fell through the female sex, humankind was restored through the female sex. A virgin gave birth to Christ; a woman proclaimed that he had risen again. Through a woman death; through a woman life. But the disciples didn't believe what the women had said. They thought the women were raving, when in fact they were reporting the truth" (Sermon 232.2).

One persuasive indicator that we are dealing with facts as they happened is that the revelation comes first to women, so unconventional an imagination for this culture. This is both confirmed and reinforced by the other Gospel accounts. So many "walls of partition" have been broken down by Jesus in his life and, now, after his death and in his resurrection. Think of it: not only is his resurrection made known first to the women, but he also reveals himself in his resurrection body first to a woman—and to a woman who is not his mother or a relative—something perhaps almost unthinkable in first-century Palestine. One powerful theme to emerge in Luke's Gospel is just this: Jesus is no respecter of persons. He does not conform to our social hierarchies and sorry prejudices.

The Revelation at Emmaus (24:13–32)

Christ is risen! Some people had heard the rumor. Some had believed it. Others suspected foul play. Such was the state of confusion and uncertainty as two of the wider company of disciples walked wearily back from Jerusalem after the Passover. They were going to a small village now gone, called Emmaus; Luke makes it sixty *stadia* from the city—just shy of seven miles (24:13).

The two are deep in conversation (*homileō*, from which we get our words "homily" and "homiletics," implies an intense discussion). They are so absorbed in this emotional dialogue (*syzēteō*) that they hardly notice that a fellow traveler has been walking along near them (24:15). When they do see him, they do not recognize him. Here, at the end, as everywhere in his Gospel, we see Luke point-ing to the crucial difference between sight and understanding, between seeing Jesus and grasping his identity. Coming to "know" Jesus is a rich theme in Luke, and he has not yet exhausted it; Jesus suddenly speaks to the two, and the form of his question itself highlights this theme: "What kind of conversation is this that you have with one another as you walk and are sad?" (24:17). How much Jesus has noticed! And by comparison, how little the two have noticed. The dramatic irony of Luke's narrative (the reader knows at this point more than the two trav-elers) heightens the thematic element still further. "What words" (*hoi logoi*) are you exchanging, as you "debate" (*antiballete*) one another? he asks. The word is another New Testament *hapax legomenon*, a term of forensics and rhetoric, har-boring a warning for theologians. (For us, too, it is possible to be so engrossed in our wearied debates that we fail to know Jesus as he is—the risen Lord whose presence is all that should matter.)

Cleopas (that he is named suggests another possible informant) asks a ques-tion that implies a judgment: "Are you the only stranger in Jerusalem, and have you not known the things which happened there in these days?" (24:18). The irony could hardly be more profound. It is only heightened when Jesus, patient teacher that he is, asks them, "What things?" The question is therapeutic, given their grief, and their response is both enthusiastic and restrained: "Concerning

Jesus of Nazareth, who was a Prophet mighty in deed and word before God and all the people" (24:19). They do not say "Chosen One" or "the Son of Man," fearful perhaps that they may be dealing with someone unsympathetic or even hostile. They do, however, clearly implicate "the chief priests and our rulers" in his condemnation and crucifixion (24:20). Gradually, they open up to the stranger: "We were hoping that it was he who was going to redeem Israel. Indeed . . . today is the third day since these things happened" (24:21). They are by this point talking much more openly, and they relate also their astonishment at the claims of "certain women" of their community, who reported finding his tomb empty and having (as Cleopas and his companion put it) had a "vision" (*optasia*) of angels there "who said he was alive" (24:23). Moreover, some of the group had gone to check out the tomb, finding it empty. Now come the disconsolate, giveaway words: "But him they did not see" (24:24). Here the tension of dramatic irony reaches to the breaking point, but still the two disciples fail themselves to *see*.

As so often, Jesus's most gentle teaching and self-disclosure begins with a rebuke; it is a more gentle rebuke than many of the translations readily suggest. The word translated "fools" or "foolish ones" is not here *aphrōn*, the derogatory term Jesus used for the rich farmer who utterly misunderstands in what good provision for the future really consists (12:20); rather, it is *anoētoi*, meaning "naïve" or "unsuspecting." (It is almost as when an exasperated teacher says to beloved but obtuse students, "You sweet dummies! How could you miss this?") How could you be, he asks, so "slow of heart to believe in all that the prophets have spoken! Ought not the Christ to have suffered these things and to enter into his glory [*doxa*]?" (24:25–26). Is not this *exactly* how it was predicted to be? And so, "beginning at Moses and all the prophets, he expounded to them in all the Scriptures the things concerning himself" (24:27). This is a remarkable sentence: "all" (*pantōn/ pasais*) is used twice, with *diermēneuō* ("interpreted") the scriptures and prophets. His discourse with them appears to have been not merely exposition but detailed analysis according to first principles; the terms remind us of the detailed, patient ordering that has characterized Luke's own *diēgēsis*, his ordered narrative of all the critical elements in Jesus's life, death, and resurrection as he has learned them.

When they come to the point on the road at which the two will turn (there is some suggestion that they are members of one family, perhaps father and son), there is about to be a parting of ways, for Jesus "made as though he would have gone farther" (24:28 KJV). This gesture, too, is pedagogical. Neither Cleopas nor his son (if that is who it is, possibly Simeon, son of Clopas, later bishop of Jerusalem after James; Eusebius, *Ecclesiastical History* 3.11; Origen, *Against Celsus* 2.62.68) is prepared to let the sweet instruction cease if they can help it. I am compelled to think here of the statement attributed to Gamaliel, but in another way than that which Gamaliel nonetheless so admirably intended it: "*Yafeh talmud torah, k'asher imah derech eretz*" ("how beautiful to study Torah, and how happy along our earthly journey" [author's translation]). The joy of this was great at the time; the memory of it later must have been immensely sweet.

Gregory the Great says that "because they could not be strangers to charity, with whom charity was walking, they invite him, as if a stranger, to partake of their hospitality" (quoted in Aquinas, *Catena Aurea* 3.2.779). Augustine put it this way: "The Teacher was walking with them along the way, and he himself was the way" (Sermon 235.1–2). Somehow they intuit presciently what they cannot yet consciously grasp; Augustine, who loves this passage, introduces what now follows: "And because they observed hospitality, him who they knew not yet in the expounding of the Scriptures, they suddenly know in the breaking of bread" (*Harmony of the Gospels* 3.25).

The theological implications of this passage, as Augustine sees, are tremendous. First, had they, preoccupied with their own grief, not pressed Jesus to stop and stay overnight (24:29), this wonderful story might not be here for us. Second, as Augustine says of Jesus on the way, "He was at one and the same time seen and concealed. . . . He was walking with them along the road like a companion, and was himself the leader. He was seen, and not recognized" (Sermon 235.2–3). It would be hard to find a theme that more clearly resonates through Luke's narrative than this. Now, a third and all-encompassing revelation: as the liturgy of the Orthodox church makes more apparent than liturgical language in the West, the "guest" is the host. Here, mysteriously, the Emmaus pair know it in the experience, for "as he sat at meat with them, he took bread, and blessed it, and broke, and gave to them. And their eyes were opened, and they knew him, and he vanished out of their sight" (24:30–31 KJV). Perhaps he had done this in their presence before; it is likely. Perhaps also the most familiar of words, following his exposition of the scriptures, and in his presence and prayer, took on a sudden sweep of meaning that opened their eyes as in an astonishing burst of light: "*Baruch atah adonai* [did the Lord say here YHWH?] *elohenu, melech haolam, hamotzeh lechem min haaretz*" ("blessed are you Lord God, king of the cosmos, who brings forth bread from the earth" [author's translation]). Perhaps they saw his nail-pierced hands. On level after level, new meaning must have sprung from this old blessing of the bread, for here, for them, the Bread of Life who had sprung from the earth had become at once their guest and host.

The church has seen in this moment one of the most cherishable evidences of the way Christ's presence comes among his faithful followers. When we invite him to break for us the bread of life, he does. He has been there all along in the exposition of the scriptures, a living presence in his word, but they have only sensed rather than recognized that in its fullness. Now, "their eyes were opened"—and just at the moment they *see*, he vanishes "from their sight" (24:31). Augustine draws the point: they know Christ in the breaking of the bread: "It isn't every loaf of bread, you see, but the one that receives Christ's blessing that becomes the body of Christ" (Sermon 234.2). This passage in Luke becomes a powerful nexus for the church's understanding of the real presence of Christ in the sacrament. In the stunning painting of the scene at Emmaus by Caravaggio, at the very moment the disciples recognize the Lord they leap up, but their eyes are fixed upon his hands and the now consecrated bread. Augustine concludes that "everything in the scriptures speaks of Christ, but only to him who has ears. He opened their minds to understand the Scriptures, and so we should pray that he will open our own" (Homily 2 on 1 John). The *Glossa Ordinaria* (Patrologia latina 114), seeing the progress from scriptural exegesis to Eucharist as prefiguring the liturgy of the church, treats the entire episode also as an exemplum of the promise of Jesus that "where two or three are gathered together in my name, I am there in the midst of them" (Matt. 18:20; cf. Bede, *Homilies on the Gospels* 11.9). The *Meditations on the Life of Christ* emphasizes the "hidden communion" of Christ's lovers with their beloved in meditation on his word and the *consolatum* of the Eucharist (Pseudo-Bonaventure 1961: 367–68). For all of these reasons this passage is of enormous importance to Christian life, and it is found only in Luke. John Wesley will see it as the scriptural precedent for his own story of conversion, the "Aldersgate Experience" in which his "heart was strangely warmed." And Charles Wesley's hymn "Talk with Us, Lord, Thyself Reveal" still echoes this understanding of the Emmaus narrative. "Did not our heart burn within us?" (Luke 24:32). The question of the Emmaus disciples reverberates through all of Christian history. A mark of faithful discipleship has always been in some measure the desire to share in the Emmaus experience, to have conversation with Jesus, and to have him, by his Spirit, open the scriptures in such a way as to enable our fuller recognition of who he is.

Revelation to the Apostles (24:33–53)

After the Lord has left them, at "that very hour" the pair return to Jerusalem, presumably arriving later in the same evening, to find "the eleven and those who were with them gathered together [*athroizō*]" (24:33), already talking in amazement about the Lord having appeared by now to Simon Peter (24:34). And so Cleopas and the other tell their story too, notably "how he was known to them in the breaking of bread" (24:35). But even while they are in this joyous exchange, flushed with the excitement and wonder of it all, suddenly Jesus is standing "in the midst of them" and saying, "Peace to you" (24:36). Despite the collective witness of previous encounters with the risen Lord, they are "terrified and affrighted" (*ptoeō* and *emphobos*—the doubling indicates extremity of apprehensive emotion) and think he is a ghost (24:37). As so often, he calms them down: "Why are you troubled? And why do doubts arise in your hearts?" (24:38). He points to his hands and his feet, inviting them to touch him, "for a spirit does not have flesh and bones as you see I have" (24:39). When he does this (24:40), they can scarcely believe for their joy and wonderment (*thaumazō* has the sense we employ when we refer to something wonderful as "fantastic" or "incredible," not meaning the word literally but hyperbolically for something so marvelous our minds cannot take it in). Luke here is as emphatic about the physicality of the resurrected body of Jesus as Paul will be later (1 Cor. 15:35–49); it is of the essence of what he is showing to have happened that every expectation of mortal nature in death has been broken through, the corruptible body having been restored and now, recognizably flesh and bones, yet an entirely new phenomenon. It can scarcely be overstressed how contrary Luke and Paul are to modernist metaphorizing and sidestepping of this absolute foundation of Christian faith and hope. John Updike, himself a modern and no pietist, nevertheless underscores this point beautifully in a poem directed against the evasive liberalism of many theologians when he insists that Jesus's bodily resurrection is the lynch-pin of any plausible Christian future: "if the cells' dissolution did not reverse, the molecules / reknit, the amino acids rekindle," he says, "the Church will fall."[3] Here again we may be grateful that an artist takes us into the heart of the matter, becoming in so doing a faithful theologian (at least in this one poem).

Luke would have liked Updike's poem for the way in which it so unequivocally grasps just how *real* Jesus's resurrection body is. Jesus asks for something to eat; the dumbfounded disciples give him "fish and some honeycomb," and he sits down in front of them and eats, as I think we may reliably imagine, with relish (Luke 24:42–43). Once again, as with the angels and the women, he reminds them all of what he has previously said to them, "that all things must be fulfilled which were written in the Law of Moses and the Prophets and the Psalms concerning me" (24:44). He has come to "fulfill the law and the prophets," and he has. Here too we have his clear indication that all of the scriptures—Torah, Nevi'im, and Ketubim—have spoken of the earth-shattering events to which they have been witnesses; he "open[s] their understanding," as he had done in Emmaus, "that they might comprehend the Scriptures" (24:45). This is another, living demonstration of the real presence of Christ in his word. It was necessary for this fulfillment, the consolation of Israel for which so many for so long had yearned, that Christ, the Messiah of God, should "suffer and . . . rise from the dead the third day" (24:46). But now a further fulfillment is necessary, namely that preaching his call to repentance and promise of the forgiveness of sins should take place "to all nations, beginning at Jerusalem" (24:47). And these very followers are first among those called to the apostolic task, to be "witnesses" of all that has happened and of its meaning (24:48).

Luke's narrative here collapses to a précis, it seems, the forty days of appearances and joyous reflection of which John gives us snatches (John 21). Calculating the space between Passover and Pentecost, forty days are typically allotted to the space Luke does not here comment upon, doubtless because he has not encountered a suitable *autoptēs* to report on it. (He repeats at the beginning of Acts, his second volume, the event now recorded here, thus tying his two volumes together.) That the following episode is a "new tiding" is indicated, as Luke does elsewhere, by the words "and behold" (*kai idou*) in 24:49 (KJV); Luke's account of the Great

---

3. John Updike, "Seven Stanzas at Easter," in *Telephone Poles and Other Poems* (New York: Knopf, 1964), 72–73.

Commission is brief and prefaced by an important caveat. The disciples are to "tarry in the city of Jerusalem" until they are "endued with power from on high" (24:49). They cannot yet know that Jesus means the coming of the Holy Spirit, which also he has previously promised. John Chrysostom notes that Jesus has all along had a clear strategy that will only in hindsight become apparent to his followers: "As a general does not permit his soldiers who are about to confront a large number [of enemies] to go out until they are properly equipped, so also the Lord does not permit his disciples to go forth to the conflict before the descent of the Spirit" (*Homilies on Acts* 1). Bede anticipates another symmetry (*Homilies on the Gospels* 1.14; quoted in Aquinas, *Catena Aurea* 3.2.791), namely that this "power" with which they are to be endued is that same Spirit that had "overshadowed" Mary at the beginning. Mary will, of course, be with the gathered *koinōnia* of disciples at the Pentecostal descent of the Spirit upon them all.

Jesus leads them out "as far as to Bethany": the Mount of Olives is the site of his final moment with his disciples as his ministry on earth draws to a conclusion. Luke records that he "lifted up his hands and blessed them" (24:50). Did they anticipate what was about to happen? For, as he did this, he was "carried up into heaven" (24:51). This is no final parting, mercifully. Moreover, now they know, as never before have they known. Filled with "great joy," they return to Jerusalem in obedience to his command and are "continually in the temple praising and blessing God" (24:53). In this observation, we may appreciate that extraordinary closure has been achieved in Luke's narrative: his great Gospel had begun in the temple, and now it ends in the temple. How striking that it should be a Gentile who would notice that, making of the evident symmetry a trace of God's hand in the story from beginning to end.

EPILOGUE

The Gospel of Luke is a special treasure of the church. In it, perhaps more fully than in any of the others, we see the intimacy of word and sacrament, the presentation of the presence of our Lord Jesus Christ entering into our history, transforming and renewing creation by his re-creation of all things in himself. Luke shows us how all of the Hebrew scriptures, the Tanak—Law, Prophets, and Writings—point to Christ and in him find their fulfillment, their fullness of expression. All of the Gospels are a witness of this great revelation of the divine plan for redemption of the cosmos, as of his people, including those of us who, like Luke, are his by adoption. But there is much that is distinctive for the church in Luke.

We can see in Luke particularly why the artists of the church have, for two millennia, seen his work as a gift of surpassing beauty. This is not merely because his narrative is so compellingly artful but because in his work we come to understand how he has himself perceived the work of God for our redemption as in itself a work of supreme beauty. He sees in the history of Jesus's life, teaching, death, and resurrection the very beauty of holiness made manifest, that beauty that is the transcendental expression of the God who himself is Beauty. Luke's work is indeed history, and he has composed it according to the standards of *diēgēsis*, a suitable genre of the Hellenistic historian, thereby granting to his account the immediacy of personal witness from many of those who were present for various of the events, as he was not. His many Hebraisms attest to his care to give these accounts verbally, much as they came to his ears. I have come to think, as the reader will have seen, that he spoke with many persons, asking of them their particular witness, their eyewitness accounts, and that a close and thoughtful reading of his narrative will suggest that not only Peter but perhaps especially Mary, the mother of our Lord, proved indispensable to him in the *diēgēsis* he has left to us. In this alone, his Gospel has become a distinctive legacy of Christ's church.

I say here that his artistry, everywhere evident, is not primarily a function of his own artistic gift, as apparent as this is. That is, Luke's special achievement is not reducible to matters of style, "Lukanisms," or even a function of his distinctively rich Greek vocabulary, suffused as it is with examples of New Testament *hapax legomena* on nearly every page. Rather, what Luke has seen into is the artistry of the divine author, the author of our faith, the one who is himself the beginning and the end of all things, even as the Apostle John records him declaring to all the church in his own spectacular, final eschatological vision (Rev. 1:8, 11, 17–18; 22:13). Making beauty an intrinsic element in his narrative is not for Luke therefore a matter of aestheticism but actually a point of deepest theological significance. God works in mysterious ways his wonders to perform, and the result is something of matchless beauty, in his re-creation not less than his original creation. How a Gentile should see all these things so acutely and completely is itself a kind of wonder. But I hope the reader of this commentary will have noticed also his compelling attention to symmetry in the divine plan of redemption itself. I mean not only the evident typology of Old Testament fulfillment, such as the first Adam/Second Adam symmetry that Luke has highlighted. Symmetry abounds in his narrative about Jesus, and his recognition of its presence as structure in the divine ordering may well account for the unique attention he gives to the annunciation, the special preparation of John the Baptist, and the nativity story. But it goes much further. Luke's narrative begins in the temple (with Zacharias longing for closure, the consolation of Israel) and it ends in the temple, with the disciples joyously praising God for his provision of the longed-for consolation of his people. At the beginning, the Spirit "overshadows" Mary; at the end of the Gospel, Jesus foretells the descent upon all those for whom Mary has become, as particularly for John but in a larger sense for all the disciples, the mother of the church. The unanswered questions about the promise of a Messiah at the beginning of Luke are answered at the end in ways that both invert and yet more magnificently confirm the hopes of the long-expectant faithful. And there is so much more of this kind of symmetrical recension: the infamous satanic temptation to the fasting Jesus to command that stones become bread is refused by the one who will become the Bread of Life, breaking bread for the sustenance of his faithful forever; the baptism in water at the dawn of Christ's ministry will be encompassed by the baptism in the Spirit for those who follow him. Those he has called in lowly provincial Galilee, and who have left everything familiar to follow him, will now be sent into all the world, to declare the good news of redemption. The glad tidings of great joy to all people announced by the angels will become the angelic proclamation of Christ's resurrection, the joy of humans and angels alike at the fulfillment of Christ's eternal victory over sin and death.

Finally, the slowly unfolding narrative Luke writes captures with unique poignancy one of the most telling facts about the coming of the Lord of the cosmos into a fallen world: recognizing Jesus for who he really is, that crucial recognition without which there can be no entering into the company of the redeemed, no real understanding of the miracle of God's grace itself, is slow to dawn upon those who ought first to have seen him as the Chosen One of God. As Luke's narrative unfolds, there is heavy irony when, other than the angels themselves, those who seem first to recognize him as divine are Satan and the demons of the possessed. Then slowly come others—unlikely others—Gentiles like the centurion, Samaritans, marginalized and ostracized people, women of uncertain repute, tax collectors, and the like. His disciples come to know him bit by bit, not fully grasping the magnitude of his identity until very late indeed, much later than we would expect. Finally, the best educated and best placed, both among the guardians of religion and the regent powers of Roman rule (with rare exceptions), seem never to understand who Jesus is at all. Perhaps it was ever thus, but Luke draws his narrative in such a way that this issue of obtuseness concerning Jesus's identity becomes a theme in his Gospel from which we can scarcely avoid drawing a warning for ourselves in our own time.

And these are but the bare lineaments, the structural symmetries and trajectories of the great story Luke tells. It is a story of longing and of fulfillment, of torment and of triumph, of sorrowing oppression replaced by a sense of closure apprehended already that makes all things new and that is the substance of things hoped for, the evidence of things still unseen, but that now we recognize, celebrate, and in the reading of the Gospel and the celebration of the sacrament renew in our common life daily. This is the substance of which Luke has spoken, and it has transformed the mere chronicle of our history forever.

BIBLIOGRAPHY

Frequently cited works are listed here. Other works are documented in the footnotes.

Modern Scholarship

Bauckham, Richard. 2006. *Jesus and the Eyewitnesses: The Gospels as Eyewitness Testimony*. Grand Rapids: Eerdmans.

Bock, Darrell L. 1994–96. *Luke*. 2 vols. Baker Exegetical Commentary on the New Testament 3. Grand Rapids: Baker.

Danker, F. W. 1988. *Jesus and the New Age: A Commentary on St. Luke's Gospel*. Rev. ed. Philadelphia: Fortress.

Fitzmyer, Joseph A. 1981–85. *The Gospel according to Luke*. Anchor Bible 28–28a. Garden City, NY: Doubleday.

Girard, René. 2005. *I See Satan Fall Like Lightning*. Translated by James G. Williams. Maryknoll, NY: Orbis.

Hornik, Heidi J., and Mikeal C. Parsons. 2003–7. *Illuminating Luke*. 3 vols. Harrisburg, PA: Trinity.

Jeremias, Joachim. 1963. *The Parables of Jesus*. Translated by S. H. Hooke. Rev. ed. New Testament Library. Philadelphia: Westminster; London: SCM.

Lightfoot, John. 1979. *A Commentary on the New Testament from the Talmud and Hebraica*. Oxford: Oxford University Press, 1859. Reprint, Grand Rapids: Baker.

Marshall, I. Howard. 1978. *The Gospel of Luke: A Commentary on the Greek Text*. New International Greek Testament Commentary. Grand Rapids: Eerdmans.

Nolland, John. 1989–93. *Luke*. Word Biblical Commentary 35a–c. Dallas: Word.

Talbert, Charles H. 2002. *Reading Luke: A Literary and Theological Commentary on the Third Gospel*. Rev. ed. Macon, GA: Smyth & Helwys.

Wright, N. T. 1996. *Jesus and the Victory of God*. Minneapolis: Fortress.

Ancient, Medieval, and Reformation Writings

Ambrose of Milan. 1998. *Exposition of the Holy Gospel according to St. Luke, with Fragments on the Prophecy of Isaias*. Translated by

Theodosia Tomkinson. Etna, CA: Center for Traditionalist Orthodox Studies.

Aristotle. 1999. *Nicomachean Ethics*. Translated by Terence Irwin. Indianapolis: Hackett.

Athanasius. 1961. *The Incarnation of the Word of God*. Translated by a Religious of CSMV. Introduction by C. S. Lewis. New York: Macmillan.

Augustine of Hippo. 1951. *Commentary on the Lord's Sermon on the Mount*. Translated by Denis J. Kavanaugh. Fathers of the Church 11. Washington, DC: Catholic University of America Press.

———. 1958. *On Christian Doctrine*. Translated by D. W. Robertson Jr. Upper Saddle River, NJ: Prentice Hall.

———. 1959. *Sermons on the Liturgical Seasons*. Translated by Mary Sarah Muldowney. Fathers of the Church 38. Washington, DC: Catholic University of America Press.

———. 1968. *Letters*. 6 vols. Translated by Wilfrid Parsons and Robert B. Eno. Fathers of the Church 12, 18, 20, 30, 32, 81. Washington, DC: Catholic University of America Press.

———. 1988. *Tractates on the Gospel of John*. Translated by John W. Rettig. Fathers of the Church 79. Washington, DC: Catholic University of America Press.

———. 1996. *The Enchiridion of Faith, Hope, and Love*. Translated by J. B. Shaw. Introduction by Thomas Hibbs. Washington, DC: Regnery.

———. 1997. *Newly Discovered Sermons*. Translated by Edmund Hill. Works of St. Augustine 3/11. New York: New City Press.

———. 2004. *Harmony of the Gospels*. Translated by S. D. F. Salmond. Revised by M. B. Riddle. Nicene and Post-Nicene Fathers 1/6. Peabody, MA: Hendrickson.

Basil the Great. 1950. *Ascetical Works*. Translated by M. Monica Wegner. Fathers of the Church 9. Washington, DC: Catholic University of America Press.

———. 1963. *Exegetic Homilies*. Translated by Agnes C. Way. Fathers of the Church 46. Washington, DC: Catholic University of America Press.

———. 2004. *Letters and Select Works*. Translated by Blomfield Jackson. Nicene and Post-Nicene Fathers 2/8. Peabody, MA: Hendrickson.

Bede, the Venerable. 1991. *Homilies on the Gospels*. 2 vols. Translated by Lawrence T. Martin and David Hurst. Cistercian Studies Series 110–11. Kalamazoo, MI: Cistercian.

Beza, Theodore. 1642. *Jesu Christi domini nostri, Novum Testamentum sive novum foedus, cujus graeco contextui respondent interpretationes duae*. Cantabrigiae: Rogeri Danielis.

Bonaventure. 2001–4. *Commentary on the Gospel of St. Luke*. 3 vols. Translated by Robert F. Karris. Collected Works of St. Bonaventure 8. St. Bonaventure, NY: Franciscan Institute.

Braude, W. G. 1968. *Pesikta Rabbati: Discourses for Feasts, Fasts, and Special Sabbaths*. 2 vols. Yale Judaica Series 18. New Haven: Yale University Press.

Calvin, John. 1972. *A Harmony of the Gospels: Matthew, Mark, and Luke*. 3 vols. Translated by A. W. Morrison and T. L. H. Parker. Grand Rapids: Eerdmans.

Chrysostom, John. 2004. *Homilies on the Gospel of St. Matthew*. Translated by George Prevost. Revised by M. B. Riddle. Nicene and Post-Nicene Fathers 1/10. Peabody, MA: Hendrickson.

Clement of Alexandria. 1954. *Christ the Educator*. Translated by Simon P. Wood. Fathers of the Church 23. Washington, DC: Catholic University of America Press.

Cyril of Alexandria. 1983. *Commentary on the Gospel of St Luke*. Translated by R. Payne Smith. Long Island, NY: Studion.

Danby, Herbert. 1991. *The Mishnah, Translated from the Hebrew*. Oxford: Oxford University Press.

Demosthenes. 1926. *Orations*. 7 vols. Translated by C. A. Vince and J. C. Vince. Loeb

Classical Library. Cambridge: Harvard University Press.

Didache (A Church Manual). 1953. Early Christian Fathers. Translated and edited by Cyril C. Richardson. Library of the Christian Classics 1. Philadelphia: Westminster.

Diodorus Siculus. 1954. *Bibliotheca historica*. 12 vols. Translated by C. H. Oldfather. Loeb Classical Library. Cambridge: Harvard University Press.

Ephraem the Syrian. 1993. *Saint Ephraem's Commentary on Tatian's Diatessaron*. Translated by Carmel McCarthy. Journal of Semitic Studies Supplement 2. Oxford: Oxford University Press.

Eusebius of Caesarea. 1984. *The Proof of the Gospel*. Translated by W. J. Ferrar. London: SPCK, 1920. Reprint, Grand Rapids: Baker Academic.

———. 1998. *Ecclesiastical History*. Translated by C. F. Cruse. Peabody, MA: Hendrickson.

Friedlander, G. 1981. *Pirkê de Rabbi Eliezer (The Chapters of Rabbi Eliezer the Great) according to the Text of the Manuscript Belonging to Abraham Epstein of Vienna*. London: Paul, Trench, Trübner; New York: Bloch. Reprint, New York: Sepher-Hermon.

Ginzberg, Louis, ed. 1968. *The Legends of the Jews*. 7 vols. Translated by Henrietta Szold. Philadelphia: Jewish Publication Society of America.

Gregory of Nazianzus. 1954. *On Preaching (The Theological Orations)*. Translated by Charles Gordon Browne and James Edward Sallow. In *Christology of the Later Fathers*, edited by Edward Roche Hardy, 128–214. Library of the Christian Classics 3. Philadelphia: Westminster.

———. 1991. *Faith Gives Fullness to Reasoning: The Five Theological Orations*. Translated by Lionel Wickham and Frederick Williams. Introduction and commentary by Frederick W. Norris. Leiden: Brill.

Gregory the Great. 1990. *Forty Gospel Homilies*. Translated by Dom David Hurst.

Cistercian Studies Series 123. Kalamazoo, MI: Cistercian.

———. 2004. *The Book of Pastoral Rule (Cura pastoralis)*. Translated by James Barmby. Nicene and Post-Nicene Fathers 2/12. Peabody, MA: Hendrickson.

Henry, Matthew. 1728. *Commentary on the Whole Bible*, vol. 5, *Matthew to John*. London, 1728. Reprint, McLean, VA: MacDonald, n.d.

Herodotus. 1920. *The Persian Wars*. 2 vols. Translated by A. D. Godley. Loeb Classical Library. Cambridge: Harvard University Press.

Hesiod. 1982. *Works and Days*. Edited by M. L. West. Oxford: Clarendon.

Hugh of St. Victor. 1951. *On the Sacraments of the Christian Faith*. Translated by Roy J. Deferrari. Cambridge, MA: Medieval Academy of America.

Jerome. 1994–96. *The Homilies of St. Jerome*. 2 vols. Translated by Marie L. Ewald. Fathers of the Church 48, 57. Washington, DC: Catholic University of America Press.

Josephus Flavius. 1926–65. *Works*. 10 vols. Translated by H. St. J. Thackeray et al. Loeb Classical Library. Cambridge: Harvard University Press.

Just, Arthur A. 2003. *Luke*. Ancient Christian Commentary on Scripture: New Testament 3. Downers Grove, IL: InterVarsity.

Justin Martyr. 1948. *Dialogue with Trypho*. Translated by Thomas B. Falls. Fathers of the Church 6. New York: Christian Heritage Press.

Lapide, Cornelius. 1639. *Evangelia II*. Translated by T. W. Mossman in 1876–86.

Lombard, Peter. 1570. *Sententiarum Libri IV*. Venetiis: Bartholomaeum Rubinum.

Lucian of Samosata. 1968. *How to Write History*. Translated by K. Kilburn. Loeb Classical Library. Cambridge: Harvard University Press.

Luther, Martin. 1990. *The Sermon on the Mount and the Magnificat*. Translated and edited by Jaroslav Pelikan. Luther's Works 21. St. Louis: Concordia.

Maximus of Turin. 1989. *The Sermons of Maximus of Turin*. Translated and annotated by Boniface Ramsey. Ancient Christian Writings 50. New York: Newman.

Migne, J.-P., ed. 1844–55. *Patrologia latina*. 221 vols. Brepols: Turnhout.

———. 1857–66. *Patrologia graecae*. 161 vols. Brepols: Turnhout.

Neusner, Jacob, ed. 2005. *The Babylonian Talmud*. 36 vols. Peabody, MA: Hendrickson.

Newton, John. 1995. *The Works of John Newton*. London: Hamilton Adams, 1824. Reprint, Southampton: Banner of Truth.

Origen. 1996. *Homilies on Luke*. Translated by Joseph T. Lienhard. Fathers of the Church 94. Washington, DC: Catholic University of America Press.

Philo. 1941. *Philo, with an English Translation*. 12 vols. Translated by F. H. Colson. Loeb Classical Library. Cambridge: Harvard University Press.

Plutarch. 1901–12. *Lives*. 11 vols. Translated by Bernadotte Perrin. Loeb Classical Library. Cambridge: Harvard University Press.

Polybius. 1922–27. *The Histories*. 6 vols. Translated by W. R. Paton. Loeb Classical Library. Cambridge: Harvard University Press.

Poole, Matthew. 1685. *Annotations upon the Holy Bible*. London: Parkhurst.

Pseudo-Bonaventure. 1961. *Meditations on the Life of Christ: An Illustrated Manuscript of the Fourteenth Century*. Translated and edited by Isa Ragusa and Rosalie B. Green. Princeton: Princeton University Press.

Tacitus. 1969. *Historiae*. 2 vols. Translated by C. H. Moore. Loeb Classical Library. Cambridge: Harvard University Press.

Theophylact. 1997. *The Explanation by Blessed Theophylact of the Holy Gospel according to St. Luke*. Translated by Christopher Stade. House Springs, MO: Chrysostom.

Thomas Aquinas. 1981. *Summa Theologica*. 5 vols. Translated by Fathers of the Dominican Province. Westminster, MD: Christian Classics.

———. 2009. *Catena Aurea: Commentary on the Four Gospels Collected out of the Works of the Fathers*, vol. 3, *Gospel of St. Luke*, parts 1–2. Translated and edited by John Henry Newman. London: Parker, 1842. Reprint, Boonville, NY: Preserving Christian Publications.

Thucydides. 1910. *The Peloponnesian War*. Translated by Richard Crawley. London: Dent.

Wesley, John. 1895. *Sermons on Several Occasions*, first series. London: Wesleyan-Methodist Bookroom.

Wyclif, John. 1975. *The English Works of John Wyclif*. Edited by F. D. Matthew. Early English Text Society o.s. 74. Oxford: Early English Text Society, 1880; rev. 1902. Reprint, Millwood, NY: Kraus.

SUBJECT INDEX

INDEX OF SCRIPTURE AND OTHER
ANCIENT WRITINGS